THE LIFE AND LEGEND OF

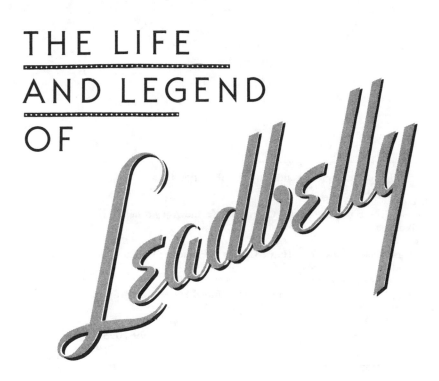
Leadbelly

CHARLES WOLFE and KIP LORNELL

DA CAPO PRESS • NEW YORK

Library of Congress Cataloging-in-Publication Data

Wolfe, Charles K.
  The life and legend of Leadbelly / Charles Wolfe and Kip Lornell. —1st
Da Capo Press ed.
    p.   cm.
  Originally published: New York: HarperCollins Publishers, c1992.
  Includes index.
  ISBN 0-306-80896-X (alk. paper)
  1. Leadbelly, 1885–1949. 2. Blues musicians —United States—Biography.
I. Lornell, Kip, 1953–   . II. Title.
ML420.L277 W6 1999
782.42162'0092—dc21   99-10989
[b]   CIP

First Da Capo Press edition 1999

This Da Capo Press paperback edition of *The Life and Legend of Leadbelly*
is an unabridged republication of the edition first published in New York
in 1992. It is reprinted by arrangement with the authors.

Designed by Barbara DuPree Knowles

Published by Da Capo Press, Inc.
A Member of Perseus Books Group
233 Spring Street, New York, N.Y. 10013-1578

To Bear and Mamou

Contents

Acknowledgments

Our search for the story of Huddie Ledbetter, or Leadbelly, lasted over three years and took us literally from coast to coast, from Oakland, California (the home of Brownie McGhee), to a cabin in the Smoky Mountains (the home of Tillman Cadle). We found a large part of the story, though, in New York City, where Leadbelly spent the last fourteen years of his life. Here we found a pensive and thoughtful Pete Seeger, at his home just north of the City, who added immensely to our understanding of Huddie. The time spent in the offices of The Richmond Organization (TRO) and with Judy Bell gathering information about the singer's copyrights and who was still performing his songs was fruitful and enlightening. The conversations with John Reynolds, who has been a Leadbelly fan, collector, advocate, and family confidant for nearly forty years, also took place in New York.

A great amount of the first-hand information we have about Leadbelly—the interviews, the recordings—was preserved through the effort of another New York City resident: Alan Lomax. He first met Leadbelly at the same time his father did: in 1933, at the Angola, Louisiana, State Penitentiary. It was Alan who gained the singer's confidence in 1934 and 1935, and who interviewed him for the long biographical introduction to the book he and his father wrote, *Negro Folk Songs as Sung by Lead Belly*. Even after the estrangement between John Lomax and Leadbelly, young Alan continued his efforts to promote the singer's career and to document his life. After he was put in charge of the Archive of Folk Song at the Library of Congress, Alan twice took the singer into the studios in Washington to record virtually his entire repertoire, as well as a vast trove of stories about his early life. It was Alan who arranged important commercial recording sessions with companies like RCA Victor and Musicraft, preserving even more songs and getting Leadbelly some sorely needed income. It was Alan who arranged for Leadbelly's appearances on network radio in the 1940s, winning him even more of a national reputation. Though John Lomax deserves the honor of "introducing" Leadbelly to America, it was his son Alan who did much of the work in documenting the rich and complex history Huddie Ledbetter had to tell. He knew the singer as well as could any white man.

Our main source of information for Huddie's life story before 1935 comes from the work of the Lomaxes, and especially from *Negro Folk Songs as Sung by Lead Belly* (1936). The middle section of our book—particularly chapters 15 through 18, which describe the hectic months from the fall of 1934 to the spring of 1935—draws quite heavily from this work.

Much of the information about John A. Lomax himself comes from his 1947 autobiography *Adventures of a Ballad Hunter*. These sections also rely on information and quotations found in the personal letters of John A. Lomax, which are part of the Lomax Family Papers housed at the Barker History Center at the University of Texas at Austin. We are grateful for Alan Lomax's willingness to assist with this book, and for his permission to quote liberally from these books and his father's letters.

The roots of Leadbelly's powerful art, though, lay in the South, and quite often we found ourselves thinking about the settings the singer knew so well: Mooringsport, Angola, Caddo Lake, Dallas, and a small town named De Kalb, Texas.

In addition to the many individuals who graciously allowed us to interview them, and who are acknowledged in the Notes, we wish to express our thanks to the following people and institutions: Mary Elizabeth Alden; Ray Allen; Archives of Appalachia (East Tennessee State University) and its staff, Marie Tedesco and Norma Myers, for help with the Cadle recordings; Richard Blaustein, East Tennessee State University; Monte Brown; Center for Popular Music (Middle Tennessee State University) and its staff, including Paul Wells, Ellen Garrison, Bruce Nemerov, and Stacey Wolfe; Elie Chandler-Fried; Larry Cohn, CBS/Sony; Norman Darwen; David Evans; the late John Henry Faulk; Folkways Archive, Smithsonian Institution and its staff, including Chris Jerde, Jeff Place, and Lori Taylor; Tony Haggert; The Haldeman Hotel; Bubba and Roma Gandy; Alan Govenar; Karen Kevorkian; Sean Killeen; Guy Logsden; Bess Hawes Lomax; Louisiana State University–Shreveport Archives; Judy McCulloh, The University of Illinois Press; Middle Tennessee State University and its staff, including Betty Nokes; John Andrew Prime; Ronnie Pugh, Country Music Foundation; John Reynolds, the tireless Leadbelly researcher and collector; Laurie Russell; Tony Russell; Ralph Rinzler; Tiny Robinson, the niece of Martha and Huddie; Becky Schroeder; Tony Seeger; Doug Seroff; Neil Slaven; Willie Smyth; TRO Music and its staff, including Judy Bell; Dell Upton; Pete Whelan; and Cindy Wolfe.

Research for this book was partially funded by the National Endowment for the Humanities, which awarded Kip Lornell a "Travel to Collections" grant in order to examine the Lomax Family Papers at the Barker History Center, The University of Texas at Austin. Much of the research was undertaken when Kip Lornell was at the Smithsonian Institution as a Postdoctoral Fellow.

This book was nurtured by Gabrielle Pantucci, our agent, and by Wendy Wolf, our editor, who hung with us through several years and many changes. Our spouses—Mary Dean Wolfe and Kim Gandy—deserve special recognition for their support and assistance in a multitude of ways. Special thanks to Elie Chandler-Fried, who generously "scanned" scores of pages. Special thanks, too, to our colleague and fellow researcher Nolan Porterfield, for his help with the Lomax Family Papers and general good counsel. The section on Bowie County and Walter Boyd could not have been written without the extensive research that Joni Haldeman of De Kalb, Texas, generously shared with us. Finally, our thanks to Alan Lomax for his generous time and advice, and for sharing with us his memories of his father, of Leadbelly, and of the era they helped define.

Preface

De Kalb, Texas, is usually pretty quiet at night, especially during the dense heat of summertime, when even at night it rarely cools off very much. July and August are generally the hottest months and a dawn with temperatures in the seventies is a godsend. In Joni Haldeman's home the fans whirled around on the high ceiling, stirring the air and bringing a hint of cool air to the house. Summer life in De Kalb has a certain rhythm to it—you know that the next day will be hot and almost certainly dry, that Wednesday will follow Tuesday, and that another load of clothes will require washing.

While we were there, the routine of daily life around the house had been interrupted by another of Joni's interesting projects, so when the phone rang at around midnight, no one was surprised. "Joni, I'm not convinced that Walter Boyd killed Will Stafford," announced the voice at the other end. Joni Haldeman and her friend, Cheryl, spent nearly an hour discussing what they knew about the murder of Will Stafford, traded conspiracy theories, and chatted about other related matters. So it went during the summer of 1991, a quest for the truth about Huddie Ledbetter—alias Walter Boyd—during his residence in Bowie County from 1916 to 1917.

Meeting Joni Haldeman in May 1991 was just one of a series of interesting, fortunate, and capricious events that befell us during the research for this book. Joni was already on the trail of Leadbelly; we ran across her by way of a chance remark made at the Bowie County Courthouse. During a futile search for Walter Boyd's criminal court records, one of the clerks (a high school classmate of Haldeman's) casually remarked that someone else had been looking for these very same records earlier in the year. Early in 1991 Joni and her twelve-year-old son, Charlie, had gone looking for the court records related to Leadbelly's troubles in Bowie County. Disappointed that they had found absolutely nothing, Charlie insightfully observed, "But Mom, if they knew him as Walter Boyd, shouldn't we look under his name?" Joni and Charlie turned around, marched back into the courthouse, and from that point, the Haldeman search moved more smoothly forward.

During the course of research you often run across people with similar interests, but Joni is out of the ordinary, the product of a fascination with local history and an inquisitive, fertile mind. She dug into the primary research with full vigor and a professional eye for details and obscure links. Throughout the summer we maintained regular telephone and postal contact with her. Our favorite package contained not only tape-recorded and transcribed interviews but also a Bowie County road map upon which Joni carefully marked the locations that the detailed map lacked. She even circled the small ad for the Bates-Rolk Funeral Homes, Inc., in red ink because they had donated the map.

———

The Gulf Coast of Texas in mid-February is utterly delightful. The cool, sunny days simply invite you outside to revel in early spring weather; at least Houston was that way in February 1991. Betty Baisley-Sorrell was waiting for the knock on the door, her greeting genuine and warm. On very short notice Betty had volunteered to take an extended lunch hour in order to tell us what she knew about her grandfather. She is Huddie Ledbetter's grand-daughter, an articulate and well-educated woman in her mid-forties who was keenly interested in meeting anyone hard at work researching a biogra-phy of Leadbelly. We spent several hours poring over the correspondence related to the legal hassles about the rarely seen 1976 Paramount film *Leadbelly* and talking about Huddie. She, too, learned many things about Huddie, as we filled her in on the fruits of our research.

Betty had recently moved back to Texas after living in San Francisco for many years. Her company offered a transfer and promotion to work in Houston. For Betty it was a return to down home—only minutes from her grandmother's home—although Houston itself had changed radically over the years. But down home also means Caddo Parish, Louisiana, about two hundred miles northeast of the modern town house. She spent her early years living near Mooringsport, until she and her mother both left Caddo Parish. Betty never knew her grandfather; she was barely out of diapers when he died. However, her mother had passed along the family stories about Leadbelly. Without reticence, Betty shared them with us.

"When I was growing up I used to hear how bad he was. He didn't take anything off of black or white. If you put your hand on his shoulder, he'd just as soon, you know, knock it off or cut you. Until I was nine or ten years old, I didn't know this was my grandfather. I remember one time we were in this little country store and something had been printed about my grand-father. They were saying 'Yeah, that was the baddest-ass nigger that we ever heard,' and so on. Of course, they said it in front of us. They could say anything they wanted to about blacks, 'cause blacks were not going to say anything [in the early 1950s]. I was a very little girl at the time and I didn't know who he was, but I didn't appreciate them talking about this man in a negative way. My mom didn't say anything then, but she said, 'Let's get out of here.' We got into the car and that's when she told me that was her father." These were clearly painful memories, though tempered by time. More acute were Betty's thoughts of her recently deceased mother. "My mother was very passive, except for her temper. She was like *her* father. She had eyes like my grandfather, large eyes and they stayed red. There was fire in them!" Almost in passing Betty remarked, "You ought to see my brother—now, he *really* looks like Huddie. Has his temper, too!"

———

In this book we sort out the myths from the truths about Huddie Ledbetter's life. In writing it we also wrestled with all types and sizes of problems that plague anyone who writes a biography, but one of the stickiest points related to the spelling of his nickname. Should it be spelled "Leadbelly" or "Lead Belly"? During the 1930s and 1940s it was usually spelled as two words, but gradually, over the past forty years, it has been reduced to a single word: Leadbelly. The family is not unanimous in its support for either form, though most would probably opt for two words. We decided, however, that current conventions should prevail because "Leadbelly" is the way most people are used to seeing it spelled today.

The Life and Legend of Leadbelly

1 New York, January 1935

Tom B. Blocker liked to think that Texans who had the misfortune to find themselves in New York City needed to stick together. This was never more true than in 1935, the sixth year of the Depression, when Texas dress and Texas food were anything but trendy, and when Dust Bowl clouds rolled across the plains west of Dallas. Tom B. Blocker was president of the New York chapter of Texas-Exes, an organization composed mostly of University of Texas alumni. These misplaced men held regular meetings to talk about old times, keep up with characters in Lone Star politics, and maybe even hear a few cowboy songs. On Friday, January 4, Blocker spent the morning putting the final touches on plans for a special luncheon the group was having at the midtown Hotel Montclair. For 75 cents admission the audience would be able to hear Texas alumnus John Lomax and his "colored chauffeur" with the unlikely name of Leadbelly, who would perform some songs from the prisons of Louisiana.

The crowd gathered earlier than usual, and Blocker began to suspect that what was planned as an easygoing, informal meeting was turning into an event. He was not truly surprised. In the four days since he had arrived in town, everyone had been talking about the man named Leadbelly (real name Huddie Ledbetter). He had impressed in private some of the city's more influential people, including the board of the Rockefeller Foundation and club owners up at Harlem—and supposedly had gotten an offer from band leader Cab Calloway himself. The *Herald Tribune* had run a major story on Leadbelly, describing how Lomax had discovered him in a Louisiana prison and how he had sung an appeal to the governor that had won him a pardon. SWEET SINGER OF THE SWAMPLANDS HERE TO DO A FEW TUNES BETWEEN HOMICIDES read the headline, and people all over town were talking about him. Many had seen Paul Muni's horrifying film *I Am a Fugitive from a Chain Gang* with its portrait of life on a southern chain gang; here was the real thing.

Reporters and photographers jostled the Texans for a place near the front of the room. A photographer from the New York *Herald Tribune* arrived first and the lead staff men from *Time* were soon in place, as were the Associated Press man and Lincoln Barnett from the *Herald Tribune*. Other reporters, booking agents, promoters, and merely the curious crowded in uninvited. After lunch, Blocker introduced John Avery Lomax, whom he noted was not only an authority on American folk songs but also one of the

1

founders of Texas-Exes. Dressed in a conservative suit and tie that did nothing to belie his banking background, Lomax also wore his customary hat that allowed the remaining fringe of his surprisingly dark hair to escape from underneath. He got up to talk about the music the audience was about to hear. "Northern people," he said, "hear Negroes playing and singing beautiful spirituals, which are too refined and are unlike the true southern spirituals. Or else they hear men and women on the stage and radio, burlesquing their own songs. Leadbelly doesn't burlesque. He plays and sings with absolute sincerity. Whether or not it sounds foolish to you, he plays with absolute sincerity. I've heard his songs a hundred times, but I always get a thrill. To me his music is real music."

Nervous about a hangover his singer was sporting from a night out in Harlem, Lomax had had the performer wait in a coat room. Now he motioned him in. Huddie Ledbetter walked forward. He was only about five-foot-eight, but he was stocky, around 160 pounds, and obviously strong, with muscles hardened from years of manual labor. He was not a young man (they would learn later he was in his late forties), and he walked with energy and confidence of a seasoned old-time performer, and dressed the part, too. He wore a rough blue work shirt over a yellow one, and old-fashioned high-bib overalls; around his neck was a red bandanna, and on his head perched a small brimmed hat, worn high up on the back. He was holding a battered old Stella twelve-string guitar, painted green and partly held together with string. It was different from the guitars most of the audience had seen before; it was large, tightly strung, and, they learned as he started to play, loud.

Leadbelly had no problem making himself heard by all. His big voice carried across the room, high and clear, honed in an age before microphones or sound systems. His speech contained an accent so powerful and dense that the non-Texans in the room had to strain to make it out. It was really a language with phrases, pronunciations, and nuances shaped by years as a black man living in the Deep South. Moreover, Leadbelly didn't sing the kind of blues played by jazz bands heard in clubs or on the radio. It was a much older music that predated both blues and jazz. There was "When I Was a Cowboy" (a story about the western plains) and the work song called "Bring Me Li'l' Water, Silvy." "Whoa, Back Buck," based on commands shouted at oxen, was followed by an old blues Leadbelly learned from a group of levee-camp workers before the turn of the century, "I'm All Out and Down." As he warmed to the occasion, Leadbelly loosened up and fed off the applause and shouts. He performed "Take a Whiff on Me," a song about cocaine. He ended with a version of his song to Governor Pat Neff, the Texas executive who had pardoned him and released him from Sugarland Prison back in 1925, nearly ten years earlier. It was a lively, complicated song, and as he sang it, people stood up to see what he was doing with his feet: Leadbelly tapped his left foot in a steady beat, while his right foot rapped out a complex, lively rhythm in syncopation. "If you don't think that's hard, try it yourself," Lomax would remark later.

The crowd eagerly asked for more. A local reporter wrote: "Two hours after the meal was over they still lingered, draining his repertoire of Negro ballads, working songs and reels and filling his ears with applause and his battered hat with jingling coins." Finally things began to wind down; the pair had another appointment at four and began to gather up their coats. The battered hat held $13.75, which the singer quietly pocketed. Promoters and bookers surrounded Lomax, wanting him to look at contracts they held out to him. A man who said he represented the Century Play Company of 1440 Broadway had in his hand a five-year contract offering the singer a weekly starting salary of $250 with the opportunity to work up to $500 a week. Of course, he admitted, Leadbelly would require "lessons in voice and elocution" before he could make a public appearance. Lomax begged off and told him to wait until Monday.

Throughout all this, John Lomax kept a nervous eye on his singer, alternately visiting and shielding Leadbelly from the people offering contracts and talking about money. "If anybody waved a $10 bill at Leadbelly, he'd follow him out the door," he explained to one reporter. It was all fodder for another round of news stories. As the pair of southerners left for another meeting with the Rockefeller Foundation and then for a six o'clock audition for NBC at Rockefeller Center, the reporters left to file their stories. The story in the *Herald Tribune* ran Saturday under the headline SONGS WIN CASH AND STAGE BIDS FOR LEAD BELLY; the *Time* magazine writer placed his in the music section, under the headline MURDEROUS MINSTREL; the Associated Press man got his on the wire by Saturday morning and watched as it went out to hundreds of local papers across the country. To many of the writers, what they had seen at the Montclair was little more than a good story, a trendy oddity that would pass. A few, though, sensed that this was something special and that the strange music they had heard was something more deep-rooted, more lasting, more elemental. They tended to agree with an editorial in the New York *Post* of January 7, which talked about Leadbelly under the title KING OF THE TWELVE-STRING GUITAR: "In the build-up for Lead Belly we see the making of a new American original. He ought to last a good long time."

The *Post* writer was prophetic. The Montclair show was in many respects the public debut of Huddie Ledbetter; it marked the first time he had played for a middle-class audience. As such, it was the start of a career that would eventually win for him not only the sobriquet "King of the Twelve-String Guitar," but a reputation as America's greatest folksinger. It would be a career that would extend from the coffeehouses of Greenwich Village to the studios of Hollywood, from a jail cell on Rikers Island to the inauguration of a president. Leadbelly would eventually be recognized as an essential link between the rich tradition of nineteenth century black southern folk music and the age of radio and television. He would also introduce several generations of Americans to their folk music heritage. It would be a complex career, full of heartbreak, confusion, struggle, and triumph. And it would be a life wrapped up as much in legend as in songs. In many ways, the news stories that came out of that dramatic week in January marked the start of the Leadbelly mythology.

But in ways none of the reporters could then understand, that week also marked the end of another story, one even stranger and more complex than Leadbelly's own tales suggested. It had roots deep in the southern past, in a world and culture vastly different from any imagined by Leadbelly's newfound admirers. That world was the wellspring of Leadbelly's art, and it was that world he tried, over and over again, to explain and to celebrate. It was a world far removed from the urban canyons and fancy hotels of New York, a world in a distant corner of Louisiana, a world surrounding a vast, brooding lake.

2 The Lake

About fifteen miles northwest of Shreveport, Louisiana, in a flat, humid corner of the United States, the state lines of Louisiana, Texas, and Arkansas converge near a unique body of water known as Caddo Lake. Sprawling across some 150,000 acres in the fertile Red River Valley, the lake extends north and south for over twenty-five miles and is equally broad as it curls west past Uncertain, Texas, and on toward Karnack. It straddles the border of Louisiana and Texas looking like a serpent on its belly.

Many claim that Caddo is the largest natural lake in the South. Its name is taken from the region's first inhabitants, the Caddo Indians, who established permanent villages with houses built of mud and straw near its banks. A primal Caddo Indian legend told of a hunting party returning one day to find the ground gently trembling. Their fear grew as the trembling became more violent. Finally the earth erupted in violence and the Red River engulfed the entire village. Caddo Lake emerged from this carnage.

But early Anglo-American settlers, who began drifting into this section of the Red River Valley during the 1830s, tell a different story of Caddo Lake's creation involving an odd natural feature in the Red River called the "Great Raft." It was a mammoth log jam, an impenetrable mass of ancient, rotted driftwood that clogged the river for some 120 miles, making the Red River unnavigable. Over the decades this mass had so fouled the river that the water backed up and formed Caddo Lake. In 1832 the War Department decided that the jam needed to be cleared; it was vital to increase trade, but even more so for the country's defense. The department hired Captain Henry Miller Shreve, who invented a special boat with a battering ram mounted on its front. He accomplished his task, opened up the area to further settlement, and lent his name to the town that eventually became Shreveport.

For generations the only people who really went into the lake's brooding backwater maze of twisting sloughs and bayous were hunters and fishermen, who were drawn to its natural wealth. The Indians for whom the lake was named had been forced westward and by 1890 were nearly only a memory. But the fishermen would brave the dangerous waters to go after perch, buffalo fish, bass, barfish, and bream. They came back with tales of the legendary Opelousas catfish, which allegedly weighed as much as eight hundred pounds! A 1940 Works Progress Administration (WPA) guidebook to northwestern Louisiana explained: "None but the old-timers here ever venture far into the lake's awesome wilderness of hidden arms and bayous with that picturesque character, the Caddo Negro guide. These local Negroes have an uncanny knowledge of the lake; not only can they find their way along the water roads on the darkest night, but they seem to instinctively know where and when certain kinds of fish are biting."

In 1910, the counties and parishes surrounding the lake in both Louisiana and Texas were home to a huge rural black population. Both in Caddo Parish, Louisiana, and Harrison County, Texas, the African Americans constituted sixty-five percent of the population—sixty thousand out of ninety-three thousand—one of the highest concentrations west of the Mississippi River. Before the turn of the century many blacks found work in the lumber industry, made possible by the thick stands of shortleaf pine. Villages such as Pineland and Pinehill in Texas or Trees, Louisiana, attest to the strength of this industry. Despite the bedevilments of the boll weevil early in the twentieth century, cotton remained a staple and cattle were quite a common sight on the south shore of Caddo Lake. A young man growing up in the region would have found himself at the very center of a thriving community with a rich, vast cultural life passed on through informal dances and all-night weekend house parties. Decades later, Huddie Ledbetter himself would recall playing at such a country dance and remark that "there's no white man for twenty miles."

It was a rather homogenous folk culture on the edge of startling changes, though. In 1906 oil was discovered in Caddo Lake and major oil companies rushed in to explore the area. Companies such as Standolin and Shoreline set up pumping plants at Tree City on the northern tip of Caddo. They quickly grabbed the most promising leases and built pipelines down to the nearby refining areas. Huge, unwieldy, cone-shaped derricks sprouted up in the lake itself and soon spread along the dirt highway running south to Shreveport. Caddo Lake, so long a domain of wilderness, rushed headlong into the twentieth century. Boomtowns sprung up. Oil City, which did not exist when Huddie Ledbetter was born, became the center of a new oil strike and by 1910 emerged as the hub of the oil business in the area. With its wooden sidewalks, muddy streets, hitching rails, and braced-up porches, it eerily resembled a town out of the Old West. Five miles south, the town of Mooringsport shared in this heady growth. Once recognized as just another stop on one of the nation's few inland water mail routes, which ran through the lake to Jefferson, Texas, Mooringsport had been an agricultural center and small port. Soon, it was nicknamed the "City of Derricks" by commercial photographers anxious to sell their scenes of the sleepy town that was suddenly sprouting oil wells like weeds.

The shining black pipelines and the derricks brought new jobs to the region as well. Between 1900 and 1910, Caddo Parish's population leaped from 44,500 to 58,200. And many of these newcomers were blacks, lured from the rural South and the parched farms of Mississippi and Arkansas in particular. The younger generation left their tedious, backbreaking work at local farms to try for a taste of the economic and social benefits of the oil boom, gravitating toward Shreveport, trading rural dances for the red-light districts centered on Fannin Street.

Among the older generation, though, who still believed in the value of the land, was a big, hardworking, lanky man named John Wesley Ledbetter. The son of slaves, he had been born in North Carolina in February 1855 and made his way into Louisiana sometime after the War Between the States. Typically, Wes Ledbetter started off by renting land. Sharecropping permitted him a toehold, into which he dug hard by working the land and shipping his cotton to Shreveport. By the late 1880s he was courting Sallie Pugh, a Louisiana girl who had been born in May 1853. On February 21, 1888, they married in Shreveport. Everyone said that Sallie was half Indian, probably Cherokee, and an exceptionally hard worker who took to the fields alongside her husband. For over ten years the couple tried to start a family, but with little good luck. The 1910 census reported that Sallie had borne four children, but that she had only one living son, "Hudy," born in January 1888.

Huddie Ledbetter always said that he entered the world on the fifteenth of January, but never said exactly where. In later years questions would be raised regarding whether or not he was actually born across the state line in Leigh, Texas. Both the 1900 and the 1910 censuses, however, clearly give his birthplace as Louisiana. And this is vehemently supported by two of his first cousins, Blanch Love and Edmond Ledbetter, who grew up in the same house with Huddie. In 1888 Wes Ledbetter was working on a farm known as the Jeter Plantation, located only a few miles from the Shiloh Baptist Church. This farm is Huddie's birthplace, "no matter what the state of Texas says," insists Blanch Love. Shiloh was a small, predominately black settlement a few miles south of Mooringsport on the Blanchard-Latex Road that runs east from Leigh, Texas, through the crossroads of Latex at the Louisiana state line, skirts south of the lake, and then doglegs northeast into Mooringsport.

Sallie and Wes Ledbetter must have had a strong sense of family, for both wanted more children, but for some reason they could not have them. They were middle-aged when Huddie was born: Wes was thirty-three and Sallie thirty-five, and about 1892 they adopted a girl, Australia Carr Ledbetter. By every account Wes and Sallie truly doted on Huddie and tended to spoil him. "No sir, my papa an' mama was *too* fine to me," he later recalled to John Lomax. "They never touched me to whip me." And their house was

almost always busy and full of relatives. Two of Wes's brothers, Bob Ledbetter and Terrell Ledbetter, often came to visit, displacing Huddie to a pallet
on the floor. His slightly younger cousins, Blanch and Edmond, became
frequent playmates when they came with their father, Bob. Even after Wes
moved his family across the state line to Texas, Huddie would often return
to spend time with his cousins in the Shiloh community.

Wes Ledbetter was fiercely determined to purchase his own land. He was
getting a reputation in the community as a hardworking, self-disciplined
man, but Wes continued to rent because that's all he could afford. His initial
efforts to buy his own place came when Huddie was about five years old;
Wes moved across the line to Texas and went into an even partnership with
another black man. For unknown reasons this arrangement failed, though
Huddie observed that "Pappa had to beat the man up pretty bad." Wes was
back into sharecropping, this time for a wealthy black man named Henry
Simms, who owned nearly four thousand acres near Caddo Lake. By the
early 1900s Wes had managed to scrape together enough money to start
accumulating his own land—around seventy acres bought at the price of
about $2.50 an acre.

It proved to be a bold move that eventually enriched the family. Unfortunately, their new land was remote and not yet cleared. And before leaving
sharecropping, Wes had to put in a final crop for Henry Simms, then build
some kind of house for his young family. Though Harrison County, Texas,
was directly across the state line from Caddo Parish, it seemed like they
were moving into another world, like they were pioneers on a wild frontier.
The work was arduous and never seemed to end. Huddie recalled how his
parents worked far past dark clearing the land. "My father would cut down
trees and my mother would cut down brush and I'd be home sleeping."
Often he and Australia would wake up long after dark and find their parents
were still working: "Sometimes I'd wake up at night way late, and watch
the fires burning off there in the bottom . . . my papa, he was a worker!"

When Huddie later proved a hard worker on the prison farms, he was
quick to credit these family lessons and the example set by his father.
Growing up in the rural South naturally taught him other real-life lessons:
how to chop cotton and then pick it in the heat of late summer, how to cut
and split wood, how to walk two miles through the piny woods to get to
school, how to ride a horse to run errands. The nearest country store was
a five-mile ride, so getting basics such as mail or coal oil for the lamps
required real effort. Huddie had to learn how to hold the full five-gallon
coal-oil can away from the saddle on the way back, far enough away so that
it would not touch the horse and spill out.

Life for the Ledbetter family was tough. Sometimes the frustrations of
providing for a growing family in rural northeast Texas broke out in domes-

tic violence. Usually Wes would take it out on Sallie. At these times young Huddie had no one to run to, and he became adept at improvising strategies for coping. "My daddy used to knock mama down if she disagreed with him," he recalled, "and I would go and stand under the shotgun on the wall until they would stop."

About 1896, when he was ready to start school, Huddie already stood broad and tall, and didn't seem to mind the two-mile walk through the close stands of pine trees to reach the nearest school at Lake Chapel, Texas. Often he trooped off in a small cluster with his cousins, Blanch and Edmond. Like nearly all of their contemporaries, the Ledbetters lived in a small log cabin, which was situated near their relatives at Swanson's Landing on Caddo Lake. This farm adjoins the very land upon which Queen Davidson, Huddie's "double cousin" (her parents were brother and sister to Wes and Sallie) still lived in 1992. Over one hundred years after the Ledbetter family moved to Harrison County, it maintains a strong sense of home and ties to the land. Even this early Huddie—or "Son," as his family called him—was prepared to fight if necessary, especially if his family, even his extended family, was involved. "Son wouldn't take on his cousins," recalls Blanch Love, "but he would fight for us. He didn't steal, he didn't bother nobody, but whenever they'd start at him, he'd fight—that he would." Another slightly older relative, Mary Patterson, also sometimes accompanied Huddie to school. Years later she recollected that he developed into a "pretty good student [who] sometimes rode a horse. He'd come down the road, singing on his beautiful pony, black, with a star on his face."

But perhaps the best account of these early school years, about which Huddie himself was somewhat reserved, comes from his childhood friend and later sweetheart, Margaret Coleman. In 1935 she wrote, "He was an apt boy in his books, was always willing to learn. . . . He was an honest boy, never meddled, quarrelled, or argued with anyone. He was plain spoken. Something about Huddie's life was quite different from other children's; he never played like the others." Even as a child Huddie appeared to others as a loner, one who observed but often stayed apart from his peers. Although he rarely precipitated conflicts or confrontations, Margaret Coleman recalled, "he did not have time for psalms although he was friendly with everyone." In retrospect, people noticed an odd intensity about this child who "never played like others, he talked of the things he wanted to [do] when he became a man." A harsh environment can make you grow up in a hurry.

Huddie attended school regularly for several years before the realities of life forced his parents to reconsider this luxury. It seems he stayed in school until he was at least twelve or thirteen, certainly until he could read and write quite well. His parents were in their mid-forties and in good health—

hardly too old to manage their farm and their daily chores. What is remarkable is that Huddie remained in school for as long as he did, or that he even
attended school at all. In 1910 over a third of Harrison County blacks were
illiterate. Huddie not only gained literacy, but his later letters and correspondence demonstrated a clear ability to read and write adeptly. Furthermore, the Lake Chapel School was located in a remote corner of Texas that
in a real sense was one of the last parts of the true frontier. It was centered
in a huge rural black enclave, surrounded by a largely white society in
which the Ku Klux Klan marched with impunity. Lynchings, though
becoming increasingly rare, were not unheard of.

Even with the occasional outburst of emotion and anger, Huddie's home
remained pretty stable. Wes Ledbetter helped his son with his schoolwork
and Sallie encouraged Wes to control his temper. Ironically, the Ledbetter
relatives sometimes felt that Wes and Sallie didn't come down hard enough
on their only son. Mary Patterson observed, "That's what his parents said,
'Everyone always picks on Son.' He had them believing that." Wes occasionally reproached Huddie, and on rarer occasions Sallie would weigh in
with her thoughts. "But if she got too tight on him, he would get on his
knees and start crying. Tears that would melt your heart," Irene Campbell,
a second cousin of Huddie's, opines. "He was really an only son, and his
mother and father were so proud of him. They'd just give him everything
he wanted, not needed, but wanted. He was just so spoiled. At 14 he started
running around." Years later Huddie himself agreed with his cousin's ob-
servations. "Wasn't nothing my momma and papa wouldn't do for me,
wasn't nothin' they wouldn't buy me, if I wanted it." Given such an attitude, it would not be hard to see Huddie deciding to leave school when he
was twelve or thirteen with few serious objections from his parents. And in
fact, an eighth-grade education for rural southern children, either black or
white, was considered quite suitable at that time.

Now that he was no longer attending school, Huddie's days revolved
around work: tough, demanding, physical labor. This fate held true for
most everyone, black or white, living in northwestern Louisiana. In the
steamy, sultry Louisiana summers, Huddie's stamina and heavyset build
became clear assets. He had been helping his father on the farm since he
was six. Blanch Love, Huddie, and the other children were all put to work
chopping cotton when they were old enough to handle a hoe. The farm
routine never varied: The cotton was chopped in the spring, then picked in
the summer and immediately taken to the gin house. "When I was a small
boy," Huddie recalled, "we'd go to the gin house and gin cotton. Bales'd
weigh 550 and 575, hundreds a bale. It would take four or five men to put
on a bale of cotton on a wagon." As he grew, Huddie became increasingly
adept at picking cotton. This was a practical point as well as a matter of

pride because there were no other male children to share the burden. Often it was simply Huddie and Wes working ceaseless hours in the oppressive fields. Eventually, Huddie "could pick more cotton than any man in Caddo Lake country except my daddy." Others, including Irene Campbell, have similar recollections. "He worked fast and steadily—plowing, chopping cotton or corn, or gathering crops. His mother said he could do as much work as two men."

Huddie attacked this repetitive field work with zeal. He did it well and with a certain flair, and even developed a distinctive style for working. His second cousin, Irene, some twenty years younger than Huddie, was impressed with his posturing, and even called him "uncle." "My first memory of Uncle Huddie Ledbetter [was] seeing him going to the field wearing starched and ironed overalls with a red bandanna around his neck and wearing a hat." This emphasis on image also was adopted by Huddie for the press and his audience when he first came to New York City in 1935. Huddie somehow persuaded his mother, and later his wives, to iron and starch his overalls so that he would have a clean, snappy pair for each day's work. Another niece, Viola Daniels, remembered the starched overalls—a new pair every day—and even his polished black shoes.

Most people now associate cotton picking and Leadbelly, but that wasn't the only type of work he accomplished as a boy. His schoolmates clearly recall his love of horses and his childhood pony in particular. Northeast Texas was clearly part of the cowboy culture, as were blacks. In a later interview, Huddie explained that African American cowboys were not unusual in those days around Caddo Lake. "There was right smart of 'em; they was just country cowboys. They wasn't professionals—go out on the ranches, but they'd [go] down in the country, you know, and drive cows." Cowboy life was enough of Huddie's life that on his sixteenth birthday Wes slyly presented him with a big horse and a fancy, well-apportioned saddle as part of his coming-of-age present.

Huddie was ecstatic but quickly discovered that the present had its utilitarian value and wasn't merely ceremonial. In his situation such presents had to serve a practical purpose. "I used to take a horse, my own saddle horse, and go down on the lake and drive up cows. Doctor Wascom, he used to have a lot of cows and he'd hire boys, give'm so much to take their horses and go and drive'm down to the lake and put 'em out on the lake for summertime so they could eat grass. Well, I had a good horse and I'd go down."

Huddie's sixteenth birthday brought another very practical present, a new pistol. Such weapons were not uncommon on this frontier, for there were wild animals to be shot and cattle to be protected. Of course, a man's honor was always at stake. Wes Ledbetter warned Huddie, though, that the gun was to be used only in self-defense. But Huddie had never been one to turn away from a fight, even when he first began grade school. His childhood friend Margaret Coleman stated, "He never tried to interfere with anyone unless they would give him a cause, then he would try to defend himself." In fact, Huddie by this time had a schoolyard reputation for being good with his fists. This reputation must have been hard-earned in a tough rural setting where fighting was part of everyday life. Something of this fighting and code or honor is reflected in a story about his youth that Huddie told in 1940:

But once when I was a boy, I was about sixteen years old and I was down around Karnack [Texas], here down South. I'd always been a good knocker, I could knock with my fists, and I run up on a colored boy at the mill. He was double-jointed. And those boys at them times, they'd get around and they'd all talk about one another, knockin' at school. And one of the boys told me, said "Leadbelly's a good knocker." I could run and knock. I always tried to get a run on and knock anything with my fist. We wouldn't hit the side of the head, we'd hit in the breast and in the short ribs. . . . My way, when I'm knockin' a man, if he ain't got nothing in his pockets, I'm going to sort of hit him in the groin there. I slap him with the back of my hand to get him to bow and when he's bowin', I meet him with a blow in the breast, like I used to jab him there.

Now I looked upon this boy and he was double-jointed. . . . He says, "See here, Leadbelly, don't you want to knock?" I says, "No, I don't want to knock." He says "Oh yes, you got to knock me." I says, "Oh, no, I'm not gonna knock you." I looked at him, kept looking at him, arms so big, and I said, "What is you, you double-jointed?" And he said "Yes," and I said, "I'm not gonna knock you. I'm single-jointed, I'm not gonna knock no double-jointed." He says "Oh, you gotta knock me. Now get out of there." "No I won't." Now I got my knife ready, 'cause I was gonna knock him or knock him with that knife. I wasn't gonna let this fellow get over me, you see. And I was gonna knock him with my knife, or a stick of stovewood or something.

There was once an old man there—old man Hunter—he was a man that'd butt you, you know. So him and another fellow got in it and old man Hunter, he'd butt you, he'd knock you out. When he aim to butt [this] man, the man reached down and got a stick of stovewood and hit him in the head with that stick of stovewood, you understand. And that was the way he won the fight. You couldn't win it with a man that'd butt, see.

Huddie was so impressed with the double-jointed man because such men were thought to have almost legendary strength. As a boy his father had pointed out to him a local character, "old man Eve Brown," who was double-jointed. "A double-jointed man, he's got two joints to your one. He's always fat and stout, and he can grab you and just tie you up like that," Huddie explained. Old man Brown could toss an entire bale of cotton, over five hundred pounds worth, into a wagon by himself. Another famous double-jointed man was John Henry, the legendary West Virginia steel driver and a titan of African American folklore. Even as early as 1900, Huddie had heard of him. "He could drive steel both ways, going and coming," he recalled.

The point of Huddie's story, though, was that such unnatural strength could be neutralized. You could gain the advantage by using a stick of stovewood, a knife . . . or a shiny new pistol bought by your father. While he was no mean bully, neither was Huddie going to let anyone take advantage of him. So much of Huddie's life reflected our vision of the Old West as much as that of the Deep South. By the time he reached adolescence, Huddie had proved himself as a hard worker, as a cotton chopper, and as a cowboy. His family was far from poor and they doted on Huddie, who learned the importance of holding up the fine name of the Ledbetter clan. These lessons stayed with him throughout his life, for better or worse.

But he was learning more than how to defend himself or how to chase cattle on horseback. As he honed these skills on his father's farm around that huge, mysterious lake, Huddie also began to discover another passion—music. This ability quickly became an even more important tool in his struggles to define himself and his place in this turbulent black frontier.

3 Marshall Lullaby

In later years, Huddie Ledbetter would always talk about the blues and how much it contributed to his own musical background. But in the complex rural black culture of Harrison County, Texas, in the waning years of the nineteenth century, there were many other musical forms and styles. Some styles—blues and gospel songs—became part of the stereotyped image that whites had of black folk music, while ballads, string band music, hollers, topical broadsides, and others almost vanished from later black folk music. All, however, were part of the musical mélange young Huddie was exposed to in the years from 1888 to 1900 and contributed to one of the most wonderfully diverse repertoires in folk music history.

Huddie apparently began trying to make music when he was as young as two years old. Irene Campbell recalled stories her grandmother told her about Huddie picking up a twig, hollowing it out, whittling holes, and creating his own primitive fife. It is quite possible that he saw older men doing something like this with larger, heavier cane, the source of fifes still played by some older black musicians in north-central Mississippi. But Huddie also was drawn to other more formal instruments as well. Again drawing on her grandmother's stories, Irene Campbell said, "He would sit in his little rocking chair. His feet could not touch the ground, but he could play tunes on the accordion and the mandolin."

When no instrument was around, Huddie used his voice—the most basic of all instruments. He vividly recalled how he would get up in the morning to go to school and race out into the yard to give a "getting-up" holler to his friends. "When I was a little boy, going to a country school, the little boys, we was living in the woods about three and four miles apart from each other. First little boy [that] gets up in the morning, he wanted to let the others know he was up, wanted to see which one beat up. They had a little echo, call it 'Ho-day,' and the first one to get up, he'd run outside and start hollering." The other boys would eventually echo this greeting.

Huddie was quick to point out that these hollers were different from the field hollers later used in picking cotton or working in the fields. These were purely celebratory hollers, ways to let your friends know that you were up and all right—or that you had managed to beat them in getting up. In an age before telephones, such communication was quite common between neighbors in the backwoods South. Some hollers became quite elaborate, and in some communities an entire repertoire of hollers developed: from distress hollers requesting help to good-morning hollers designed to celebrate a new day. Certain people became acknowledged experts at complex hollers that could be heard for long distances. Huddie and his friends even knew hollers that verged on becoming little songs, replete with blueslike lyrics:

> *One dollar bill, baby, won't buy you no shoes.*
> *One dollar bill, baby, won't buy you no shoes.*
>
> *Dollar bill, baby, won't buy you no shoes.*©

School itself even offered different types of music to a young boy fascinated with sounds and rhymes. During recess most of the boys played ball while the girls would organize "play-parties" or "ring" games. Sometimes the boys would join these activities that combined actions and songs into an infectious game, which could be expanded to fit a specific length of time. Such games fascinated young Huddie and gave him one of his first opportunities to actually sing about some part of his life. The "play" that he best remembered was one that later became one of his favorite musical pieces, "Ha, Ha Thisaway." Though he later recorded numerous different verses of the song, one of the most cogent was:

> *I'm gonna tell you, tell you, tell you,*
> *I'm gonna tell you, to save my soul.*
> *Teacher's gonna fail you, fail you, fail you,*
> *Teacher's gonna fail you, so I was told.*©

There was also, at the Lake Chapel School about 1900, a teacher with a strong interest in music named George Summers. He organized a little band among the students there. Karnack native Mary Patterson, who was about the same age as Huddie, recalls how Summers taught Huddie some of the rudiments: "He had me playing a little old string instrument, a mandolin. There was three or four of us in that little band. Huddie played the guitar." Nobody knows exactly what kind of repertoire the "little band" played, but it was probably full of dance music and waltzes. Summers's instruction, probably the only formal teaching in music ever received by Huddie, most likely concentrated on tuning, keeping time, and chord positions. A few of the songs that Huddie recalled in later years, such as the vaudeville piece "Lindy Lou," were known to have been in the repertoires of black string bands from the Deep South.

At home Huddie's interest in music pleased both parents. Though he was not a singer, Wes Ledbetter certainly liked music and apparently could even play a little on the guitar. Sallie, whose fine voice often led the choir at the Shiloh Baptist Church, sang lullabies and spirituals to her young son. But the real role models for music making came from his two uncles, Bob and Terrell. Both lived nearby (though Terrell eventually settled in, ironically, a town named Terrell, Texas) and worked full-time chopping cotton and plowing. They also enjoyed local reputations as guitarists and vocalists of the kind Huddie later referred to as "songster." This term denoted a person who was a noted singer, played a stringed instrument, and possessed a wide repertoire of sacred and secular music. Songsters like Uncle Terrell sometimes roamed about, picking up songs from traveling minstrels and vaudeville stages as well as from their peers. He eventually taught Huddie the work song "Looky Yonder Where the Sun Done Gone" and the pan-Southern drug classic "Take a Whiff on Me," which was equally popular in both black and white circles. The latter song was about cocaine—still a legal drug at the turn of the century—and warned, "Cocaine's for horses and not for men,/ the doctor say it kill you, but he won't say when." Uncle Bob stayed closer to home, mostly around Oil City. John Lomax recorded him for the Library of Congress in 1940, including the "Cleveland Campaign Song" about the election of Grover Cleveland in 1884. Bob's son, Edmond, became a songster and he would often play with Huddie when they were both teenagers. Margaret Coleman wrote that "through all this there was an unfinished duty he looked forward to, so he talked it over with his parents to get him some kind of an instrument so he could learn music." When Huddie was seven this dream came true when Uncle Terrell dropped by the house, returning by mule from Mooringsport. A "windjammer" (a small button accordion) hung from his saddle and he gave it to his excited nephew. Huddie worked on it all evening and into the night, trying to find the proper combination of rhythm and buttons to make a tune. His experimentation wore down Sallie and Wes's patience, but they understood his enthusiasm. By morning Huddie had mastered a rough version of "There's No Cornbread Here." A few days later his mother taught him an old jig called "Dinah's Got a Wooden Leg." Soon she was adding to his repertoire some of the lullabies and spirituals she sang in church and Huddie was learning that the windjammer could be as much at home in the church as at the local square dance.

During the next several years, Huddie began to find out that he had a special talent for remembering the words and melodies to the songs he heard in his community. They were not only the church songs and simple jigs and reels he had started with, but the whole range of contemporary southern black folk music. Though he was later called a bluesman, at this date blues were just emerging as a musical genre separate from others such as ragtime, work songs, and dance tunes.

Other instruments came his way and Huddie displayed an aptitude for them all: harmonica, piano, Jew's harp, and even the old reed organ at the Shiloh Church. Soon he was being asked to come to the country dances to play his accordion. Huddie would mount his pony, hook the windjammer to the saddle horn, and ride far into the countryside. By 1903, he had become a fixture at the sukey jumps, which paid him fifty cents a night. Huddie gradually grew more fascinated with stringed instruments, especially with the drive and rhythm he could generate with them. His early experience with the mandolin and guitar in the Lake Chapel School had only whetted his appetite. "He loved music," Mary Patterson said, "but he liked string music even better."

In addition to learning from his uncles, Huddie learned some music from two local boys, Bud Coleman and Jim Fagin, who played for country dances. One played the guitar, the other the mandolin, and Huddie soon followed them to every dance at which they performed. He begged his father to buy him a guitar, and after a day during which Huddie was particularly persuasive, Wes relented. As with the accordion, Huddie stayed up the entire first night trying to pick out the tunes he'd heard Coleman and Fagin perform: "Green Corn" was the first tune he learned. It was an old dance song often played by white fiddlers at square dances—the "green corn" of the title refers to newly run moonshine whiskey carried in a "jimmy-john"—and Huddie would keep it in his repertoire the rest of his life. From Jim Fagin he learned "Po' Howard," a song about a legendary black fiddler from the early Emancipation days.

———

Huddie probably got his guitar around 1903, about the time the instrument was experiencing a real surge of popularity in the rural South. Throughout much of the previous century, the guitar was known as a genteel parlor instrument, suitable for strumming by the lady of the house or the unmarried daughter wanting to entertain a suitor. President Andrew Jackson's wife Rachael owned a guitar and in the 1870s and 1880s music publishers issued dozens of books and sheet music pieces that made the guitar resemble the staid, classical instrument it once was in European culture. There are a few scattered instances, though, of the instruments falling into the hands of folk musicians: a foot soldier in the Civil War, a black entertainer in a band in a St. Louis tavern at the turn of the century, a cowboy accompanying himself in a ballad in the New Mexico territory. Generally, though, it was not a favorite instrument with nineteenth century blacks. In a survey of musical instruments mentioned in interviews with former slaves done by the Works Progress Administration in the 1930s, the guitar was seldom mentioned in comparison with the fiddle and the banjo. While 205 ex-slaves mentioned fiddles and 106 recalled the banjo, only 15 talked about guitars.

Suddenly, at the end of the century, all this began to change when companies like Gibson and the new mail-order house of Sears, Roebuck began to manufacture inexpensive guitars.

Huddie lacked neither mentors nor partners with whom to pick. His first cousin, Edmond Ledbetter, Uncle Bob's son, remembered the kind of music he and Huddie used to make. "We were kids together, used to make music. Sometimes he played a mandolin and I'd second him with a guitar and sometimes we played the guitar together. Used to play all 'round here, up to Mooringsport, over to Leigh [Texas], and back to the Jeter Plantation." The two boys were so close that people often thought that they were brothers. Often they were joined by Starling Myers, another part-time songster who also worked as a local guide for Caddo Lake fishermen.

Huddie demonstrated an immediate aptitude not only for learning music but for learning it quickly and skillfully. Though he was good at school, Huddie was even better with music. Soon he was out in the country playing music for parties and dances, but he always came home in time for work and school. But there was a lot yet to come—new songs, emerging styles of music, new ways to sell himself to an audience. Huddie was starting to emerge as a brash and self-confident teenager who was beginning to sense some of the possibilities for his music.

Most of the parties and dances that Margaret Coleman talked about were held in rural houses miles from the nearest town and often miles from the nearest white homestead. "They called them sukey jumps," Huddie recollected many years later. *Sukey*, or *sookie*, was apparently a Deep South slang term dating from the 1820s and referring to a servant or slave. A sukey jump, therefore, was once a dance or party in slave quarters. Huddie himself once explained the term by saying, "Because they dance so fast, the music was so fast and the people had to jump, so they called them sooky jumps." *Sookie*, Huddie thought, was derived from the field term for cow and was used to call a cow, too. Whatever the case, these late nineteenth century country dances gave Leadbelly the first public platform for his music.

Often the dances were held in private homes, which the owners had prepared by moving most of the furniture outside or up against the wall. By dusk, a big bonfire would be started out front, both to help cook the food and to alert people about the exact location for the dance. Zora Neale Hurston, the famed writer and folklorist who later came to know Leadbelly in New York, described such a dance in the book *Mules and Men:*

You can tell the dances are to be held by the fires. Huge bonfires of faulty logs and slabs are lit outside the house in which the dances are held. The

*refreshments are parched peanuts, fried rabbit, fish, chicken, and chitter-
lings. The only music is guitar music and the only dance is the ole square
dance.*

In another account, she noted that many times the only music was performed on a guitar, and while "one guitar was enough for a dance, to have
two was considered excellent. Where two were playing one man played the
lead and the other seconded him. The first player was 'picking' and the
second 'framing,' that is, playing chords while the lead carried the melody
by dexterous finger-work."

Mance Lipscomb, the Texas songster and bluesman who was some ten
years Huddie's junior, also spent an apprenticeship at rural house parties,
mostly along the Brazos River in Texas. As a youth, he went to the dances
in order to learn new material. "I wasn't out there for nothin'; I was
catchin' them songs," he recalled. Later he began to play his guitar for the
dances, sometimes with three different sets of musicians who were set up
in shifts so that the dance could go on all night without interruption.
Lipscomb remembered:

*The first crew was eight o'clock. I played an hour with them. They had
everything in bloom. Long about twelve o'clock, here come another crew
in there. Fresh crew! I fan them out. Played all night till four o'clock, in the
morning, sometimes eleven o'clock on a Sunday. Setting right in one chair.
And they had me settin' up there, and wasn't no electric lights. Had old
lamp lights. No electricity. No fan. And I'd get down there an' set by that
window to get a little air. Lots of nights I played all night long, didn't have
nothin' on but my pants. No shirt at all. Just sweaty as I could be. Trying
to stay cool. And long about twelve or one o'clock, you'd hear a gun
somewhere, in the house or out the house. "Boom!" Somebody died.*

The earliest dances that Huddie remembered featured music played on
the fiddle or accordion, or windjammer. Years later he could still play some
of the old dance tunes on his accordion, pieces such as "Sukey Jump" and
the minstrel show song "Jawbone." Like so many of the old fiddle tunes,
they were primarily instrumental, with a few vocal choruses thrown in for
variety's sake.

*Jawbone eat and Jawbone talk,
Jawbone eat with a knife and fork.*

But the most interesting description of a late nineteenth century sukey
jump comes from Chris Franklin, an ex-slave from Caddo Parish interviewed about his musical activities in 1937:

De white folk 'low dem [allow them] to have de frolic with de fiddle or banjo
or windjammer. Dey dance out on de grass, forty or fifty niggers, and dem
big girls nineteen years old git out dere barefoot as de goose. It jes' de habit
of de times, 'cause dey all have shoes. Sometimes dey call de jig dance and
some of dem sho' dance it, too. De prompter call "All git ready." Den de
holler, "All balance," and den he sing out "Swing your pardner," and dey
does it. Den he say "All promenade," and dey goes in de circle. One thing
dey calls, "Bird in de Cage." Three join hands round de gal in de middle,
and dance around her, and den she git out and her pardner git in the center
and dey dance awhile.

One old fiddle song—one borrowed from the African American fiddle
tradition, not necessarily from whites—was Leadbelly's version of the familiar "Give the Fiddler a Dram," which he called "Gwine Dig a Hole to Put
the Devil In." This hard-driven breakdown with simple, expandable verses
could easily be drawn out to a fifteen- or twenty-minute set. Whites had
often sung about giving the fiddler a dram of liquor; the line among black
performers dealt with the concept of digging a hole for the devil. Huddie
explained that "long years ago that was when they see the boss comin', you
know, and the boys would see the boss comin', well, they didn't like him,
you know, but they'd be together, nothing but Negroes, all piled-up there
together. When they see him comin' they say 'Well, we gonna dig a hole to
put the Devil in, boy they 'started to jumpin.' "
These turn-of-the-century gatherings featured a number of different
styles of dancing. The older people preferred the classic Texas square dance,
which had been developed from the French cotillion and contra dance
decades earlier. "They called the sets all the time when they danced," said
Huddie. "They called 'Shoo Fly,' uses 'shoo fly' mean square dance." It
worked this way: a couple would get on the dance floor and, on cue from
the caller, begin to circle to the right. And then, said Huddie,

when you get back to your home [starting place], grab your partner, the
first man on the head "shoo fly." When they begin to "shoo fly" then they
holler:

> Shoo fly, shoo fly,
> Shoo fly, shoo fly,

Then they commence hollering:

> One dollar bill baby, won't buy you no shoes,
> One dollar bill baby, won't buy you no shoes,
> One dollar bill baby, won't buy you no shoes.©

Then the next man would "head shoo fly": get his partner and circle around. This continued until each couple of them had circled to home; they then would make a ring and circle again, find their partners, and began to "dance on ahead and dance toward the candy stand."

Younger partners preferred a faster beat and a faster tune, and did a complex set of dance steps that Huddie later referred to as "breakdowns" or "the old buck and wing": "You got to do it real fast. And when you breakdown you ain't tapping, you just working your legs. Now a long time ago my grandfather, great grandfather, say you ain't dancing 'til you cross you legs." The Baptist church tried to discourage African religious practices among slaves. It forbade not only drumming, but any kind of dancing—with dancing defined as movement that involved crossing the legs. Thus these rural dances were not just an incidental part of Huddie's growing up; they were deep-rooted links to his African American heritage and a vital part of the rich musical culture that was nourishing him.

Another account from the turn of the twentieth century describes a dance called the Dog Scratch being done by two individuals surrounded by a circle of men who shouted encouragement, and clapped and eventually joined in. Mance Lipscomb recalled seeing two dancers engaged in "cutting contests . . . seein' who could outdance the other one. You ever see two roosters flappin' up alongside on another? It was like that." Leadbelly also recalled a step called "Knockin' a Pigeon-Wing," which he asserted went well with a song like "You Can't Losa-Me Cholly." The Pigeon Wing was, in fact, one of the most enduring of these old dance steps; dancers scraped and shaked one foot, then another, fluttering their arms like an awkward bird trying to fly. Then there was the Eagle Rock, which Huddie later celebrated in a barrelhouse piano solo for Capitol Records. This was yet another "bird" dance, descended from an even earlier plantation dance called the Buzzard Lope. (Mance Lipscomb remembered dancers doing this step at some of his parties, but it pretty much died out by the 1930s.) In the Eagle Rock, the dancer rocked his body from side to side while making preening, winglike movements with his arms. This dance made it into the dance halls and bordellos of urban areas in the region; veteran New Orleans cornet player Charlie Love recalled that he and his friends danced the Eagle Rock to the music of Buddy Bolden, the legendary cornet player who laid the groundwork for New Orleans jazz.

All of these things young Huddie took in, and the hours he spent watching dancers in all manner of dusty cabins and tin-roofed farmhouses were not lost. He, in fact, became a dancer himself, and his early reputation was built as much on his dancing as on his singing or guitar playing. He did the old buck dances and square dances and he could "cut" the Pigeon Wing along with the Short Dog along with the best of them. But the dance that he really specialized in was a newer dance derived from these old steps, the tap dance. His niece, Irene Campbell, recalled some of the Saturday night get-togethers the family or the community would have, and how Huddie would be the center of attention: "He did tap dancing. He was the first person that I ever saw do tap dancing. It was very much like they have today. It was entertainment, sometimes just for the family. You know that we would come by. They would have competitions to see who could 'cut it,' called it 'Cut the Pigeon Wing.' "

In later years, Huddie recorded a sample of the kind of dancing he did for such affairs, under the title "Leadbelly's Dance." It was fast and complex, involving the feet, the hands, and slapping "hambone" on the body. Parts of it combined storytelling with dance. For one sequence, he explains, "My mama used to make flapjacks and here's the way she's make'em up"; for another, Leadbelly says, "I used to walk down to the levee with my gal and here's the way she'd walk."

In fact, Leadbelly seems to have done what most dance historians call a "soft shoe," the older forerunner of tap-dancing that was done without the actual metal taps. This kind of dance probably came from a merging of English-Irish jigs and clog dances with African American solo dances. An ex-slave named James W. Smith described "jigging contests" held on plantations about the time of the Civil War in Texas, where one of the dancers could "make his feet go like triphammers and sound like the snaredrum." Early minstrel show dancers soon began to make distinctions between the clog and the soft shoe, and during the days following the Civil War, black minstrel stars like Billy Kersands began to feature a version of the soft shoe he called Essence of Old Virginia. Influential later dancers such as George Primrose popularized "leather soles" even more, and traveling circuses, tent shows, and vaudeville revues took these innovations deep into the hinterlands. In a sense, they returned them to the folk tradition.

Huddie probably learned from what he had seen of the soft-shoe dance on stage and copied it. A few years later, when young Huddie spent time with the blind bluesman and songster Blind Lemon Jefferson, one of his jobs was to do a soft-shoe tap dance while Jefferson played a guitar instrumental such as the ragtime-styled "Hot Dog" (which he later recorded for Paramount Records). Dancing was clearly intrinsic to Huddie's music.

Huddie always worked during the week, and Saturday night was the night to really kick back and let off steam. But there was another side to that coin on Sunday morning. The Ledbetters attended the local Shiloh Baptist Church. "He used to be a secretary. . . ." Huddie said of his father years later. "And my mother used to lead prayer meetings and my father, too, they always worked their hymns out, the Baptists do." The old Shiloh Baptist Church is just south of the Jeter Plantation, where Huddie was born, and it was at this church he heard the old hymns and spirituals. "Death is slow but death is sure, Hallelu, Hallelu," he would sing as a lad, listening to his father "line out" the songs, call out the words line by line before the congregation sang it. This was a stark but evocative body of songs, rich in imagery and strong in melody, and it took its place in young Huddie's imagination, alongside the old folk ballads, reels, and field hollers. During the first years of Huddie's popularity in the middle 1930s, most of his fans and admirers overlooked this aspect of his music, but in later years Huddie made up for the oversight by recording dozens of religious songs and including them in his programs.

Huddie grew up in the church, although he did not actually join a congregation until he was around twenty. He became thoroughly familiar with the different styles of prayer meetings, revivals, Sunday services, singing styles, and even the techniques for preaching a sermon. Huddie became adept at imitating the singsong, emotional chants of the old preachers and in 1943 he recorded such a parody for a New York record company:

> There's a lot of pretty girls up in Heaven—
> That's going to make everybody want to go to Heaven—
> Going up there to see the pretty girls—
> There's a big stream of molasses,
> run right down through heaven—
> It may sound funny, it don't cost money—
> But there's a big stream of honey
> running down through Heaven—
> And there's lots of flapjacks
> and a lot of good butter—
> And a good sharp knife sittin' on each side—

Huddie also learned the essential elements of song leading, how to "line out" a song, and how to understand the age-old types of poetic meter used in the songs, such as "common meter," "long meter," and "short meter." Such metrical schemes referred not to the musical notation but simply to the number of syllables in each individual line of a song. Leadbelly explained that "Must I Be Carried to the Sky on Flowered Beds of Ease" was "the long meter. You see, I didn't cut that off at all . . . [in] common meter you cut off between them two verses. You got to always cut off between the verses to make it common. And to make it long, you sing two verses right at once on the long time."

As Huddie's reputation as a singer grew, he began to find himself more in demand to sing in church. One of the big events in the church year was the "tracted meeting," annual revival services that lasted for several days. The meetings were almost a form of folk theater, in which the congregation participated as much as the preacher, improvising with passion, blurring the boundary lines between singing, preaching, praying, and testifying. Huddie once described such a prayer meeting on a recording for the Library of Congress:

Now, they sing that first song at the beginning of the prayer meeting, [then] they'd get down to prayer. Now, they open up but they keep on all night. They call on one brother or one sister to pray and when they call on some of the sisters to pray they just shakes, you know, some of 'em be so nervous, you know, they can't hardly pray trembling in their voice. Well, some men be like that. Now, that's the way they carry on their meeting down South, at my home.

After the first round of prayers, they would sing again—"they'll sing, they goin' around to the mourners, everybody goin' get around the mourners and start singing for a while and then the preacher going [to] preach." Later, when the men were done praying, the "Amen corner" sisters started out:

The Amen corner sisters, the ones who do this moanin', starts out, the whole church can help 'em. But they starts out, and when the preacher, and when the men is prayin', to give 'em some spirit, they'd moan behind 'em and that would make 'em pray and the sisters would holler "C'mon and mon there Sister Sally."

Of course, the same kind of talent and fame that helped him fill the collection plate through his singing eventually brought him into the bad graces of some of the older church members. As his reputation as a "rounder" and a party-goer grew, some of the women got a little nervous. Sallie Hooks, a long-time resident of Mooringsport and cousin of Martha Promise (later to be Huddie's wife), saw Huddie in church as a child and thought of him as a "worldly man":

He could play church songs. I remember when we first got our organ at church. I was a little girl back then and he played the organ. We didn't have nobody else could play and lots of old folks liked to have had a spell because he didn't belong to the church. My daddy and all got around the old sisters wouldn't let them bother him.

Although the image of the young, strapping teenager being protected from a posse of "older sisters" seems a bit odd, the story of Huddie playing the first organ at his church remains a familiar legend in western Caddo Parish. Huddie's niece Pinkie Williams agrees with the story, but views it from a slightly different angle. She recalls that Wes Ledbetter was a "secretary" for the church and that the entire family was active in the church. "The whole family was in the church. Huddie was the first organist at the Shiloh Baptist Church; his name is on the church record. He could play just about anything."

Wes and Sallie undoubtedly pressured their son to go to church, to join the church, and to become a Christian. Huddie, however, never did actually join until after he left home. His interests seem to have been in the music, rather than the spiritual message. "I never led no prayer," he remarked. "I just used to lead singing. They never would call on me to pray. Of course, I could do it all right . . . I can pray and preach, too. I can *sure* pray."

How much of the church Huddie truly believed in and how much of it he viewed as mere theater is debatable. His two nieces Viola and Irene Campbell both feel that he was more serious about his beliefs than many thought. "He had a deep-down . . . belief in religion. Because if someone would come in and they would be cursing and using profanity, wrong language, Huddie would say 'Look, you don't do that here. These are my nieces and you don't do that here!' And usually when he would speak like that, people would move."

But gradually Huddie began to slide away from the church. By his mid-teens, Huddie Ledbetter had become, in the eyes of some church members, a "backslider." "That was when somebody done belong to the church and done turned back," remarked Huddie. At revivals and prayer meetings, the members would sing, "Backslider, fare you well, I will meet you on kingdom's shore." Yet Huddie himself never really felt any dramatic isolation from his church, or from his religion. He later said, "I believe I got as good a religion as I ever had before but I just liked music and singing, you know, and dancing. I just went on back and started doing it."

And years later, hundreds of miles from the Shiloh Church and Mooringsport, he could vividly recall and sing the songs he learned there: "Get on Board," "Let It Shine on Me," "Must I Be Carried to the Sky on Flowered Beds of Ease?," "Down in the Valley to Pray," "Run Sinners," "Ride On," "The Blood Done Signed Your Name," and others. It was a music as rich as that he heard at the sukey jumps, as steeped in tradition, as passionate, as memorable; it was a ballast that would help him through the stormy seas ahead.

4 Fannin Street

By the time he was fourteen, Huddie had won a reputation for his guitar playing and singing, and was much in demand for the sukey jumps and house parties. Offers to play now arrived on a regular basis. Margaret Coleman remembered, "As the time rolled on, the white people with stores and drugstores asked Huddie to play Saturday evening and nights at their places to draw the crowd. In that way he made nice change." Though he had grown up in an almost exclusively black community, he was getting a chance to perform for a wider audience, a different audience, the kind of audience he would later learn to cultivate in New York. He also began practicing the craft of entertaining, learning how to sell himself and his music to an often rowdy crowd. Much of it came naturally to him.

For a time he worked on a regular basis Saturday nights at a saloon in Leigh, Texas, out a few miles west on the Blanchard-Latex Road. Huddie was trying hard to grow up—he was a big, strapping boy with muscles toned from working in brutal weather on his father's farm. But he soon realized he wasn't as sophisticated as he thought. A story Huddie told years later illustrates this awareness: "Every Saturday I'd go out to Leigh, Texas, and I'd carry my guitar. Some of them would give me money when I'd get to the saloon, then the man would give me beer and money, too. But I had a good friend, her name was Early Bennett, she would call me 'Six-Shooter,' and Early, she would stash the beer for me; every time somebody would give me some beer, I'd give it to Early and she'd keep it for me." Huddie couldn't abide the raw, bitter taste of the beer, though, and he could hardly bring himself to drink it—though he felt he had to. Finally he hit upon a solution. "I'd get some sugar from my momma at home, you know, and put it in a paper, and put it in my pocket. So when I'd get through, me and Early would get behind the saloon. Early, she drank hers straight, but I had to put a little sugar in mine."

In 1902 this part of Texas and Louisiana was still very much a frontier, a land of bootleg whiskey, disputes over women, knife fights, and shootings. With so much violence a part of everyday life, it was hardly surprising that Huddie soon got caught up in it. Irene Campbell recalled, "At 14 he started running around. I can remember later when he came to his mother's all cut up. He had been out all night, and he had his guitar strapped to his back." There was "blood all over the front of his clothes and his jaw was hanging open because someone had barely missed his eye with a cut on his jaw from top to bottom." Such scenes became more and more familiar, and though Wes and Sallie were upset about them, Margaret Coleman—who was by now his steady girlfriend and confidante—was more sympathetic and more willing to listen to Huddie's side of things. Margaret insisted that it wasn't the life Huddie lived, nor his character which caused him problems. Instead, it was nothing "but jealousy in the heart of the people because he could beat them playing and dancing and made more money. Some began picking on him, telling wrong things. Huddie, being big-hearted, would laugh and try to keep down the confusion. He would say to them boys 'I don't care what you say about me, don't hit me.' He would try to defend himself, regain friendship with his enemies." Another friend of Huddie's, Mary Patterson, agreed this was the official line that reached his parents, but thought there was more to it. "That's what his parents said, 'Everybody picks on Son.' He had them believing that. But I think that . . . he was always crazy about women. They were jealous of him, I guess, but he sure would fight about the women." Another childhood friend from this time, Sallie Hooks, added, "He wouldn't take nothing off of nobody. He didn't go 'round just starting things, but if somebody looked like they want to start, he'd be ready." Obviously, Huddie was a quick-tempered boy in a violent society. His ability to talk his way out of trouble with his parents could mask this only so far.

After a few more nights of watching his only son come home bleeding from cuts and bruises, Wes Ledbetter knew that he had to take some kind of action. When Huddie turned sixteen, Wes presented his son with a typical coming-of-age present in the frontier South of 1903—a pistol. The gun was a Protection Special Colt that comfortably fit under Huddie's coat in a holster. Years later, Huddie could recall his father's exact words when he handed him the weapon. "Now son, don't you bother nobody, don't make no trouble, but if somebody try to meddle with you, I want you to protect yourself."

The gift did wonders to lift Huddie's self-image. And it didn't take him long to try it out. At a neighborhood sukey jump a few weeks after his birthday, Huddie asked a girlfriend named Eula Lee to ride home with him on his new horse. She readily agreed. As they were preparing to leave, however, another boyfriend stepped up and insisted that Eula Lee ride home with him in his new buggy. This boy had been talking big all night, Huddie recalled, and had been thinking that this new buggy made him the "boss over the whole world." An argument developed that quickly evolved into a struggle; the boyfriend grabbed the girl by the arm and she grabbed Huddie to hold on. Huddie remained silent, but as the other boy kept getting louder and more abusive, he eased his hand under his coat, feeling for the Protection Special. He felt the chilly steel, its cold weight reassuring. Huddie listened to the tirade and finally, when the braggadocio's talk "got too big," he lashed out with the gun and pistol-whipped the youth on the side of the head. He went down and Huddie leaped on him, straddling him with Colt in hand. Then he pulled the trigger. The gun misfired—a bad cartridge. Before Huddie could recover from his surprise, the badly shaken boy managed to squirm away and take off around the side of the house. Huddie fired two quick shots in his direction, but it was too late.

Huddie took Eula Lee home, then rode over to his own nearby farm, woke up his father, and told him what had happened. Wes quickly got dressed and rode over to the sheriff's office, only to discover that the parents of the other youth had already arrived. They were crying that somebody had been killed, that Huddie had to be arrested right then. Fortunately, the sheriff was acquainted with Wes, knew of his good reputation in the area, and was willing to cut his son some slack. He eventually fined Huddie $25 for carrying a concealed weapon and let him go with a warning.

For the rest of his life this incident stayed with Huddie; it wasn't the first time he had met violence at a frontier dance, but it was the first time he had truly asserted himself . . . and the first time he had gotten himself into a potentially lethal situation. This was apparently his first brush with the law, and but for the chance misfiring of his Colt, it could have resulted in something far more serious. As it turned out, the episode became a lesson to him—a lesson about how quickly violence could erupt in a frontier settlement and how easily one could get caught up in it. This lesson was reinforced a short while later when Huddie drew his gun once more. He saw his girlfriend and another boy sitting together in a nearby house; without thinking, Huddie fired his Colt through the door. The bullet apparently flew harmlessly, but it meant another visit with the sheriff.

Huddie was now a grown man. His friend Mary Patterson joked, "Huddie was a good-looking nigger. He wasn't a real good-looking person; had dark skin and pearl white teeth. He wasn't ugly, but he wasn't pretty. Nice looking young man." Huddie Ledbetter was about five feet eight inches tall. He had a smooth and very dark complexion and a muscular, athletic figure. Even then Huddie had developed a sense of style. Though he often spent arduous days working in the fields, when he went out at night he was cleaned and well dressed, sporting his eventual trademark red bandanna around his neck. Completing this outfit was a guitar strapped across his back.

The country girls found him irresistible: He had developed into a witty, talented, good-looking young man from a respectable family. He was a "musicianer"—a term used by rural blacks to refer to a performer who had instrumental as well as vocal skills. As such, he was special—a cut above the other farm boys and mule drivers at the local dances. His first real girl was Margaret Coleman, the daughter of a neighboring farmer. By 1903, when Huddie was fifteen and a young man with a Colt and horse, Margaret became pregnant by him and gave birth to a girl. The child died in infancy. The community was much upset both by her pregnancy and the infant's death. Margaret's parents pushed hard for the couple to get married. Huddie apparently had no real objection to this, but Wes and Sallie had big plans for their son, which didn't include Huddie being trapped into becoming a family man and a dirt farmer at the age of sixteen.

The Colemans finally backed off. Margaret certainly harbored no ill will toward her lover. Her later letters held nothing but respect for Huddie, and affection for his "poor, hard-working" parents. She also continued to see Huddie—and in another year she became pregnant again.

The second baby was another girl, who came out big and healthy. Margaret gave her the name Arthur Mae, but this time, perhaps in self-defense, Huddie denied that he was the father of the child. But his protests fell upon deaf ears and the Colemans were up in arms, rousing much of the community against Huddie. Pressure began to mount for Huddie to either marry Margaret or leave the area. The Colemans themselves soon relocated to Dallas, where Margaret raised her daughter. Huddie continued to deny his paternity, but soon found that his bad reputation with the older folks around Mooringsport was something not easily overcome.

Despite his feelings for Margaret, she was now out of the immediate scene—and Huddie was not often without a girlfriend for very long. However, he found out that the older folks had long memories when he fell in love with a girl known as "Sweet Mary," the sister-in-law of Alonzo Betts, who was a half brother to Huddie. Irene Campbell thinks Huddie felt pretty strongly about Mary—certainly more than for Margaret—and even proposed marriage. Mary's family wouldn't agree to the marriage, though, possibly because of Huddie's growing reputation as a womanizer. Later, after he moved to New York, Huddie wrote and recorded a song for Capitol Records, "Sweet Mary Blues," in which he sings about "going all around the world trying to find my sweet Mary." Although there's nothing in the song specifically referring to Marshall or Mooringsport, his older relatives who still live in the area still believe the song is a lament for this early failed love affair.

Huddie turned sixteen in January 1904. He was still living on the farm with his parents, working in the fields during the day, doting on his ten-year-old adopted sister Australia, occasionally even attending church. Yet he was also a father himself; a respected singer, musician, and dancer; a brawler and scrapper; and a ladies' man, but all of this was only in a small farming community near nowhere. This teenager grew more and more anxious to test himself in the outside world, in a world where the girls weren't so shy, the music not so monothematic, and the dances not as tame as the Buzzard Lope.

Down the road, on the far side of Cross Lake's swampy shores, crouched in an arm of the old Red River, lay Shreveport. It was a mere nineteen miles from Mooringsport in distance, yet decades away in development. In 1904 Captain Shreve's town was still two years away from the Caddo Lake oil strike that would by 1910 turn it into a boomtown and an oil center. But before then it remained a center for the cotton trade, as it had been before the Civil War, a place where planters from a hundred miles around brought their cotton. Shreveport was a town that "gave itself over to cotton," in the words of one guidebook: The very streets and sidewalks were piled with bales of cotton and the talk in shops and restaurants and hotels centered on cotton prices and cotton futures. The cotton was once shipped out on the boats moored along the docks of the Red River, but now traveled recently on the new rail connection to places like Dallas.

In 1900 Shreveport's census showed an official population of 16,913 (a figure that would double over the next decade); about a third of these residents were black. It was second in population only to New Orleans; in fact, the Chamber of Commerce during these early days even sought to imitate New Orleans' famous celebration by staging their own Mardi Gras on Fat Tuesday. Like New Orleans, the town was a loose and open gathering place for all kinds of businessmen and traders from the Ark-La-Tex. Down along the waterfront, especially on Strand Street and on the corner where Gross Bayou spilled into the Red River, was the red light district, just a few blocks from the new Holy Trinity Church and even fewer from the businesses along Commerce Street.

This eventually bothered the city fathers, anxious to move Shreveport forward into the twentieth century and to dispel the image of their town as a collection of frontier saloons. In late 1902 the city council formed a committee to choose a section of the town to serve as a "red light district for the habitation of women of immoral character." They settled on an area west of downtown, away from the riverfront, in a triangle bordered by Fannin Street, Common Street, and the Texas and Pacific Railroad tracks. It was called St. Paul's Bottoms, after the old St. Paul Methodist Church on Caddo Street, and it was a low-lying part of town where the humid summer breezes were few and the mosquitoes numerous. This was hardly choice real estate; the streets and alleys were muddy, the saloons were rough, and the houses were shabby rental properties, many of them taken by black families. In February 1903, the council designated the area as the official red-light district—"the red light district of the city of Shreveport to the exclusion of all others." From all over town, madams loaded up their belongings and began to move.

The center of the new nightlife was Fannin Street, which began on the east side of the bottoms and ran eight blocks downtown, ending at the riverbank. At the head of Fannin, where it ran into Cane (now Baker) Street, stood a sumptuous new two-story house owned by the city's most popular madam, Annie McCune. At the opposite end of the block on Fannin was another fancy house, a late Victorian palace dripping with elaborate gingerbread decoration, run by a redheaded madam named Bea Haywood—"as fine a looking whorehouse as there was down there," recalled a former professional gambler. Tricks cost $3 each, or two for $5, and the fancy parlors had all kinds of modern conveniences, such as the new player pianos that reeled off the latest turkey trot for a mere quarter. Within a year after the big move, the bottoms had at least forty whorehouses, not counting the little shotgun houses and dens where individual girls plied their trade. There were also dozens of saloons, dance halls, gambling houses, and even an opium den run by a character named "Ol' Bob" and a smoke house in the back of a Chinese restaurant.

White madams operated the big Victorian houses and they featured white girls. Farther down on Fannin Street, though, were houses featuring black or "mulatto" girls. An elderly white customer recalled that "some mulatto girls as you call them—the high yallers—ran places . . . for white men—didn't allow nigger men in their places. If a nigger got in there they came in by the back door." Some of the famous madams were black, such as Baby Jane, who erected a brilliant electric sign in front of her house on Caddo Street, a block over from Fannin, who had a collection of red, green, and purple wigs, and who had a reputation for letting her drunker customers sleep it off on the premises. Fannie Edwards, another black madam, had a huge house filled with girls and over the years used her insider knowledge of local politics to build up impressive real estate holdings. Another building on Fannin Street housed the Octoroon Club, with many of its women imported from New Orleans—a point upon which its owners capitalized. Working-class customers who could not afford the $3 charged by the big houses could find dozens of independent black entrepreneurs working out of little shotgun houses for as little as a dollar a trick.

Just a block down the street from Annie McCune's Victorian palace were two places run by blacks for blacks, joints which a contemporary newspaper described as "the most notorious dives in the bottoms." These were the establishments of Caesar Debose and George Neil, described by local historian Goodloe Stuck as "the center of Negro nightlife—and crime." DeBose's place was next to a Chinese restaurant; its ground floor was a long saloon, but upstairs were rooms reserved for girls and for gambling. It was the scene of frequent shootings and stabbings, and a regular hunting ground for police and federal agents after wanted men. Though smaller, George Neil's place included not only the usual bar and gambling rooms, but also a dance hall, a stage, and an eatery. Neil, at one time the wealthiest black man in northern Louisiana, sought only black clientele, and on occasion even complained to the police when whites wandered into his place.

One Saturday night a retired police chief who had jurisdiction over the bottoms took some visiting newspapermen to Neil's dance hall and described what he found:

The musicians, if so they may be called, were thumping out a hot dancing rhythm as I led the way around the edge of the floor. We backed up against the wall by the side door. The orchestra stopped for a moment and then swung into a rollicking cakewalk. The dancers responded instantly and Negroes certainly do shine in a cakewalk. There was no master of ceremonies, no calling the next stunt in advance; it was a sort of catch-as-catch-can, the kind of dance being controlled by the orchestra.

The chief's rare description of the dance he saw suggests that the new "uptown" Fannin Street dances were in fact not all that far removed from the rural dances of the backwoods sukey jumps.

After a general showing off for a while, a sort of pattern appeared. Pairs of dancers would dance into position directly in front of us and proceed to do their stunt, breakdown, hoedown, double-shuffle, buck-and-wing and many another step for which I knew no name. . . . One couple in particular attracted our attention. The man was undersized and coal-black. He was shovel-footed, buck-kneed and agile as a cat. The woman was chocolate colored, broad, rather squat, bulged high in front and low behind, sort of a shed-room-rumped effect, and badly pigeon toed. They faced each another and danced, turning 'round slowly, his huge foot slapping the floor with loud thwacks and her feet keeping time with a sort of forward and drag back movement. It was really comical.

In such places, a young Huddie Ledbetter could see that, while music was extremely important, the dancers often took center stage, and they managed to merge courtship, celebration, and tradition into some new and exciting synthesis. There was, of course, an uglier side to places like Neil's. The Shreveport *Times* complained that in Neil's "police have been openly assaulted by Negroes" and that there had been so many fights and scrapes that "the walls of the dance hall are peppered with bullet holes." In a violent age, Fannin Street was a crucible of violence. In some ways, the dens and dance halls of the bottoms were as far removed from the courts and the police and due process as were the remote hamlets around Caddo Lake; blacks in the bottoms tended to settle problems by themselves, by skill with a knife and quickness with a gun, and this, too, was an impressive lesson for a young teenager just in from the swamps.

In the story he inevitably told to accompany his famous song "Fannin Street" (or "Mr. Tom Hughes' Town" or "Follow Me Down"), Huddie implied that he had never been able to go to Fannin Street until he was sixteen. "I been wantin' to go down on Fannin Street all my life," he says in his Folkways recording of the story; his mother, however, heard the stories about the newly created red-light district and was afraid for him to go. It was only when his folks finally allowed him to put on his long pants—a frontier rite of passage—that he got up enough courage to defy his mother. "When you put on long pants you ought to act like a man, if you ain't no man." In fact, his song about Fannin Street has very little about the bottoms in it; most of it revolves around the act of defying his mother. It describes both his mother and his "l'il adopted sister," Australia, begging him not to go; it broke his mama's heart, he sung, and she walked away from him with her hands behind her, crying. Unable to stand the sight of her crying, Huddie went to her, fell to his knees, and begged her to forgive him—but then walked away "with tears runnin' over the back of my head."·

The scene described in the song doubtless took place and was probably every bit as traumatic as Huddie remembered it; but in a later interview he admitted that this trip to Fannin Street was by no means his first. Huddie had gone there with his father when he was just a small boy, when Wes Ledbetter had taken his cotton to sell in Shreveport. When he was sixteen, he said, he had gone there when his father had given him some money for the fair. But Huddie went to Fannin Street instead, defying his father, not his mother:

My papa would take me to Shreveport on some bales of cotton. He'd lead me all around in Fannin Street, that's what I'd like, you know, see people dance, and play and sing and pianos, and the women dance. (I love to see women dance anyhow.) And so my father carried me down there, I was a little boy, I wasn't much knee high to a duck at that time, but I was staring. Sure, your children don't forget nothing. My father'd lead me around by the hand in the daytime, and then he'd put me in the wrong yard, too. 'Cause I'd be sleeping, and he'd be gone. When I'd wake up and he'd be gone, it'd run around in my mind (I was a little boy, too), he's going right back down there where he carried me that day. So I say, well, when I get to be a man I'm going down there, too.

And when I got to be about sixteen or seventeen years old, see, I was wearing long pants at that time. So my father put me on a bale of cotton and carried me to the train, and give me forty dollars in my pocket. I was a big shot, too, when I had that forty dollars. Sent me to go to the fair, five times, he says, "Son, don't go down on Fannin Street none at night.". Just thinking about Fannin Street, and I said "No, sir, Papa," and that was just where I was going. I wasn't going to tell him. He shouldn't have asked me.

Anyhow, when I got to Shreveport, I never did forget how to go down on Fannin Street 'cause there's a little hill you drop off. I knows exactly where the big place sitting up on Texas Street—I guess it was a church, I don't know what it is, I never did pay that much mind—'cause when I was getting ready to go down that little hill, I was studying about that church. But I knowed how to go down there. So I went on down on Fannin Street, and that's where I'd go every time I'd leave home.

It was a whole different world to a boy from out in the parishes, and as he walked along beside his father, his eyes grew large at the marvels of Fannin Street. In the store windows were dress mannequins, staring at the boy with unmoving eyes. Huddie admired them as he and his father walked past, and when they returned a couple of hours later he noticed they were still there—in the exact position, in fact, their eyes still staring. "Papa, don't these people never go home and get nothing to eat?" he asked, to the great delight of his father. "No, son, that's fashions."

Later on, he would pretend to be more sophisticated:

I was down there, and two girls, you know, high browns, and I was so young, and they asked me, "Where'd you come from?" And I told 'em, "Chicago." Well, I was dead out of the country, and I knowed it, but they didn't have to know where I come from. When they found out, they said, "Daddy, take us up there and buy us some beer." So I took 'em up, you had to get beer in a pigeon-hole, you know, wouldn't let women inside of a bar (a saloon what they call it down there). So I ordered three glasses, these big tumblers, and so when they got up the beer, the women says, "All right, let's drink, Daddy." So I grabbed my glass and got on to it, and I got a big mouthful, but I went to spitting it out on the floor. They said, "Oh Daddy, you from Chicago and can't drink beer." And I said, "No I can't drink it, stuff's too bitter for me. You got to put some sugar in it!" And so the women jived me a whole lot.

They jived him, but Huddie soon became a favorite of the girls at Neil's and DeBose's; his work on his father's farm had made him strong, and his naïveté added to his charm. He learned about women on Fannin Street, but he also began to learn more about his music. This was one of the big reasons he kept thinking of going into town on Fannin Street: the attraction of pianos and guitars in the barrelhouses.

Shreveport did not have the rich kind of early jazz culture that the downstate city New Orleans enjoyed, but a number of the better pianists and singers were on a circuit that took them through Shreveport. As he listened to them, Huddie began to hear some new sounds to add to his own music. One was an early form of the blues; he remembered a singer and piano player named Pine Top Williams, who boomed out off-color versions of "The Dirty Dozens" and sang it "right to a gal in the audience." He also sang versions of "Take Me Back" and one of the early archetypal dirty blues, "Salty Dog." Huddie later could still recall fragments of Pine Top's song:

> Baby, let me be your salty dog,
> I don't want to be your man at all, you salty dog.
> Yes, honey babe, let me be your salty dog, your salty dog.
>
> Little fish, big fish swimming in the water,
> Old man, can I marry your daughter, you salty dog?
> God made woman, made her mighty funny,
> Kiss her 'round the mouth, sweet as any money.

Another blues he learned very early—one which he said was his very first blues—was "I'm on My Last Go Round," which he recorded for Bluebird in 1940. The blues songs, he found, were more popular on Fannin Street that the older country songs, work songs, and ballads he had been singing. He quickly added the blues to his repertoire.

His guitar playing also took a new turn. Though he was still playing a six-string at this time, he could adapt the barrelhouse piano style to it. He said, "Boogie woogie was called barrelhouse in those days. One of the best players was named Chee-Dee. He would go from one gin mill to the next on Fannin Street. He was coal black and one of the old-line players and he boogied the blues. At that time anyone could walk into a barrelhouse and just sit down and start playing the piano. I learned to play some piano myself by picking it out." At dances and in saloons he would always sit near the piano so he could hear the rolling bass, what he called "walking the bass." This was novel in 1904 or 1905, and quite the rage. Huddie recalled, "It was about 1904, 1903, piano players were walking the bases. [You'd] walk up to a man and tell him, 'Walk the bases for me,' give him a drink or something." Some of the best of this new style can be heard on his Shreveport song "Fannin Street," a dense, complex composition that became a Leadbelly standard.

Whether or not Huddie, as some early biographies have suggested, was "kept" by some of the girls in the Fannin Street houses, or whether he was simply a familiar figure and favored entertainer, he stayed there almost two years. What other musicians he might have met, what other girls he could have loved, what scrapes he fought his way out of there, remain unknown. But he always remembered the street, always spoke and sang about it as if it were one of his most vital formative experiences. By 1909 efforts were being made to clean up the district (prostitution would be legally voted out in 1917), but by then Huddie was miles away and entering another chapter of his life. His mother had been right about one thing: It was a testing time for him, and when he came back to Caddo Lake, after two years, he came home a man.

5 Banished Away

Back home, Huddie soon found his reputation hadn't improved at all. Sallie and Wes were glad to have their son back, but the good people in the community were still muttering about Margaret Coleman's babies. Now they added to that fresh gossip about what Huddie had been doing on Fannin Street, and what kind of new trouble his quick temper, his womanizing, and his pistol might get him into. But Huddie didn't stay long. "At eighteen," he explained, "I was banished away and went out in West Texas."

Actually, it took him two years, from about 1906 to 1908, to get there on a trek throughout north-central Texas and beyond. He explored the land between Harrison County and Fort Worth, stopping over at Marshall, Longview, Tyler, and Dallas. At some point Huddie wandered to New Orleans, where he said he heard more of that new, raw music that so fascinated him, and where he saw Jelly Roll Morton playing in a Rampart Street dive. In Dallas about this time he heard his first true jazz band, one led by the legendary black stage star Black Patti. She toured the South from the turn of the century to 1917, often with vaudeville troupes sponsored by the Consolidated or TOBA (Theater Owners Booking Agency, also known as "Tough on Black Asses"). On this show she had brought with her a band from New Orleans, an eight-piece band highlighted by a strong, syncopated rhythm section. "That's the first jazz band I heard," recalled Huddie. "I got more kick out of piano and I thought I could understand it more."

Huddie, in fact, continued to learn from piano players as he moved from bar to bar, from bordello to bordello, enjoying life and listening to music. What would eventually become a distinctive Texas-Louisiana blues piano style of artists such as Son Becky, Rob Cooper, and Alex Moore, was then just forming. Many of the men that Huddie listened to around 1907 represented some of the deepest roots of this style. He recalled Pine Top Williams, Dave Alexander (whose son, now known as Omar Hakim Khayyam, is a well-respected blues piano player in the San Francisco Bay area), and Dave Sessom, then working in Houston. None of these early barrelhouse piano players recorded—they were one generation too early for that—so we have no clear sense of just what they did that so impressed Huddie. In 1942 he tried to explain this fascination "we always called ragtime, well, when you played fast music that was ragtime, and when we hit barrelhouse, we got blues. Out in Alabama they need to sing: 'Rag is in the bag, we got the

37

blues—we're in the barrelhouse now . . .' Then they come out on it with their lowdown dances." Some of this rough, rural country ragtime was doubtless feeding into the more polished and composed "classic" piano rags of Scott Joplin, James Scott, Tom Turpin, and others that was then sweeping the country. The African American traveling vaudeville shows set the stage for "classic" blues that would eventually be made famous by Ma Rainey and Bessie Smith. Black music at the dawn of the century was ready to break out on a number of fronts, and Huddie was soaking up a surprising amount of it as he moved around Texas.

   Some who knew Leadbelly in later years eventually came to believe that during these early days he picked up a wider variety of songs than his postprison shows and recordings indicated. Frederick Ramsey, who extensively recorded and interviewed Huddie in the late 1940s, wondered if Huddie for a time was "a kind of song plugger on the road travelling through the South and singing current hits, and contemporary songs of the early 1900's." He observed that when Huddie was totally relaxed and simply performing, he would often include old popular songs in addition to the folk and blues. "Travelling in the South even singing for Negro Audiences you would get requests . . . , people who could know about the current popular songs even though they [were] Broadway and white inspired or Tin Pan Alley songs, and he had quite a few of them in his repertoire." Ramsey noted that songs such as "Bully of the Town" enjoyed favor among vaudeville entertainers during this period; in fact, this song was popular as early as 1890 and was made famous on the stage by comedienne May Irwin, who recorded it for Victor around 1910. Huddie's "Hawaiian Song" is a similarly unlikely borrowing, as is "Hesitation Blues." Certainly Huddie picked up many popular songs in later years and there is little reason to doubt that some of his ecletic habits were formed this early. Though the mass media of records and radio were a full generation away, the commercial music industry was in full flower at the turn of the century. This industry was making its growing presence felt even in the dusty, out-of-the-way towns of Texas and Louisiana.

———

Some of the time during these years Huddie supported himself by picking cotton and doing farm work. However, as Huddie's musicianship improved, he found increasing work playing for dances. And there were fringe benefits. After Fannin Street it became more difficult for him not to take women for granted; he was, after all, big, handsome, and had a way with words. Moreover, Huddie's self-confidence and brashness grew, and his skills with the guitar could not be matched by many of the local players. The country girls responded and Huddie viewed them as a valuable natural resource that was his for the taking. He later told the Lomaxes: "I used to

be terrible with women, terrible rough. I'd treat 'em every whichaway. And
I had trainloads of 'em, trainloads, sometimes eight or ten at a dance.''
Huddie routinely would take a woman home, but would ''put her out'' on
the road in the middle of nowhere if she ''wouldn't be with me.''

By 1908 some of this sexual touring caught up with Huddie and he came
down with what he described as a ''serious illness.'' He managed to make
it back to Harrison County to his parents' home near Caddo Lake. Sallie and
Wes successfully nursed him back to health, but the ordeal lasted for six
months and there were times that he hovered near death. His folks became
greatly alarmed and thought the best plan was to take him to a physician.
Huddie himself went along with this, though he gradually grew impatient
with the slow progress of orthodox medicine. He finally took matters into
his own hands and went to see an old granny-woman he had heard about.
She began treating him with a patent medicine named ''Lafayette's mixture,'' supposedly invented in the United States sometime during the days
of the American Revolution and named after the Marquis de Lafayette.
Although Huddie never specified the exact nature of this illness, the contemporary pharmaceutical register described Lafayette's mixture as a remedy
for a number of maladies. It was primarily used to treat gonorrhea, however, and the six-month treatment time he describes fits the disease's pro-
file.

Despite the fact that he fully recovered, the illness scared Huddie. His
family certainly saw it as an omen and they tried to get him to see it all as
a warning to stay home, settle down, find a decent girl, and join the church.
The carousing, rambling, and wanderlust all had a price, and Huddie was
lucky to get off with such a token payment. Huddie apparently took much
of this to heart, and for a short while he reformed his life-style to more
closely conform to his parents' wishes. He later told the Lomaxes that he
even attended Bishop College in nearby Marshall for a year and a half.
Bishop was one of the two black schools in Marshall (the other was a
Methodist school called Wiley College) and would have been the local
choice for Huddie because it was maintained by the Northern Baptist Convention. It had been established in 1881, was coeducational, offered degrees
in liberal arts, theology, and music, and maintained an enrollment of about
four hundred students. Bishop College officials have never been able to find
any records to show a Huddie Ledbetter ever attended there. But the
registrar of the college, J. D. Hurd, noted in 1956 that ''perhaps Mr. Ledbetter was a grammar student and no such records were kept at that time.'' In
fact, since Huddie never completed high school, it would have been quite
natural for him to have enrolled at a grammer school level—most likely at
the eighth-grade level.

He quit Bishop, Huddie said, in order to get married, and for this first marriage there is a definite date. On July 18, 1908, a marriage license was issued in Kaufman County, Texas, some thirty miles east of Dallas and one hundred miles west of Marshall, near the home of one of Huddie's uncles. It authorizes the rites of matrimony between "Juda Ledbetter" (a Spanish-tinged misunderstanding of Huddie) and "Miss Aletta Henderson." The marriage itself took place two days later, performed by J. C. Chappeel, witnessed by Paul Smith. Most remember Aletta's name being Aletha or simply Lethe, and nobody seems to remember how she and Huddie met. It was most likely during his ramblings between Dallas and his Harrison County home. Lethe (as we will call her) had been born in Grigg County, Texas, in September 1890, the fourth of Orange Henderson's six children. She was a stout, hard-working girl who could hold her own picking cotton in the fields with Huddie. The 1910 census records show them living in Harrison County with the rest of the Ledbetter clan. Huddie is listed as a "farmer," while his wife was considered a "farm laborer." Curiously, there were no children yet, but his wife seemed to be making some progress in stabilizing Huddie's life.

There was even a brief fling with the Baptist church. "When I joined I was twenty years old," Huddie recalled. "I was married. Had my first wife then." When they found out how well he could sing, the congregation made him a song leader. "I used to lead'em in church at night, and when they going to take up a collection they'd call on Brother Ledbetter to sing, so I go up there and sing for 'em." Huddie later recalled he also served as the organist for his church; it was a little pump organ into which he breathed life during the services. One night, though, he got more than he bargained for. All of his life Huddie had watched with a certain detachment as members of his mother's church would "get religion" and "go to shouting." Now he himself got caught up in the excitement, and got the spirit. "I was Jumpin' Judy—jumped all over the place, all around there. Everybody's trying to hold me, just jumping and shouting," he recalled. "I was feeling pretty good then, cold chills running all over me. Like my hair was standing up on my head." He then sang:

> Ain't you glad, ain't you glad,
> That the blood done signed my name?

Huddie had a new wife, he had survived a major illness, which for the first time in his life underscored the fact that he would not live forever, and he was reconciled somewhat with his parents. It was enough to cause a rounder to get religion, at least for a short while.

The lure of the sukey jumps and dances had diminished, but it didn't go away entirely. Shortly after joining the church, Huddie traveled to Leigh, Texas, where he been used to playing for the people at dances. "The people, all of 'em merchants, asked me about my guitar and I wouldn't know what to do about it," he remembered.

They asked me "Say Huddie, where's your guitar." I say "I done joined the church now." "Oh, what you go and do that for? You ain't gonna give us no more music on Saturdays?" I say, "Well, I don't know Mr Wenson." So I got back home again and think. And people going to church, you know, lots of people going to church with such a good religion, so next week they raised so much sand around there, between one another. So I got to thinking about my guitar [and] next Saturday I went out to Leigh, Texas, with me riding my horse, had my guitar sitting on my leg, and I went back and started playing the guitar and entertaining and picking up a little change. And so I been entertaining ever since. I didn't go back to church. . . . They called me a backslider, that means you turned back. You done left the church and gone back on the same road you was going when you joined, said you had religion.

This very brief stay with the church—Huddie once said that he was actually a member little more than one week—must have been exceptionally painful to his mother. It didn't seem to have upset his relationship with his wife, however. Shortly thereafter, probably late in 1910, they moved back to the Dallas area. The pair settled into a routine that permitted Huddie and Lethe to take advantage of their cotton-picking and farming experience, while letting Huddie keep his hand in music. In summers, both would hire out to the farmers north and east of Dallas, around Terrell or Rockwall, mainly to pick cotton as seasonal laborers. They would work places like Gus Edwards's farm, beginning at dawn and working in the broiling Texas sun all day. Lethe worked right next to Huddie, keeping up with him. "She was a little, low woman," Huddie reminisced, "but Godalmighty, she could pick cotton!" When the work got overbearing and the sun intolerable, Lethe would ask Huddie to sing one of the old work hollers like "Ain't Going Down to the Well No More," and he would "raise it up right sweet." They'd "pick cotton till you couldn't hear nothing but the bolls rattlin'. " At other times, Huddie would take work plowing, usually in the spring, and bragged he could wear out two teams of mules in a day and dance all night, all the while seeing after the women. In the winters, the Ledbetters would move to Dallas and enjoy the city life: Lethe would get some temporary job, and Huddie would earn what he could by playing and singing.

In 1900 Dallas had a black population of just over ten thousand and by the time Huddie and Lethe moved to the area, probably in December 1910, it had more than doubled. Rural blacks were flooding into the town in amazing numbers; the rural south-central Texas farm economy, beset by the boll weevil disaster and the decline of the sharecropping system, was on the verge of collapse, and thousands of African American farm laborers were out of work. Many of them made for the nearest urban areas in eastern Texas, the Dallas–Fort Worth area. In this fledgling metroplex some found work as day laborers and others commuted to field jobs in counties to the north of the city. Many settled in or around an area called Deep Ellum, a neighborhood north and east of downtown where Elm Street intersected Central Avenue. When Huddie saw it for the first time, he must have compared it to Fannin Street, and might have noted that it was not quite as unabashedly bawdy as the Shreveport neighborhood. Deep Ellum was not an official red-light district, and it was not exclusively devoted to bars and bordellos. It included small businesses: pawnshops, cafés, tailors, used clothing stores, and shoeshine stands. But there were also juke joints, gambling dens, dance halls, and whorehouses. A news story from a 1930s black paper reported that the neighborhood was "the one spot in the city that needs no daylight savings time because there is no bedtime, and working hours have no limits. The only place recorded on earth where business, religion, hoodooism and gambling and stealing go on without friction." If it was not Fannin Street, it was close, and it had a musical climate that was even more exciting.

Huddie joined in when he met up with one of its most colorful figures, the singer and guitarist Blind Lemon Jefferson. Though Jefferson had only a regional reputation when Huddie met him, he would within fifteen years or so become the nation's first real country blues star. His best-selling records would make him the most influential and popular of all the pioneer country blues singers, and Lemon's strange life and mysterious death in 1929 would make him the first of the great blues legends. Lemon was a rural busker who knew everything from old ballads to gospel songs, but he was first and foremost a blues singer. And with him, Huddie was for the first time in the presence of a master musician who lived, ate, and slept the blues. Josh White, who later became a friend of Huddie's and who helped guide Blind Lemon around, recalled that after the singer would return home at the end of the day he "would lie on the bed with his guitar and shout his blues into the night air." In later years, as he talked about his early days, Huddie would single out Blind Lemon over and over again as his great teacher—indeed, Lemon was about the only one he would acknowledge by name or through his songs.

Everyone seems to agree that Lemon Jefferson was born near Wortham, a hamlet of about eleven hundred in the very corner of Freestone County, some sixty miles south of Dallas. He was the youngest of six children of cotton farmer Alec Jefferson and his wife Classie, but aside from this, little is known about his childhood or musical training. The 1900 Freestone County census contains the family of Alex and "Classy" Jefferson, and among their children is one identified as "Lemmon B. Jefferson," whose birth date is September 24, 1893. It is assumed he had been born blind, but older musicians who knew Jefferson in the 1920s suggested he was not totally blind. In later life, he wore large wire glasses—not dark glasses—and his songs were full of strong visual images that suggested that he had some vision at one point in his life. He was probably nineteen when he met Huddie in 1912, still five years younger than his Louisiana counterpart.

Before he met Huddie, Lemon had won fame singing in local churches. His parents were members of another Shiloh church, quite different from the one Huddie attended—Shiloh Primitive Baptist Church. Jefferson might have received his earliest training there singing gospel songs. We know he was once hired to sing at a picnic sponsored by the General Association of Baptist Churches in Buffalo, Texas, and that his first commercial recordings were of religious songs. Before he made his way to Dallas, he wandered through the streets of small towns—Groesbeck, Marlin, and Kosse—all stops on the local H & TC Railroad that ran north and south through Wortham. Gradually his reputation spread, though we have no idea who taught him or what other singers he might have heard. The few witnesses who recall him during those days remember only that he, like Huddie, had varied musical tastes. "That was one thing about Lemon," recollected the retired Wortham postmaster Uel L. Davis, Jr. "He'd be singing in a church one day, singing at a house of ill repute the next." Like so many early blues singers, Lemon appears to have regularly mediated between the church world and the blues culture, finding solace and usefulness in both.

About 1910 Lemon decided to try his luck in the Deep Ellum section of Dallas. By this time he was heavy, about 180 pounds, stood approximately five feet eight inches tall, and was able to get around amazingly well. "A little chunky fellow," musician Sam Price described him. "A big stout fella" and "big loud songster" with a "tin cup wired on the neck of his guitar," remembered another contemporary, Mance Lipscomb. For a time, after Lemon got married, he also worked as a bootlegger. His hearing, which allowed him to tell when a customer tried to stiff him by putting a nickel into his cup instead of a quarter, also informed him if his wife had been into his bootleg stock while he was gone. "He'd take the bottle and shake it," said Price, "and he could hear that there were two or three drinks missing. And what he'd do, he'd beat the hell out of her."

In 1925, a good decade after he stopped working with Huddie Ledbetter, Blind Lemon Jefferson began to win nationwide fame through his recordings. Most of these were done for Paramount, an odd, minor league record company that was a subsidiary of a chair company in Wisconsin. Paramount 78s were not recorded very well, suffered from poor pressings, and lacked a comprehensive national distribution network. But the company was adept at working a market that many of the big companies had not yet figured out: down-home country blues. His friend Sam Price had put Lemon in touch with the company, and after a couple of lesser releases, the guitarist recorded two pieces—"Got the Blues" and "Long Lonesome Blues"—for a single 78 in February 1926. The former showed off his unique guitar playing and high, forceful voice, and spotlighted lyrics that were as typical of blues as they were misogynistic:

> Ain't so good-lookin', teeth don't shine like pearls.
> Ain't so good-lookin', teeth don't shine like pearls.
> But that lyin' disposition'll carry her through the world.

This recording exploded like a bombshell on the fledgling blues scene in 1926. Sales of over one hundred thousand were rumored, and the metal masters Paramount had made had worn out in three months; Lemon had to return to the studios to rerecord his two-sided hit. Within a matter of months he would travel north to Chicago to record every three or four months; the company eventually created a special label for him, one trimmed in bright lemon yellow. Between 1926 and his untimely and mysterious death around December 1929, Blind Lemon Jefferson recorded over a hundred titles. Many of these records were not only best-sellers in their time—they were featured in display ads in big northern newspapers like the *Chicago Defender*—but they became blues standards, reissued and copied by later generations of bluesmen and folk singers. The best known include "Matchbox Blues," "See That My Grave Is Kept Clean," "Easy Rider Blues," "Broke and Hungry," and "Jack o' Diamonds." Their success won him the title "King of the Country Blues" and opened the door for the commercialization of this music.

All this would come later, though. When Huddie first met Lemon in Dallas, the blind singer was still in his teens. Though Huddie liked to talk about his days with Lemon—it was one of the few subjects concerning this part of his life he would later discuss with friends and interviewers—he was inconsistent as to just exactly when this was. He claims to have met Blind Lemon as early as 1904 and to have run around with him for as long as eighteen years! On yet another occasion, Huddie dated their work together at around 1912; he remembered the date because one of the songs they did together in the streets was a ballad about the *Titanic* ("Fare Thee Well, Titanic"). The *Titanic* tragedy spawned a series of folk ballads in both black and white traditions, as well as a cycle of folk tales about the ship's last hours. If Huddie and Lemon sang this song together, it means they were at least performing together in Dallas after the ship went down in 1912. If anything, Huddie was the senior partner, and probably had more musical experience and a more diverse repertoire than Lemon. While he certainly learned something from the blind singer, it is equally probable that Lemon learned from him.

Huddie left some vivid memories (on his *Leadbelly's Last Session*) of just what Blind Lemon was like. "Him and me was buddies," Huddie began. "Used to play all up and around Dallas–Fort Worth. In them times, we'd get on that Interurban line that runs from Waco to Dallas, Corsicana, Waxahachie, from Dallas. Then they had that Interurban that run from there to Fort Worth." The line was almost certainly the T & NV line that ran southeast toward Lemon's home county. "We get out two guitars; we just ride . . . anything. We didn't have to pay no money in them times. We get on the train, the driver takes us anywhere we want to go. Well, we just get on and the conductor say 'Boys, sit down. You going to play music?' We tell him, 'Yes.' We just out collecting money, that's what we wanted—extra money. And so we'd sit down and turn the seats over, you know. He's sitting in front of me, and I'd sit down there and we'd start."

Some places they performed at were more memorable than others. One was the rough suburb of Silver City, which they could reach by bus. "There's a lot of pretty girls out there, and that's what we were looking for. We like for women to be around, 'cause when women's around, that brings men and that brings money. 'Cause when you get out there, the women get to drinking, that thing fall over them, and that make us feel good and we'll tear those guitars all to pieces." He later celebrated Silver City in one of his "jazzy blues" called "Silver City Bound"—in which he sang "me and Blind Lemon gonna ride on down."

For a time, perhaps several years on and off, the pair managed to make a decent living, running a route that included many of the saloons, dance halls, and whorehouses of east Dallas and as far out as Kaufman County. Sometimes their weekend take was as much as $150 and their travels would take them as far as the rough-and-tumble oil town of Groesbeck, some seventy miles south of Dallas on the H & TC Railroad. Blind Lemon attracted special attention by playing what was then called "Hawaiian guitar," a type of open guitar tuning with which he usually used a bottleneck, knife, or short metal cylinder to slide along the strings. Huddie himself learned this style, but when he was with Lemon he quite often played a mandolin or a windjammer. Sometimes Huddie would strike out on his own and organize a band to go strolling through the more proper residential sections of Dallas, performing for tips from white folks. Depending on who he could round up on any given day, Huddie would have to play guitar, mandolin, or accordion, and on the rare occasion even the mouth harp and bass fiddle.

Though the popular success of Lemon in the 1920s forever associated him almost exclusively with the rural blues—he was without much question their most popular proponent—there is quite a bit of evidence to suggest that he performed other types of music. Like Huddie, he was a "songster," as were most buskers of the day: He learned a variety of music, folk as well as the current favorites, sinful as well as religious, ragtime and dance tunes as well as ballads. Indeed, Lemon Jefferson's recorded repertoire includes songs drawn from diverse sources ranging from the current Tin Pan Alley song "Beggin' Back" to the ancient British ballad "Three Nights Drunk." Huddie remembered singing, with Blind Lemon, songs like "The Titanic" and "Careless Love," which Huddie said had been first popularized in his area by Lemon. At times when Huddie would dance to stir up a crowd, Lemon played a guitar solo that was a version of "Dallas Rag," a song that would be made into a popular Columbia "race" record—the term used in the 1920s to designate black music—a decade later by the Dallas String Band, another serenading band from the Deep Ellum area. During World War I, the pair liked to sing a rollicking parody of "The Darktown Strutter's Ball" called "I'll Be Down on the Last Bread Wagon." Like most street buskers, they also did their share of out-and-out topical songs about the events of the day. "The Titanic," of course, was one of the most popular, but especially relevant in Dallas were songs about the boll weevil. Both men later recorded versions of songs about the insect that was causing such displacement among the East Texas cotton fields.

Then, of course, there were blues. How many of them Huddie knew when he met Blind Lemon is unclear; years earlier he had first heard the term *blues* when his grandfather applied it to a song called "I'm All Out and Down," and he learned his famous "Roberta" down on Fannin Street. But many of the true blues in Huddie's songbag seemed to date from his time with Lemon. There was "C.C. Rider," derived from the phrase "easy rider," which referred either to a woman or to a guitar, whose shape suggested the easy curves of a Silver City girl. When he recorded it in 1926, Blind Lemon renamed it "Corinna," complicating matters by giving it the title of yet another well-known blueslike song. "C.C. Rider" would survive into the rock era, and become a standard at the hands of singers like Chuck Willis, Laverne Baker, and the Animals. "Matchbox Blues," with its memorable line "Sitting here wondering would a matchbox hold my clothes," was used by both singers and also eventually survived into the rock and roll era, when a buddy of Elvis Presley's, Carl Perkins, used it to create a rockabilly classic for Sun Records in the 1950s; later the Beatles followed suit. "Fort Worth and Dallas Blues" was a song particularly demanded at the Big Four Club near the rail terminal in Dallas. When the pair would start singing "Got the Fort Worth blues and Dallas heart disease," reminisced

Huddie, "the women would come running! Lord have mercy! They'd hug and kiss us so we could hardly play." More evocative, more suggestive, was "Black Snake Moan," which they later recorded commercially. Huddie's version began:

> Ohh, black snake crawling in my room,
> Ohh, black snaking crawling in my room,
> Better tell somebody,
> Better get this old black snake soon.
>
> Oh, it must have been a bedbug, because a chinch
> couldn't bite me that hard.
> Oh, it must have been a bedbug, because a chinch
> couldn't bite me that hard.
> Asked my sugar for fifty cents, said Leadbelly, ain't a
> child in the yard.

"Blind Lemon Blues," recorded by Huddie for the Library of Congress, was an odd narrative blues that Huddie learned from Lemon and named after his friend. It is about a seventy-five-year-old man who takes a notion to leave home; after three years his wife dreams he has returned. She awakens, hears him at the door asking for forgiveness, promises her preacher she will hold the line and not take him back, but finally relents. At its end, the rambler comes in and his children each play a tune on the piano for him. Though the song might relate in some way to Lemon Jefferson's life, "Blind Lemon Blues" is more likely a piece Lemon simply liked to play, and which had enough drama and machismo to appeal to Huddie, who himself had wandered a lot while married to Lethe.

The two also shared the prison songs or prison blues. Huddie created most of the prison songs in his own repertoire, he admitted, after his own jail time. We don't know if Lemon ever spent any serious time in jail—aside from an occasional vagrancy or drunkenness charge—but he certainly featured songs about prison in his recorded repertoire. There was "Hangman's Blues," with its description of the "mean old hangman wanting to tighten that noose"; "Lockstep Blues," with its line "Every morning I come walking down this big long hall"; " 'Lectric Chair Blues," with advertising copy that read " 'Lectric chair is the next place he's gonna sit down in, and he ain't tired either, so he don't want to sit down." Most included grim and realistic details that evoked southern prison life. Even if none of these specific titles showed up in later Leadbelly recordings, the older singer must have heard some of them by way of Lemon and must have learned how effective prison life was as a theme for the blues.

No one knows exactly how long Huddie and Lemon worked together, but at its longest the partnership could not have lasted more than five years, from 1912 to 1917. And, as we shall see, that span of time was probably interrupted on more than one occasion. But however long it lasted, the relationship had a significant influence on Huddie. In later years he talked often of Blind Lemon and recorded at least five different songs in tribute to him. "Blind Lemon Blues" was the first, in 1934 and 1935; perhaps Huddie was name-dropping with all his songs and reference to the blind singer, but in 1934 Lemon was not as widely known in the white community as he became later. The Lomaxes knew of him through their backgrounds in Dallas and knowledge of blues records, but the average white listener would not have recognized the name enough to be impressed. Huddie was no doubt sincere in his appreciation of Lemon Jefferson and honest in his debt to him.

Huddie also was specific about one technique that he learned from Lemon: how to play the slide guitar. Ironically, Huddie utilized it more in later life than Lemon himself did on his recordings. But beyond this debt was a greater and more subtle one—Lemon taught Huddie a lot about how to play the blues on guitar and how unorthodox playing techniques and unusual singing styles could be molded into a powerful and creative music. And it is quite likely that Huddie, five years Jefferson's senior, taught the younger man some of the music that later appeared on his records. As they traveled around Dallas, up and down its dusty streets and wooden sidewalks, singing, drinking, boozing, and whoring, they stimulated and challenged each other, making a living but forging a new way of expressing what Huddie liked to call "that old feeling."

6 Stella and Irene

Sometime during his wanderings—probably late in 1910, when he was living near Dallas—Huddie acquired his first twelve-string guitar. It proved to be more than just a casual acquisition; the unique sound of the big instrument would have a profound effect on his singing style and repertoire. Though he could play, and continued to play, a variety of other instruments like the windjammer, the mandolin, the harmonica, the piano, and even the string bass, the twelve-string guitar soon became his favorite. From the very start he seemed to sense that it would become his trademark. Over the years Huddie told several versions of how he started playing the twelve-string. Here is one:

Well, I used to just have an ordinary guitar. One night I was playin' in a place—one of them sukey-jump places—and people was drinkin' and some was dancin' and it was warm. I was playin' there and one of the strings broke. I jest went on playin', though. Then a pretty gal come along and boy! She was a high-brown. Wow! She came over to where I was sittin' and playin', and she come and leaned down close. Jest then another string broke, but I didn't let on. I jest went on playin'. It was hot, and she jest leaned down over my shoulder and pushed against me—you know. And another string broke, but I couldn't stop now. Not no how! So I jest kept on playin', 'cause she was nice—fine as wine in summer time. And then you know what? Another string broke, and I jest had one string left. I played that one string 'cause I liked that thing. But I made up my mind right then that I'd go out and get me a 12-string guitar.

Colorful as it is, this account smacks of the kind of yarn spinning that Huddie liked to do in later years to entertain his audiences up north; he told it while strumming a guitar accompaniment, playing off the common association of the guitar as "easy rider," and the equation of musical prowess with sexual ability. He had discovered that a twelve-string guitar can help you cope with sexual challenges as much as musical ones.

A few months earlier, Huddie had told a less fanciful account of his first twelve-string guitar: "I saw one of the old 12-string Stellas sitting in the window of a Dallas store. The year before I'd heard a man play it in one of those travelling medicine shows where they sold a cure-all for fifty cents a bottle." Captivated by the loud, ringing sound of the instrument, Leadbelly had spent the rest of the night hanging around the medicine show tent listening to the man play. Shortly thereafter, when he finally saw one of the twelve-strings for sale; "the price of the guitar was $12," he recalled, "and I knew I had to have it." That week he approached a local farmer who knew of his cotton-picking expertise and hired out to earn the money of the guitar. The going wage was $5 for every thousand pounds of cotton picked and within a week he was able to return to the store and purchase the Stella.

Years later, in the 1920s and 1930s, the Stella twelve-strings were to become the favorites of several notable blues recording artists: Barbecue Bob (Robert Hicks), his brother Charlie Lincoln, and Blind Willie McTell. These Georgia musicians worked the streets of Atlanta as buskers and were attracted to the twelve-string because of its volume and power—doubtless one of the great appeals the instrument had for Huddie. Another of its attractions was its fresh sound; in the first decades of this century the Stella was very new to the scene. The twelve-string in general was introduced into the United States from Mexico and Latin America, which had a long and complex history of double-stringed instruments. By 1900 a company called Lyon and Healy was producing them for sale in the states, and a 1928 catalog listed five different models under various brand names.

Ironically, the Stella company itself, which was to have such a great appeal to rural southern musicians, was headquartered not in Memphis, Dallas, or Atlanta, but at 87 Ferry Street in Jersey City, New Jersey. "Stella" was one of several trade names used by the Oscar Schmidt Company, established sometime between 1879 and 1893 and incorporated in New Jersey in 1911. Thus, the Stella that Leadbelly bought in Dallas could not have been very old and might well have been one of the earlier models brought out by the company. The Stellas in general were hardly top-of-the-line instruments. They were not especially durable, and they suffered from an interior finishing that was, in the words of one historian, "crude and hastily completed." The exteriors looked good, though; they were done in Honduran mahogany for the sides and back, and German spruce for the flat top. The tough bridges were made of rosewood, but the fret board was usually constructed of birch or maple that had been stained or painted black (which eventually caused rot). The instruments had a sound much better than they should have and new models sold for around $15. Unlike the more expensive Martins or Gibsons, the Stellas eventually fell apart and few of them survived more than a couple of decades. Huddie would go through several in his career, and even in later years, when he was nationally known, he still remained true to the Stella brand name. In fact, he even referred to his instrument playfully as "Stella," causing some of his fans to think the name was a nickname he himself had bestowed on the guitar.

Once he had the twelve-string, it didn't take Huddie long to realize that it was not just bigger and louder than the conventional six-string models he had played at sukey jumps and on Fannin Street. By coincidence, Huddie's interest in the guitar in general had come just about the time the instrument itself had undergone a major change. Its movement away from being a parlor instrument to an instrument of the people had been accompanied, about 1900, by a movement away from the older, European-style gut string to the steel strings. Huddie's generation was the first to really absorb and understand the style of playing on steel strings and helped forge the style of blues playing that would remain popular for decades. The steel strings had a brighter, louder sound, but were harder to play and demanded more tension on the guitar. Like the twelve-string guitar, the use of steel strings probably came into Texas and Louisiana from Mexico, and it is quite likely that blacks in the area had been experimenting with them long before the guitar makers began to switch over to them in 1900.

The twelve-string complicated these new demands even more. Huddie soon learned to prefer very heavy gauge strings, and learned that he could play best when he used a bone pick for his thumb and a steel pick on his index finger. Tuning of the six pairs of strings roughly corresponded to that of a six-string guitar. The two high pairs of strings Huddie tuned in unison, giving them a tone resembling that of an organ or accordion; the lower pairs he tuned an octave apart, dramatically enhancing the bass runs he became so fond of using in his music. These techniques yielded a loud, almost strident sound that could easily compete with the fiddle and banjo duos heard at the sukey jumps—something that the standard guitar could hardly do. Furthermore, this unique, booming sound attracted the attention of listeners on street corners or in roadhouses. The tight strings demanded strong hands to properly note and strum them, hands that Huddie's years of work picking cotton had built up. This sound was complemented by his strong, assured, high voice, which Huddie's field hollers and country singing had helped develop. It was hard in rural Texas to find good steel strings in those early days, strings that would hold their pitch at the high octaves Huddie liked on the high pairs. He solved this problem by occasionally tuning his guitar down two tones, pitching his vocals a bit lower and creating a loose action with less demand on the strings.

Huddie's only comments about this tuning process came in a 1942 interview. At first when he tried to play the twelve-string his fingers got to "mashing too hard," but when he finally got his Stella to Dallas, his own twelve-string, he took it to a dance that very night. "I put my foot on the doorstep and my finger of the strings and said 'Here's Leadbelly!' " From this point forward Leadbelly never seems to have seriously considered any other instrument as his main accompaniment. Within a few years he was

referring to himself as "King of the Twelve-String Guitar," years before he
met John Lomax in Angola Prison.

One of the first songs Huddie set about adapting to the twelve-string was a
lilting waltz that he liked to call "Irene." He was apparently singing the
song as early as 1908 or 1909; family folklore has him creating the song
while singing lullabies to his seven-month-old niece Irene Campbell in
Leigh, Texas, near Marshall. Huddie was twenty then, freshly married, and
charmed by his little niece, who was so small that she had to be kept on a
pillow. Starling Myers, Huddie's old buddy "who wanted to be like him,"
told Irene Campbell years later, "I was there when he wrote that song. He
was entertaining you while your mother was getting you some food."
According to Myers, Huddie was casually strumming and "he just stumbled
on that song. That's the way he did. He could just make up songs." Huddie
liked the idea of a song named for a niece and continued to sing it to the
baby. It became such a favorite that he persisted in performing it until
Irene's mother rose up in arms, announcing that she would not have a child
"named for a reel" and tried to resolve the problem by adding the name
Matilda to baby Irene. It worked for a while, but as soon as she was old
enough, Irene took her original name back and stuck with it.

The true origins and history of "Irene," though, is more complex and
more enigmatic than this family tale. Huddie assured the Lomaxes that he
had first heard the song—or at least the refrain and a couple of verses—
from his Uncle Terrell, his guitar-playing uncle from West Texas. Terrell
had been the source for several other good songs—"Boll Weevil," "Take a
Whiff on Me," and "Looky Yonder, Where de Sun Done Gone"—and
seems to have been the one who brought the song "Irene" into the Ledbetter family. In October 1940, after Huddie had gained his fame in the north,
John Lomax traveled to Oil City, near Mooringsport, to make a series of
field recordings by Bob Ledbetter, another of Huddie's uncles. Uncle Bob
had grown up around Mooringsport, singing the hollers and reels his father
before him had sung. Unlike his nephew, Uncle Bob never rambled much,
preferring Mooringsport. In contrast to Leadbelly, Bob Ledbetter commented to Lomax that "I've never had no trouble in my life. I ain't never
been fined, ain't never been arrested, never been to the jailhouse but twice
in my life, ain't been to the courthouse but twice." He voted twice in his life,
once for whiskey and once in the presidential election for Grover Cleveland.
He sang for Lomax a version of a Cleveland campaign song, a version of
"When the Sun Goes Down," a brief ditty called "What She Ate," and his
version of "Irene." His was virtually identical to the song as sung by Huddie, and after he was finished, he recalled, "I learned that from my brother,
the one that's out west. He brought it home to me. That's first how I heard

it. That was Terrell, about 19 or 20 years ago." When Lomax directly asked him if Huddie had made up the song, Uncle Bob answered categorically, "No sir! It came from my brother. I don't know who made it up. Huddie got it from us."

The song itself is a tender, moving waltz about the courtship of a young girl whose mother says she is too young to get married. And the famous chorus wistfully laments, "I'll kiss you in my dreams." It certainly sounds nothing like a blues or a work song, and though several of the verses Huddie and his uncles sang resembled commonplace stanzas that had been floating around in oral tradition for years, the song itself seems to point to a parlor song of Tin Pan Alley origin. John and Alan Lomax must have suspected this when they transcribed Huddie's song for their book in 1936. They showed the song to various friends and got a variety of leads: One man remembered hearing it on a West Texas ranch about 1916; another said the melody came from Flotow's popular nineteenth century opera *Martha;* music historian Sigmund Spaeth was not familiar with it but agreed that it certainly had some kind of written origin. In the years since, no one has been able to track down any printed Victorian song that exactly matches the words and music that the Ledbetters sang. There is evidence, nonetheless, that the chorus, at least, was circulating among other folksingers besides the Ledbetters. In November 1936, the exact month and year that the Lomax book came out, a Library of Congress field recording unit came upon Gilbert Fike in Little Rock, Arkansas. Fike was originally from Louisiana and sang a song called "The Girls Won't Do to Trust," which used a set of unusual misogynistic verses to set up a familiar chorus:

> The girl will chew tobacco, but she will raise a fuss
> The girls will drink good whiskey, boys, but they
> won't do to trust.
>
> Irene, goodnight, Irene,
> Irene, goodnight, my life,
> I'll kiss you in my dreams.

While it is possible that Fike had heard Huddie sing a version of the song or, far less likely, received an advance copy of the Lomaxes' book, it is probable that both Fike and Leadbelly heard the song as it circulated among rural singers in Texas and Louisiana.

Another intriguing piece of the puzzle surfaced in the 1950s: a text of a song called "Irene, Goodnight!" in a souvenir songbook published by a touring minstrel show called Haverly's American-European Mastodon Minstrels. The date on the book was 1888, its origin of publication "The Courier Company, Show Printers" in Buffalo, New York. J. H. Haverly was a major minstrel show producer during the years of Reconstruction, creating lavish, well-orchestrated spectacles that featured satiric or "comic" songs. He toured widely and had contracts with some of the era's best songwriters. In 1880, for instance, he signed an agreement with singer-composer James A. Bland, who was famous for his songs "Oh, Dem Golden Slippers" and "In the Evening in the Moonlight." Equally important was the fact that Bland was African American. In fact, Haverly had bought out an entire minstrel company in 1878, enlarged it to include over one hundred members, dubbed it "Haverly's Colored Minstrels," and set out to tour the United States (including the South), and, in 1880, England. It is entirely possible that one or more of his touring groups got through Louisiana in the 1880s and we know that they toured through at least part of the state by 1891. Could they have impressed the local singers with their version of "Irene"? In the souvenir booklet (which appears to have been for a white troupe, not a black one), the song is reprinted with the headnote "As sung by Lew Randall":

> *Irene, good-night!*
> *Think, love, of me; my pretty Irene,*
> *Good-night! good-night!*
> *Irene, good-night—*
> *Keep me alway* [sic] *in thy dreaming';*
> *Think, love, of me.*
> *When the night closes day with its twilight*
> *Irene good-night!*
> *Softly the moonlight gleaming,*
> *Would I ne'er could leave thee,*
> *My pretty Irene, good-night!*
>
> *I'll count the moments and the hours*
>   *That pass so slowly by,*
> *Until I see your sunny smile*
>   *And gaze into your eye.*
> *O, let me hear thy tender voice,*
>   *As oft I've heard before*
>   *O, precious one, loved one I adore!*
>
> *Irene, good-night!*
> *Keep me alway* [sic] *in thy dreaming;*
> *Think, love, of me.*
> *When the night closes day with its twilight.*
> *Irene good-night!*
> *Softly the moonlight is gleaming,*

Would I ne'er could leave thee,
My pretty Irene, good-night!

Nothing has surfaced about the singer Lew Randall, and the Mastodon booklet does not have any musical notation. Though the basic chorus and idea of the song are the same as the Ledbetters' and Fike's, Randall's song is full of flowery nineteenth century diction ("Would I ne'er could leave thee") that is far removed from the kind of verses Huddie sang. It smacks of the language used by early Tin Pan Alley songwriters, some of whom were enamored with Victorian prose. Nonetheless, the songbook provides evidence that a much earlier song about Irene was popular in the decade of Huddie's birth and that its popularizers were doing shows in the general area in which he grew up.

Recent research has added another unexpected twist to the song's story. Historians delving into the lives of nineteenth century popular songwriters have learned that the composer of the Lew Randall "Irene, Goodnight!" was Gussie Lord Davis.

Gussie Lord Davis (1863–1899) was a prolific and successful songwriter who died at the height of his popularity. Maxwell F. Marcuse, a Tin Pan Alley historian, noted that, "In an era of 'sing 'em and weep' melodies, Davis did more than his share to open up the tear ducts of America." The composer of a remarkable string of sentimental favorites that became immensely popular with early country musicians and folk singers, Davis scored with "Maple on the Hill," "In the Baggage Coach Ahead" (reportedly a million seller), "Little Footprints in the Snow," and "The Fatal Wedding." Like Bland, Davis was an African American—one of the first black songwriters to really become a financial success. He began his career in Cincinnati ("a Cincinnati boy of color," the newspaper of the day announced), writing for local publishers about 1880.

In 1886, Davis published "Irene Good Night" in association with a Cincinnati white man named George Propheter—one of the three hundred songs the two published together. In 1892, the same song was reprinted, giving Davis credit, by a major publisher, Witmark and Sons, in New York City. "I have made a specialty of waltz songs," he told a reporter for the New York *Evening Sun* in 1888. "They are more sun to-day than any other. The day of Negro and jubilee songs is over . . . women as the supports of the music dealers. A man goes to the theater, hears a song, likes it, but is content to gain snatches of it, and whistling suffices him. A woman buys it and sings it at home." At the time, he reported, he had numerous songs "in all minstrel troupes in the country," including "Irene, Goodnight"—"and the singers prefer them now rather than the lively songs of the South." One of the singers, certainly, was Lew Randall from Haverty's troupe, who later that very year would publish "Irene" in their book.

Significantly, the Haverty's text is nearly identical to the original sheet music published by Davis and Propheter. The fact that several other Davis songs, including "Maple on the Hill" and "The Fatal Wedding" entered the repertoire of southern singers, and were later collected by researchers as folk songs suggests that his "Irene, Good Night" was the primary source for Huddie's song. Either the Ledbetters or other anonymous singers stripped its archaic diction, simplified the text into a standard verse and chorus pattern, and added new verses derived from other black folk-song stanzas. Many such lyric songs had sets of stanzas that were free-floating and interchangeable, and a creative singer like Huddie could have easily grafted some of them into the foundation of the older, composed song. The music for Davis's printed version is also somewhat different from the melody Leadbelly sang. The Davis melody is in ¾ (waltz) meter, whereas Huddie's was in $6/4$. Despite the different time signatures there are enough basic similarities between the two to suggest a relationship and to argue that Davis's music, like his words, indicates a prototype for Leadbelly's version. Yet the differences are there, enough to make us wonder if some anonymous musician, possibly in Texas or Louisiana, rearranged the Davis song and near the turn of the century created a song that was much closer to the one Terrell Ledbetter carried on horseback during one of his visits to his kinfolk.

Huddie knew the song was a love song, and when he started singing it during his rambles and farm life in northeast Texas, he would perform it in a high, crooning tenor voice. His big Stella generated a strong, inexorable rhythm of its own, and the song soon became one of his favorites—even though it had little in common with the rest of his repertoire. It was a modular song, one that could be lengthened or shortened depending on the circumstances, and as he sang it he added new stanzas that he either wrote or adapted. The first time he recorded the song on disc, in 1933, he sang only two verses and two choruses, including the slightly ominous refrain "I'll get you in my dreams." A year later he recorded it with four verses and four refrains. By the time the Lomaxes had transcribed the song for their 1936 book, it had grown to six verses and the same number of refrains as well as an extensive spoken part. In short, "Irene" slowly evolved into a rather sprawling, complex conglomerate that would display Huddie's ability to take different parts of an old song and yarn and create something new and unique out of it. And though Huddie couldn't know, it would eventually become his most famous song.

7 Harrison County Chain Gang

By the summer of 1915, Huddie and Lethe had moved back to their old haunts at Harrison County, not far from Marshall and only a few miles from his parents' farm near the shore of Caddo Lake. This suited Wes and Sallie Ledbetter, who were entering their sixties and finding the demands of subsistence farming, raising cotton, and running cattle increasingly demanding. Australia had left home by now, and even though relatives were nearby, the farmhouse was getting lonely at times. And even though much of the Western world was at war, life in eastern Texas was little affected by European battles.

Though Huddie was twenty-seven, married, and a father, Wes and Sallie's old instincts to nurture and spoil him remained as strong as ever. Sallie worried about him attending church and wondered why he so rarely used his voice to lead the Sunday morning singing, while Wes grew increasingly concerned with his fighting and drinking. Both parents wondered why Huddie and Lethe hadn't been able to have any children of their own after seven years of marriage. The fact that Huddie was continuing to build his reputation as a musician in the area was probably the very least of his parents' concerns.

Wes was proud of his farm, a nice spread of sixty-eight and a half acres of land in Harrison County, not far from the Louisiana state line. The hardworking couple had purchased most of it from A. B. Waskom, a local white farmer whose family was so well established that a nearby town was named after them. Henry Coyle sold them a second parcel of land in 1911, thus completing their holdings. For most of the early years of the century, they watched with curiosity and interest as the oil boom developed in Caddo Lake. With land so close to the lake—site of the world's first over-the-water oil derricks, which are now so commonplace—it was only a matter of time before developers began to look at the Ledbetter farm itself. Beginning in May 1908 three separate entrepreneurs, Phil Draiss, Henry Coyle, and the J. M. Guffy Petroleum Company, approached them regarding oil leases. A token $1 fee for drilling rights was paid on the spot to Wes and Sallie, and one of the contracts provided for "free gas" to them as long as they made their "own connection." Unfortunately, although oil virtually surrounded them, none was discovered underneath their land. So Wes continued to make the best of it through farming.

All this routine was shattered in June 1915 when Wes and Sallie received word that Huddie was in trouble once more—big trouble. He had been arrested and incarcerated in Marshall. By now Huddie was no longer the teenager the sheriff could straighten out by talking to; he was a twenty-seven-year-old man and in jail. The Ledbetters went down to Marshall, some nineteen miles away, to see what they could learn and to get help for their son. Exactly what Huddie did is still not perfectly clear. When the Harrison County Courthouse was relocated to new facilities in the 1960s, most of the early Harrison County court records were destroyed or lost. Huddie himself later contended that early in his life "I never served a jail sentence anywhere. I have been arrested for fighting once but only got a fine of thirty dollars for it." Yet there are enough official documents surviving to suggest that this 1915 affair was something more than a $30 offense.

Rumor and family legend say that Huddie got into trouble as the result of a fight over a woman. The Lomaxes say the incident began when Huddie physically attacked a woman who had rebuffed his advances in Marshall. Given Huddie's track record, either explanation seems plausible. The fact is that after his arrest he remained in jail for several weeks with no formal charge lodged against him. Whatever the sheriff was thinking about, it must have been serious enough to really scare Sallie and Wes. They began negotiating with a Marshall law firm operated by a father-and-son team, W.C. and William Lane (Lane and Lane), and soon began to appreciate the seriousness of Huddie's offense. They quickly learned just how much legal advice could cost in rural Texas in 1915. Wes and Sallie had to think about the terms for a while: In lieu of cash payments, Lane and Lane would defend their son if the Ledbetters would sign over their farm. It was a difficult choice, but the outcome was inevitable. For most of Huddie's life they had been getting him out of trouble, and once again they didn't hesitate to make this final selfless sacrifice. They soon made up their minds and drove back to town in order to sign the official papers. Within a few minutes they were done; the Ledbetters were sixty-eight and a half acres poorer and much of the homestead they had worked hard to acquire was gone. On June 21, 1915, the land was signed over to the Lanes "in consideration of legal services."

This incident became part of the Leadbelly legend, for in later years many people made reference to the story of how his family sold all their land to keep him out of jail. Most, however, think this incident occurred in 1917 following Huddie's second and more notorious brush with the law. But surviving documents clearly show that the loss of the farm happened two years earlier. Yet exactly what happened in Harrison County that summer remains to this day open to specualation.

On July 26, 1915, just over a month after the Ledbetters hired Lane and Lane, Harrison County finally filed the official charges against Huddie. A new trial date of September 8, 1915, was set; when it was all over Huddie had been convicted of simply "carrying a pistol" and sentenced to thirty days in jail. In keeping with the practice of the time, he was actually placed on the county road gang for the duration of his sentence. Moreover, he had incurred $73 in court costs, including $34 in witness fees (to reimburse witnesses for the time they lost from work) and $31.50 for the clerk, sheriff, and county attorney. On September 26 his sentence began.

Because he knew pretty well what was in store for him during the next thirty days, the very thought of life on the Harrison County chain gang made Huddie shudder. He didn't fear the grueling dawn-to-dusk physical labor—he was used to that—nor was he too worried about the rough company or about food that even a dog would refuse. Even the weather might not be too bad—early autumn in East Texas can be quite lovely. But Huddie was a man used to virtually complete freedom of choice. As he watched the guard whip his bridle reins on the necks and hands and heads of the prisoners who didn't move fast enough, Huddie began to sense that there were some things he couldn't take. He had his pride, and he liked to say that he always gave as good as he got—no man had struck or insulted him and gotten away with it. Furthermore, there was the matter of spiritual abuse: Huddie had already spent much of the summer in jail for an offense he had questioned. Even more time in this harsh, lockstep routine was too much. He rattled the chain that yoked his legs together and wondered just how fast a man could run by taking such awkward, mincing steps.

The answer came only three days into his sentence. The gang was working on a country road outside of Marshall, and as Huddie weighed his chances, he remembered that part of his turf. He had grown up in Harrison County, worked on some of the farms there, played for innumerable sukey jumps, and walked down almost every dirt road in the county. He knew, moreover, how and where to cut cross-country, and who lived on even the most remote farms. As the morning wore on, he slowly edged toward the end of the chain gang, estimating how far it was through the nearby plowed field to the distant woods. When the guard was distracted, Huddie made his break. Grabbing his chain so it wouldn't clink, he started an awkward, comic crabwalk across the field. For just long enough, the guard didn't turn around and Huddie got almost fifty yards before he stumbled and dropped his chain. This alerted the guard, and he quickly spurred his horse around and shouted an alarm. Huddie broke for the woods, running as fast as he could manage with such a major handicap. The guard pulled out his old Winchester and began firing. Shots plowed into the ground near Huddie's leg and he could actually hear shots spin past his ears. With a leap, he made the woods, crashing through the underbrush, finally out of the guard's sight.

He ambled through the pine forest as quickly as he could, occasionally stumbling over the scrub bushes. But he managed to stay ahead of the law and the dogs they were using to track him down. Soon he was out of the trees into another field. A black man was plowing, and he looked up with alarm as Huddie approached. Huddie beseeched him to cut his chains, but the frightened field hand shouted, "Pass by, nigger, pass by!" Huddie was luckier in the nearby woods, where a group of field hands were clearing pine trees. One of them swung his ax, breaking Huddie's leg chain in half. Now he was able to really skim the ground, but at the same time Huddie began to hear the sheriff's dogs sounding on his trail. He had hunted enough to know what to do next; coming to a stream, he jumped in and splashed several hundred yards downstream. Exhausted, Huddie finally climbed up from the stream bed, made his way up the small bank, and collapsed. Huddie heard the guards handling the dogs, heard them yelping as they lost the scent, and heard the entire group move on away into the woods on the other side. Huddie was free again, and not too far from his father's farm near Karnack.

Wes and Sallie knew nothing about all this; they were still in shock from the trial, the conviction, the loss of their land. But Huddie's niece recalls a family story about that night. As evening wore on, Sallie had had a "dread premonition" about her son. Later that same evening, Huddie "burst through the door in chains and leg irons fresh from an escape off a country road crew." Wes himself could hardly have been too surprised to see Huddie—his attempt to hire a lawyer was probably in part motivated by fears that his son would do something like this. But he knew that hiding him would be hard and that the farm was the first place the deputies would search. For the first couple of days, Wes managed to hide his son in a thick cane patch. They decided that it was only a matter of time before the authorities came by, so they finally and regretfully sent him on his way to New Orleans. It was just in time. Two hours later the sheriff rode by to see if Wes knew anything. "The last I heard, he was on the chain gang," Wes said. "You're a damn old liar," the sheriff spat out, but rode down the dirt road.

The train trip to the "Big Easy," as New Orleans was called, took most of a day, but it was far easier than outrunning the sheriff and his dogs. Huddie looked forward to his new home. On the surface it appeared to be Fannin Street on a larger scale: It had music, good food, mild climate in winter, and the fast women who worked in the bawdy houses of Storyville. Even Deep Ellum paled in comparison to the storied nightlife of New Orleans. At the clubs trumpet masters King Oliver and Freddie Keppard were playing a type of music that would eventually be known worldwide as jazz. But Huddie cared little for New Orleans and was horrified at some of the grotesque side effects of the sporting life there. He told the Lomaxes, "You go down to Rampart Street and you are liable to see anything. You see a man without no legs and a woman doesn't have a nose." In less than a week Huddie was heading back home, back to the family farm, where he found Lethe waiting for him.

The family pondered what to do next. Huddie certainly couldn't stay on the farm, only nineteen miles from the sheriff's office. But where to go? One logical answer presented itself. For years the Ledbetters had maintained ties with relatives in and around De Kalb, Texas, in the northeasternmost county in the Lone Star State. Some of the Bowie County Pughs were related to Huddie's mother—occasionally some of them made the eighty-five-mile trip by horse or train between De Kalb and southern Caddo Parish. Some of the local Pughs lived near Mooringsport, Oil City, and Tree City, just to the east of Karnack. Another old friend of the family, Frank Bridges, had moved from Caddo Parish to De Kalb, and in the last ten years a group of cousins named Stafford had made the move, too.

Bowie County held several other appeals for Huddie. It verged on the eastern fringe of the frontier and actually adjoined the old Indian nation that had become the new state of Oklahoma only eight years before. While it wasn't the proverbial frontier town like those that existed on the West Texas plains, De Kalb was reminiscent of the Wild West. It was still wide open and free, though not entirely lawless, and had definite reminders of the classic West of old. Most everyone carried a gun for both self-protection and everyday use and violence was commonplace. Sam Bass, a famous Texas outlaw, had to hide out from the law along the banks of the Red River in northeastern Texas a few years earlier. It was normal for a man, even a black man like Huddie Ledbetter, to carry a gun at this flashpoint of the frontier.

A spur of the old Chisholm Trail ran just to the west, through the far edge of adjacent Red River County, and thousands of cattle were still being driven through there a scant decade before. Western Bowie County begins to flatten out and the vast expanses of prairie begin only ten miles west of the county lines. Many of the farms in Bowie County used horses both to work the fields and for basic transportation. In addition to being on the frontier, De Kalb offered steady employment for a strong man like Huddie. Cotton was king, although the boll weevil was slowly working its way to the northeast. Huddie and Lethe knew only too well that sharecropping was a grim, losing proposition, but it still beat the Harrison County chain gang.

The eighty-five-mile expanse between De Kalb and Marshall contained dozens of small towns and two counties, but it was distant enough to make Huddie feel comfortable. He was still a fugitive, though, and escapees from a Texas chain gang were not dealt with lightly. With his twelve-string guitar, musical talent, and imposing physique, Huddie was not exactly inconspicuous. He and Lethe decided he would "lay low" with his music for a time, in order not to attract the attention of visitors who might report to the sheriff in Marshall about a brawny twelve-string guitar player entertaining at dances up in Bowie County. Also, his name was not exactly common among the residents of Bowie County, and Huddie began casting about for an alias. Seizing on one of the most common names in the area, the young couple were soon introducing themselves as Mr. and Mrs. Walter Boyd.

8 They Called Him Walter Boyd

The Bowie County that Huddie and Lethe moved into in late 1915 was the nexus of a large black rural community that ecompassed most of extreme northeast Texas, and that included the counties of Red River, Cass, and Morris. The 1910 census classified the entire area as from twenty-five to thirty-seven and a half percent black—not as high as the sixty-two to seventy-five percent density found in Harrison and Marion counties to the south, but enough to make it one of the state's largest African American enclaves. In Bowie County itself, some thirty-four percent of the 34,800 residents were black, and almost a third of these were listed on the census as "illeterate." The nearest town of any size, Texarkana, straddles the Arkansas-Texas border to the east. Twenty miles due west a trio of towns with the confusing names of New Boston, Old Boston, and Boston form a triangle near the county's geographical heart. New Boston acts as the county seat and since the late 1980s its shining courthouse complex proudly has abutted Interstate 20, which connects Little Rock and Dallas.

By early 1916 Huddie and Lethe had settled themselves on a small sharecroppers' farmhouse near Beaver Dam, just to the northwest of De Kalb. Bowie County itself is bound to the north by the Red River, which also forms the Lone Star State's border with Oklahoma and Arkansas. The town of De Kalb, named after a German general who fought for the American Revolution, sits near a low ridge slightly above the rather flat land that is dotted with the small farms and plantations of western Bowie County. Many black people lived around De Kalb, Dalby Springs, Oak Grove, and other small communities; some of these, such as Oak Ridge, barely exist today. But these settlements were home to many of Bowie County's African American residents who worked as tenant farmers or sharecroppers.

Huddie and Lethe—now Walter and Lethe Boyd—were among those second-class citizens who lived by farming someone else's land and growing their own garden. They knew this life-style all too well. Even the land reminded them of the cotton-producing expanses of Kaufman and Rockwall counties. On the positive side, though, they had family around De Kalb. Not only did they find some of Sallie's relatives there, but Huddie's half brother, Alonzo Betts, lived within a mile of their home near Beaver Dam. Also nearby was Huddie's cousin, Mary "Pig" Walker, who was married to a fun-loving man of about Huddie's age named Will Stafford. Huddie and Will quickly struck up a friendship, albeit a short-lived and tragic one, destined to play a major role in Huddie's future.

Will had apparently lived for much of his life in Caddo Parish and married Mary sometime around 1913. By December 1915 they had settled on a sharecropper's farm near Beaver Dam. It was near a swamp, in sight of the cottonwood trees that lined the banks of the Red River. In fact, the house rented by the man known as Walter Boyd was only a quarter mile away, within easy eyesight of the Stafford residence. Will Stafford stood about six-foot-one and had a medium build. A big wide-brimmed western hat usually sat atop his head—not an unusual affectation in country that was still part of the frontier. He had the reputation of being a tough guy and more than an average horseman. Like Huddie, Stafford liked women, and he didn't mind wagering some of his money on cards. He was light-skinned but deeply tanned by years of working in the fields and with the cattle, so that strangers couldn't tell if he was a black or a white man. In fact, the entire Stafford family was quite light-skinned—Will's son Presley shared this trait as well. Even in the late twentieth century the Staffords in western Bowie County are among the more light-skinned and fair-haired members of the African American community.

As his friendship with Stafford developed, "Walter Boyd" found that he had little trouble getting farm work in the area. The years had honed his ability to pick cotton about as fast as any man around, and his strength and endurance soon impressed his bosses. But unlike many of his contemporaries, who worked for one family for many years, Walter Boyd was employed by an unusually large number of white families in northwestern Bowie County. Howard Farris, who was a boy at that time, recalls his father saying that Boyd was a "mean nigger," who caused trouble and didn't last long on their farm. Two of these families, the Farris and Hamilton clans, have remained prominent landowners well into the late twentieth century. For a while Huddie worked for a German family, the Fromms, who had settled not far from De Kalb. He even worked for a well-to-do black man, Jim Jones, who also employed him as a musician. In 1917 the Ledbetters had settled to work on the farm of John Cowen, a white landowner who lived on Rural Route 4, De Kalb. It was called the Marsh Place because of the wet marshland that permeated the farm. About two miles to the east lived Ellic Griffin, who worked on the John Wright farm—another man named Lee Brown also lived close by. Each were peers of Huddie's and soon started a friendship that flourished in the hours when they did not have to work the land.

At times it must have seemed like quite a change from the bright lights, high rolling, and rich musical life of Fannin Street or Deep Ellum. In the spring they planted the cotton, hoping the spring rains would replenish the rich soil of the Red River delta. During the summer the cotton required tending and worming, with the occasional thundershower keeping everything from becoming totally parched. By early fall black tenant farmers were straining their backs stooping and picking the bright white bolls. The old cotton sacks, dragged by a harness over the shoulder, extended ten or twelve feet behind them, and wide-brimmed straw hats, for both Lethe and Walter, kept the broiling autumn sun off them. A portable tripod on the row lanes held a scale for weighing the sacks before they were dumped into the tall, iron-tired, mule-drawn wagons. Though the couple worked many difficult and tedious hours a day, money remained as scarce as a cool breeze on an August afternoon in East Texas.

Even today, many decades after Huddie worked in the Bowie County fields, old-timers still recall his capacity to pick huge amounts of cotton—up to five hundred and six hundred pounds a day. In later years, Huddie would sing one of his most famous songs about how it was to ''Pick a Bale o' Cotton.'' Texas farmers will laugh at this, though, and point out that a bale of cotton is usually fifteen hundred pounds, and that no man, regardless of how fast he is, can pick more than five hundred or six hundred pounds. There was often, apparently, a competition among the pickers to see who ''weighed out'' the most cotton at the end of the day, and Walter Boyd was certainly in the midst of this competition. Huddie later insisted to John Lomax that he could ''snatch eight or nine hundred pounds a day—when I want to,'' but Lomax, who knew firsthand what cotton farming was like, didn't believe a word of it. Huddie had learned to ride and rope back in Caddo Parish, and in the frontier hamlet of De Kalb he found he could sell these skills as well. His reckless determination also made him good at breaking and training wild horses, and white families in the county would sometimes hire him to perform this dangerous task. Barton Hamilton's family lived a few miles to the south and he remembers that Huddie ''was a bronc rider [who] broke a horse for us one time and rode it for my uncle, up on the Hamilton Place above Springhill. [It] threw him and he got up and caught that horse and rode it.''

There was a demand for music, too, and Huddie often turned to his guitar in order to break up the monotony and earn extra money—even at the risk of attracting attention. In this remote frontier community, people soon learned that young Walter Boyd was quite a hand with music. Zeola Vaughn recalls that ''he helped my daddy a lot but, my oldest brother [Zollie] would talk about it—everywhere he went he carried this guitar. If he went to the field, he had it, that was his life. He'd have this cotton sack rolled up and on his back, it had a strap and this guitar with him every where he went. And if he took a notion to sit down and pick it, the folks gathered and sang.'' Ellum Park, located at the base of a small rise known as Jim Jones Hill, became the most important gathering point for major social events in the black community between 1914 and 1919. It was here that many people came to dance to the insistent rhythm of Huddie's booming twelve-string guitar.

One of the special celebrations held there was a unique African-American holiday known as Juneteenth. The name comes from the date of June 9, 1865, when a major general named Gordon Granger, assigned to command the District of Texas after the Civil War, proclaimed emancipation for all blacks in the state. A popular legend has it that the date was so late because an earlier messenger bringing the news was killed on the way to Texas. By 1866 blacks in the state began celebrating in a major way on June 19th (though blacks in other states celebrated the more established days of July 4 or January 1) with everything from parades to baseball games to picnics to dances. Juneteenth gradually spread to black communities in Louisiana, Arkansas, and Oklahoma, but has remained especially strong among blacks in East Texas. Zeola Vaughn remembers that "my papa would give big picnics for the 19th of June, what they call Juneteenth. He'd give maybe a two or three day picnic and have a fiddlers stand and things up there. My daddy played the fiddle at this place, there was one man who played the mandolin at this thing. And [Walter Boyd] would pick this guitar. And if he was gonna be there everybody know he could pick and sing and they anxious to get there." Because the barn, barbecue pit, and dance platform at Jim Jones Hill were shared by black and white citizens alike, they maintained separate facilities. Today all that is left of the grounds is a small round pond, but during the years around World War I, Ellum Park was a hub of activity.

Huddie soon established a circuit of weekend dances and juke joints to play as well. He couldn't realize much actual cash playing for weekend dances at the local jukes, but it gave him a respite from the daily grind of farm work, in addition to special status in his community. The black communities in Bowie County could get rough on a Saturday night. The local joints and informal house parties catered to the crowd that liked to drink, bet on card games like "coon can," and listen to music. People also came to learn and improvise on the latest dances. In 1917 the "Grizzly Bear" and "Eagle Rock" were among the favorites. Huddie later recorded "The Eagle Rock" for Capitol Records in 1944:

> Love you baby and don't care what you do.
> Love you baby and don't care what you do.
> Oh Lord, lovey you baby and don't care what you do.
> Dop, dop, don't leedle dup.
> Stop! Do that eagle rock.

Many of the joints were located along the Red River, which separated Oklahoma from Texas. According to the county court records and contemporary reports in the newspapers, black-against-black weekend violence was a normal course of events.

The man known as Walter Boyd soon became a popular figure at jukes in northern and western Bowie County—most weekends would find him at one of the joints in which he felt especially mellow. Drinking and gambling continued to appeal to him. His prowess on the twelve-string guitar was without peer and the unusual nature of his instrument helped to bring him even greater notoriety. Women were attracted to Huddie not only because of his love for this life-style and his ability to make that twelve-string "talk," but for his good looks. He possessed physical strength, a trim physique, and a roguish charm accented by his gift for making small talk with women. But not everybody in the family approved of this life-style. The young niece Viola Betts Daniels overheard Wes Ledbetter warning his son about what was wrong and right. He admonished Leadbelly about the fast life and the ruination that his "starvation box"—his guitar—would bring. But Huddie didn't listen to his father and "was always picking up that gun he carried. My father didn't like that because you were looking for trouble!"

During nearly eight years of marriage to Lethe, Huddie must have slept with countless other women. Some were the "noted riders" he referred to in his songs; others were simply local women who came to the jukes from the surrounding farms. Leadbelly simply found it difficult to resist these Bowie County women; in true southern blues tradition, he claims to have had women by the "trainload." Just how much of this was middle-aged braggadocio and how much of it was accurate may never be known. In spite of what he said, or regardless of how many flings he had, he always seemed to come back to Lethe. She was doubtless used to his forays and to his cavalier attitude about them, and she always seemed to be there for him.

By this time Huddie looked on women as a natural resource to be plundered. If any were so bold as to refuse his advances, he'd merely toss them aside. Some women no doubt became wise to his tricks, but others were quite willing to step into their place. One story Leadbelly later recounted in graphic detail illustrates just how deeply this attitude had become ingrained in him. One night, he said, he offered a woman in Bowie County $5 to be his "special friend." Later, when he came around to consummate their relationship, he became incensed to find another man at her house. She refused to return his money after several requests, and finally he lay in wait for her. Catching her alone in the woods, Huddie beat that "black devil" with a wooden switch until it was "frazzed to pieces." "I whipped the dress right off her back," he bragged. Shortly thereafter, the girl's mother came looking for Huddie, going first to his house to ask Lethe of his whereabouts. As it happened, he was down in the field plowing, and the old woman stalked down there and finally found him. She stood on the other side of a drainage ditch and hollered at him. "You some chief devil, ain't you? You been going with my daughter, too, ain't you? You talk like a deacon, and a child of you's born ever weekday and two on Sundays. The Lawd's gonna strike his fire in your heart someday to get rid of that murdering pride of yours." Huddie, surprised by the tirade, let her have her say. At the end, she even went to the sheriff to have him arrested, but Huddie knew that the sheriff wasn't going to bother him over something like this. Word of the incident spread, though, and soon he found that no women would take his money.

Women were not the only subject of confrontations in the community. The juke joints themselves bred animosity between men, often played out in an obscene insult game called "joinin' " or "playing the dozens." During this hurling of insults, your honor and pride was at stake. Pride severely enough wounded often resulted in fights with fists, switches, knives, and even guns. Later blues recordings of "The Dirty Dozens" and its cousin, "Dirty Mother For You," celebrated this tradition in song form. John Lomax noted these verses performed, but not recorded, by Huddie:

> You was born in the ditch,
> Your head got hitched,
> You're a dirty mother-fucker,
> You the chief cock-sucker.

There was another side to Huddie, though, and about this time he revealed it—he became a surrogate father to three young nieces and nephews. Though he and Lethe had no children of their own, for most of 1917 they took in three children of Alonzo Betts—Viola, Irene, and Alonzo, Jr. When the children's mother had died, they had been sent to live with relatives in Louisiana. This arrangement somehow worried Huddie. Viola recalled, "Some way or another Uncle Huddie would always get in touch. He heard about us out there and sent his wife to see us and visit us, and we was so happy that he told her to bring us back." The children and Lethe soon arrived at the Beaver Dam farm, where Huddie and Lethe were living in a "cottage down a path," where he was farming, and where "he had good money, too." Viola was only ten in 1917, and her sister Irene—the one family legend says the song was named after—was just nine. When Huddie was home, the sisters remembered the good times sitting around the fire during the cool autumn evenings and singing. The year quickly passed, and in early December the children went back to Mooringsport for Christmas. After the holidays, Viola was scheduled to enter the preparatory school at

Bishop College in Marshall, while the others returned to the De Kalb area. But it didn't work out that way. Viola recalled:

During Christmas we got the news that Will Stafford was killed. And the sad part of it was that our Uncle was the one that did it. We sisters were shocked, but couldn't find out much about what had happened. Our Grandpa went back there [to Beaver Dam] and brought our things back. That's the only person that went back, and if he heard anything, well, people didn't talk to children in those days.

9 The Rollin' Sonofabitch

Even today, more than seventy-five years after it happened, the exact circumstances of the death of Will Stafford are not much clearer than they were to Viola and Irene in the Christmas of 1917. Old-timers in Bowie County still talk about the event, and they have passed on enough tales that it has become something of a local legend. There are old court documents and yellowing newspaper stories about Huddie's arrest and trial. There are tales told by the Ledbetter clan about odd details brought out in the trial, and there are things about Huddie's capture that don't make sense. There are Huddie's own memories of the event, told with some reluctance to interviewers like John Lomax, Ross Russell, and Charles Edward Smith. The one thing that is certain is that on or about December 17, 1917, Will Stafford was killed and the man calling himself Walter Boyd was arrested and tried for his murder. Rightly or wrongly, Huddie found himself facing serious prison time, and the settled life he had been leading in rural Bowie County was tossed into sudden disarray.

Late in the fall of 1917 the pressures of farm life were slightly diminishing. The surviving cotton crop had long passed through the gin and gone to market. The late fall chores demanded less time, though the daily routine continued. November is usually a gentle, mild time of the year in northeastern Texas. Christmas was coming up soon and everyone was looking toward the holidays as a long break from work. The days between Christmas and New Year's were especially relaxing because there was a square dance at someone's house almost each night. They literally rolled up the rug, if they had one, moved out the furniture, and danced till dawn. Because these gatherings involved families, generous amounts of homemade food, and there was no work to be done during the day, these parties were more relaxed than usual weekend reveries.

December 13, 1917, was a Thursday, and four men—Ellic Griffin, Will Stafford, Lee Brown, and Huddie—were on their way to a dance at the Red River bottoms. Because of a tantalizing new woman, Chammie Jones, tensions between Will and Huddie ran high. She was about thirty years old, and though witnesses never described her as beautiful, she was seductive and tempting. She was especially appealing to Huddie and was equally frustrating. Chammie Jones was actually living at Will Stafford's home as part of an odd and complex relationship between Will and Huddie. Will's wife, who was Huddie's cousin and had the nickname Pig, remained at home sharing the house with Chammie, which must have annoyed Pig to a point beyond distraction. This was not Will's first extramarital relationship; he had had one child by Clara Boyd, another local girl. And later Clara's sister, Iola, would become involved not with Will, but with Huddie. Like a Greek tragedy, such a sordid love affair could only result in a tragic ending.

The four men walked along the lonely, quiet dirt road that led to the school for black children at Beaver Dam, where the dance was to be held. The road there narrowed to what was virtually a dirt path, with the swamps almost touching on either side. There was almost certainly talk and banter, probably about work, life, and women—especially Chammie Jones. Soon tempers flared and the situation quickly escalated out of hand as Will and Huddie confronted each other. It was well known that Huddie carried a pistol, and most likely he now reached for it. Within seconds Will Stafford fell dead, rolling to the low side of the road.

The other three men fled. According to newspaper accounts published during the trial itself, Huddie, alias Walter Boyd, forced the other two men to accompany him. Brown, who might have been slightly injured during the gunfire, and Ellic Griffin were certainly not about to argue with a man who had a gun that he had used with such impunity. They fled north toward the river and soon arrived in Pat Gibbons Bottoms, a 457-acre black settlement alongside the Red River slightly less than three miles from where they'd abandoned Stafford's body. At this point, Huddie was on the banks of the river that also formed the state boundary between Texas and Oklahoma; by crossing it, he could have escaped the jurisdiction of the Texas authorities. In the late fall and winter, the Red River is often little more than a trickle. Although the river has been controlled by a dam for several decades, springtime often means another round of highly destructive floods. In December a man can literally walk the forty yards across to Oklahoma. Huddie must have realized that had he crossed, he would be miles from the scene of the crime by daybreak. A truly desperate man standing on the banks of the Red River in mid-December could have found a way to cross the border. Technically speaking, once he set foot in the Red River, Huddie would have been in Oklahoma. It is possible that he was paralyzed through fear and indecision. Perhaps, as he later argued, he felt that he had nothing serious to fear because the shooting was self-defense and he would easily be vindicated. Possibly he had insisted that Griffin and Brown accompany him so he could have them as witnesses. For whatever reason, he didn't take this chance to escape and soon allowed both men to go their own ways.

Not surprisingly, no one reported the crime that night. However, the next morning a group of children walking along the road happened across Stafford's body. Only one person in the community had a telephone, so a rider on horseback was dispatched to the Farris house in order to call the sheriff in the town of Boston to ride the twenty-odd miles to investigate the murder.

Later that night Sheriff Jim Baker paid a visit to Ellic Griffin, who had made his way home. Margaret Cornelius was fourteen years old at the time and within two years she would marry Richard Stafford, Will's brother. She was living in the Beaver Dam community when this all happened and "can remember when the law come that night and picked him up and arresting him [Ellic Griffin]." During this tense situation everyone stood their ground when the sheriff arrived and took Griffin away. They were not frightened, exactly; they just didn't know how else to react. The family felt vindicated when Griffin returned the next day a free man.

The police apparently believed Griffin's version of events—that there was a fight between Huddie and Stafford followed by Will Stafford's murder at the hands of his buddy. Huddie apparently remained at a house at Pat Gibbons Bottoms, because that's were Jim Baker and his men found him on the evening of the eighteenth. They arrested him, brought him in chains to the Farris residence that night, and then transported him to the De Kalb holding jail by wagon. The following morning the man called Walter Boyd lay in the Bowie County Jail charged with murder and assault to murder.

Will Stafford, meanwhile, was about to be buried. The family did not tarry with the funeral, and within two days Stafford was laid to rest in the Beaver Dam cemetery. Along with Ellic and Annie Griffin and other friends, Margaret Cornelius attended the ceremony and recollects that "it was a team and a wagon, that's the way they carried the corpse to the cemetery. When they brought Mr. Will to the cemetery, Miss Chammie was sitting on the coffin in the wagon." While Chammie Jones rode atop her lover's coffin, Stafford's widow sat quietly on the spring seat at the front of the wagon. It was a scene from the most hackneyed southern gothic novel.

Huddie soon began to sense that this time he was in real trouble and that he couldn't count on his father's resources. Since he was unable to afford an attorney, the state of Texas turned to its roster of pro bono lawyers. The law firm of Mahaffey, Keeney, and Dalby drew the case. Though the two primary attorneys specialized in business law, one of their associates, a Mr. Thomas, was assigned the case on the basis of his experience, albeit limited, in criminal law. J. Q. Mahaffey, the son of one of the partners, recalled that his father was reluctant to take the case; he felt that the firm was stepping beyond its expertise. Mahaffey recollected that it was not only a clear-cut case, but that Huddie wouldn't receive a fair trial because at that time a black man in Bowie County was treated as the "equivalent of a stray dog."

The times were particularly bad for a black man seeking justice in Texas. Mahaffey, Thomas, and most of the residents of Bowie County that winter were very much aware of the bloody riot that had occurred in Houston a short time before. Some new black recruits, ushered into the Army as part of the country's buildup for World War I, found themselves stationed in Houston. Many of them were from the north and were suddenly being asked to play the kind of subservient role Texas blacks had been playing for years. They had revolted against their officers and began a rowdy march toward the downtown Houston business district. Shooting erupted, the mob went wild, and there were casualties on both sides. Thirty-seven blacks were hanged as a result. The word spread through the state and left both black and white communities tense and worried.

Huddie, alias Walter Boyd, remained in the Bowie County Jail in Boston for nearly six months while the legal system crept forward. Shortly after his incarceration a very frightened and powerful Leadbelly broke out by overpowering the jailer, confiscating his gun, and fleeing into the countryside. After three days of freedom, Huddie was recaptured and returned to jail. The taste of freedom was tantalizingly sweet, but it came back to haunt him.

According to official Texas State Penitentiary records, prisoner #42738 was Walter Boyd, who had never previously been arrested. Huddie also insisted that his wife was named "Allie," that she was presently living in Mooringsport, and that he had been in school for five years. He was obviously trying to maintain his alias in hopes of concealing his earlier conviction. As it was, District Attorney Hugh Carney, who later became a district judge, sought an indictment charging Huddie with the murder of Will Stafford. On January 29, 1918, a grand jury of Bowie County indicted Walter Boyd on this charge, accusing him of killing Will Stafford by "shooting him with a gun." There was also another charge that District Attorney Carney filed: one count of "assault to murder." This charge apparently refers to an assault Huddie made on either Brown or Griffen the night of the incident. Huddie decided to plead guilty to both charges. It was a day and age when nobody suggested a plea bargain, especially for a black man.

The trial on the murder charge occurred on February 21, three weeks after the indictment. It was somewhat of a local sensation and was covered by two newspapers—the Texarkana-based *Four States Press and Texarkana Courier* and *Daily Texarkanian*. On February 22 the *Daily Texarkanian* reported:

Boyd put up a rather novel defense, attorneys state, wherein he tried to fix the responsibility on two other negroes for the killing. The claim was made that Boyd and two other negroes were out at night on the date of the killing when they had some words with Stafford. Boyd was walking ahead of Stafford, and the evidence showed that he turned and shot Stafford. In

*testifying Boyd claimed that one of his companions shot Stafford. It was
proven, however, that neither of these had a pistol or revolver; where upon
Boyd is said to have asserted that the one who really killed Stafford over-
powered and disarmed him and shot him with his own gun.*

Later that day the jury was ready to render its verdict. Foreman Cookman
stood and announced their verdict: "We, the Jury, find the defendant,
Walter Boyd, guilty of murder, and assess his punishment at twenty (20)
years confinement in the State Penitentiary." These words were chilling
enough, but Leadbelly still had to wait for the verdict on the assault to
murder charge. This trial would not take place for several months.

How fair was the trial? No transcript survived the years and the courthouse's move to a new building in the 1980s; thus, only circumstantial
evidence exists. The trial was certainly fast—one day—and not many witnesses could have been called. Huddie himself later only commented that
Stafford shouldn't have crossed him, an ambiguous comment that could
refer to either self-defense or attempted murder. He once said that the
original fight started over Griffin "jiving" Will Stafford about his girlfriend
and that Boyd's name only came up later in respect to the girlfriend. Blanch
Love, one of Huddie's first cousins, told a different version of the case.
According to her, after Stafford was killed the other men ran, but Huddie
hung around because of his friendship with the dead man. When the law
came the next morning, they found "tennis shoe" prints around the body,
and when they found Huddie, he was wearing shoes that matched the
prints. This, supposedly, held up as one of the strongest pieces of circumstantial evidence against him. But Blanch insisted that when the other men
involved in the fight were picked up, "come to find out they all had on them
tennis shoes like Huddie was wearing." Whether or not this was ever
brought out in the trial is not clear, but apparently enough about the
proceedings bothered pro bono defender Thomas that he immediately filed
a motion for a new trial—exactly the proper course of action by modern
standards. The state of Texas considered this petition for several weeks, but
on March 13 turned it down. It also suggested that Walter Boyd also serve
a "term of not less than 5 nor more than 20 years." The court did allow Mr.
Thomas and Mr. Boyd ninety days "to prepare and file in this cause a
statement of facts and bills of exceptions." In short, they were being given
time to present a stronger case for a new trial. A $5,000 bond would have
permitted Huddie his temporary freedom, but it proved impossibly high.

Spring had arrived by the time Huddie's second trial began, and on April
22, 1918, he was found guilty. The jury recommended ten years of confinement. A month later at his sentencing hearing, the court assigned him,
still calling him Walter Boyd, a term of "not less than two no more than ten

years," a sentence to run after the murder charge. All told, Huddie faced a minimum of seven years and a maximum of thirty years in the notorious Texas penal system. Had Huddie murdered or assaulted a white person, he almost certainly would have been a candidate for capital punishment.

Thomas attempted a final legal maneuver on May 22, 1918, when he filed an appeal to revise or reverse the judgment of both sentences. On June 7, 1918, the Court of Criminal Appeals dismissed the appeal and sustained the original judgment partially because Walter Boyd had "made his escape pending appeal." It further required that Boyd pay all of the costs related to the appeal. Finally, it mandated that Walter Boyd be turned over to the state of Texas immediately.

Shaw State Prison Farm received Huddie directly from the Bowie County Courthouse. Located about ten miles northeast of De Kalb at the end of the road just beyond Almont, the prison farm sat on the border of Arkansas, Oklahoma, and Texas. In 1913 the state of Texas had purchased the 2,715 acres of land from Gus Shaw for $100,000 and for the next fourteen years used it as a prison for black inmates. The meandering Red River formed its northern and eastern border, a barrier that was at times difficult for even the strongest swimmer to cross. This was a working facility, literally a farm where all of the convicts worked. Most of them labored in the fields and Huddie faced a minimum of seven years of picking cotton and hard physical labor with no chance of reprieve. Always looking for an angle, an alternative, Huddie considered his fate: "Here I was, the king of Fannin Street, rotting in that pen for killing old Alex Griffin [sic]."

After a year of incarceration at Shaw, Huddie began finding it hard to control his restlessness. He really wanted his freedom back. On August 15, 1919, he saw his opening and escaped with a fellow convict. "I didn't like the way the white folks was beating up on everybody. They didn't bother me too much 'cause I was the number one roller on the number one gang. But I never did like them chain gangs." The first chance he got, Huddie and the other convict slipped into the underbrush while working in the fields and got a good start before the overseer missed them. Lacking his physical stamina, Huddie's buddy fell out and was soon captured. Determined to escape, Huddie pushed on farther into the woods and outdistanced his pursuers. His downfall came when a white man happened upon Huddie while he rested in some rushes next to the Red River.

The sheriff was notified and surprised Huddie at the makeshift camp. Huddie awoke surrounded by a pack of vicious, growling, tracking dogs; the "dog boy" in charge was barely able to hold them back, and when one lunged at Huddie, the boy got him back only by hitting him with a stick. "Come on, Walter, let's go," ordered the man with the dogs. Huddie shook his head; nothing was worth going back. One of the white trackers drew his pistol. "Come on back here, nigger, or I'll shoot your black heart out!" But Huddie paid him no mind to that, either. Slowly he got up and turned his back on them. Walking deliberately, Huddie quietly waded into the Bend Lake near the Red River, for he had no intention of returning to Shaw. He later told Gordon Parks, "I just kept on walking up over my eyeballs, drinking up that nasty river [sic]. Then one of the dogs come in after me. I took him and choked him good and slung him under the water and held him there till he was through. When I kept going under, they come in and yanked me out."

They wouldn't even let him drown. The water reached his chest before they hauled him out and began to revive him. "Water was runnin' outta every hole," he remembered. They kept asking him how he felt, but he couldn't speak. Finally they got him up, walked him around, and decided he was ready to go back to camp. The men put him on the wagon and the entire party slowly made its way back to Shaw State Prison Farm. "After I dry out they wanted to beat me but I wasn't having no more of that, so I picked up a hoe and stand the old captain off with it. He took out his Winchester and points it at me saying 'Nigger, put down that hoe or I'll kill you!' But I just look at him like I'm crazy. I'm ready to die, to go all the way." Huddie eventually calmed down, but he must have wondered if the less than twenty-four hours of freedom was worth the retribution that he faced.

When he got back to camp, his immediate supervisor, Captain Francis, kept him out of the fields for a week. As he rested and felt his strength returning, Huddie had time to reflect. As important as freedom was, survival was even more so. Over and over he had gone up against the system, and the system had always won. As vital as his pride and reputation was, Huddie was learning hard truths about a black man in a white man's world, and he was realizing that there might be other ways to deal with the problem: Instead of confrontation, he would use the age-old prejudice against itself. This involved a technique that later blacks would call "yessing them to death." But it involved, he must have now realized, playing the stereotype prejudice cast him in. Huddie could no longer be the bad nigger who stayed around after a murder expecting justice, who perversely walked into the lake to drown, the abject roustabout. Captain Francis assured him that if he worked hard and kept out of trouble, nobody would bother him. And Huddie decided to live by a new plan, to become a "rollin' sonofabitch," the hardest-working man in the Texas penal system.

Soon he became the leader of a hoeing squad on the lead row. It reflected not only his hard-won working ability, but his new attitude. His days of trying to escape, to evade the system were over. But it was draining, demanding work. He had to keep the men in line and take grief from the "walking boss" who supervised the field workers. He occasionally chafed under the ongoing brutality and insensitivity of the prison farm employees, some of whom felt that every black prisoner needed a "taste of the leather" whip. One time he had to stand up to Captain Francis when he was wrongly accused of loitering on the job and not working the men hard enough. The tense confrontation lasted for several minutes but ended peacefully and in compromise. Huddie knew that, in the final analysis, he was powerless to change his own situation and had to use the system if he was to be a free man before his appointed time.

Huddie not only confronted his pride, but his manly past. A man who liked women, he'd had his share before he got into serious trouble. The most lasting outcome of his early philandering, Taleta "Panthy" Boyd, was born on August 7, 1918, on the Pat Gibbons Bottoms on the banks of the Red River. Her mother, Iola Boyd, who lived in Beaver Dam, had a brief interlude with Huddie shortly before he was incarcerated in mid-December 1917. Iola Boyd was born in 1902 and had a comic-tragic childhood. The Boyd family appeared to be stable enough except for her father, Nick Boyd, who "cracked up and lost his mind. The creek was up and he couldn't cross the bridge; not having a good mind he forded on the mule and somehow got off the mule and was drowned. He was just going around the country. He wasn't bothering nobody . . ." Apparently Nick Boyd was something of a cut-up and Zeola Vaughn remembers when "he came down to the house one late evening and told them he had come to play and he had a guitar and was singing, 'Come go with me to Reveille' and when he got to a verse he called her Sister Jones and sang 'Sister Jones come and go with me' and when he put her name in it she wanted some one to come and get him." Zeola Vaughn came to the end of this story with a laugh and she recalled Nick Boyd with more than seventy years of detached irony. "It was real funny afterwards but at the time we were all scared of him. We had heard about him being crazy, so he was just going place to place."

Unlike Huddie's first child, Arthur Mae, the new baby girl seemed to hold no interest whatsoever for Huddie. It was not a surprising turn of events given his status as a guest of the state of Texas. Panthy grew up and remained in Bowie County all of her life. In 1991 she lived a quarter mile from the Beaver Dam Cemetery, where Will Stafford found his final resting place. Even today people recall her reputation as a blues and gospel singer and as the daughter of Walter Boyd. Until her death by a heart attack on December 6, 1991, she was Huddie's closest living relative and last surviving child.

Huddie remained at the Shaw farm for nearly two years. Captain Francis respected him enough to formally ask that the Board of Pardons clear his record of the escape charge. Huddie had found a niche at Shaw and was learning how to survive in this tough, often brutal system. Just as his life was settling into a somewhat tolerable routine, Huddie found himself uprooted once more. This time it was a transfer to the Central State Farm, located just to the southwest of Houston: a place known to most simply as Sugarland.

10 "The Midnight Special"

Bud Russell was known throughout the state of Texas as "the transfer man." He was big—six feet tall, two hundred pounds—and his job was to move groups of prisoners between various jails and prison farms in the state. He would escort them from the local jails to the big prison at Huntsville, and then take them on down to the prison farms on the Brazos and Trinity river bottomlands. Russell was a familiar figure in folk songs from Texas, and "the folk image of Bud Russell is one of an evil spirit wandering the land, kidnapping the men into slavery." One local jailer still remembers him as a "very strong man with a very big knife." He often took charge of a large group of prisoners by himself. Russell liked to use chains, and on one occasion chained sixty-four prisoners into one long line and marched them through Houston to the train station. He was the only guard for the entire group. In 1920 it was Bud Russell who appeared at Shaw to take charge of Huddie and escort him to his new home at Sugarland. Years later Huddie would remember the trip; he had not wanted to go, but there was no choice and Bud Russell put chains around his neck and hauled him away.

Fort Bend County lies nearly three hundred fifty miles southwest of Bowie County, a trek that in any place other than Texas would have crossed several state lines. The prison farm was located in the Brazos River bottomland, about twenty miles west of Houston. Today that site is well within the city's metro area; then it was out in the country. It was officially called Central State Prison Farm, but was also referred to as Fort Bend, Brazos Bottom, or, most often, Sugarland—from the nearby town built around the tall building of the Imperial Sugar Company Refinery, which operated day and night to process the locally grown sugarcane. The buildings of the prison camps dot U.S. Highway 90 about a mile outside of the small town. It was a different world from Shaw, which looked across to the Oklahoma and Arkansas border. What Texas tourist promotions liked to call "the balmy breezes of the Gulf of Mexico" rarely made it into the swampy Brazos River bottomland. A line from a popular local blues song was more accurate: "That Fort Bend County bottom is a burning hell." Farther south than some towns in Mexico, the Sugarland farm was muggy, oppressive, and bleak: its very presence was designed to break the spirit of men.

When he arrived at Sugarland, Huddie was thirty-two years old, was used to hard work and brutal conditions, and was as strong, tough, big, and

fit as any man in prison. Yet the routine at Sugarland was a challenge even
to him; there were long summer days in July and August when by three
o'clock it seemed like the sun just stopped in the middle of the sky. Because
of his experience and endurance, Huddie was made a work group leader.
As he put it in the work song "Go Down Ol' Hannah": "Number one leader,
I was rollin' some/ I was rollin', honey from sun to sun." The tight, precise
rows of corn, cotton, and sugarcane stretched out for miles across the flat
bottomland. The "man on the end" oversaw the individual gangs of workers and didn't hesitate to use his whip to "tighten them up" if the work
wasn't going fast enough to suit him. The weak fell from heatstroke and the
desperate tried to escape; most endured.

Huddie's relationship with Lethe had been strained even before his conviction. Now the emotional distance between them grew greater. Even with
his 1918 conviction, she might have stayed with him as long as he was held
at nearby Shaw. When he was moved more than three hundred miles away,
however, even Lethe began to have doubts. Huddie later sang that when he
left his wife for prison, he would probably "never no more see her" and she
should "do the best she can." Apparently Lethe took him at his word and
their marriage totally disintegrated, though there is no evidence that they
ever formally divorced.

The distance to Sugarland also meant that Wes and Sallie had little hope
of seeing their son much more. Both were in their sixties now and their hard
life was beginning to take its toll on them. Still, their protective instincts
died hard. About one year after Huddie arrived at Sugarland, Wes appeared
at the main gate, asking to see the manager, Captain Flannigan. He had
managed to get his hands on some more money by selling his last few acres
of land, which he had somehow accumulated after Huddie's first scrap with
the law in 1915. Now he shoved the cash across the table at Flannigan,
asking him to take what he wanted but to let Huddie go. Wes was getting
too old to handle his farming chores and Huddie was his only male child.
Huddie was desperately needed to work the farm in Harrison County.
Flannigan stared back at the old man with a mixture of wonder at Wes's
forthrightness and sympathy for his plight. Although Flannigan had the
reputation as a tough but fair boss, business wasn't done that way anymore.
This was the Texas penal system, not the Bowie County sheriff's office, and
Huddie had no choice but to serve out his term. Flannigan shoved the
money back to Wes. The older man saw Huddie later that day, before he left
to return to Mooringsport. "They must think you need a lot of punishment," he told his son. Wes recounted his meeting with Flannigan and of
his attempt at bail. Both men sensed that Huddie would be at Sugarland for
a long, long time. At the end of their talk, Wes said his farewell. "Don't
reckon I'm gonna see you again, boy. I know I ain't got long to live." He

left and started the long trek back to Mooringsport to give the bad news to Sallie. Four months later, Huddie learned that his father had died.

None of these events stopped Huddie from playing. Both the inmates and the overseers soon recognized he was a superb and entertaining musician who could bring a spark of life to the long, dreary weeks. Soon Captain Flannigan was letting him travel around unguarded to other camps on the farm every Sunday. Huddie would entertain the men with songs and spin yarns; in short, he was able to somewhat replicate the type of performing he had done for years at saloons and house parties in northeast Texas. Initially, Huddie was a little nervous about this, preferring to remain a regular line worker. But the lure of having at least a little freedom on Sunday afternoons was strong, and it provided a chance to hone his old songs and learn new ones.

The prison camps, as folk song collectors would later learn, were rich repositories of older songs, handed down by word-of-mouth through generations of singers. Because of their relative isolation, the camps were islands of archaic African American culture that were largely removed from the modern world and its musical fads. During the specific years Huddie was in Sugarland, blues and jazz were becoming a national craze. In 1920 a black vaudeville singer named Mamie Smith had recorded the first blueslike song, "Crazy Blues," for the OKeh Record Company. It became a huge hit. Three years later trumpet greats "King" Oliver and a young Louis Armstrong made their first records together as the Creole Jazz Band. Piano player Jelly Roll Morton, whom Huddie had seen several years before in New Orleans, also made it into the recording studio. These musicians helped to popularize jazz for millions of Americans who had grown up on the brass bands led by John Philip Sousa. Bessie Smith, arguably the greatest blues singer of them all, started recording in 1923, spreading her music beyond the tent-show stage to a fascinated new mainstream audience. "The Jazz Age" was not misnamed and had Huddie been able, he would have been right in the middle of it. As it was, he heard little of it and continued to sing songs that were old in styles that were old, and only his own creativity within this enforced tradition kept his juices flowing. He didn't know it at the time, of course, but this isolation would in the end serve him well and form a distinctive repertoire that would win him his fame.

It seems certain by this time that Huddie was commonly being called Leadbelly. He himself had implied that he had used this nickname in Dallas as early as 1912, when he got his first twelve-string guitar, but it certainly seems like a prison nickname more than anything else. There were two other well-known singers at Sugarland, both of whom were probably there at the same time as Huddie. James Baker and Moses Platt were later to record their songs for the Library of Congress. Baker was known as "Ironhead," while Platt used the name "Clear Rock." These names are similar in style to "Leadbelly" and the name probably refers to his strength and vocal ability rather than to his original name. Leadbelly himself said that nicknames in Sugarland were nothing casual; a man without a nickname in prison was like a little bug on the floor with no pallet to sleep on. "He's nobody with nothing. But give that little bug a pallet and he's somebody with something." His own nickname came from his ability to act as the lead man for the convict gangs that worked the cotton fields at Sugarland. He himself worked at a fast pace, and the songs he knew and sung helped make the work go smoother for all of them. One day the chaplain of the prison, the Reverend "Sin Killer" Griffin, came to him. "He says to me, you're a hard-driving man. Instead of guts, you got lead in your belly. That's who you are, old Leadbelly!" Whatever the case, Huddie seemed proud of the nickname and used it himself enthusiastically.

———

Many of the songs that Leadbelly later made famous came from his days at Sugarland. Most came directly from prison life and lore, like the song about Old Riley, a legendary convict who years before made a near-miraculous escape from the prison farm by outrunning the dogs and the horses of the guards who chased him. He managed to outrun the most vicious of all the dogs, the pack leader dubbed "nigger-eatin' Rattler," and "walked the Brazos River like Christ." Somehow, the story goes, he got across the flood-swollen river and shouted "bye-bye" to grim-faced guards. The legendary Riley is related to the hero of another black folk song, "Long Gone," about an escaped convict who was "long gone from Kentucky/ Long gone, got away lucky." Interestingly, one of the first commercial recordings of this song in 1928 was by another Texan, Dennis "Little Hat" Jones, whose nickname suggests that he might have been a former convict. Leadbelly sang two songs about this escape: one was titled by the Lomaxes "In Dem Long Summer Days," though Huddie called it simply "Old Riley" when he recorded it for Folkways. The other was "Old Rattler," a song about the lead dog which had been known in black circles for years, and was made into a song about a coon-hunting dog by white singers. It later became a hit record for Grand Ole Opry star Grandpa Jones in 1947.

"Shorty George," which Huddie would record no fewer than four times in his career, is about a "short train" that ran out of the farm from Houston. On Sundays it brought wives, families, and lovers to the men at Sugarland. As Huddie sang it in his 1935 commercial ARC recording:

> Well, Shorty George ain't no friend of mine.
> Shorty George ain't no friend of mine.

He keep's a-takin' all the women,
Keep all the men behind.©

Such sentiments were well known to many of the singers and most of the men at the farm, but Leadbelly liked to add a personal touch to the familiar song:

Well, I can't do nothing, hon, but wave my hands,
Well, I can't do nothing, hon, but wave my hands,
Got me a lifetime sentence,
Down at Sugarland.©

Others were work songs and chants, like "Billy in the Lowlands," an ax-cutting song that became one of Leadbelly's favorites. Not to be confused with the Anglo-American fiddle tune "Billy in the Low Ground," this was a work chant designed to coordinate the fall of axes or picks in a work crew. The leader sings "Billy in the lowlands," the group comes in by adding "Oh, Lawd, lawd," and the axes fall. Later verses can be added or changed according to the leader's whim. Huddie liked to add a verse about "Yonder come the captain, Captain Flannigan," and another explaining the title of the song: "Poor Billy got fevo', hundred an' nine, suh." A familiar holler was one Huddie called "Dicklicker's Holler." He learned it from an inmate at Sugarland, one with the prison name of Dicklicker, who liked to "holler" it while he and Leadbelly would be sitting in the "bullpen," a central room that opened into the various cells. It was basically a lament about women—hardly a true work song—but it stuck with Leadbelly and he liked to sing it years later when he was living in New York City. "Go Down, Ol' Hannah" was a widely circulated work holler that commemorated a bit of prison history: an especially hot day back in 1910 (a full decade before Huddie came on the scene) when several Texas convicts died of sunstroke and others risked shotgun blasts while trying to escape.

Of all of the songs he learned at Sugarland, however, by far the most popular was "The Midnight Special." Leadbelly did not write all of the song, though he probably did add some elements to it. He did popularize it through numerous recordings; his version became the one younger folksingers adapted in the late 1950s and 1960s. Parts of the song were clearly circulating in folk tradition prior to Huddie's encountering them and he may have known of it before his days in Sugarland. But it was in that prison that the form of the song as we know it today came together. Eventually Huddie came up with a fairly stable set of verses for his "Midnight Special." It included "Yonder come Miss Rosie," "get up in the morning," "better walk right," "Jumpin' Judy," and a final quatrain in which he begins to worry about "my great long time" yet to serve.

The title alludes to a Southern Pacific train that left Houston every night a few minutes after eleven for San Antonio and points west. As it rolled westward and entered Fort Bend County about twenty-five miles from downtown Houston, it crossed the Brazos River bottomland and passed near the buildings of the prison farm. Often its lights flashed through the cell windows and its whistle echoed across the prison farm. To the men who nicknamed the train the "Midnight Special," it became a cruel, tantalizing, and regular reminder of life beyond the Sugarland fences.

The inmates saw the train as a potent symbol and soon added other verses about prison life and about local incidents concerning the Houston police, including Bud Russell, the "transfer man" who had taken Huddie down to Sugarland. A stanza that Leadbelly almost always sang in his version of the song was:

> Bason and Brock will arrest you,
> Payton and Boone will take you down,
> The judge will sentence you,
> And you Sugarland bound.©

A. W. Brock was the chief of police in Houston for a time and the team of George Payton and Johnnie Boone was a pair of city detectives who specialized in working the black sections of town. Leadbelly himself had not spent much time, if any, in Houston before his Sugarland stay, so this stanza either dates from the years there after his release or was created after hearing other Sugarland inmates describe the conditions in Houston.

Other singers from Sugarland, such as Ironhead and Clear Rock, sang many of the same songs that Huddie did, and even recorded them for the Library of Congress, as did Huddie. And whereas other singers were passive about accepting the old songs and passing them on, Leadbelly couldn't stifle his churning creativity. He had to put his stamp on many of the songs, do them his way, add and change to fit his personal view of the world.

Leadbelly most often added to commonplace blues stanzas new material reflecting his trouble with women that eventually landed him in jail. In Sugarland, he found his captive audience loved it when he personalized songs, bringing in familiar local figures like Captain Flannigan. He began to build on this and found it was an easy step from making up localized stanzas to creating entire songs. And if prisoners liked to hear such local, personal references in songs, might not his keepers find the same delight?

His chance to find out came sooner than he expected and it resulted from some odd terms in Texas politics. In 1917, the year Huddie was arrested on the murder charge, the governor of Texas was James E. ("Big Jim") Ferguson. Coming from a farm background, he had emerged in 1914 as a champion of farm and rural education reform and had been elected to two terms as governor. During his second term, though, Ferguson became involved in a number of shady activities, one of which was selling pardons. In 1917, he was impeached and various reform candidates moved into state politics. One of these was Pat M. Neff from Waco, who found himself in the governor's chair in 1923 and 1924. In the fall of 1924, though, Ferguson's wife, "Ma" Ferguson, decided to avenge her husband by running for the office and—after an angry fight in which she and her husband took on the Ku Klux Klan—won and prepared to take office in January 1925. In the meantime, Neff, who had campaigned in 1920 on a law-and-order platform that specifically promised no more pardon selling, had been true to his reformist zeal. The pardons indeed had dried up; during his four years as governor, Neff pardoned only five men. For a convicted felon in Sugarland, chances for relief did not look good.

But then, about January 1924, Governor Neff decided to begin a tour of the various prison camps around Texas. One day he and his wife and a delegation of other women arrived at Leadbelly's camp, and the captain summoned the singer to provide some evening entertainment. By this time Huddie had become quite well known as a prison entertainer and was even being allowed to keep money he made as a result of his performing. Here was his best chance for an audience yet, and he eagerly seized it.

Leadbelly claims that he kept some white suits "creased up and everything," ready for special occasions.

I paid another boy a nickel to wash them, that's all he charged. And my clothes would be all ready to go. Pat Neff came and there were four cars, all of them would be women, except for the chauffeurs. And these women would have these little automatics in their pocketbooks; they didn't take no chances. When the Governor come, they come down in the field; I'm way down in the field, leading the boys. Coming down to get Ledbetter, so I could get my "glad rags" [white suit] on. I went and got ready, and we had an eight piece band and we all get ready to go out there. Now I got my songs all in the back of my mind. The way I made this song up ["Governor Pat Neff"], I lay down at night trying to get the right words, you know, kept a pencil and paper under my pillow. I'd be laying there, everybody'd be snoring and I'd doze off a little. I'd dream of a good word and I'd write it down a little. . . . When we went up there that night, Governor Pat Neff and the women was sitting on the front porch. He was sitting with his legs crossed and his arms folded. He wore these tall collars and a bow tie, looked a little like a priest, you know. When I go in I wouldn't tell nobody what was on my mind. I put my guitar on my shoulder, had my twelve-string Stella.

All the other guys went by the Governor. The Governor greeted me, "How you doing, Ledbetter?" "I'm just fine." "How you feeling?" "You're honor, I feel alright." "Still dancing?" "I can dance all night." He said, "You are some nigger!"

Part of Huddie's act consisted of a comic dance called "The Sugarland Shuffle" in which he imitated a man dashing up and down rows of cotton, picking like a demented, frantic, crazy parody of the kind of fast picking that Leadbelly himself had done to earn the respect of his overseers. He later remembered that he "picked the guitar some for the Governor and sang songs, not the barrelhouse kind, but songs like 'What a Friend We Have in Jesus.' The Governor asked me to play 'Ole Dan Tucker,' 'Down in the Valley,' and other hillbilly tunes." Fortunately, Leadbelly's repertoire was eclectic enough that he could do this. Huddie, however, had greater plans than simply entertaining Neff and his entourage.

I sat down near the piano player and the bass player. Old Stack O' Dollars, he sing, you know, we had eight pieces. We'd play and sing. We sang "Midnight Special" and then the captain said, the Governor wants to hear a song. I sat down at a place where I could really see him. I was watching him, but I was watching the women, too. Before I start to sing that song, he talked to me. Then the women would ask me some questions. While we talking, they had some whiskey in there. He'd pour out some whiskey, in a plain glass. He gave it to a woman to give to me. She brought it over, but she wouldn't look at me. The girl sat down the whiskey and look over there. I drank about half of it then, set it back down. It wouldn't be long before I drink the rest of it because I wanted to finish it before I start playing. Finally I started my song. I put Mary in it, Jesus's mother, you know. I took a verse from the bible, around about the twenty second chapter of Proverbs, around the fourteenth verse: if you forgive a man his trespasses, the heavenly father will also forgive your trespasses. But if you not forgive man of his trespasses, the heavenly father will still forgive you of your trespasses. Then I start singing:

> *In nineteen hundred and twenty three,*
> *when the judge taken my liberty away from me.*
> *In nineteen hundred and twenty three,*
> *when the judge taken my liberty away from me.*
> *Say my wife come, wringing her hands and crying,*
> *Lord, have mercy on that man of mine.*©

Making no reference to his crime, or to his guilt or innocence for it, he built the entire song on sentiment by explaining how hard parting from his wife had been and how happy everybody would be if he could go back home. The date of his judgment was not exactly right, but he needed a rhyme. And his wife had been Lethe, but Mary (the name of his prison girlfriend) apparently had a more Christian ring to it. Despite a few histori- cal inaccuracies in the pardon song, Governor Neff was delighted at this instance of apparent on-the-spot ballad making and with Huddie in general. Huddie said that the governor told him, " 'I'm going to turn you loose after a while, but I'm going to keep you here so you can pick and dance for me when I come down.' I thanked him and wanted to go right then, but I was glad that I could please him. I just stayed in the field cutting cane, wouldn't take no easy job." He knew that the governor had another whole year to serve before his term was over, but he could hope that Neff would keep his word. During this period, Neff came back several times: "He came down one time and had a party, built a platform right out in the yard. They had all the musicianers out there and the yard was full of people. I reckon that we had thirty five or forty cars come out of Houston. And Governor Pat Neff sat right down on the grass, green grass, where he could look. After every- one got to dancing and everything the Captain came round and said for me to sit down for a while and let the other boys 'go to town.' I'd danced on the set, one boy played the piano and I danced the buck and wing. Later the Governor wanted me to play his song again."

Then weeks passed with no word from Neff. It was starting to look like another cruel hoax and Huddie's friends began to kid him about his opti- mism. White governors, they contended, don't remember scruffy black prisoners they heard sing once or twice and they surely don't give them pardons. The election came and passed, and still no word. Then finally, on January 16, 1925, in one of his last acts in office, Neff signed a full pardon for Huddie, as Walter Boyd. The prisoner, it read, had served six years, seven months, and eight days of his sentence of from seven to thirty years. And though Neff was obviously impressed with Leadbelly's music, and though this pardon was one of only five he granted, it remains curious that Huddie had almost completed the seven years that were the minimum for his sentence. Certainly Neff was protecting himself to some extent from later criticism and certainly there was no question of Huddie "buying" his pardon. Ironically, Neff's casual, generous act done at the tail end of his tenure was to be the act for which history best remembers him.

Huddie received the news one morning when Captain Flannigan called him into his office and told him he was a free man, that his plea had actually worked. Amazed at the potency of his music, Huddie packed his meager belongings and headed out the gates for Houston. He had every intention of heeding the words to his own "Midnight Special": "If you ever go to Houston/ Boy, you better walk right."

11 " 'Fo-Day Worry Blues"

With $115 in his pocket that he had earned from enter-
taining in prison, Leadbelly hunted up his girlfriend Mary
and began his new life in Houston. Temptations were all around him, in a
city bigger and rowdier than even Shreveport, but he made an effort to land
a steady job. Somehow he got on at the Houston Buick agency and learned
how to work as a driver as well as a laborer in the lot. There were minor
scrapes with the local law and soon he earned a reputation with the local
police. A former chief of detectives, T. K. "Kirk" Irwin, knew Leadbelly
during these days. "I remember a great big fellow. Always played guitar and
sang when you'd take him in. Some of the boys would see him on the street
and pick him up just to hear him make up songs."

His day job left his nights free and he used them to moonlight by playing
his music. During the time he had been in prison, the blues had become a
national fad. No longer was it confined to the cathouses and saloons of the
red-light district; now it could be heard at vaudeville theaters and on records. Leadbelly soon found his way to the local theaters that featured this
music and began to hear some of the new generation of professional blues
singers that were causing such a stir. He heard Ethel Waters, Ida Cox, and
Eva Taylor for the first time. Huddie especially recalled Bessie Smith's
singing, but it was Clara Smith's (no relation) "Death Letter Blues" he
added to his own repertoire. He himself started out working the local
barrelhouses and juke joints, and for a time might have even joined a
vaudeville circuit himself.

Yet Houston wasn't Shreveport, where Huddie had family and friends
and where people knew who he was. His relationship with Mary (no one
seems to remember her last name) always remained casual, and after several months he began to think there was little to really hold him in Houston.
Besides, his father was gone and his mother was having to fend for herself.
The climate was nice in the winter, but eternally hot and sticky during the
rest of the year. Word from Mooringsport told of jobs, even for African
Americans, that could be had in the booming oil industry there. All in all,
it seemed like a good idea to head home to Caddo Parish.

In the meantime, Leadbelly was still marveling at the changes that had
taken place in black music while he'd been in prison. His own forty-one
years had seen a revolutionary shift in the nature of black music, and in how
it was perceived by both black and white audiences. At the turn of the

century, as Huddie approached manhood, most black musicians were what were called "songsters," with rich and diverse repertoires that included old dance tunes, ballads, gospel songs, and even folk adaptations of old sentimental songs from Tin Pan Alley. Huddie's own early repertoire reflected much the same mixture. During the 1920s, some of the last of these old songsters got a chance to record for the new phonograph record companies: Henry Thomas (from Texas) and Charlie Patton (from Mississippi) were two that were quickly establishing reputations. By the time Huddie got out of Sugarland, though, a generation of younger black musicians were developing a new style of music that everybody was calling the blues.

Though its precise origins remain obscured by time, it is clear that blues developed in the Deep South around the turn of the century. The first blues were almost certainly sung at the turpentine camps, tenant farms, and cotton fields that stretched between central Texas and western Alabama. Ku Klux Klan activity was on the rise and threatened some blacks who tried to use their voting rights; many of the gains made during the course of Reconstruction were slowly eroding away through both legal channels and social customs. The musical form and language of the blues is one quite dramatic reaction by the black community to these harsh conditions. And it swept across the entire South within ten years, carried east and north by part-time musicians moving to new locations for work or itinerate musicians employed by traveling shows. By the close of World War I, the blues were firmly established as part of the African American musical vocabulary.

Huddie must have been surprised and somewhat jealous to hear Blind Lemon Jefferson's Paramount records, the first of which became available about one year after Huddie was released from the Texas penal system. Lemon's songs for the Paramount Record Company sold well and he was among the earliest of the "down-home" blues singers to explore this electronic medium. *Down-home*, in this context, refers to a guitar-accompanied male singer. Lemon and his rough-and-tumble colleagues, such as Walter "Furry" Lewis, Blind Willie McTell, and in later years Robert Johnson, each made recordings. The first country blues recording by Ed Andrews, "Time Ain't Gonna Make Me Stay" and "Barrelhouse Blues," was issued by OKeh Records in the summer of 1924. Slowly, the number of down-home blues recordings increased, but most blues musicians really made their living by playing music on street corners, for house parties, or at clubs called "jukes," where booze, gambling, and loose women were on tap and available. On Friday and Saturday nights these ramshackle joints were packed with eager patrons who stayed until the break of day. Such joints were commonplace in the country around Caddo Lake, and Leadbelly frequented them quite often as a featured musician and well-known rounder.

The commercial recording of blues really began in 1920 when OKeh Records released "Crazy Blues" by Mamie Smith. It caused a sensation and proved that a strong market for vernacular black music existed and could be exploited for commercial gain. After a moderate downturn of the economy in 1921 and 1922, the record industry made a comeback with the rest of the economy. This time the record executives cast their nets wider, looking for musical talent they thought would appeal to an increasingly affluent black population. They initially went after talent similar to Mamie Smith: female singers with piano or small jazz combo accompaniment. By early 1924 two stars, Bessie Smith and Gertrude "Ma" Rainey, had emerged. The established record companies like Columbia and OKeh, as well as upstarts such as Paramount and Gennett, struggled to locate black talent. They also slowly learned how to sell their records to a market they had never before targeted.

The record companies were almost all white-owned and were all located in the north, far from the culture that produced and nurtured this music. They assumed—incorrectly, as it turned out—that the people who bought records by Smith and Rainey were all African Americans. Predictably, most of their new blues records were released in specifically designated numerical series that were advertised in black-oriented newspapers. The term *race records* came into being as a merchandising label to describe these new series, and crudely stereotyped graphics were used in advertisements that appeared in the Norfolk *Journal and Guide*, Chicago *Defender*, and other newspapers that reached black readers across the country. These were the first records produced with a black audience in mind. The concept of a record store had not yet developed, so customers purchased these products through the mail or at furniture stores. Because furniture stores sold wind-up Victrolas, they also carried a stock of the shellac 78 rpm records to play on these early phonographs.

By 1926 the blues market had expanded to include male blues singers, whose music appealed to urban blacks who had migrated northward as well as those who remained down home. The classic female singers were relatively easy to locate—they sang on the vaudeville stage, tent shows, or other professional venues. But men performing in southern juke joints or on street corners in Shreveport were more difficult to scout. After months of internal debate and faltering about, a system for finding talent slowly emerged. Because they were in touch with paying customers on a daily basis, the same men who sold hand-cranked Victrolas and records became the first talent scouts. The record companies built permanent studios in New York and Chicago, but they also decided to use portable studios to conduct field sessions in major cities across the South: Atlanta, New Orleans, Dallas, St. Louis, and Memphis. Even smaller cities such as Greensboro, North Carolina; Bristol, Tennessee; and Augusta, Georgia, were eventually chosen as sites for recordings done on portable equipment. These sessions recorded not only race talent but hillbilly singers, local hotel bands, and popular singers.

The approach of going to the musicians themselves in order to record American vernacular music clearly worked. As early as 1890 anthropologist Jesse Walter Fewkes brought a primitive cylinder machine to Maine and recorded the music of Passamaquoddy Indians. During the intervening years a handful of dedicated scholars recorded a wide variety of Anglo-American, Native American, African-American, and other ethnic music. Robert Gordon of the Library of Congress hit the field to record American folk musicians on a cylinder machine during the middle 1920s. Ironically, this very tack eventually helped to get Leadbelly out of jail when John and Alan Lomax of the Library of Congress met him at Angola.

Leadbelly himself heard these commercial records, for they contained the type of music that he loved. Whether he purchased the records, heard them at friends' homes, or learned them secondhand from other musicians is unimportant. Blues songs that he absorbed from recorded sources ultimately became an important part of his repertoire. Many of his blues or blueslike songs, including "Alabama Bound," "Easy Rider," "Bully of the Town," and "Good Morning Blues" likely evolved from oral tradition. But "Back Water Blues" (Bessie Smith), "Its Tight Like That" (Tampa Red), "Midnight Special" (Sam Collins), and "Outskirts of Town" (Big Bill) all appeared on race records long before Leadbelly recorded them.

Of course, Leadbelly was not the only blues singer playing around the Ark-La-Tex. At least four local blues players made their debut long before Leadbelly made his first commercial recordings for the American Record Corporation in 1935. Elzadie Robinson, a rough-voiced vaudeville singer, recorded for Paramount between 1926 and 1928. Another female singer from the same period, Lillian Glinn, recorded "Shreveport Blues" for Columbia in 1929 and may well have been from a background similar to Leadbelly's.

Oscar "Buddy" Woods and Eddie Schaffer were closer to Leadbelly's brand of blues. Both men played the guitar on their laps using a broken bottleneck that they used to "fret" the guitar. This style of playing is sometimes found in the Mississippi Delta and may stem from the interest in Hawaiian music that began in the 1890s following the appearance of such musicians at the 1893 Chicago World's Fair. Black musicians, in particular, favored this approach to guitar playing. Leadbelly used this style on several of his recordings, though he held the guitar in standard position and placed the bottleneck on his left pinkie.

Another Ark-La-Tex musician to record during this time, Jesse "Baby-face" Thomas, still lives in Shreveport. Thomas came from a musical family that included an older brother, Willard, born in Logansport, Louisiana, in 1902, who eventually recorded twenty selections for Paramount and Victor between 1928 and 1932. "Ramblin'," as he was called, often recorded using a slide guitar technique and spent his time traveling through northeast Texas. He died sometime in the late 1930s.

In 1940 John Lomax came to Shreveport as part of a recording project for the Folksong Archive of the Library of Congress. He recorded not only Buddy Woods but three other Caddo Parish musicians who had become part of the local scene. Kid West and Joe Harris, two of Woods's buddies, were also street singers who worked the "black bottom" area of town. They'd been playing for several decades and revealed strong songster roots in their versions of "Baton Rouge Rag," "Nobodies Business," and "Bully of the Town." Harris, from Bunkie, Louisiana, was the guitar player, while West picked mandolin. Both men sang and proved to be effective vocalists on the blues: "Kid West Blues" is an ironic look at marriage, while Harris's "East Texas Blues" reminds one of Blind Lemon Jefferson. In "Out East Blues" Harris talks of an earlier life in southern Louisiana and his "woman in Franklin, one in Donaldsonville," both of which are located fairly close to his Avoyelles Parish home. Fannin Street remained at the heart of activity for blues musicians, though joints like Jerry's Saloon on Texas Avenue, which bridged the Red River between Bossier City and Shreveport, also appealed to black musicians. Bossier City, home to Barksdale Air Force Base, remains an unsavory part of greater Shreveport with its pawnshops, strip joints, and clubs that cater to servicemen.

By way of contrast, Noah Moore remained around Mooringsport all of his life until he was killed in World War II. Moore was born in 1907 and made his living sharecropping around central Caddo Parish. An avid fisherman, he also loved to play the guitar and learned some songs from his cousin, Leadbelly. His playing, though not directly patterned after his famous cousin, does have some of the rhythmic intensity that Huddie so often displayed. Moore also displayed something of a songster tradition in his repertoire, but his Library of Congress recordings suggest that he was more of a blues man. "Oil City Blues" is a fine example of his artistry, for it features a series of "floating" verses derived from a variety of sources that are so commonly found in this music. But Moore personalizes the song through numerous local references:

> Baby, here I am in your Oil City town.
> Baby, here I am in your Oil City town.
> If you find some other man, you got to turn me down.

I stood on the corner, till my feet got soakin' wet.
I stood on the corner, till my feet got soakin' wet.
I was trying to make friends with every Oil City gal I met.

Oil City town is the place I long to be.
Oil City town is the place I long to be.
I've got a brownskin gal waiting there for me.

Given the recording success of these other singers from the Shreveport area, it seems strange that Leadbelly didn't really try his hand at commercial recordings at this time. He was in Houston and Shreveport from 1925 to 1930, during the high-water period for commercial recordings of Leadbelly's style of music. Hoping to cash in on the success of Blind Lemon Jefferson, the Memphis Jug Band, Jim Jackson, and others, every single major record company sent talent scouts and recording teams to the South. Over fifty field recording sessions were held during these five years, from Dallas to Atlanta, from Memphis to New Orleans. OKeh Records even held sessions right in Shreveport and nearby Jackson, Mississippi, in 1930. For most years between 1925 and 1930, the combined companies released an average of five hundred new blues or race records a year—many drawn from the sessions held at portable studios in hotels or auditoriums in these cities. In their desperation to come up with a salable product, the companies recorded dozens of mediocre blues singers and seemed willing to give almost anybody a trial record or two. Yet none of the company files shows any reference to Huddie Ledbetter or Walter Boyd or Leadbelly. No one recalls Huddie ever going for an audition at any of these sessions or being recommended by the numerous talent scouts that roamed the area.

Was he too old-fashioned? Other songsters of a similar age, such as Stovepipe #1 (Sam Jones), Will Bennett, and Jim "Mooch" Richardson, were being recorded. Did he not know enough blues? By now he had become an accomplished blues singer with his months as apprentice to Blind Lemon, which would seem to be impeccable credentials. Did he lack "original" material, a common complaint of record talent scouts back then? Hardly—his penchant for adapting and making up new songs was one of the things that everybody liked, even the Houston policemen who rousted him. Was he simply disinterested? A few years later, when offered the chance to record for the Lomaxes, Huddie was eager enough to record for days on end. Were the field tryout sessions simply not held anyplace close enough to him? Dallas and New Orleans, the locations for more than a dozen sessions, were a mere day's train ride away; for a man used to rambling as far and wide as Huddie had, that was not a major obstacle.

In February 1930 the local radio station in Shreveport asked the OKeh recording unit to come, in order to record a local announcer. They obliged, but also recorded a handful of selections by an African American string band from the area, the Mississippi Sheiks. Ironically, though, Huddie had been arrested only a couple of weeks before, and the very days the OKeh crew were recording, Huddie was watching the jury hear evidence against him. It was the ultimate in bad timing. Leadbelly himself never commented on his failure to record. He did tell Ross Russell that his first commercial record was for Columbia, and mentioned two titles: "Pig Meat Papa" and "East St. Louis Blues." Only the former selection appears in the American Record Corporation (ARC) session he did in 1935. Was there possibly an earlier tryout that yielded two test pressings for Columbia or was Huddie confusing the two companies? By 1935 a corporate relationship did exist between the two companies. The Columbia files show nothing at all like this, further compounding the mystery of why Huddie couldn't—or didn't—seize his first chance to really do something with his music.

Despite his later lack of commercial success, Huddie remained a highly respected musician after his release from the hot fields of southern Texas. Gigs were plentiful, but still not enough to support him full-time, so Huddie had to figure out what to do and where to go. Once again he returned to Caddo Lake, where he was well known. Huddie lived in Mooringsport, but played his twelve-string guitar in the nearby small towns such as Blanchard, Greenwood, Oil City, and Vivian. Because it supported a bank, several doctors, a large hotel, and a drugstore, Mooringsport served as the hub for central Caddo Parrish.

But good jobs were scarce for all. Exactly how Huddie supported himself is unclear. Some say he worked for the Gulf Refining Company, possibly as a maintenance man or a truck driver delivering pipes. Others contend that odd jobs and some part-time farm work paid his bills. Some of the time, at least, he got money by making illegally distilled liquor. One of Huddie's friends from this time, Booker T. Washington, had always found good jobs during the oil boom, but the only job he could find in 1927 was watering the streets "to keep the dust from settling in the stores. The streets wasn't paved like they are now. Then I used to carry mail from the post office to the depot 'cause a train came through here called the Flyin' Crow."

Music provided some relief from these oppressive conditions. Where there was music, home-brewed liquor was not far away. Leadbelly drank bourbon when he could get it, but Booker T. Washington said that "it was mostly bootleg. We would hide our liquor if the sheriff came . . . put some leaves over it. He'd be hunting for the whiskey and walk right over it!" Often they walked or rode their horses several miles west to Texas because the Harrison County sheriff wasn't as strict on people who broke the Prohibition laws.

Blues and the other types of music Leadbelly played were heard not only at late-night parties. Washington remembers "one time we had a ball game and my daddy barbecued a pig. He couldn't sell the pig out, so he sent somebody down to Huddie's. Huddie would bring a gang up with him to my daddy's house; played the guitar and sold that meat out. I didn't last one hour, sold out in about thirty minutes! There were so many people, they broke the porch down! If people heard that Huddie was going to play, they'd come if they had to walk."

It was probably at one of these after-hour dances that Huddie met Era Washington. With Lethe long gone, Huddie had drifted from woman to woman. Most were one-night affairs, others stayed with him for longer periods. Era was different because she remained part of his life for many years; for close to five years in the late 1920s they were steady lovers. Despite their close and caring relationship, Leadbelly still felt confined and his violent nature sometimes surfaced. He later wrote that "she was all time worrying when I'd go out and play. Sometimes I wouldn't come home til 'fore day . . . I'd be out playing for the niggers, drinking good whiskey, foolin' with the women, and having a good time. She got so mad with me one time that she broke up my twelve string box. I would have killed her then, but I know they'd put me in the pen." The guitar had cost him $20, though, so he settled on beating up Era "pretty bad" and then making her wash clothes for three months to pay for another guitar. On occasion, he would feel remorse about the way he treated his common-law wife, and guilt about the way she tolerated him. He wrote one song about their relationship " 'Fo-Day Worry Blues," recorded both for the Library of Congress and for the commercial ARC (" 'Fo-Day" referred not to "four days," but to "before day"—the time just about dawn when Leadbelly would often return from his various ramblings, often with other women.) He said he had first learned the song from Era, one particular morning as she stood in the kitchen fixing his breakfast and crying about the way he treated her.

By that time Sallie, who had grown rather feeble, lived part of the time with her son. Era kept house for both of them, frequently staying home to mind Mrs. Ledbetter. Sometimes Era and Huddie went out to dances together and at one house party across the lake from Oil City Huddie was nearly killed while he concentrated on playing "Mr. Tom Hughes' Town." He was attacked from behind by a man who stuck a knife to his throat. A second assailant pushed his way toward Huddie with pistol in hand. Huddie defended himself against the knife wielder, while Era fought the gunman like a "regular wild cat." Between the two of them, Huddie and Era handled the situation well. But Huddie severely punished the gun-toting assailant by "playing a tune on his head with that pistol." Afterward, he dutifully reported to the police station, still "bleeding like a hog" from his knife wound. The police merely shook their heads, told him to get out of there, and advised him not to play in Oil City anymore. The wound healed, but left a nasty scar that would stay with him for the rest of his life—a scar that became one of his more prominent features.

———

Close as Leadbelly and Era remained during those years, he could not keep away from other women. He was like a magnet to women around Caddo Parish, and Anna Lee Ford of Mooringsport was one of his girlfriends. Even until her death in 1988 she bought all of Huddie's records and spoke fondly of the salad days some sixty years before. But there was one woman, Lizzie Pugh, who caused a serious rift between Huddie and Era Washington.

Lizzie, born in 1905, had known Leadbelly "most all of my days. My step-father who raised me, was his cousin. [Huddie's mother was a Pugh.] We used to go to dances . . . and he used to play; most of the time he played by himself. I'd see him sometimes, but my mama didn't like him. I don't really know why. She tried to be nice and make me see it then. But I didn't have sense enough to see it. In those days I just liked the idea of getting out, 'cause my mother didn't let us get out too much except to [New Zion Baptist] and back." But Lizzie did get out sometimes and she especially liked the dances. If one of the older neighborhood girls went, then Lizzie could go, too. She went for the home-cooked food, good-time music, dancing, and to see Leadbelly play his twelve-string guitar and sing.

"He mostly had his eye on me," she said. For a quiet twenty-two-year-old girl, the attentions of a local legend must have been quite flattering. Despite the watchful and mistrustful eye of Era Washington, Huddie managed to get Lizzie off by herself. It was cool weather, around the time of the break between Christmas and New Year's, when they consummated their relationship. Lizzie refuses to comment about the extent of this liaison, but it lasted long enough for her to become pregnant. On September 18, 1927, Jesse Mae Ledbetter was born.

Like so many other unwed young mothers from this era, Lizzie did not have her child at home. She spent the latter part of her pregnancy in Port Arthur, Texas, along the Gulf Coast. This "extended vacation" covered the fact of her pregnancy, though she returned to Caddo Parish not long after Jesse Mae's birth. In fact, she remained a single mother until the early 1930s, when she married Wilbur Carey. Lizzie remained in or around Mooringsport for many years, though she later worked as a maid around Marshall, Texas.

Throughout Jesse Mae's early childhood, her grandmother Lucy Davis tried to protect her and her mother from even seeing Huddie. She felt convinced this good-for-nothing, irresponsible rounder had no business even visiting Jessie Mae. But for some reason, Huddie's paternal instincts surfaced more with Jessie Mae than they had with any of his earlier illegitimate children. He really began trying to see her, and occasionally even Lucy's best efforts were not enough. Huddie's interests were clearly in Jesse Mae; he now had virtually nothing to do with Lizzie, in part because of pressure from Era and his other friends.

His music, meanwhile, led Huddie into a vivid, diverse range of settings. At least once, he even worked for a preacher. It wasn't at a formal church service, though, but a "brush arbor" revival. Jack Keasler was there and wrote that "in 1928, I was one of about 20 oil field roustabouts under the Rev. Cosmo Dufilo's brush arbor on the shore of Caddo Lake one Sunday when he showed up with his big 12-string guitar to play and sing and enjoy Olvazina's fish fry." Leadbelly had been invited by Reverend Dufilo to "take time out from singing in the barrelhouse at Oil City to sing at the fish fry."

But violence continued to be a fact of Huddie's life. Shortly after getting the vivid scar across his neck, he got into another saloon fight in which he was whacked over the head with a bottle; Huddie didn't go to a doctor, even though his head had been laid open, and for a year he felt numbness in his fingers from this altercation.

From time to time he and a distant relative named Eddie Packard made some moonshine whiskey. One time Era, Huddie, and Eddie were off on one of the Caddo Parish back roads working at the still when they were surprised by the police. The trio split, running in different directions. During a wild dash through the dusk, Eddie lost his balance, fell, and hurt his leg. Era was caught, too, and both were taken in, but Huddie made it to safety.

In 1930, however, an incident occurred that was much more serious. It began a chain of events that has been the center of much confusion and speculation and has become the subject of several different versions and local legends. Two things seem clear, however: something happened involving a Salvation Army band and it had racial overtones. Huddie was accused of assaulting thirty-six-year-old Dick Ellet, whom Sheriff Tom Hughes described as a "splendid white citizen of Mooringsport," with a pocketknife on January 15, a Wednesday night. A few hours after Huddie had been taken to the parish jail, things turned really nasty. Ellet had been taken to the Highland Sanitarium for treatment of his serious cuts, and as news of the attack on a white man by the "drunk-crazed negro" spread, a mob began to form. Angry whites began talking about lynch justice—a very real fact in the South of the 1920s. Tempers flared and the mob got nastier. They moved toward the parish jail and later that night the thing local police feared happened: The mob stormed the jail. The Shreveport *Times* of the next day described what happened next: "The negro, Huddie Led Better [*sic*], 43 years old, is in the parrish jail charged with assault with intent to

murder and only the prompt response of the sheriff's office for help saved
the negro from mob violence at the hands of a band of men who stormed
the Mooringsport jail Wednesday night. The mob was held at bay by officers
Stewart and Arnold until Bert Stone and A. C. Collins, deputy sheriffs,
arrived. Elliot's [sic] condition was said not to be critical by hospital attend-
ants Wednesday night."

As Ellet's condition improved, things calmed down, though one can only
guess at the effect the mob must have had on Huddie. He had certainly been
in jail before and had been no stranger to violence, but now, for the first
time, he had attacked a white man and was finding out just how different
the rules were for that. He apparently never mentioned this incident to the
Lomaxes or to other white writers who talked to him. It must have been
traumatic, but it must have also been the kind of incident that he knew
would frighten certain whites. It was one thing to relate to Huddie as a
knife-fighting ex-con whose victims had themselves been black; it was another to see him as one who had "sassed" whites at something as respected
as a Salvation Army concert and who had actually attacked a "splendid
white citizen."

Leadbelly himself told the Lomaxes, the writers for *Time* magazine, and
Frederick Ramsey that it was his "stabbing six negroes in a fight over a can
of whiskey" that led to the conviction that put him in Angola. Leadbelly's
old friend Booker T. Washington stated the event had to do with a local high
sheriff, Mack Flannagan. One day Flannagan, said Washington, "was walking down the street and he didn't want Huddie to walk on the sidewalk.
Huddie said he'd walk where he want to walk, and they had an argument
about that. You know how narrow the sidewalk is. He just come up to you
and tell you to get out in the street, that the sidewalk made for white folks.
Said, 'Niggers is supposed to walk out in the road.' " Apparently Dick Ellet,
a local citizen, came along at this time and got involved. More words were
exchanged and, recalled Washington, Huddie "drew his knife out" and
"cut him from side to side"

Blanch Love, one of Huddie's cousins, tells a dramatically different family story that began on a Saturday night, when Huddie and many workers
from the nearby oil fields hit town for some R & R. The local Salvation Army
band was playing on the porch of a store called Croom's, a drugstore on a
popular downtown corner. Huddie enjoyed their version of "Onward Christian Soldiers" and began tapping his feet to it—almost dancing, in fact.
Several white men standing nearby took exception to this; "they must have
thought it was irreligious," Blanch remembered. One of them told Huddie
to move along and he did relocate, but he still kept up his dancing. The men
followed him and physically moved Huddie themselves. Several knives were
pulled and Huddie pulled his in self-defense; blood was drawn and then the

police arrived. "All them folks around was white and Huddie was black; so when the law jumped on him, he sassed them back."

The Shreveport *Journal* of January 16, 1930, described Huddie's arrest and explained: "The trouble with the negro started when he, while in an alleged intoxicated condition, was disrespectful to a Salvation Army meeting that was in progress on a Mooringsport street. According to reports, Ledbetter insisted upon doing a dance during the service, which aroused a group which included [Dick] Elliot [*sic*]. In a scuffle which followed, Ledbetter drew a knife and slashed Elliot's arm." The Shreveport *Times* of January 16 confirms the stabbing of "Elliot" (his name was eventually corrected to Ellet) by Huddie, but asserts that "Dick Elliot, 36 years old, is in the Highland sanitarium suffering from severe cuts inflicted by a drunk-crazed negro who attacked him late Wednesday afternoon at his home near Mooringsport where the negro was butchering a hog. The negro, Huddie Ledbetter, 43 years old, is in the Parish jail charged with attempt to murder . . . A bottle of rubbing alcohol was found on the negro with more than half of its contents gone. Ledbetter incurred a gash on the top of his head during the altercation that took place."

The fact remains that three weeks later, on February 7, L. C. Blanchard, the district attorney for the First Judicial District of Louisiana, filed charges against Huddie: The charges read that on the fifteenth day of January 1930, one Huddie Ledbetter "in and upon Dick Ellet feloniously did make an assault, with the intent, then and there, him, the said Dick Ellet, willfully, feloniously, and of his malice aforethought to kill and murder." The trial soon followed. It was swift, lasting but a day. Within minutes following the completion of testimony the jury found Huddie Ledbetter guilty of "assault with intent to murder." The February 19 issue of the Shreveport *Times* reported that "Huddie Ledbetter, negro, was convicted Tuesday by a jury in the District Court of assaulting to murder Dick Ellet, a resident of Mooringsport. The verdict was reached a few minutes after the completion of the testimony. Judge T. F. Bell will sentence the negro next week."

On February 25, 1930, almost exactly five weeks after cutting Dick Ellet's arm with a knife, Leadbelly was sentenced to "hard labor, for a period of not less than six (6) years nor more than ten (10) years, subject to the commutation provided by the law." Two days later he was received by officials in Angola, Louisiana, a facility that made Sugarland look like easy time. They assigned him to Camp A and Leadbelly was now known as prisoner LSP #19469.

12 Angola Penitentiary

"Intolerable," "a swampy hell," "uninhabitable," and "racist" are a handful of the more polite descriptions that have been used to describe Angola State Penitentiary. Sixty years ago this penal institution clearly deserved its reputation. Tough criminals allegedly broke down when they received a sentence to Angola, one of the nation's most notorious prisons. None of them wanted to be sent to a prison where one of every ten inmates annually received stab wounds and which routinely seethed with black-white confrontations.

Today it looks more like a large working plantation than one of the most notorious prisons in the United States. Because so much of its acreage is under cultivation, Angola employees still patrol the grounds on horseback; however, the primary roads that crisscross its vast expanse are now paved. Proper heat and air-conditioning has been installed in the inmates' living quarters, the modest dormitories that are divided into "camps" and scattered across Angola. At noon the prisoners' noncommercial FM radio station begins its broadcast day in the same building that houses its weekly newspaper, the *Angolite*. Near the state's training center for guards, which is located in Angola's northwest corner, the inmates maintain the only nature preserve located on a penitentiary. It is, in fact, now closer to a model prison than the festering pit to which Huddie Ledbetter was sentenced to what must have loomed as a veritable lifetime of interminable hard labor.

Characteristically, Huddie himself never spoke much about Angola State Penitentiary. Huddie arrived at Angola near the beginning of the Great Depression. The oppression of its already harsh system was only amplified by cost cutting imposed by the state in its desperate effort to save money. The little money that was appropriated by Louisiana to run Angola often mysteriously found its way into other state projects.

Angola State Penitentiary was probably as close to slavery as any person could come in 1930. Tucked away on a bend of the Mississippi River about fifty miles northwest of Baton Rouge, the facility remains far away from public awareness. Even in the 1990s its entrance can be found only at the dead end of a winding, often muddy state road. In 1930 it was even further removed from decent civilization. And that's the way the state of Louisiana wanted it, for Angola held some of the meanest inmates. Its lean staff of ninety employees ran the prison like it was a private fiefdom and the inmates were all looked upon as "niggers" of the lowest order. The employees' word was final and strictly enforced by a band of gun-carrying convicts serving as guards. These trusties enjoyed their special status and would go to any length to keep the small privileges afforded to them.

Leadbelly was put to work almost immediately. His strength and physical endurance had sculpted muscles of steel, but even these were strained by the harsh demands of the Angola system. Arriving in the late winter meant that Huddie had it relatively easy compared to the future demands that would be placed upon his powerful back. February in southern Louisiana can be warm and forgiving, but the weather can also turn cold, brutally cold at night in the poorly heated barracks. At least the work hours were shorter than Leadbelly was to endure in a few months. Angola prisoners worked from "kin to can't," which means they labored from the time you could see at dawn until it became impossible to see after dusk. Leadbelly spent the first two months preparing the rich delta humus for the cotton and other crops that were annually planted.

Angola State Penitentiary was designed to be as self-sufficient as possible. This cost the taxpayers less money, which made politicians like Governor Huey P. Long look better. It was not only a farm that raised food staples and cash crops, but a miniature community with its own mail system, sugar mill, canning factory, dairy, repair shops, and small ranch. Today the Angola inmates even eagerly look forward to the Angola Prison Rodeo, which has been held since 1965.

With the Mississippi River bordering the penitentiary on three sides, levee control was another task to which Leadbelly and his fellow inmates were sometimes assigned. This was a life-and-death matter because the almost annual spring arrival of high water posed a real threat to the physical plant. You can be certain that if the levee were to break, the inmates were to provide the final line of defense against the onslaught of the Mississippi River. At this point in its course the river truly is mighty: A straight shot across to the other side is almost exactly one mile. Many men have tried to escape by swimming through the swift and silty waters; few are known to have survived. Most are presumed drowned, their bodies never recovered.

Assigned to Camp A, located almost near the center of Angola, Huddie was housed with about seven hundred other African American inmates. Even under these dire conditions, the social rules regarding segregation were strictly enforced. Riots would almost certainly have erupted if black and white prisoners were suddenly integrated. A hundred and thirty women, mostly black, lived in Camp D and worked under the same conditions as the men.

Leadbelly's daily life was miserable. He rose before dawn, which by the summer of 1930 was at five. The breakfast rations varied little from day to day; in fact, his daily diet consisted almost entirely of white or red beans, grits, greens, sweet potatoes, blackstrap molasses syrup, cornbread, and water. Other fresh vegetables—cabbage, corn, or peas—were occasionally available during the summertime. Meat was an almost unknown luxury, although pork was sometimes thrown in to flavor the beans. This fare kept down the cost of operating Angola because the prisoners almost always ate what they could grow.

As the quality and variety of the food increased, so did Huddie's misery because better food also meant that the year had slipped into summertime. By seven A.M. all of Camp A's inmates were in the fields tending to the cotton crop and within a few hours the conditions became unbelievable. Straddled by a major river and situated about 125 miles north of the Gulf of Mexico meant that the weather from May through September consisted of almost unrelenting heat and humidity. Daytime temperatures of ninety to one hundred degrees with nearly equal relative humidity are common-place. Except for the occasional water break, Leadbelly labored through the morning with his hoe in hand and the rows of cotton yawned in front of him like unrelenting waves on the ocean.

Shackled together like slaves, Huddie and his fellow sufferers wore iden-tical "white uniforms . . . of stiff, unyielding 12-ounce cotton that chafed them raw—most of them would leave the heavy shirts on the headland (a 'commons' near the field) and work bare-back in the hot sun. They wore crude black shoes made by the Camp E shoe shop of cheap, split leather, the uppers nailed to the soles. In the summer, they were issued cheap farm straw hats, but nothing else—no socks, underwear, or even belts to hold up their pants."

Following a brief lunch, which they ate in the unshaded heat of the fields, it was back to work until at least five P.M. During the cotton-picking time of late summer, relief sometimes came earlier if each man picked his quota of 250 pounds of cotton before "knockin' off" time. Dragging their long cotton sacks behind them, the inmates constantly stooped to pick the bolls off the short plants. It was backbreaking work, but Leadbelly was used to such labor and he was among those who often finished by noon. Many others completed their assignment by early afternoon, though the occa-sional straggler sometimes kept all of them in the dry, dusty fields until dusk.

After a supper of unremittingly predictable staples, Leadbelly tumbled onto a corn-shuck mattress that lay on the wooden floor of his dormitory. Showers were a weekly luxury, so he almost always stumbled into bed in his smelly wet uniform. Although totally exhausted, Huddie would some-times awaken at night in order to slap at the mosquitoes that buzzed around the room. The windows stayed open at night for ventilation, but in order to save money the state did not provide the money for screens. Huddie would also snap awake at night during the winter in order to draw his blanket closer around him because the state also failed to provide the dormitories with adequate heat. Each of the forty-foot by eighty-foot brick and cinder block dormitories in Camp A held about seven hundred men. The lights were on twenty-four hours a day, 365 days a year. Each of the camps was surrounded by barbed-wired fences, which were both rusty and exceptionally sharp.

These conditions provided a great deal of security for those running the penitentiary, but the prisoners had virtually no privacy. They were shackled day and night. Consequently, Leadbelly was surrounded by members of Camp A day and night. The dormitory bathroom facilities consisted of a "slop jar" in the corner and an outhouse. Like his daily routine, the lack of privacy was equally unremitting. And for a man used to years of rambling and a roustabout life-style, the strict rules at Angola State Penitentiary proved to be a particularly difficult adjustment for Huddie. He was also quite proud and independent, two qualities that spell trouble for any prisoner. Sometimes it became too much for Huddie to bear and on two occasions he paid the price. On November 21, 1931, he received ten whip lashes administered by Captain Pecue. The reason given in his prison records is "laziness." This punishment was followed by further confrontations and on June 27, 1932, Captain Pecue administered fifteen lashes to Huddie because of his "impudence."

But Huddie was not always in trouble with the system. Within several months after his arrival, the authorities noted that Huddie was generally well mannered and his reward was to be placed on the eligible list as a waiter at Camp F. Two years later he was moved to a tailor's job working at Road Camp 5. These jobs provided him with some relief from the tedium and physically destructive field work and they further suggested that he might do better to work within the system. Huddie Ledbetter was a shrewd man. He realized that the trusty inmates would just as soon shoot or whip him as take his money in one of the high-pressure poker games that kept the inmates occupied during their precious spare time.

Like many other inmates, Leadbelly remained aware of the events outside of Louisiana State Penitentiary. He wanted his freedom back so badly, he could almost taste its sweetness. But everyone at Angola watched as the real world virtually collapsed under the oppressive weight of the Depression. Banks had closed, unemployment had skyrocketed to unprecedented heights, and many people's lives were spun into almost unfathomable chaos. It became harder for inmates at Angola, for the state saw Angola as a place to save money. But they not only cut back on the institution's already bare-bones budget, they were actually letting some inmates out early!

Weighing his Texas prison record and his subsequent full pardon from Governor Pat Neff with his current status, Leadbelly decided that any chance at legitimate freedom came with higher odds than an escape from Angola. Since Angola's beginning, when it was purchased from private individuals in 1901 after the state ceased its convict leasing program, successful breakouts were virtually unheard of given the long and treacherous Mississippi River that created much of its border. The rugged, tangled Tunica Hills that bordered Angola to the east offered the best route for escape. But slipping away into the tangled Tunica Hills was impossible because of omnipresent guards. The dormitories were completely surrounded by barbed wire and were so well guarded at night that tunneling beyond the encirclement provided the only possibility. But almost all such digging was discovered long before the inmates could reach their goal, or the wet soil collapsed, burying its exhausted occupants in a dark, rich ooze. Given these unappealing options, Huddie decided to try to use the legal system to his advantage.

Perhaps it was a fear of the "Hole" that scared Leadbelly the most. This small, rectangular-shaped building housed the Camp A inmates that were put in isolation. If a prisoner became incorrigible or broke a serious rule, he went to the Hole for a period determined by Camp A's captain. The food was limited to one meal of a single biscuit, some greens, and one cup of water each day. During hot weather isolation prisoners were severely weakened by dehydration. In the corner was a bucket that served as its privy. Angola records clearly indicate that Leadbelly avoided the Hole during his four-and-one-half-year tenure.

Given his options for early release, almost exactly two years after arriving at Angola Huddie prudently chose to formally ask the Louisiana Board of Pardons to commute his sentence. He eagerly awaited word from Baton Rouge. In June 1933, the Pardons Board deliberated and sent him the good news: He would be set free on June 26, 1934, if Governor O. K. Allen signed his petition. Leadbelly was ecstatic, for he thought that he would be free in one year under a new state rule called "double good time."

By this time Huddie's musical talents had gained the well-deserved respect of his fellow inmates. Weekends provided a desperately anticipated respite from work for Angola prisoners; they had Sunday off and sometimes part of Saturday afternoon. On their day off they could read the Bible, laugh, clown around, surreptitiously gamble, or sing, for it was the one day that they didn't have to work for "Mr. Charlie." Anyone who could play music was in demand. On Sunday Huddie remained busy playing music for as long as his fingers lasted or anyone was interested enough to listen.

Sometimes he just played for his own entertainment. The word soon got around this closed community: Leadbelly was a first-class guitar player with a gruff voice that carried above the din. When Leadbelly brought out his twelve-string guitar, most people, including the guards, paid attention.

By the early summer of 1933 even Warden L. A. Jones had heard of Huddie's talents, which was quite fortuitous because he had just received a unique request. John Lomax from the Library of Congress was touring the South in search of folk songs. He wondered if Warden Jones could recommend some talent for him to hear. Certainly there were many talented men among the prisoners under his attention, but the Lomax letter suggested that Lomax was looking for someone just like Huddie Ledbetter.

Indeed, John Lomax and his eighteen-year-old son Alan were looking hard for musicians like Leadbelly. They were on a quest for "pure negro folk songs" to be placed in the recently established Archives of Folk Song in the Library of Congress. John Lomax figured that they would have the best luck looking in prisons for oppressed men and women removed from the mainstream and who still sang older folk songs. "Alan and I were looking particularly for the song of the Negro laborer, the words of which sometimes reflect the tragedies of imprisonment, cold, hunger, heat, the injustice of the white man." It is unlikely, though, that John Lomax used such language when he contacted Warden Jones.

13 The Dollar-a-Year Man

In the early 1930s, folklorist, platform lecturer, college professor, and former banker John Avery Lomax was trying to recapture a sense of direction for his life. For two decades he had enjoyed a national reputation for his pioneering work in collecting and studying American folk songs; no less a figure than President Theodore Roosevelt had admired his work, and had written a letter of support for him as he sought grants for his research. He had four books to his credit, and had given lectures at venues ranging from Yale to the Chautauqua Institute at Lake Chautauqua, New York. More recent years, though, had brought a series of setbacks and personal crises. The stock market crash had, by Lomax's own admission, reduced his income to its lowest level in years—its lowest level since he had been a young college student just before the turn of the century. Now in his sixties, he himself had been hospitalized with a serious illness, and in 1931 had had to cope with the long illness and eventual death of his wife, Bess. He still had two children—Alan and Bess—who were young enough to depend on him for their welfare, and he felt this responsibility keenly. Money was so scarce that on one particular lecture trip to New York City, he and his eldest son, John Jr., camped out next to the road and cooked their meals over an open fire. He had always dreamed of finding a way to make a living by doing the thing he loved best, collecting folk songs, but he was now beginning to wonder if he would ever realize that dream.

Though John A. Lomax was always associated with Texas and Texas culture, he was technically born in Mississippi in 1867, and came with his family to central Texas when he was two years old. His parents settled on a farm south of Fort Worth, on the Bosque River near Meridian, and he grew up here, one of five boys who worked hard to help the family scrape by. It was not an easy life, as Lomax later described it in his autobiography, *The Adventures of a Ballad Hunter*. The farm was bottom land, and had to be cleared of trees and underbrush before it was ready to farm; as a boy, Lomax helped out the family by hauling stovewood from the bottoms into Meridian. His customers told him later that when they saw his wagon coming, "they knew that Johnny Lomax was somewhere back up the road, hauling to town another load of firewood." It was a hard, frontier life, not at all unlike the one Huddie Ledbetter had had; if anything, John Lomax's early life was even harder. Leadbelly's folks were reasonably well-to-do and he was an only child; Lomax's were small farmers, and he was the youngest of the five boys. Leadbelly was given a horse by his father on his fifteenth birthday; Lomax had to sell his pony to get money to attend a local college.

The Lomax family were Methodists, and attended camp meetings when they could; the old Wesley hymns and newer revival songs awoke in young Johnny a fascination with what we today would call folk music. The songs remained vivid in his memory years later, as did the preaching. (One particular preacher he heard was even the subject of a local joke; when asked how well the man could preach, a local wag quipped, "No, he can't *preach* much, but he can *sing* religion into a Comanche Indian.") Such experiences instilled in him an abiding interest in religious music and preaching, and eventually led him to chronicle these types of folk performance.

An even more important type of traditional music for him, though, was the cowboy song. Though the Frontier was very much still alive in the 1870s and 1880s, and though dime novels and Wild West shows were feeding the public's appetite to know more about the West, nobody had thought much about the cowboys as sources for folk songs. Lomax began to. In his autobiography, he says he first really listened to a cowboy sing when he was only four, and that he began to write down some of the songs when he was a "small boy." His work would later open up the entire field of study for this distinctive American folk song type.

He also became interested in the African American musical culture that surrounded him in central Texas. When he was only nine, he met an eighteen-year-old bond servant, a black youth named Nat Blythe. They began a close friendship, an attachment Lomax characterized as one of "fierce strength and loyalty. I loved him as I have loved few people." They remained best friends for three years, a friendship "that perhaps gave my life its bent," he wrote. Young John helped Nat with his reading and writing—even love letters written to Nat's sweetheart—and Nat in turn taught John black folk songs like "Big Yam Potatoes in a Sandy Land" and dance steps like "Juba." When Nat was twenty-one, he took his savings and left; Lomax never saw him again, and heard rumors that he had been murdered. For years after, he always looked for Nat when he traveled around the South.

Lomax's interest in black music continued, though. By 1904, he was writing his fiancée about singing he had heard at a black normal school at Prairie View. "The singing is perfect," he noted, "yet the old time negro trill is gone." This suggests that even this early, Lomax was familiar with African American traditional singing, and that he was already concerned about the erosion of these older styles in the face of progress. Two years later, back at Prairie View, he wrote that he was "the sole white man (wholly so) among nearly a thousand negroes." Though it would be his work with

cowboy songs that would win him his early fame, he was also one of the first
folk music scholars to sense the uniqueness of the African American music.

———

Lomax sensed that one way out of the grueling farm life was education, and
in 1887 began attending a local college and teaching in a one-room school.
By 1895 he had made it to the University of Texas, where he raced through
an A.B. degree in two years. He stayed on at the University after he got his
degree, working as the school's registrar, the steward of the men's dormitories, and secretary to the president; he also founded an alumni association
called the Texas-Exes, which would later play a major role in his work with
Leadbelly. His interest in ballads continued, but he began to think his future
lay in what he described to a friend as "problems connected with the
administrative life of large educational institutions." This is not surprising,
since the vocation of folklorist or folk song collector hardly existed then;
Lomax, however, was about to help invent it.

    In the summers, Lomax usually went off to schools in the North or East
to beef up his academic credentials; he had married in 1904, and from 1903
to 1910 had taken a position of professor of English at Texas Agricultural
and Mechanical College at nearby Bryant, Texas. In 1906 and 1907 he was
at Harvard (where he got an M.A.); there he found that his professors were
not only sympathetic to his interest in cowboy songs, but they felt it was
vital, important work. Harvard, in fact, had become the center for folk song
study in the United States, largely due to the massive collections of ballads
assembled by Francis James Child and the subsequent critical studies done
by his disciple, George Lyman Kittredge. It was Kittredge who pioneered
modern methods of ballad study, and who encouraged collectors to get out
of their armchairs and library halls and get out into the countryside to
collect ballads first-hand. When he met John Lomax in 1907, this is what he
encouraged him to do; the cowboy songs Lomax had been writing down
were glimpses into a whole new world, and Lomax should follow up on his
work. "Go and get this material while it can be found," he told the young
Texan. "Preserve the words and music. That's your job." He helped Lomax
get funding support, and by summer of 1907 Lomax was back in Texas
gathering songs. Some he gathered by sending out a form letter to thousands of newspaper or magazine editors, and to various individuals; the
response was overwhelming. Others he gathered by traveling through
Texas, catching up with real cowboys on trail drives or round-ups, in saloons, and around lonely campfires at night. He also tried something else
unique: recording some of the songs on Edison cylinders. His 1907 trip
yielded some twenty-five fragile cylinder recordings—the first folk songs in
English to be recorded by any American. During the next three years, he
would make even more recordings on his trips, and become convinced that

sound recordings done in the field were an essential part of the collecting process. In this, too, he would become an innovator.

All his work bore fruit in 1910 when he published *Cowboy Songs and Other Frontier Ballads,* a remarkable collection that appealed both to scholars and laymen alike and that made John Lomax a national figure in the field of folk song. It included several songs that became quintessential cowboy favorites; two of them, "Git Along Little Dogies" and "Home on the Range," had been collected from a black man—a retired trail cook—in 1908. The book emerged as the major collection of western songs, and had a profound effect on other folk song students. One historian has noted that the book's publication "sparked a great surge of interest in folk songs of all kinds, and, in fact, inspired a search for folk material in all regions of the nation." A few months after the publication, Lomax was elected president of the American Folklore Society, and he used his prestige to travel widely and to help in the founding of many state folklore societies. He was among the first scholars to present papers about American folk songs to the Modern Language Association, the nation's leading organization of teachers of language and literature. For the next several years, too, he hit the lecture circuit, traveling so often that his wife Bess Brown had to help him with his schedules and even some of his speeches.

During most of this time, Lomax had continued his work at the University of Texas, but in 1917 he got caught up in a Texas political purge of the school, and was fired. He returned a few years later to become secretary to an alumni association, but was forced out of that job when he complained too loudly about the university's emphasis on football. He continued to collect ballads and to correspond with other singers and collectors, but the increasing family obligations and need to make a steady living made it difficult to do this full time. A former student helped get him into the business and banking world. For a couple of years he even moved to Chicago, but eventually got back to Dallas, where he sold bonds for a local bank until the stock market crash.

During all these moves, Lomax continued to dream about what he would like to do with folk music. He wanted to embark on a nationwide collecting project, resulting in as many as four other volumes, and "complete the rehabilitation of American folk-song." Eventually these plans were modified to where he envisioned a book tentatively called *American Ballads and Folk Songs,* designed to survey the whole field. It called for first-hand field collecting, and would especially focus on the neglected genre of the black work song. By 1932, at a nadir in his personal life, Lomax traveled to New York, and stopped in to see a man named H. S. Latham of the Macmillan Company. He informally outlined his plan to Latham, and read him the text of an earthy African American blues ballad called "Ida Red." Latham was

impressed, and two days later Lomax had a contract, a small check to bind it, and an agreement to deliver the manuscript about one year later. The spring of 1932 began to look more green, lush, and full of promise.

Lomax immediately set to work. He traveled to libraries at Harvard, the Library of Congress, Brown University, and elsewhere in order to explore unpublished song collections and to canvas the folk song books published over the past ten years. During his stay in Washington, D.C., Lomax became friendly with Carl Engel, Music Division chief of the Library of Congress. Engel felt that Lomax had the necessary background and energy necessary to someday direct the Archive of Folk Song. Through funds provided by the Council of Learned Societies and the Library of Congress, Lomax ordered a state-of-the-art portable electric recording machine. More importantly the Library of Congress agreed to furnish blank records and to lend their name to his collecting; Lomax simply had to agree to deposit the completed records at the Library of Congress. He did so with no hesitation.

The Library of Congress eagerly courted Lomax because of his reputation and their dissatisfaction with Robert Gordon, then the nominal head of the Archive of Folk Song. Gordon himself wanted to see his type of work continue at the Library of Congress, but the Depression in general and specifically a lack of tangible results placed his position in jeopardy. Despite the fact that he largely raised the money for his own salary and the library's own support for folk music remained tenuous, Gordon wished to see Lomax affiliate himself with the Library of Congress. This eagerness impressed John Lomax, Jr., who wrote to his father in December 1932 following a visit to Gordon: "I found Mr. Gordon at work at the Library of Congress. He received me most cordially and stated that he would rather see *you* than any other person in the country. He says that he wants to have a session with you, which he is willing to have last for 48 hours on the first stretch. Therefore, he was most delighted to find you are coming soon." The two men got along well and Gordon readily agreed to provide Lomax with research funds for *American Ballads and Folk Songs*. But soon the personal, political, and financial situation at the Library of Congress became so desperate that by early 1933 Gordon was gone. Circumstances were finally smiling on John Lomax and he stood poised to cement a formal relationship with the Library of Congress. On July 15, 1933, Lomax was appointed an "honorary consultant" for a dollar a year.

By the time of his appointment Lomax was already on the road with his eighteen-year-old son Alan, then a junior at the University of Texas. The machine they really wanted was still on order when they departed from Dallas in early June, so they carried a dictaphone recording machine with them. Camping some of the time, they were laden with cots, bedding, and

cooking equipment in addition to clothing. Although they were to travel across the entire South, their first stop was in Texas.

The duo had begun a grand adventure to collect songs for *American Folk Songs and Ballads,* a task that was to last for many months. Lomax's library research had reinforced his belief that a dearth of black folk song material existed in printed collections. This fact, along with his early appreciation for African American folk culture, perhaps nurtured through his friendship with Nat Blythe, led John Lomax to decide that black folk music from rural areas should be the primary focus. This bold determination resulted in the first major trip in the United States to capture black folk music in the field. In order to fulfill their quest, the two men concentrated on sections of the South with a high percentage of blacks. They also pinpointed laboring camps, particularly lumber camps, which employed blacks almost exclusively. But prisons and penitentiaries also emerged as a focal point for research.

Locating musicians isolated from mainstream culture and insulated from white traditions was their rationale for this methodology. It was a simple but effective strategy. In the *Adventures of a Ballad Hunter,* Lomax describes the fundamental premise for their trip: "[Black] folk singers render their music more naturally in the easy sociability of their homes and churches and schools, in their fields and woodyards, just as birds sing more effectively in their native trees and country." Work songs held a special fascination for Lomax, who was most eager to capture examples of these "fast-disappearing gang songs of labor."

In June they traveled across East Texas, stopping at places that John had contacted in advance as well as locations recommended to them during their journey. Their first stop was at Terrell, now on the eastern edge of the Dallas–Fort Worth metroplex and only thirty miles from their home. They recorded a lovely version of "Wade in the Water" from a black woman who took a break from washing clothes in order to sing for them. From there Alan and John Lomax drove southeast to visit their first prison, Huntsville, the headquarters for the entire Texas system. Lomax was well acquainted with Superintendent Lee Simons, who unfortunately had been called away. His stand-in wanted nothing to do with the Lomax project and they were sent down the dusty road, south to a small town just outside of Houston.

They were again stymied at Prairie View State Normal College, a school dedicated almost exclusively to educating black Texans to teach in secondary schools. Greeted with curiosity and courtesy, the Lomaxes found themselves staying in comfortable quarters that the college reserved for distinguished white visitors. However, the students themselves were much less warm and forthcoming. Lomax observed that they "seem suspicious of us and somewhat ashamed of the creations of their people. . . . Because some of these songs sound tawdry and cheap, these critics of their own people are apt to be blind to the beauty of the music."

Their next stop was only about thirty miles from Prairie View, still well within the hot, wet Brazos bottomland. They had traveled to a remote community to look for examples of spirituals and other religious songs. They spent the entire late June day recording songs and after a country supper of chicken, corn, and peaches, slept on their cots in the front yard of a house. The next day they took one of the musicians to a party, where he played until midnight. John Lomax was moved by the music and he recalled that the "steady, monotonous beat of the guitars, accented by handclaps and the shuffle of feet—the excitement growing as time went on, the rhythm deeper and clearer—again I felt carried across to Africa, and I left as if I were listening to the tom-toms of savage blacks."

The Lomaxes passed their days searching for black folk music in the heat of the south Texas summer. On July 2 they went to the Gulf Coast, spending several days among the African American longshoremen. The Fourth of July found them at the Duncan Farm in Egypt, Texas, thirty miles southeast of Houston, where they heard many fine spirituals and sermons. At Sugarland they encountered a wonderful singer, James "Ironhead" Baker. John Lomax was so impressed they he later called him a "Black Homer," and returned several times in later years to record him again. "Central State was where we recorded 'Old Hannah,' 'Rattler,' and many more work songs," recalled Alan Lomax. They were to be some of the most powerful songs the two recovered.

Their trek took them to the north and east toward Louisiana to the lumber camp at Wiergate, Texas. On that steamy July 10 day John Lomax finally heard the work songs that he sought and his eloquence regarding the incident is unsurpassed:

I heard for the first time the wail of the Negro woodsman as a fine tree that he is cutting sways and then falls to the earth with a shuddering crash. Shrill, swift, wavering, the shout swings to a sudden and dramatic conclusion. . . . There is music in that cry, and mystery, and wistful sadness. After we had listened for a while, a group of glistening ebony figures, their torsos naked, came and sang the requiem of the falling pine into our recording machine.

In retrospect, they found a wealth of wonderful material in Texas, recording black protest songs like "Working for Mr. Charlie," in addition to the song types they expected to find.

By mid-July they arrived in Baton Rouge. The Library had shipped them a new recording machine, the one ordered months ago but just now on its way to them. The cylinder machine made only scratchy and squeaky sounds, but their new disc-cutting machine was the best portable machine on the market. These were long before the days of magnetic recording tape, transistors, and digital sound. Their new behemoth weighed a hefty 315 pounds. Alan recalls that the machine consisted of one large amplifier, a cutting turntable, two Edison batteries (the only source of power), a loudspeaker, and the discs themselves. The latter were twelve inches in diameter, and were of annealed aluminum ("we had tried cellulose, but they were too brittle"). In addition to the machine itself and a modest supply of discs—which were hard to find anywhere in the United States—they carried spare bulky alkaline batteries and extra cutting and reproduction heads.

Their Ford car was already crowded, but this new load of equipment, welcome as it was, proved to be almost too much. Later that year, in fact, they remodeled the back portion of the car in order to accommodate the five hundred pounds of equipment. This technology was so new that not all of the commercial studios had it, and no other folk song collectors in the United States had access to anything quite like it. Both John and Alan took to it quickly, and were pleasantly surprised at how good the results were; they investigated the advantages of different microphone placements and other, more subtle alterations to the recorder itself. During the summer of 1933 the sound quality of their discs steadily improved as they became more familiar with the recorder.

After several days of rest and initial experimentation with the disc cutter, they drove about two hours to the northeast. They were bound for Angola Penitentiary, situated about sixty miles from the capital. Texas had some of the toughest prisons in the country, but the Lomaxes were told that Angola rivaled anything the Lone Star state could offer. John and Alan Lomax arrived at the front gate of Angola on a typically sweltering summer's day in southern Louisiana. Their terse reception surprised them, though by now they were quite used to being searched upon entering a prison. The guards eyed them with unusual suspicion and searched them with the utmost care; because of a recent prison escape they were among the first visitors to the penitentiary in almost one year.

The Angola staff itself was cordial and no doubt bemused by these Texans and the search. For four days the Lomaxes listened to and recorded male and female inmates, including the prison's blacksmith, who performed two spirituals. John was disappointed that the inmates were not allowed to sing as they worked. Then, one drizzling, rainy Sunday Captain Andrew Reaux of Camp A brought Huddie Ledbetter to entertain them. His music impressed them straightaway. Both sensed something important was happening. John wrote that "we found a Negro convict so skillful with his guitar and his strong, baritone voice that he had been made a 'trusty' and kept around Camp 'A' headquarters as laundryman, so as to be near at hand to sing and play for visitors. Huddie Ledbetter . . . was unique in knowing a very large number of songs, all of which he sang effectively while he twanged his twelve-string guitar."

The original discs from that day are still preserved in the Library of Congress, and though they are too cracked and decayed to be reissued for the public, they still give an idea of the kind of music the session produced. Leadbelly sang seven different songs, starting with "The Western Cowboy" and a song about cocaine, "Honey, Take a Whiff On Me." It was precisely what the Lomaxes were looking for. "We were looking for the genuine oral tradition—not a type of song," recalls Alan. "And we were experienced in recognizing it." Next came "Angola Blues," a song interesting enough that they recorded it twice, and the long version of "Frankie and Johnny" Leadbelly called "Frankie and Albert." These took up one side of disc number 119-B, and a second, labeled 120, was started. The singer continued with an old dance tune, "You Can't Lose Me Cholly," and a badman ballad about Dallas saloons called "Ella Speed." In between, the singer pulled out a song they hadn't heard before: a gentle, lilting waltz called "Irene." As Leadbelly sung it in a high, almost tenor voice, both men were struck by its simplicity and beauty. They recorded it a second time, and then a third. They had no way of knowing that eighteen years later the song would be the most popular in the country, or that it would become a standard in both pop and folk music.

A shrewd, resourceful man used to living by his wits, Leadbelly was probably already thinking of some way this new and truly unexpected connection could help set him free. The Lomaxes were clearly sympathetic. Huddie also impressed them with his life story as well as his music. Lomax clearly understood that Huddie Ledbetter was special when he later wrote that "one man almost made up for the deficiency. He knew so many songs which he sang with restraint and sympathy that . . . I quite resolved to get him out of prison and take him along as a third member of the party." Lomax eventually backed down after he learned that Leadbelly had already served part of a sentence for murder in Texas, and he was almost certainly unaware of Leadbelly's attempts to gain early release through a pardon petition.

John and Alan Lomax left Angola in order to continue their southern tour. From south Louisiana they headed even farther south, back to New Orleans for several days, and then up the Mississippi River. On August 9 and 10 they set up their bulky recording equipment at the state penitentiary at Parchman, Mississippi, also known as "Parchman Farm." Some of their best recordings from this trip were a series of thirteen work songs recorded by a convict group from Camp D that included inmates nicknamed Rat,

Tight Eye, and Double Head. After packing their car, they made the half-day drive due north on Highway 61 to Memphis, Tennessee. After one day in the Shelby County Workhouse, John and Alan Lomax headed east on "Old 70" to Nashville, where they recorded what Alan called "some of the finest things we ever found" at the state penitentiary. After a stop in downtown Richmond, Virginia, home to that state's penitentiary, the Lomaxes returned to Washington, D.C. While the Lomaxes filled their blank discs and notebooks, most of the men and women who shared their music remained trapped within a cruel system—an irony both appreciated.

The recordings of Leadbelly made by the Lomaxes had historical significance beyond the fact that they were the first ones of a man who would become a major figure in American music. The whole idea of using a phonograph to preserve authentic folk music was still fairly new. Most of John Lomax's peers were involved in collecting songs the classic way: taking both words and melody down by hand, asking the singer to perform the song over and over until the collector had "caught" it on paper. In 1932, just the year before, English folk song scholar Cecil Sharp's *English Folk Songs from the Southern Appalachians* was published, and many hailed it as a high-water mark of the old collecting style. John Lomax sensed at once the limitations of this kind of method, especially when getting songs from African American singers, whose quarter tones, blue notes, and complex timing often frustrated white musicians trying to transcribe them with European notation systems.

The whole concept of field recording was, in 1933 and still today, radically different from the popular notion of recording. Field recordings are not intended as commercial products, but as attempts at cultural preservation. There is no profit motive, nor any desire to make the singer a "star." As have hundreds of folk song collectors after him, John Lomax had to persuade his singers to perform, to explain to them why their songs were important, and to convince the various authorities—the wardens, the trusties, the bureaucrats—that this was serious, worthwhile work. He faced the moral problem of how to safeguard the records and the rights of the singers—a problem he solved in this instance by donating the discs to the Library of Congress. He had to overcome the technical problems involved in recording outside a studio; one always hoped for quiet, with no doors slamming or alarms going off, but it was always a risk. His new state-of-the-art recording machine sported a new microphone designed by NBC, but there were no wind baffles to help reduce the noise when recording outside. Lomax learned how to balance sound, where to place microphones, how to work echoes and walls, and soon was a skilled recordist.

Finally, like so many field workers after him, Lomax had to figure out how to get funding for his work. With no profit potential to interest investors, he had to look to corporations and foundations—and be willing to pay a great deal of his costs out of his own pocket. His recording of the voluble prisoner named Huddie Ledbetter was thus part of an important experiment on several fronts—part of a pioneering effort to use the new disc-cutting machines to preserve a fast-vanishing culture. He did not take the easy route and set up his machine in genteel parlors or comfortable hotel rooms. He went directly to where he thought the best and most powerful music was: the prisons, the work camps, the lonely Texas ranches, the swampy bayous of Louisiana, the deep hollows of Kentucky. It was almost as if he was finally realizing his dream, after sixty-six years of getting ready for it.

14 Angola Blues Again

At first Leadbelly's soggy, blistering summer days passed as quickly as a Saturday night on Fannin Street. But then he began to despair because no word of his freedom followed on the heels of the good news from Baton Rouge. He knew that he had to get the governor's attention. But how? Despite the prison's close proximity to the capital, the governor never came to inspect Angola, so that Leadbelly couldn't personally get to the governor. Early in December 1933, Leadbelly finally decided that he would try to convey his artistic sense to Governor Allen through a poem. If his music helped him to get out of Sugarland, then a poem seemed like his best surrogate now in lieu of a personal performance.

John Lomax suggests this poem was first sent to Huey Long, governor of Louisiana in 1931. Lomax wrote, "So touched was Huey that he had the song published in the newspapers as Long advertising, and that was the last Leadbelly heard of it." However, no trace of this poem has turned up in the Baton Rouge papers from 1931 or 1932. Nor was it printed in Long's own newspaper, *The Citizen Advocate*, which was published from 1930 until his term as governor expired in January 1932 and he moved into the U.S. Senate.

But fully aware of the fiscal problems and his chance at a commutation, Leadbelly did send a plea to Governor Allen. The opening stanza began, "If you were me and I was you—I would see what I could do to get a pardon through." Full of hope, Leadbelly sent it off to Governor Allen by way of Mr. R. L. Himes, general manager of the Louisiana State Penitentiary, Baton Rouge. Perhaps intrigued by this unusual request or ever the efficient bureaucrat, Himes answered him promptly:

December 6, 1933

Huddie Ledbetter, No 19469
Camp A, Angola, Louisiana

Dear Ledbetter:

I have your letter and your poem to the Governor, I think I must have told you before that because you are a "second termer" you can not be reprieved. You will be eligible to parole in February, 1936. The only relief other than this is through the Board of Pardons. The small paper which I enclose will explain to you exactly how to proceed to bring your case to the attention of the Board of Pardons.

Very truly yours,
R. L. Himes
General Manager

This response is obviously just one of a series of exchanges between Huddie Ledbetter and R. L. Himes. All of them concerned Huddie's desire to be a free man. Leadbelly later disputed Himes's point that he was a "second termer," claiming that he was never imprisoned at Sugarland. He even said that the fingerprints lied and that he was not the "Walter Boyd" in question. Huddie appealed to Himes's sense of family by pointing out that he had a wife and a child to support. Himes was steadfast and continued to point out that the rules for commutation held Huddie's only hope.

———

The winter of 1934 gradually waned and spring eventually returned to southern Louisiana. Leadbelly's daily routine continued with monotonous regularity. His trusty status helped to reduce the physical burden of life in Angola, but Huddie wanted to get out. He knew that his quickest road to salvation lay with an early release that simply had to be signed by Governor Allen. His failed attempt at reaching Governor Allen through his music fell upon deaf ears and he must have despaired of getting his petition signed. Then word reached the Angola community that the Lomaxes were returning in early July and Huddie sensed an opportunity.

In the spring of 1934, John and Alan Lomax returned to the South in search of more folk songs for the Archive of Folk Song. Again, black American songs and music were their primary focus and they immediately drove to the deep South. Their plan was simple: From early April through August, they would comb rural areas and stop by some of the prisons they'd missed the first time. In addition to looking for blues, work songs, and sacred songs, John and Alan would visit the French-speaking section of Louisiana and make some of the first recordings of Cajun ballads and songs, as well as of dance songs of black Creoles. This hybrid French patois, which was later known as "La La," combines elements of black American folk songs with their French ancestors and is the direct antecedent to our present-day Zydeco music. While in the Cajun section of southwestern Louisiana, John Lomax thought about returning to the Louisiana State Penitentiary. He wrote the following letter:

New Iberia, Louisiana
June 20, 1934

Dear Mr. Himes:

Will you kindly let me know if Ledbetter, the 12 string Negro guitar player is still in Angola? We now have a greatly improved machine on which we wish to record some more of his songs for the Library of Congress. I hope it will again be possible for you to let us see him. You will recall that our mutual friend, Professor A. T. Prescott, is my sponsor. Kindly address me here, General Delivery.

Sincerely Yours,
John A. Lomax

Himes wrote affirming Huddie's continued presence at Angola and granted them permission for a second visit.

"In nineteen and hundred and thirty-two Honorable Governor O. K. Allen, I'm pleadin' to you" Huddie sang for the Library of Congress's disc cutter.

Now this song I compose in nineteen and thirty-two. I sung it on up into nineteen and thirty-four. And the first day of July, the good, cool, kind boss, better known as Mr. John A. Lomax, they come down on Angola, it was raining one Sunday, an' he tol' me, says, "This song that you made about Governor O. K. Allen, if you sing it through the microphone I'll take it to Governor O. K. Allen for you." I thanked him I says, "Boss, if you take it to Governor O. K. Allen, I sho' believe he gonna turn me aloose." And sho 'nuff, boss, I sung this song to him an' he taken it to Baton Rouge, and one month from that day Governor O. K. Allen told me to go home.

This spoken vignette, recorded by Leadbelly nearly one year after his release from Angola, clearly suggests that he had been thinking about his fate. On July first when the Lomaxes returned to Angola, he immediately sang his song "Governor O. K. Allen" into their microphone. At this point he also approached John Lomax with his case: If Leadbelly obtained Governor Allen's signature, his sentence would be commuted and he would immediately be freed. The paperwork was at hand; it merely required Allen's okay. Leadbelly apparently asked the Lomaxes to intervene by hand-carrying this disc to Baton Rouge and presenting it to Governor Allen himself.

Here the exact circumstances of the Lomaxes' involvement become muddied. The legend is that John Lomax pled Leadbelly's case to Governor

O. K. Allen and eventually gained a parole for him. The facts clearly belie this scenario. In John's own words, "Through a twist of circumstances, just a month after our second visit to Angola, Leadbelly was set free." Apparently, after recording "Governor O. K. Allen" he "took it over to the Governor." Alan recalls that when they drove to Baton Rouge, his father left the disc with the governor's secretary and did not speak directly with Allen. The fact is that on July 25, 1934, Governor O. K. Allen signed a routine order commuting Huddie Ledbetter's sentence to three to ten years. Because of the special "double good time" provision, Huddie was freed on schedule on August 1, 1934.

This scenario is confirmed in a letter written by Warden L. A. Jones in 1939. In response to a letter from the city of New York's Probation Department requesting information about the reasons behind Huddie Ledbetter's release from Angola, Jones wrote:

Mr. Irving Halpern
Chief Probation
Officer
Court of General Sessions
New York, New York

This man has been the recipient of wide publicity in various magazines of national circulation, the story usually being that he sang or wrote such moving appeals to the Governor that he was pardoned. Such statements have no foundation in fact. He received no clemency, and his discharge was a routine matter under the good time law which applies to all first and second offenders.

L.A. Jones
Warden

It was shortly thereafter that John Lomax discovered this was not Huddie's first prison term. Evidently, Huddie had not been forthcoming with the details of his previous brushes with the law. Whatever he might have told John Lomax, he left the Texan wondering, because on February 12, 1935, John Lomax wrote to Himes asking for more information about Ledbetter's past.

In Himes's response, dated February 15, 1935, he explained that Leadbelly had not actually been pardoned, but had been released through a policy called "good time." If he ever got into any trouble in Louisiana in the future, and if he was ever sentenced to any more jail time, he would fall under the provisions of the "Hog Law." This meant that before he could start serving any new sentence, he would have to serve the balance of the time still owed the state from his earlier sentence: in this case, five years, six months, and twenty-three days.

Other people with a vested interest in Huddie Ledbetter also became concerned about his changed status. On September 26, 1934, Sheriff Tom Hughes from Shreveport wrote to Mr. Himes. Hughes reiterated that "Hughie" [*sic*] had committed "assault to murder, on Mr. Dick Elliot [*sic*], a splendid white citizen of Mooringsport." He wanted to know if Huddie Ledbetter had been released. Himes was compelled to answer in the affirmative.

15 "Your Servan, Huddie Ledbetter"

According to popular legend, Leadbelly left prison and went almost immediately to John Lomax, showing up unexpectedly and offering his services as a driver and valet. The truth is more complicated, and not quite as dramatic. Huddie was indeed released on August 1; the prison gave him a pair of coveralls and an ugly pair of yellow shoes. Captain Reaux, one of his overseers, himself gave him ten dollars, but Huddie spent it his first night out. Then he made for Shreveport, his old stomping ground; he originally planned to go on to Dallas, to stay with his daughter Arthur Mae, who was now in her thirties. She had written him in prison and had a house on Tuskegee Street in Dallas. If this plan didn't work, he hoped to stay with relatives in Kilgore. Apparently it didn't; either he gave up the idea of Dallas or went and then returned to Shreveport in a couple of weeks. The times were not as good as when he had gone to Angola four years before; the Depression had hit the refineries and oil fields, and jobs were scarce—especially for an ex-con.

By early September, Huddie had started staying with a Shreveport woman who was to have a profound effect on his life and his music: Martha Promise. Martha had been born in the community of Longwood about 1906 and had known Huddie and his family all her life. Though she was a good deal younger than Huddie—by eighteen years, making her younger than Huddie's own daughter Arthur Mae—she had dated him as a teenager. Family stories tell of Huddie courting both her and her sister Mary, and of his defending Mary's honor at a local dance.

When a boy grabbed Mary and pulled her onto his lap, Huddie supposedly stopped his music, leaped up, and smashed his guitar over the boy's head. Martha herself grew into a quiet, patient, hardworking religious girl who was best known as leading soprano in the Shreveport Silver Leaf Jubilee Choir. She had been attracted to Huddie for years, in spite of his reputation. Now, in September 1934, she was working at a local laundry and making a modest $4 a week. When Huddie got back to town, he was broke, ragged, hungry, disheartened, and alone. His mother had died while he was in Angola, and the deepening Depression made things even grimmer. He and Martha had been seeing each other before he went to Angola, and in desperation he turned to her now. She didn't hesitate to take him in. "I'se had all kinds of women an' the best kind to get is one who loves you and you can trust," he later told the Lomaxes in tribute to her.

Casting about desperately for something to do, some job to take the pressure off Martha's $4 a week, Huddie thought back to his benefactor—the man he credited with getting his release. The first time he had met Lomax, in 1933, he had begged him to help him get a parole by hiring him as his "man." Leadbelly offered to drive the Lomaxes' car, cook meals, and wash clothes. And on July 20, ten days before his release, he had written to Lomax in Austin, again lobbying for a job. He suggested that Lomax send him a ticket and he would go directly to either Dallas or Austin to meet him, not even going by first to see his "wife," Martha. He wrote that he had to make some money after he got out, and even asked Lomax to send him some money. The letter was signed, "i'm your Servan, Huddie Ledbetter." A second letter followed on August 10, ten days after his release. It was from Shreveport, and in it he insisted that he was looking for Lomax, and that "i am going to work for you." Lomax was apparently interested enough to respond, but his letters were returned by the post office. Confused and becoming worried, Huddie wrote again from Shreveport on September 4. He was not living in Mooringsport anymore, he wrote, but hoped Lomax could come and get him; he hadn't gotten any job and did not have much money. A fourth letter, written on a petty cash voucher form from a local plant, followed six days later. He had sent three letters, he wrote, and had not heard anything. If Lomax could not come after him, Leadbelly asked to be sent a ticket. The letter was addressed to "Dear Boss Man," a phrase he would continue to use with Lomax during the next six months.

Lomax in fact did need help. He was preparing to leave on another song-hunting expedition partially funded by the Carnegie Foundation through the Library of Congress Music Division. This support was bare-boned at best. His machine—the same one he had used before—occupied a platform in the back of his Model A. As with his earlier trips, Lomax had agreed to deposit the records he made with the Library of Congress. He was convinced that the prisons of nearby Arkansas held a wealth of black folk songs and his plan was to use the method he had used in Texas, Louisiana, and Mississippi: gain access to the prisoners with letters of recommendation from the appropriate governor or state official. The problem was that his teenage son Alan, who had gone along to help on the earlier trips, was now sick in bed and unable to travel.

Faced with the prospect of making a long, tiring journey alone, Lomax recalled Leadbelly's skills. He was a good driver and mechanic—his experience working for the Houston Buick agency served him well here—he could help with the heavy machine; and, best of all, he could serve as liaison with the African American singers and prisoners Lomax was wanting to record. All in all, it sounded like a good idea. After he got Leadbelly's last letter, he wired Leadbelly to meet him at the Plaza Hotel in Marshall on September

22. "Come prepared to travel," he said. "Bring guitar. . . ."

Huddie did, and found Lomax at the hotel experimenting with his recording machine. As Lomax described in his book, and in the later *March
of Time* newsreel about Leadbelly, he came bluntly to the point—Texas
style. He asked his new employee if he was carrying any weapons, having
been worried about Huddie's reputation of carrying a pistol. "Only this
knife, Boss," Huddie replied, bringing out a razor-sharp knife with a long
blade. Lomax took it and balanced it in his hand. Down in Austin, he said,
he had a wife and daughter, and hoped to live a long time for their sakes.
"Whenever you decide that you are going to take my money and car, you
won't have to use this knife on me. Just tell me what you want and I'll give
it to you without a struggle." This direct, pragmatic response appeared to
startle Huddie. "Boss, suh, don't talk that way. . . . I'se yo man. You won't
ever have to tie your shoes again if you don't want to. I'll slip in front of you
if anybody tries to shoot you. I'm ready to die for you."

This somewhat reassured Lomax. He explained to Huddie that he
couldn't afford to pay him much money, but that he would pay for his food
and lodging; Huddie would get to help in collecting other folk songs, a
subject which intrigued the singer. The rest of the morning Lomax tried to
make some test records of the singer. He wanted to try out the new and
complicated machine with its state-of-the-art studio microphone, which
remained frustratingly sensitive to wind noise. Though by now an experienced recordist with a good ear, Lomax was not entirely pleased with the
results. Eventually he gave up and went to lunch. The next morning he
wrote to his wife, "Ledbetter is here and we are off." He also asked her to
send some old clothes for the singer: an old black suit of Lomax's own,
some old ties, and something to serve him as a suitcase. "Don't be uneasy,"
he concluded. "He thinks I freed him. He will probably be of much help."

They hit the road to Little Rock, some two hundred miles to the northeast, Leadbelly driving, Lomax worrying about what an unusual pair they
made and whether he would be able to keep the singer on the job. They
arrived there on September 26 and, while waiting to see the governor, met
a couple of black street musicians. Lomax rented a tourist cabin three or
four miles out of town so they could bring any black musicians they found
to make records. The two street musicians, known as Blind Pete and George
Ryan, recorded several old-time songs, accompanying themselves on the
fiddle. The songs were not blues or work songs, but were fine examples of
the kind of black hillbilly music Leadbelly had grown up with. Leadbelly
himself continued to sing, occasionally making a record so that skeptical
local singers could see how it was done; his songs also served to show others
the kind of material Lomax was looking for.

They finally got a letter from the governor giving them permission to record, and set off down Highway 65, some seventy miles to the southeast to Gould and the Cummins Prison Farm. There the local warden received them and set up a room for Lomax to stay; he was a Texan by birth, and was the only white official in the camp of over two hundred. Lomax promised not to mention to the hosts anything about Leadbelly's prison record, but an hour after they had arrived, all the convicts seemed to know about it. Leadbelly was fed and housed with the black guards and trusties who did the day-to-day work of running the prison farm. Lomax wrote to his wife on October 1 that he had high expectations: There were three camps in the general vicinity, and he had hopes to interview as many as eight hundred inmates.

Once again, to set the tone and give a sample of the kind of music they wanted, Lomax asked Leadbelly to sing for some of the men. In his book *Negro Folk Songs*, the collector gives a vivid description of one particular afternoon when Leadbelly and he sat in the "run-around," explaining and performing songs.

We sat at a point in the run-around while the men were crowded inside as close as possible to us, peering out between the iron bars. So eager were they to hear and see Leadbelly that at times some stood on the shoulders of others. When the twanging of his guitar strings rang out, supporting his rich booming voice, silence fell in the rows of cells suddenly and completely. The crap games ceased, the cooncan players dropped their cards, while from dim corners, where groups were mumbling prayers and songs and religious preachments, poured all of the worshippers, including the black ministers. For the moment Leadbelly's "sinful songs" became more powerful than the "spirituals."

Especially effective was Leadbelly's version of the Dallas murder ballad "Ella Speed." At the climax, when Bill Martin finally shoots Ella with his "colt 41," Leadbelly would shout out, "Don't none o' you boys kill no womens. . . . When you kill a woman you is gone." Men would silently nod their heads in agreement. Lomax reflected that in all the prison concerts Leadbelly gave, this was the only song he did in which he pretended to offer any advice to the inmates.

The first week at Gould was a nightmare of logistics. The fussy recording machine broke down over and over, and inmates who had been gathered to sing and record were complaining about the delays. Finally things seemed to be ready, and Lomax and Huddie set up the machine outside near a barn and next to a stack of pine logs. The men came in from the cotton patch, and a group of them led by a big man named Kelly Pace stepped up to sing and swing their axes.

Oh, the Rock Island Line is a mighty good road,
Oh, the Rock Island road is the road to ride.

Pace led the group of seven men through the song, and Lomax knew he had found a song he had never heard before. One of the men had done an imitation whistle as part of the performance, and when they heard their work played back on the record, they shouted and threw down their hats. The whistler beamed with pride; he claimed that they could hear that whistle clear to Washington.

Huddie liked the song as well, and before he quit work that day, he had learned it, too. He knew little of the history behind it—that it had originated in the early 1900s, when the Rock Island Company had purchased the rights to cut across Arkansas, through Little Rock and into West Memphis, dividing the state in half; most of the early versions tell of a railroad run between Little Rock and Memphis. Huddie knew a good song when he heard it, and quickly appropriated it. It would become one of his most famous songs. He would not record it until 1937, but in later years he would do it for RCA Victor, Capitol, and Folkways, and make it a regular part of his repertoire. In later years folk groups like the Weavers and singer Lonnie Donnegan would make it into a pop song hit as well.

In his spoken introduction to his 1937 Library of Congress version of the song, Huddie recalls how impressed he was with the ax-cutting team in Arkansas that produced the song. "They cuttin' by axes, there's about ten or twelve men on the log and they cuttin' four-foot wood. One man on the right side and one on the other, each man's got a poleax, and this man what cut right-handed, he step on the other side. The one that's left-handed, he's right over next to him, but he's on the other side. They cutting in the same chip. You can't cut your ax in there and leave it, you got to pick it up in the rhythm with the saw as I cut down, and you bring it up. . . . The boys swing the axes. One man, he give the word and they catch him down the line, just like coaches, and all on down the log." As he continued to work with the song over the years, though, Leadbelly gradually dropped the work song references and replaced them with a narrative about an engineer who fools the "depot man" about what kind of freight he is carrying. This story Leadbelly did not add to the song on recordings until 1942, with the Asch recording of the song, but he tended to use it thereafter. The later populariz-ers of the song used the story of the engineer as well, making it a purely railroad song instead of a prison work song.

Some twenty songs were eventually recorded at the Cummins Farm in Gould, including another memorable one by Kelly Pace called "Jumpin' Judy." A women's convict group—Huddie had performed before them, too—sang some gospel songs. Other groups whose names were never writ-

Leadbelly

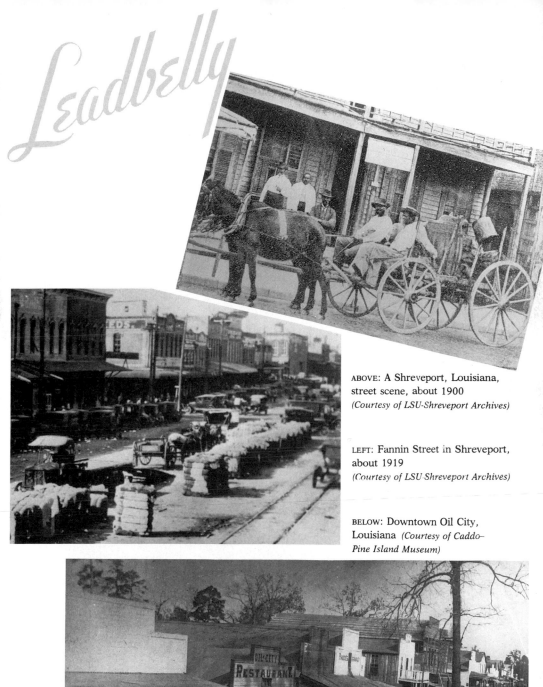

ABOVE: A Shreveport, Louisiana, street scene, about 1900 *(Courtesy of LSU-Shreveport Archives)*

LEFT: Fannin Street in Shreveport, about 1919 *(Courtesy of LSU-Shreveport Archives)*

BELOW: Downtown Oil City, Louisiana *(Courtesy of Caddo–Pine Island Museum)*

ABOVE: Governor Pat Neff of Texas, about 1924 (*The Texas Collection of Baylor University*)

LEFT: Huddie Ledbetter's Texas Prison System pardon (*Courtesy of the American Folk Life Center's Archive of Folk Culture, Library of Congress*)

Leadbelly at Angola in 1934, at right, and standing hatless under the window at the far left in the picture below (*Courtesy of the Library of Congress*)

LEFT: John A. Lomax, in a portrait by
J. Anthony Wills (*Barker History Center,
University of Texas, Austin, and Bess
Lomax Hawes*)

BELOW: The trunk of John Lomax's car with his
recording equipment, about 1934 (*Courtesy of the
American Folk Life Center's Archive of Folk
Culture, Library of Congress*)

Alan Lomax (*Courtesy of the American Folk Life
Center's Archive of Folk Culture, Library of Congress*)

Huddie Ledbetter and Martha Promise Ledbetter in 1935 *(Courtesy of the Library of Congress)*

Leadbelly's stationery from the late 1930s (center) and an advertisement for Huddie's 1940 collaboration with the Golden Gate Quartet (above) *(Courtesy of the American Folk Life Center's Archive of Folk Culture, Library of Congress)*

RIGHT: Sheet music for Gussie L. Davis's "Irene, Good Night" (1892) *(Courtesy of the Library of Congress, Music Division)*

Leadbelly entertaining children in the mid-1940s *(Courtesy of LSU-Shreveport Archives)*

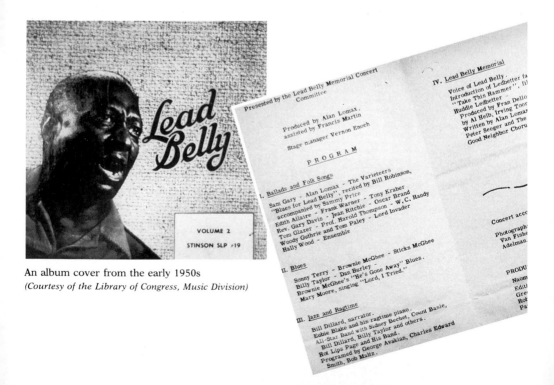

An album cover from the early 1950s
(Courtesy of the Library of Congress, Music Division)

VOLUME 2
STINSON SLP #19

Presented by the Lead Belly Memorial Concert
Committee

Produced by Alan Lomax,
assisted by Francis Martin

Stage manager Vernon Enoch

PROGRAM

I. Ballads and Folk Songs

Sam Gary - Alan Lomax - The Varieteers
"Blues for Lead Belly", recited by Bill Robinson,
accompanied by Sammy Price
Edith Allaire - Frank Warner - Tony Kraber
Rev. Gary Davis - Jean Ritchie - Oscar Brand
Tom Glazer - Prof. Harold Thompson - W. C. Handy
Woody Guthrie and Tom Paley - Lord Invader
Hally Wood - Ensemble

II. Blues

Sonny Terry - Brownie McGhee - Sticks McGhee
Billy Taylor - Dan Burley -
Brownie McGhee's "He's Gone Away" Blues.
Mary Moore, singing "Lord, I Tried."

III. Jazz and Ragtime

Bill Dillard, narrator.
Eubie Blake and his ragtime piano.
All-Star Band with Sidney Bechet, Count Basie,
Bill Dillard, Billy Taylor and others.
Hot Lips Page and His Band.
Programed by George Avakian, Charles Edward
Smith, Bob Maltz.

IV. Lead Belly Memorial

Voice of Lead Belly.
Introduction of Ledbetter fa
"Take This Hammer", fil
Huddie Ledbetter
Produced by Fran Dello
by Al Helb, Irving Toor
Written by Alan Lomax
Peter Seeger and The
Good Neighbor Choru

Concert acco

Photograph
Van Fishe
Adelman.

PRODU

Naom
Edit
Gre
Rob
Pa

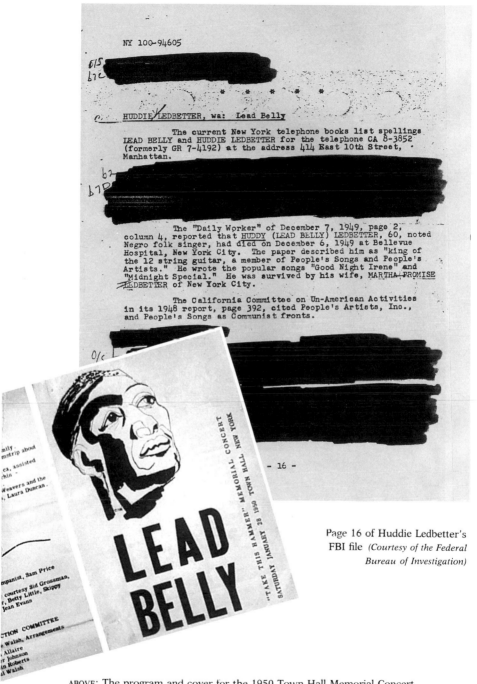

NY 100-94605

* · * · * · *

HUDDIE LEDBETTER, wa: Lead Belly

The current New York telephone books list spellings LEAD BELLY and HUDDIE LEDBETTER for the telephone CA 8-3852 (formerly GR 7-4192) at the address 414 East 10th Street, Manhattan.

The "Daily Worker" of December 7, 1949, page 2, column 4, reported that HUDDY (LEAD BELLY) LEDBETTER, 60, noted Negro folk singer, had died on December 6, 1949 at Bellevue Hospital, New York City. The paper described him as "king of the 12 string guitar, a member of People's Songs and People's Artists." He wrote the popular songs "Good Night Irene" and "Midnight Special." He was survived by his wife, MARTHA PROMISE LEDBETTER of New York City.

The California Committee on Un-American Activities in its 1948 report, page 392, cited People's Artists, Inc., and People's Songs as Communist fronts.

- 16 -

Page 16 of Huddie Ledbetter's FBI file *(Courtesy of the Federal Bureau of Investigation)*

ABOVE: The program and cover for the 1950 Town Hall Memorial Concert *(Courtesy of the American Folk Life Center's Archive of Folk Culture, Library of Congress)*

TOP: "Ledbetter Heights," on Fannin Street, Shreveport, today *(Kip Lornell)*

CENTER: Huddie's daughter, Jessie Mae Baisley, at left, and Lizzie Carey in 1988 *(Courtesy of Betty Sorrell)*

LEFT: Panthea Boyd King, Leadbelly's daughter, 1991 *(Kip Lornell)*

ten down in the files did songs like "Job" and "It Makes a Long Time Man Feel Bad." To make up for the lost time, the pair worked sixteen-hour days, getting up at five, and then eventually finished their work. Lomax was impressed with Leadbelly's work in the camps; he wrote his wife that their success was due to the singer's being in a familiar environment. Confirmation of all this seemed to come the day they left Cummins; as they pulled out in their Plymouth early that morning, Leadbelly lowered his voice and explained that they didn't have to worry about gas; he had bribed one of the guards to fill up their tank from the state of Arkansas pumps at the farm. Lomax lectured him briefly on the morality of such things, but they kept on down the road.

The following week (October 7–13) they returned to Shreveport. Huddie was already lonesome for Martha—he had complained about this even before they left for Arkansas—and he wanted to show off to her the suit that Lomax's wife had mailed to him. Besides, he admitted he was nervous going back into so many prisons so soon after his term at Angola; he was tired of looking at black people in penitentiaries, he told Lomax. There were better places to be, and he was anxious to drive the big Plymouth down Fannin Street and show it off as well. It was a trip of some four hundred miles, but Huddie was eager to drive it; surprisingly, Lomax agreed to the detour.

The stay in Shreveport rejuvenated Huddie, and Lomax followed it with a brief trip home himself. By the middle of October they were on the road again, headed for Alabama and the prison systems there. A short stay in New Orleans yielded a few recordings, but Huddie's old nervousness about the city surfaced; he refused to go out "carousing," as was his custom, and instead spent a quiet night or two going to bed early. "I don't like these New Orleans niggers much," he told Lomax. Soon they were on the road to Mobile. Throughout the time they traveled together, Lomax had never seen his companion read a newspaper or look at a road map; except for their return to Shreveport, Leadbelly had shown little interest in what direction they were going, what their destination was, or when they would arrive. His old instincts as a rambler came back into play, and he was happy simply to be driving down the open road, free from confinement, headed someplace new.

One particular late October afternoon they found themselves driving along the Gulf of Mexico. There was an especially breathtaking sunset over the clouds, and Lomax was interested in Huddie's reaction: His driver had never seen the ocean before. As the car continued east on the highway near the bluff, Huddie kept looking at the water, trying to take it in, and then finally exclaimed that it was the biggest river he had ever seen. He asked if the river would extend as far as Mobile, and then craned his neck to try to see across it.

After a time he mused that he couldn't see any trees or anything on the opposite bank, and couldn't see how a person could get across it; he never commented on the sunset, the clouds, the lighthouses winking in the distance, the rolling waves. Lomax was puzzled by this reaction, but finally wrote it off to the fact that his companion had been locked up for twelve years and had lost his appreciation for natural beauty. However, after he wrote up the incident for *Negro Folk Songs* he decided to delete it from the final draft, perhaps feeling that it made Leadbelly seem like an accommodating "Stepin Fetchit." In fact, as we shall see, the Gulf might have made more of an impression on the singer than he had let on to his benefactor.

The plan in Alabama was to follow the methods used successfully in Arkansas: a trip to the capital Montgomery to get a letter of permission from the governor, and then to regional prisons at Birmingham and Tuscaloosa, working south from there. Things got off to a good start; Leadbelly went out of his way to be the perfect valet, waking his boss on time in the morning, fixing his coffee, polishing his shoes, brushing his suit. In Birmingham they used the technique they had tried in Little Rock, simply driving around the town looking for street musicians; and, indeed, they found a couple of black buskers who sang and played guitar, and decided to record them. By October 26 they were at the Roosevelt Hotel in Montgomery, planning to go into Kilby Prison the next morning to record more work songs. (They actually wound up recording six gospel songs by another group of "unidentified convicts.")

It was here, though, that the fragile alliance between collector and singer threatened to rip apart. Lomax had been in the habit of letting Huddie take off on his own when their work day was done. He didn't really even want to know where he went, but did try to talk Huddie into occasionally leaving his guitar under the bed in the hotel room—both to protect the guitar and to keep Huddie from showing off too much. (This strategy seldom worked.) Some days Huddie would be late rolling in by seven o'clock in the morning, when Lomax liked to leave, but Huddie always had interesting excuses and nothing serious had come of it. But on the twenty-eighth of October, a Sunday morning, the pair was scheduled to go back to Kilby, and Leadbelly didn't show up at all. Lomax waited for two hours, then drove to the black section of town where Huddie had been boarding; still no luck. Finally he drove on out to the prison by himself, spent the day running both the record machine and coordinating the singers, and returned exhausted at eleven that night. An hour later Huddie showed up at the front desk; he had finally arrived that morning late and had found Lomax gone. Since his employer always gave him his $1 daily expense allowance in the mornings, Huddie had found himself with no money and had had nothing to eat all day. He had even wired Martha in Shreveport for money.

Lomax was furious; all the small irritations of the past month boiled up, and he delivered a blistering lecture to the singer. Huddie took it all, and then confessed that he was "nothin' but a nigger" and that "there never was a nigger that would keep his word." He begged for a second chance and for something to eat, and Lomax, moved by his genuine compassion for Leadbelly and impressed by the "poor nigger" speech, finally agreed. Only later did he learn that Leadbelly had money in his pocket at the time.

A few days later, while driving in downtown Montgomery, Leadbelly pulled out into traffic and ran through a red light, almost causing a wreck and setting off a cacophony of angry honks. Outraged, Lomax ordered him to stop the car and asked him what he thought he was doing; Huddie replied that he thought Lomax had told him to run the light. This was too much for Lomax, who felt legally and morally responsible for Huddie—the last thing Lomax wanted was serious trouble over a minor traffic infraction. He ordered the singer to get his guitar and step out of the car right then. Without a word, Huddie got out and vanished into the crowded streets.

Lomax went on with his work, fully expecting that Huddie would show up at the hotel that night. He didn't. A day passed, then two, then three. This time, apparently, the rift was complete, the parting final. Lomax was regretting his sudden outburst, wondering if there had been some kind of genuine misunderstanding about the red light. But he had no idea where to even start to hunt for the singer so he could make amends. He had about given up and finally decided to leave Montgomery to go to the Atmore Prison Farm, far to the south near Mobile. At a final stop at the post office, he stood on the steps reading mail and looked up to see Leadbelly nearby. He called to him.

The singer offered no explanation about where he had been for the last three days, but he did not seem as desperate or hungry as he did after the earlier incident. (Later Lomax found that he had been taken in by some local women and that the local relief board had helped him with money for food.) Lomax offered a gracious apology and conceded that the misunderstanding about the light might have been his fault; he then asked the singer if he still wanted to drive for him. "I surely do, boss, I surely do." Within minutes they were on their way again.

Leadbelly proved his value to the collecting project again at Atmore. At the prison farm they found a group that sang old folk ballads like "The Boston Burglar" and gospel songs like "Where You Building Your Building"; they also happened upon a splendid soloist named Albert Jackson, who sang the classic badman ballad "Stagolee." One inmate delivered a chanted prayer and a sermon for the disc-cutting machine. Then one Saturday night (probably November 3) the machine, as usual, broke down right in the middle of a session. Throughout the trip, the prisoners had generally been more than eager to put their music on the discs and were delighted to hear it played back. They were disappointed this time that they couldn't finish, and to make up somewhat for all their wasted preparations, Leadbelly was asked to give an impromptu concert.

He was happy to do so, but had not counted on the size of the prison. He sang one batch of songs, his strong voice booming down the halls of the dormitory. But there were other dormitories, and they didn't want to be left out. Good-naturedly, he moved over to the next one and repeated his concert. Then to another, and another, and another—eventually seven in all. Lomax was worried about the strain on his voice, but Huddie wasn't: he could sing all night long if he needed to, he bragged. At the end, someone passed the hat among the prisoners; there was not much, but they had been paid their weekly 25-cent cigarette allowance that day, and the hat came back full. ''A few nickels an' more than three hundred pennies,'' Leadbelly bragged later.

A couple of days later Huddie was back with Martha, and Lomax was on his way home to Austin. One adventure with Leadbelly was over, but in fact he was already laying plans to take it a step further. He had been invited to speak at the annual meeting of the Modern Language Association, to be held between Christmas and New Year's in Philadelphia. On October 25, in the midst of the Alabama trip, he had written to President Aydelotte of Swarthmore College, the official host of the 1934 meeting, and suggested that Leadbelly come along with him and sing at a ''smoker'' at the meeting. The entertainment committee of the MLA no doubt recalled the stirring presentation given by Lomax at their previous meeting in St. Louis; and Alan had described the fieldwork and played selections of recent field recordings for the meeting. This was the first time that recordings of black vernacular music had been heard at an MLA meeting and his bold move caused an immediate sensation. Now one of the organization's favorite speakers came up with another innovation: presenting a real folk singer for a live performance. On October 31 Townsend Scudder III wrote to Lomax to say that the MLA liked his ''generous suggestion'' that his ''talented aborigine'' sing for the guests at the ''smoker.'' Furthermore, Lomax had apparently mentioned all this to Leadbelly before he dropped him off in Shreveport; on November 7, Martha wrote to the collector saying that she and Huddie were well and that she hoped ''you all will make the trip to Philadelphia as well as you made this one.''

16 The Sweet Singer of the Swamplands

Before Leadbelly continued on to Philadelphia with Lomax, the pair traveled through Georgia, the Carolinas, and Virginia for an already scheduled series of stops at prisons. It was to be John Lomax's last fieldwork for many months. Ironically, his book *American Ballads and Folk Songs* had recently been published by Macmillan and was quickly gaining public notice. Many of the songs in the book had been collected on his 1933 trip, the one where had first met Leadbelly, and in fact a number of them had come from him. Included were Huddie's version of "Frankie and Albert," "Bill Martin and Ella Speed," "Honey Take a Whiff on Me," and "When I Was a Cowboy," all of which had been recorded in Angola in 1933. (Curiously, one song, "Julie Ann Johnson," which was not recorded in the first session, was included in the book, even though Lomax specified that most of the songs were transcribed from the discs they had made.) Leadbelly by no means dominated the collection, but his name appeared often in the headnotes of his songs, and in the introduction, where Lomax mentions him as an important source. He is one of the "group of Negro 'boys' " who that summer "gave up for the time their crap and card games, their prayer meetings, their much needed Sunday and evening rest" in the various penitentiaries to sing for him. Since people interested in folk song study—which included not a few members of the Modern Language Association—were talking about the new book, it would be an appropriate time to show off one of the prime sources.

Alan was by now recovered from his illness and was planning on joining his father on the trip. In *Negro Folk Songs* John gives credit to Alan for insisting that he bring Leadbelly along. This reinforced the request that came from the MLA, as well as "almost daily" letters from Leadbelly himself, begging to be taken along. Yet the correspondence in the Lomax papers clearly shows the MLA trip was Lomax's idea, and hardly a spur-of-the-moment decision or a giving in to pressure from Alan and Huddie. At any rate, Lomax had a mechanic modify the Plymouth so there was room for a backseat in which he could ride next to the recording machine. They met Huddie in Shreveport, he took over the driving, and they pulled out, waving to Martha as she stood beside her laundry.

December 10 found them in Atlanta, where they wrangled with the prison boards of both the state and federal facilities before getting permission to record. They found some seventeen songs at Bellwood camp, including early versions of "This Train" and "The Longest Train," both of which were later to become folk music standards. The problems Huddie and John Lomax had had in Alabama seemed to be behind them; the singer was cheerfully teaching Alan guitar licks, doing virtually all the driving, and even making repairs on the car. Lomax wrote his wife: "Leadbetter is a treasure so far. I could not ask for more considerate thoughtfulness. The days I left him out in the cold at Shreveport were certainly good for him—just as I intended. . . . Yes'sum, we are making progress in the department of personal relations."

One problem with the Georgia prison boards was that they were angry about a recent series of articles written by northern writers who had come into the area, gained access to the prisons, and then written exposés about the terrible conditions they found. By now the prison boards were suspicious about anyone with connections to the federal government (even the Library of Congress) coming into the camps. It took all of John Lomax's considerable powers of persuasion to finally convince them that the trio was hunting songs, not reform. In truth, none of Lomax's letters make any comment about especially harsh conditions; he and Leadbelly had both seen much worse in prison farms of Arkansas, Alabama, and Texas. Soon they were able to visit the main prison site at Milledgeville, where they recorded a huge number of songs—some thirty-two. Alan, however, fell ill with some kind of flu—the doctor on the spot thought it was a recurrence of malaria—and Leadbelly found himself again promoted to "first assistant." It worked well, though Lomax began to think that Leadbelly was using Alan to manipulate him on occasion, getting at him through his son, who was developing a real rapport with the singer. Leadbelly continued to "prime the pump" at prisons by singing and playing the kinds of songs Lomax wanted, and stimulating the local singers to come forward. This, too, was working well, and Huddie was picking up quite a bit of knowledge about folk songs and the nature of traditional music.

After a week, Alan began to feel better and the team found itself staying at the Reed Prison farm, fifty miles or so out from Columbia, South Carolina. Leadbelly had recently developed a severe toothache, and the constant pain was making him surly and irritable. One afternoon Lomax had to leave him in the car outside the prison gates, and he came back to find the car splattered with blood. "Leadbelly had been trying to pull his molar with the automobile pliers. 'I couldn't get a good holt,' said Leadbelly; 'the pliers kept slipping off.' " Finally Alan was able to find a black dentist who was able to kill the nerve to the molar.

After a final stop in the state prison at Raleigh, North Carolina, the team rolled into Washington, D.C., on Christmas Eve. It was here that the wave of publicity about Leadbelly really got its start. The night they arrived he sang for a Major Issac Spalding and a party of selected guests; the following day, he entertained two groups of newspaper people who had gotten wind of the unusual discovery Lomax was bringing to the MLA meeting. Yet there was some time for a little last-minute relaxation; Lomax saw some old friends (including Senator Tom Connally, Speaker of the House, and Dr. Vance of the Law Library), and then took Huddie to the zoo. That night he returned the singer to the hotel and then treated himself to a show: Katharine Hepburn and Donald Crisp in the new film version of *The Little Minister*. There was time for sleep in a decent bed and, for Alan and Huddie, some more guitar lessons. There was a Christmas tree, with presents—including three for Huddie. He was moved; it was the first time, he said, that Santa Claus had thought of him in five years.

They drove to Philadelphia on the afternoon of the twenty-sixth and checked in at the Benjamin Franklin Hotel, which was buzzing with last-minute preparations for the huge MLA meeting. As usual, because of the Jim Crow laws, Huddie had to seek lodging elsewhere and wound up at a room on 1126 Pine Street. The next day Lomax began running into old friends; he was a familiar and popular figure at the MLA meetings, and was well aware that the organization had sponsored, in one way or the other, many of the American ballad studies that had been done. He met his old professor Barrett Wendell from Harvard; the brilliant scholar Tom Pete Cross; and Harold Thompson from Cornell. Many had, of course, read Lomax's new book, and they showered him with plaudits and congratulations. Too soon, though, the local reporters sought him out, and their eager questions about Leadbelly and the sensational aspects of his pardon consumed much of his day.

One of the odder interviews took place the following day (Friday the twenty-eighth) when Kenton Jackson, a reporter for the *Philadelphia Independent*, one of the country's leading black papers, caught up with the singer. Entitled "Two Time Dixie Murderer Sings Way to Freedom," the result was one of the first substantial stories based on interviews with the singer, as opposed to Lomax, and was the very first time a black newspaper printed Leadbelly's story. It read, in part:

Interviewed Friday for the first time by a Negro newspaper, Ledbetter, sitting nonchalantly on a bed at 1126 Pine street, where he stopped while in this city, told The Independent how he strummed and sang his way to freedom from behind the cold, gray walls of prison in the not-so-sunny south.

Down in Texas, not too long ago, Ledbetter looked out in the distance and saw the huge Gulf of Mexico. The ripple of the waters enthralled him. He picked up his trusty guitar and strummed a tune or two. Something seemed to grip him. He sang an extemporaneous song, the strains of which enchanted the guards of the Imperial State Prison at Sugar Landing, where he had been confined.

Thought of Paul and Silas

Asked what inspired him to sing to attract the attention of Governor Pat Neff, Ledbetter said he thought of the Biblical "Paul" and "Silas" in prison. He reviewed how they both sang and prayed at the midnight hour after they had been thrown into prison and how the earth trembled and the walls of the prison shook, the locks on the cell doors fell and they walked out free.

Ledbetter visioned the Biblical miracle and it seemed as if the very locks on the prison cell were dropping. But they weren't. Then he sang a song he had composed himself. He waited until Governor Neff made his regular visit to the prison and then serenaded the Texas chief executive with his composition which ended with the lines, "If I had you, Hon. Governor Neff, where you got me I'd wake up in the morning and set you free."

The rest of the story recounted the singer's meeting with Lomax and their field trips to prisons. "In these excursions to the penitentiaries Ledbetter proves a great help. Dr. Lomax has him sing a folk song or two to show the convicts what kind of a song he wants."

Granted, the journalist might well have garbled some of the details; but it is remarkable the way Leadbelly apparently embroidered some of them. He did in fact see the Gulf of Mexico, but while he was traveling with Lomax, not while he was in Sugarland; indeed, the Gulf is some forty miles from the prison farm. And while Lomax was disappointed in Leadbelly's reaction to the Gulf, it apparently made more of an impression than he revealed at the time. In the account he now gave, Leadbelly started something he would become noted for in later years before northern audiences: taking bits of history and embroidering them into self-dramatized vignettes. Thus he here merged his vision of the Gulf with the story of the Sugarland songs. He also added the account of Paul and Silas, making himself appear a devout Christian unjustly imprisoned and clinging to his faith. There is little of this quality in Lomax's notes, and such piety would likely have surprised some of the guards and trusties who knew him in Sugarland.

The Modern Language Association was—and is—the nation's largest organization of scholars of literature and language; their meetings routinely included papers on every aspect of literature, as well as language, linguistics, history, and folk balladry. This was to be their fifty-first annual meeting; Lomax and his son had addressed them the year before, presenting the results of their pioneering 1933 recording trip. The audience would include many of the scholars then interested in folk songs, many ranking among the country's leading teachers and researchers. The 1934 program included a predictable mix of esoteric topics like "Milton's Autographs" and "The Barker Theory of Detached Consonants," but also included not one but two sessions in which Lomax and Leadbelly were scheduled to appear.

The first appearance was at the Friday evening smoker (December 28), listed on the program as a "subscription dinner and smoker," to be held in the elegant Crystal Ballroom at the Benjamin Franklin Hotel at seven-thirty. The MLA president, Professor Frank Aydelotte of Swarthmore (the host school), presided over some fifteen hundred members anxious to be entertained. Leadbelly's name did not actually appear on the formal MLA program for this session; it was listed as:

Negro Folksongs and Ballads, presented by John Lomax and Alan Lomax with the assistance of a Negro minstrel from Louisiana.

The entire evening program was out of the ordinary. It wasn't just a case of Leadbelly and Lomax holding forth; the session was begun with a set of "Elizabethan Ayres to the Virginals," presented by Mary Peabody Hotson from Haverford College; it ended with her husband, Leslie Hotson, leading the group in a sing-along featuring sea chanties. In between, just after the Elizabethan madrigals, came informal speeches by Henry Seidel Canby, editor of the well-known *Saturday Review of Literature*, and Marjorie Nicolson, the dean of Smith College. When the MLA entertainment committee earlier wrote to Lomax to set up the program, Thomas Scudder III had explained: "Now it occurs to me that if your negro, with his folk songs, and the Hotsons with their Elizabethan music, divide the program, the members will have furnished for them a treat of uncontaminated 'original' music which should live in their memories." The entire musical part of the program was set up to last forty minutes—twenty minutes for the Hotsons and twenty for the sea chanties—but with Leadbelly added, they would cut down on the sing-along. It was a good choice. Huddie performed in fine form, sitting at the center of the head table and entertaining his largest audience yet. Even Lomax admitted later that others might feel that it "smacked of sensationalism," but it served its purpose. It was a radical, history-making experiment, and it brought home to one of the nation's largest gathering of academics a sense of the living folk music tradition. And as he had started doing after Leadbelly's prison concerts and impromptu Washington concerts, he let the singer pass his hat at the end. Instead of pennies and nickels, though, the MLA crowd filled his hat with silver coins and dollar bills. History is silent about what Huddie himself thought of the "Elizabethan Ayres" or the sight of a room full of formally dressed scholars bellowing out sea chanties.

The next morning, a Saturday, Lomax and Leadbelly were up early to make another appearance, this one at the nine o'clock discussion group of "Comparative Literature II (Popular Literature)." This time the program makers saw fit to at least list Leadbelly by name:

"Comments on Negro Folksongs" (illustrated with voice and guitar by Negro convict Leadbelly of Louisiana).
                                   —*John A. Lomax, Library of Congress.*

For one of the first times in his public career, Huddie was identified by the name Leadbelly instead of Huddie Ledbetter; possibly this was a reflection of the fact that Lomax had used the Leadbelly name in *American Ballads and Folk Songs* and was trading on the current popularity of the new collection. Possibly, too, he had decided that if he was going to go public with the singer, the name would be more colorful and appropriate.

This time Leadbelly found himself in a program consisting of talks by some of the country's leading scholars of folklore. Edward F. Hauch talked about the then-current debate over how old ballads might have originated, Indiana University's Stith Thompson talked about his studies in classifying folk tale motifs, and Lomax's friend Reed Smith of the University of South Carolina summarized recent activity in collecting and studying American ballads. This group only numbered about ninety, but they were much more understanding of Huddie's music; in fact, they represented the cream of folk song experts in the country at that time. Their names included Ralph Boggs, Phillips Barry, Arthur Davis, Louise Pound, Henry Belden, and R. W. Gordon—most of whom had collected and/or published books about American folk music. Huddie's appearance before them was well received, but more importantly helped spread his name among people who really counted in the field of folklore. It would help Huddie personally in months to come, but it would also serve to expand the idea of just what a folk song was. Most of the members of that study group were still preoccupied with the nature of ballads, especially those that could be traced to Great Britain. Now here was Lomax and his "Negro convict" opening the door to a whole different vista of folk music: African American folk songs. Once again Leadbelly's old hat was passed, and filled. For the two appearances, the members of the MLA showed their gratitude to the tune of $47.50.

Before the group left for New York, there was time for one final appearance: a Sunday afternoon "tea" at the deanery at Bryn Mawr. Janice Reed Lit, from Haverford, had written Lomax ten days before and invited Lomax to come to a tea and give a talk; his old friend Owen Wister (author of the cowboy classic *The Virginian*) would be there. By the time Sunday arrived, the gathering had grown to include a "distinguished audience of Philadelphia literary and artistic elite" and Leadbelly had been included in the invitation; Lomax was nervous about the whole thing, more so than at the MLA meeting, and feared he would do what he tended to do when nervous—talk too much. That afternoon he drove to the campus and found their destination: the home of the college's former president, Thomas. As usual, Leadbelly wasn't the least intimidated; he recognized the campus as "one of the famous women's schools" and then commented, "Well, maybe they don't know it, but they is about to hear the famousest nigger guitar player in the world." In spite of his nerves, Lomax was impressed; he later asserted that it was that remark that made him think Leadbelly might be of interest to bookers and managers in New York, and that maybe he might have a career on his own. He put the thought aside for now, though, and introduced his singer to the group at hand. Dressed in formal evening clothes, they listened politely as Leadbelly sang songs like "Dicklicker's Holler" and "Whoa, Back, Buck." Later Mrs. Lit wrote a gushing letter, thanking him for the afternoon, proclaiming him a genius to have been able to see the importance of Leadbelly, but complaining about the fact that Lomax, against her specific request, had still let Leadbelly pass his hat. It infuriated Lomax that Leadbelly had not been paid for the performance in front of some of the wealthiest people on the East Coast and his hat passing had only netted $10.

If the Gulf of Mexico didn't excite Leadbelly, New York did. "Run under a mile of water to get in it!" he said, laughing, as the trio drove into the city on the afternoon of the last day of 1934. The stories of Fifth Avenue, the elevated railroad, the subways, the crowds, the taxis, all had penetrated even to the distant prison farms of Texas and Louisiana, and Leadbelly now felt he was indeed entering "the capitol of all the states in the world." The problem that had plagued the trio throughout their journey immediately presented itself again: how to work out lodgings for Huddie. Lomax was especially nervous about leaving him alone in New York, but soon found that no hotel or rooming house south of Harlem would let Leadbelly stay with them. Conversely, the Negro YMCA in Harlem would not let the Lomaxes stay with Leadbelly. Grudgingly, they agreed to separate, at least during the nights.

On the evening of New Year's Day, Leadbelly gave his first informal concert in New York. It was for a gathering of Columbia and New York University professors, as well as various writers and news reporters, hosted by a woman named Mary Barnicle. Barnicle was then a professor at New York University with a keen interest in folklore and folk song study, a graduate of Bryn Mawr and one of the most popular and controversial teachers in the city at the time. She had met John Lomax the year before as he was finishing *American Ballads and Folk Songs*. As Alan Lomax recalled: "When my father and I came to Macmillan Publishers in the fall of 1933, with our new songbook, we met Margaret Conklin, who was, at the time, the roommate of Ms. Barnicle." Conklin was a manuscript reader for Macmillan, and, like Barnicle, an enthusiast of folk culture. "Conklin took us home to meet Barnicle and we hit it off so splendidly that she invited us to talk and play records and sing for her classes the next day. . . . Between her and the Lomaxes it was a case of love at first sight. We came for supper and were invited to move into their big, bookfilled apartment for as long as we stayed in the city. My father was deeply moved by her appreciation of what he was trying, with very little support, to accomplish."

Now, on their return trip to the city, Barnicle arranged for the Lomaxes to stay with one of her friends, and set up the New Year's gathering. As usual, Leadbelly passed his hat and took in around $14; that, though, was not the biggest fallout from the party. Alan Lomax recalled that "the New York *Herald Tribune* rather accidentally wrote a feature story about Leadbelly that brought him national publicity. . . ." The story, indeed, came about under hectic circumstances. After the Barnicle party, Huddie had decided to go out on his own and sample some of the nightlife in Harlem. Lomax was nervous about this, for he and the singer had an appointment the following morning with George Brett, president of the Macmillan Company; he was interested in a book of Leadbelly songs as a sort of follow-up to *American Ballads and Folk Songs.* "Tomorrow is the most important day of your life," he told Leadbelly; it was essential that he get to their Washington Square apartment by eight o'clock, in time to get ready for the interview. Leadbelly promised, and then headed back uptown to Harlem.

Up until now Leadbelly had been nervous about the big city and had stuck close to the Lomaxes. By now his confidence was up, though; flush with hat money from his concerts, his ego boosted by the interviews and attention, he decided to sample the nightlife. He must have made it to the world-famous Cotton Club, where Duke Ellington won fame, and where now the headliner was bandleader Cab Calloway. Calloway's band and his singing—especially his highly mannered scat singing on songs like "Minnie the Moocher," "Reefer Man," and "Kicking the Gong Around"—were the hottest act in town. (It would be six months before Benny Goodman would make swing a national fad.) Leadbelly saw him, hit many of the bars in the area, and alternated gin and whiskey throughout the night. He never got to bed, and finally showed up at the Lomaxes' room two hours late. To make matters worse, a newspaper reporter from the *Herald Tribune* chose that morning to visit the trio. Huddie staggered in the door, tired and drunk, saying that Cab Calloway had offered him a thousand dollars to sing in his show. "If I wasn't so drunk," he muttered, "I could make a million dollars today."

Lomax got him to bed to sleep it off, and went on with the newspaper interview. The result appeared in the issue of January 3, right next to Walter Lippmann's column. It was probably the most important article in Leadbelly's career, as it introduced him to New York and to the world at large. It also would be the source of much of the Leadbelly legend in later years.

Lomax Arrives with Leadbelly, Negro Minstrel

SWEET SINGER OF THE SWAMPLANDS HERE TO DO A FEW TUNES BETWEEN HOMICIDES

Sniffs at Cab Calloway

WHY, HE HIMSELF HAS SUNG WAY TO 2 PRISON PARDONS

John A. Lomax, tireless student and compiler of American folk songs, has arrived in New York with his son, dozens of records made by them for the Library of Congress on a year's tour through the prisons and plantations of the South, and a walking, singing, fighting album of Negro ballads named Lead Belly, self-acknowledged king of the twelve-string guitar.

Lead Belly, born Huddie Ledbetter, of the Louisiana swamps, is a powerful, knife-toting Negro, who has killed one man and seriously wounded another, but whose husky tenor and feathery, string-plucking fingers ineluctably charm the ears of those who listen. Twice has Lead Belly sung for the Governors of Southern states, and twice has he been pardoned by them from serving long terms in state penitentiaries.

The sweet singer of the swamplands was sleeping off the effects of his first trip to Harlem yesterday when a visitor called on Mr. Lomax and his son, Alan, at the home of a friend at 181 Sullivan Street. Mr. Lomax apologized and said that Lead Belly would sing at a luncheon of alumni of the University of Texas at the Hotel Montclair tomorrow noon.

"BIG BOSS" AND "LITTLE BOSS"

To Lead Belly, Mr. Lomax, whose massive book "American Ballads and Folk Songs" was published by the Macmillan Company two months ago, is "Big Boss." His son and collaborator is "Little Boss." For these two the

Negro minstrel bears an undying affection which led him on September 1 to pledge to them his life and services till death should part them. He has followed them everywhere as chauffeur, handyman, and ever-ready musician and has asked for nothing but the privilege to continue.

All of this has proved at times a little embarrassing for "Big Boss" and "Little Boss," as Lead Belly's voice causes brown-skinned women to swoon and produces a violently inverse effect upon their husbands and lovers. A large scar which spans his neck from ear to ear bears witness to his dreadful charm and a knife that was fortuitously dull. Big Boss fears that in Harlem something catastrophic may happen when Lead Belly starts to sing.

Mr. Lomax was very much relieved when his faithful retainer returned unscathed yesterday morning from his first expedition to the metropolitan black belt. Lead Belly claimed that Cab Calloway was bidding for his services, even as agents and band leaders in Philadelphia had done when he sang there a few nights ago. For the famous orchestra leader and scat singer himself, however, Lead Belly expressed the greatest contempt.

"I can beat Cab Calloway singin' every time," Lead Belly told Big Boss and Little Boss, shedding a prodigious tear. "He don' know nothin' 'bout singin'."

So saying, he fell asleep with a big red bandanna over his face, and he was still in his slumbers several hours later when Mr. Lomax related the events leading up to their present association.

LEAD BELLY FOUND IN PRISON

"We were in Louisiana," he began, "continuing our work of making records of these unwritten folksongs of the road-gangs, the cotton pickers and the barrel-house singers for the Library of Congress on a grant from the Carnegie Corporation. We had discovered that the southern prisons were treasure troves of these ballads, for the convicts were encouraged to sing at their work. One drizzling rainy Sunday we visited the Louisiana State Prison at Angola, where Lead Belly was serving ten years for assault with intent to kill.

"He was dressed in stripes and for the entire day he played his guitar and sang for us. He has a repertoire of at least 500 songs which he knows by heart. Many of them he claims to have composed himself. There is no question as to his ability. He's better than any radio character I ever heard.

"At the end of the day he told us that he had written a song begging Governor Allen of Louisiana to pardon him. He had written to the Governor several times asking permission to sing it to him, as he had sung to Governor Pat Neff of Texas six years before when he was pardoned from serving forty years for murder in the Texas State Prison. We agreed therefore to make a

record of his petition on the other side of his favorite ballad, 'Irene.'

"I took the record to Governor Allen on July 1. On August 1 Lead Belly got his pardon. On September 1, I was sitting in a hotel in Texas when I felt a tap on my shoulder. I looked up and there was Lead Belly with his guitar, his knife and a sugar bag backed with all his earthly belongings. He said, 'Boss, here I is.' I took him up to my room and asked him what he was doing there and he replied, 'Boss, I came here to be your man. I belong to you.'

"I said, 'Well, after all, I don't know you. You're a murderer.' He said, 'Boss, it wasn't my fault. They attacked me. I had to fight back.' I told him that as a matter of fact I did need a driver for my car and might be able to use him, but I added, 'If some day you decide on some lonely road that you want my money and my car, don't use your knife on me. Just tell me and I'll give them to you. I have a wife and children back home and they'd miss me.'

"Well, at that tears came to his eyes and he said, 'Don' talk that way, Boss. Don' talk that way to me. I came here to be your man. You needn' ever tie your shoes again if you'll let me tie them. Boss if you ever get in trouble and some man tries to shoot you I'll jump in front of you and take the bullet before I let you get hurt.'

"Well, I suppose he was dramatizing a situation, but anyway I told him he could come along and he's been with us ever since. He's a fine driver and he keeps the car looking like new. There's not a lazy bone in his body. He's enormously powerful and claims that he has never been tired and never had a headache, though I suspect he has one now."

Mr. Lomax said that Lead Belly had been of great value to him on subsequent visits to the prisons. The authorities had always had great difficulty in explaining to the convicts just what sort of things he wanted. Thereafter, however, Lead Belly sang for the convicts and then asked them what they could do in turn.

"The only trouble after that," Mr. Lomax related, "was that the convicts were overeager. They all wanted to 'get on the record,' and they delayed me at times. We couldn't make them stop."

Lead Belly made a tremendous hit when he sang before the Modern Language Association in Philadelphia last Friday. He is scheduled to sing next week at Yale and a few days later at Harvard University, where Mr. Lomax is to lecture on his work. Mr. Lomax does not quite know what to do with him after that. Lead Belly, he explained, was a "natural," who had no idea of money, law or ethics and who was possessed of virtually no self-restraint. He is tremendously pleased with himself, and when Mr. Lomax told him before an appearance at Bryn Mawr a few days ago that he was about to sing at one of the most famous girls' colleges in the country, Lead Belly replied, 'Well, do they know they're goin' to hear the famousest guitar player in the world?' ". . . .

Mr. Lomax is one of America's authorities on balladries. He conceived an interest in folk songs when as a boy he heard cowboys sing on the Texas plains at night. Upon his graduation from Harvard he received the Sheldon Fellowship for the Investigation of American Ballads. In "American Ballads and Folk Songs" he includes the words and music of more than 200 such pieces. In the last year he has recorded 1,000 folk songs from all parts of the South for the Carnegie Corporation. His grant is exhausted, but he says he intends to continue on his own resources and to do a comprehensive job will require at least five more years. His home is in Austin, Tex.

Both Lomaxes were shocked when they saw the article, and especially how much the newspaper played up the sensational aspects of the story. "We hated that!!" recalls Alan. Both began to learn about the nature of big-city tabloid journalism, and how easily stories could get out of control. The irony was there, too: the very publicity that they needed could be bought only by emphasizing the violence in the singer's past.

But there was little time to reflect on this. The next day, the fourth, Lomax resumed the hectic schedule he had laid out for both he and Huddie. And first on it was an appearance, set up some weeks earlier, before a group Lomax had a special entrée to: the Texas-Exes.

17 Martha

The first two weeks in January saw a hectic round of meetings and performances that exhausted John Lomax and exhilarated Leadbelly. Many of these were private affairs given for foundation boards, publishing companies, university faculty gatherings, and gatherings of artists and writers—the cream of the city's philanthropic and cultural community. They exposed Leadbelly's music to a small but influential audience. But other performances resulted in serious and far-reaching publicity. The *Herald Tribune* story of January third, with its now-notorious "Sweet Singer of the Swamplands" leadline, was the first widely read newspaper account about the singer. The Texas-Exes gig on the fourth was the first real public appearance for Leadbelly. Now, a contact made at that event led to a third event the following week, one that netted Leadbelly even greater exposure: his first radio broadcast.

As a result of the Texas-Exes show, NBC had asked Leadbelly to audition for a guest shot on Rudy Vallee's network radio show. The audition was with Vallee's music arranger at two P.M. on Monday, January 7. On the surface, it would be difficult to imagine a more unsuited pair of musicians. Vallee was a Yale veteran who specialized in crooning (through a megaphone) songs like "Life Is Just a Bowl of Cherries" and "My Time Is Your Time." His weekly radio show, *The Fleischmann Hour*, was one of the nation's most popular, and helped promote the careers of Eddie Cantor and Burns and Allen. What his people thought of Leadbelly's booming voice and powerful guitar can only be guessed at. Even Leadbelly himself was intimidated; Lomax wrote to his wife that he saw Leadbelly "frightened" for the first time during the audition, and that he "did not do so well." And, in fact, the Vallee staff never got back to them.

In the meantime, another radio program had approached them: CBS's *The March of Time*, which aired nationwide from New York on Friday nights. A reporter and photographer from *Time* had seen Huddie at the Texas-Exes and done a story on him (which would not appear until the fourteenth), but in the early 1930s *Time*'s circulation manager Roy Edward Larsen had established a weekly radio show based on the magazine's most dramatic news stories of the week. In an age before cassette recorders and sound bites, preserving the actual sound and interviews of news events was next to impossible; to remedy this, Larsen invented a technique he called "newsacting," whereby professional actors impersonated newsmakers, reading from scripts and accompanied by sound effects and even music. (One actor learned to impersonate President Franklin Roosevelt so well that the White House finally complained, saying that the chief executive was tired of having to answer to comments that he had never actually made.) Over all the scripted news loomed a stentorian announcer proclaiming that "Time marches on"—and plugging the current issue of the magazine.

On January 8, the program managers met with Leadbelly and Lomax and decided they had enough character and personality to carry off the segment of the show about them in person, without actors. There was a rehearsal at the Columbia studios on Thursday, and here Huddie did not seem intimidated; he sang well and enjoyed the excitement of a big-time radio rehearsal. The show had a staff of about seventy-five, including a full orchestra and an elaborate sound effects team, and was done live. By now it had become one of radio's most popular shows, sent out all over the country; *Variety* described it as "the apex of radio showmanship." It would be Huddie's first exposure to a genuine nationwide audience.

The show went off with no problems on Friday evening at nine over WABC. The featured story was a dramatized news report on the story that had dominated the New York papers ever since Leadbelly had arrived: the Bruno Hauptman trial. Hauptman had been charged in the kidnapping and death of the Lindbergh baby, and papers were running several pages a day of the trial transcript and the latest sensational revelations. The wreck of the luxury liner *Havana* and the opening of the New York automobile show were other stories covered. Then it was time for Leadbelly and Lomax; the latter narrated and "named" the songs, and Huddie sang. Once again the chain gang story was dramatized, simplified, and sent out to a huge audience—except this time the audience was not just in New York, but nationwide, in literally millions of homes. Roy Edward Larsen invited the group to come home with him for an informal party, to meet other *Time* writers and to meet a Mr. Loew of Loew's theater chain. Leadbelly, John Lomax, and his two sons Alan and John, Jr. (who was in college nearby and had brought about twenty friends to the radio broadcast), all attended. Lomax was a bit put out by this—he stipulated that they would have to leave early to catch the train back—and didn't care much for Loew and the other "theater magnates," calling him "hard-faced," and "repulsive." It was a jaded audience, and one that was hard for Leadbelly to win over, but by now he was learning how to ingratiate himself with such audiences. "He conquered them completely," wrote Lomax the next morning, and as usual the fans showered the singer with cash, including two $5 bills. "Leadbelly of this moment is the most famous [black man] in the world," Lomax wrote his wife, "and I the most notorious white man."

Leadbelly had always had an eclectic repertoire that had included jazz and pop songs, ragtime, turn-of-the-century sentimental songs, parodies, and the like; now he also began to add some of these to his programs. He was especially fond of "That Silver-Haired Daddy of Mine," the big cowboy hit of 1932 that Gene Autry had popularized. (In fact, Huddie loved Autry's music and eventually got a chance to meet him.) He was also fond of doing songs associated with Jimmie Rodgers, "America's Blue Yodeler," who had died in 1933; Rodgers's songs were full of yodels, and Huddie could imitate these perfectly. (He once called Lomax and, to prove he was sober and in good voice, yodeled to him over the phone.) He also performed an occasional jazz song, like "I'm in Love with You, Baby." Such songs bothered the Lomaxes, and Huddie could never understand why they didn't like them; they felt he was only a poor imitator in these songs, and encouraged him to stick to his prison songs and older folk songs. They were the "money-getters from his white hearers," wrote Lomax.

By the morning after the *March of Time* radio show, after twelve days of the New York whirlwind, both Lomaxes were worrying about whether all the success and adulation was going to Huddie's head. He was, after all, suddenly making more cash money than he ever had in his life; Lomax was by now refusing any engagement unless Huddie was allowed to pass his hat. He was hearing the kinds of offers that theater, radio, and record company agents were making; and he was winning approval from the wealthy and powerful of all sorts. No country singer had ever hit it bigger or any faster. Lomax often reminded reporters of something that obviously impressed him: that barely five months before, Huddie Ledbetter was simply another convict sweltering in Angola Prison. It would have been a miracle if some of it had not gone to Huddie's head.

Nonetheless, in a letter to his wife, Lomax confessed that he and Alan were "disturbed and distressed at his beginning tendency to show off in his songs and talk, when his money value is to be natural and sincere as he was in prison." If the trend continues, he added, Leadbelly "will lose his charm" and become only an ordinary Harlem black. Lomax was still nervous, too, from what he called the "terrible debauch in Harlem" that occurred the night they had arrived, when Leadbelly staggered in drunk with the offer from Cab Calloway. Lomax didn't let the singer forget that he had missed an important appointment with Macmillan over that, and Leadbelly was his usual contrite self over the incident. Still, it preyed on Lomax, and he seemed to worry about losing his influence over the singer.

John Lomax's role in the presentations was far more than that of just an emcee. He was still a well-known and popular lecturer, a polished and spellbinding speaker of the old school. Though he was by nature a shy man, he had taught himself over the years how to captivate an auditorium, and how to entertain as well as instruct. Many of the colleges that were now

wanting to book him and Leadbelly had in fact booked Lomax himself
earlier, and they knew he was an effective "act" who could draw and please
crowds. It was not only Leadbelly that was booked, but Lomax and Leadbelly as a pair. Alan Lomax recalled of these early programs that his father
"introduced Leadbelly, interpreted his utterly novel material, made it un-
derstandable, just as do modern [folk festival] presenters, but with far more
charm."

Off-stage, Lomax did all the booking, relying on his own reputation as a
speaker and, in many cases, his contacts in the college community. He also
did publicity, handled the money, and "protected" his partner from various
dubious offers which he would inevitably get. "We have to keep Leadbelly
away from the crowd and whisk him off as soon as he is done playing and
passing his hat," he wrote to Ruby Terrill. All in all, Lomax was far more
than just a manager or booking agent for Leadbelly.

The frantic pace was starting to take its toll on the sixty-eight-year-old
Lomax. He was, after all, overweight (about two hundred pounds), had a
temperamental stomach, and was having to deal with Alan's illness as well.
"Up to now this experiment has been a sort of nightmare," he wrote. "I
hate the hard faces of the gold hunters. I despise the female cranks and
celebrity hunters." Lomax was by no means a country boy being thrilled by
New York, but that was part of the problem: He knew enough to see
through many of the phony offers and claims, and he was perceptive
enough to see loopholes in a contract. But the sheer intensity of the round
of meetings, performances, interviews, rehearsals, and a telephone that
never stopped ringing would have taxed a veteran publicity agent. By January 15, he was writing to his wife in Texas: "I have sought no publicity; in
every way I have avoided and run from it." By then he was turning down
all social engagements, even with old friends like Dorothy Scarborough. "I
must save myself and meeting strangers and engaging in small talk makes
me utterly miserable and on a nervous strain." A letter to his wife was so
sad and discouraged that Lomax asked Alan to append a note to it, apologiz-
ing for its tone and explaining that he was "entirely weary" over everything.

Lomax never really explained his exact motives for bringing Leadbelly
into New York. Alan Lomax is not at all sure that his father had originally
planned to have Leadbelly perform in New York City. After all, Leadbelly
was his driver and he may have simply needed his services while he traveled
around visiting various foundation boards in his search for funding. Lomax
was clearly in a situation where he was having to improvise. All that is
certain is that at some point during these early days, Lomax realized that
Leadbelly might be able to actually make money in performing if he were
"presented" properly to a northern audience and managed properly.

To that end, Lomax presented Leadbelly with a management contract on January 5, the day after the Texas-Exes concert, with all its various offers. In it, the singer agreed to have Lomax represent him as "exclusive manager, personal representative and advisor." In consideration of "past services" to Leadbelly, and in respect to radio, stage, concert, phonograph records, and recitals, the singer agreed to have Lomax represent him for a period of five years. For this service, Leadbelly agreed to give to Lomax fifty percent of all money earned, and empowered him to receive the funds and deduct any commissions or expenses before turning them over to the singer. During the five years, the singer could not accept any jobs without his manager's written consent. A couple of weeks later a supplement to the original contract was signed; it added to the management the services of Alan Lomax and changed the percentage. Now Leadbelly was to get only one third of his income (after expenses), with the Lomaxes getting two thirds. The agreement seems outrageous by modern standards, but Lomax probably had little to guide him; he had just seen dozens of eager promoters trying to sign Leadbelly up at the Texas-Exes concert, and felt a real sense of urgency to protect his "client." Had he taken the time to talk to other promoters or agents to see what they were charging, he would have found that his agreement was not far out of line with the industry norms of the day. Commissions of between forty and fifty percent were not unusual and, of course, the Lomaxes' role was far more complicated than simply sitting in a New York City office suite and booking engagements for Huddie Ledbetter. Lomax was half the act, and he worked as hard on his part of the program as Leadbelly did on his. Leadbelly knew only that his "Big Boss" had taken care of him for the last three months, borne all of their expenses out of his own pocket, brought him to the big city, and made it possible for him to pass his hat and get more money in one night than he used to see in a year of backbreaking work. With no hesitation, he signed.

Lomax decided to give New York another week; if he didn't sign some contract that meant "real money" by the twelfth, the team would return to Washington and sort out the field recordings from the last three months that had been shipped there. His best bet was some sort of long-term radio deal, but if that didn't materialize, he was hoping for a book contract. He had been talking to Macmillan about a quick book that would be called *Leadbelly and His Songs*, and on the seventh he and Leadbelly had performed before a gathering of fifty Macmillan employees. The hat had yielded only $14.30, but the editors, led by Margaret Conklin, had been enthusiastic. As it turned out, none of the radio prospects panned out, nor did any of the possibilities for theater work. Initial contacts were made, though, for a series of commercial records with the huge American Record Company. Leadbelly would make some twenty double-faced records and receive a royalty of 2 cents a record—actually a good offer for that day and time. "In time this should make some income," Lomax wrote his wife. But more important to Lomax was an offer that came from Macmillan, an offer not for one, but two books: a volume on his adventures while song collecting, and the book on Leadbelly. The latter was to be done first, of course, to take advantage of the intense publicity surrounding the singer. Lomax felt that the whole book could be whipped up in no more than a month or so of intense work and decided to stay in New York in order to complete it. Meanwhile, Leadbelly could continue to do shows in the area to pick up spending money. The only problem was how to find peace and quiet to do the writing.

During these early days in the city, Alan and John Lomax had been staying in the big book-lined apartment of Mary Barnicle and Margaret Conklin, and Leadbelly had been staying in the Harlem YMCA. Conklin and Barnicle knew that little work would get done on the book as long as their guests were there; too many reporters had their phone number, and the logistics of getting Leadbelly back and forth were tiring out everybody. As it turned out, the two women also shared a summer house out in Wilton, Connecticut, about fifty miles from New York on the Norfolk River. Here was a place where the three could stay together and have the kind of solitude needed for the book; the house didn't even have a phone. The women offered it to the team, rent free, for the rest of the winter. Lomax gratefully accepted, and on January 8, a Tuesday, Barnicle took the day off to drive out and open the place up. Leadbelly and Alan and John Lomax followed the next day.

The day before the Connecticut move, Lomax made another far-reaching decision. In a letter written the morning of the eighth, he told his wife, "If Leadbelly is not drunk this morning, I have promised to wire today money to bring Martha to him." He had been thinking of this earlier; at another point, he wrote that as soon as he and Huddie made their management contract, he would do this. Certainly he felt Martha would help control his singer, help stabilize his wanderings. Though he had actually had little trouble since the Harlem escapade, Lomax constantly feared that Leadbelly would start drinking again (he claimed gin helped clear his voice for singing) and take off on another night out. With the move to the country, she would help ease the boredom for the singer and would also serve as a cook and maid for the team. Huddie was delighted at the news, "shouting happy over Martha's coming," but they ran into a problem almost immediately. Leadbelly did not like the idea of sending money directly to Martha; for reasons of his own, which he never explained to anyone, he felt she couldn't be trusted with such an amount (around $40). Lomax then tried to find someone in Shreveport who could receive the money and make sure Martha got on the train; some banker friends refused outright, but finally Macmillan came through by having one of their representatives contact C. M. "Red" Leman of the Shreveport firm of Hirsch and Leman. The firm agreed to make the travel arrangements and visit Martha; in the meantime, the Shreveport *Times* got hold of the story and ran a major article about it. They assumed, as perhaps did Leman, that Martha and Huddie were already married.

Thus began a strange comedy of errors. Martha told Red Leman that she couldn't leave at once, that she had to get rid of her household goods; there was no way she could go until January 17, eight days later. Leman dutifully wired this to Lomax on the ninth. By this time, the team had gotten very busy and Lomax did not feel especially worried about the delay. Leadbelly, though, was angry and disappointed, and decided to take things into his own hands. He sent a wire directly to Martha:

Martha Promise I wants you to come on to New York now. When I tell you something means I want you to do it and not wait. Shut your doors and come on. Some other Shreveport wimmen will come when I say come. I looks for you want to marry you at once as you are[.]
Huddie Ledbetter

(Oddly, in the next day's *Tribune* a slightly different text of this telegram was given, omitting the "other Shreveport wimmen" reference and adding that "Boss and Little Boss and I will meet you at the train and take you to our home, where you and I will cook and keep house for them.") Not satisfied with this earlier message, Leadbelly later that day sent a second:

Hurry up we are all waiting for you don't be frightened I'll be at the train steps waiting to kiss you just as soon as you arrive in New York.

Whether it was the fact that she was hearing directly from Huddie, the promise of marriage, or the sense of urgency in the tone of the wires, it worked. Martha agreed to leave on Friday, the eleventh, and Leman got her the tickets and put her on the train. Then he wired New York that Martha would leave at five P.M. on the Illinois Central, arrive in Washington at seven-fifteen Sunday morning, and get into Penn Station just after noon on Sunday. She was sitting in an Illinois Central railroad car Friday night when Leadbelly made his radio debut on *The March of Time*.

Lomax described Martha to a *Tribune* reporter:

Martha Promise is an intelligent, sweet-faced Negro woman with some education and an admirable character. She is not a kept woman, but rather *a woman who has been keeping a man. When Leadbelly was hungry and broke, after getting out of jail, she took him in out of the cold, though her salary in the laundry wherein she worked was only $4 a week. I promised her at the door of the laundry when I last saw her a few months ago that if Leadbelly would behave himself I would feed him, clothe him and give him a good bed to sleep in every night, and deliver him back to her safe and sound. I also told her that if Leadbelly made any money I wouldn't give it to him and let him waste it, but would keep it safe and bring it back to Shreveport to buy them a home where they could spend the rest of their lives in comfort.*

The promise to Martha, he added, had been the "strongest restraining influence on the boy" during the trip. Her frequent letters to him had constantly admonished the singer to "stay by Boss."

And, in truth, Martha was a much more interesting and complex woman than most of Leadbelly's liaisons. She was older, had known him for most of her life, and was a stable member of the Shreveport community. She seemed to have a good sense of what Lomax was trying to do as he worked with Leadbelly in his travels, and supported it. The fact that she had taken in the singer when he was just out of jail suggests she cared deeply for him—enough to risk her reputation as a choir singer and good citizen. The wire from New York must have come as a shock to her; neither Lomax nor Huddie seemed to appreciate just what they were asking Martha to do. With virtually no warning, she was expected to quit her good job, close up her house, pack, and take a long, punishing train ride to a huge, intimidating city she had only heard of. She had no idea of how long the move was to last. Still, she did it. It was a leap of faith, and a powerful testimony to her feelings for Huddie. Thus on Sunday an odd delegation stood on the train platform at Pennsylvania Station. Huddie, who had slept little the night before, was dressed for the occasion. He wore a double-breasted tan suit with red pinstripes, a tan shirt, and a dark red tie; around his neck was a white silk scarf, which he planned to present to Martha. Lomax, cigar in mouth, dressed in his usual suit and vest, stood nearby (Alan was ill and stayed in Wilton). Standing a little off to the side was a group of newspaper writers, photographers, curious onlookers, and a coterie of redcaps who worked at the station and were curious about what was attracting all the attention. Martha's arrival had been trumpeted in the papers for the last three days, yielding headlines like HOMICIDAL HARMONIZER AT THE TRAIN FROM DIXIE and SWEET SINGER OF THE SWAMP GRINS ALL OVER AS "BOSS" LOMAX WIRES FOR BRIDE. Now it was nearing noon, and Huddie was pacing up and down on the platform for Track No. 8, where the 12:05 from Washington was due in on time.

The train pulled in, doors opened, and passengers began to spill out on the platform. Huddie broke away from Lomax and dashed down to the end of the platform. No Martha. He ran back to the other end, searching among the people coming out of the front cars. By now he was looking worried, and even Lomax was frowning in puzzlement. As the passengers made their way upstairs and the platform began to empty out, Huddie's search became more frantic. The photographers lowered their cameras, waiting to see what was going to happen. By now Huddie was looking through the empty cars of the train, moving from one to the other. Still there was no Martha. John Lomax was concerned as well: perhaps all his complicated plans with Martha had gone askew; perhaps she had gotten on the wrong train.

Finally the pair, still trailed by reporters and photographers, walked over to ask if there was another train due in from Washington soon. In fact, another train was due in soon—in just twenty minutes. Huddie decided that Martha had somehow missed her regular connection and would be aboard this one. Lomax was dubious, but agreed to wait for the 12:35 and see. A *Tribune* reporter later described the next few minutes:

> . . . *they go upstairs to the cafeteria for a cup of coffee. Leadbelly, too heartsick to eat, sits glumly with his head bowed above the rising fumes. Mr. Lomax, sympathetic and worried, drinks his coffee and lights a new cigar. The minutes crawl, but 12:35 finally comes and again hopefully the two men stand upon the platform. Leadbelly toys with his white silk scarf, after he has flashed it in the public eye for a few hours, he proposes to present it to Martha.*

Once again the train from the South hissed to a halt; once again the doors opened and passengers spilled onto the platform; once again, Huddie ran from car to car, searching for the familiar face. Once again, there was no Martha.

Dejectedly, the small band climbed back up the stairs. Some of the photographers were starting to pack up, convinced the show was over. Lomax and Leadbelly conferred; Lomax was concerned about his sick son Alan, left alone in the old farmhouse, and wanted to get back to him. Huddie was determined to find out what had gone wrong with Martha. He would stay at the station all night, if necessary, and meet every train that came up from the South; he had promised Martha he would be there, and he would. It seemed a good plan; but before he left, Lomax decided to check to see if any communication at all had arrived from Martha or from Red Leman. He went off to call Margaret Conklin to see if anything had arrived at Macmillan; he asked Huddie and the *Tribune* reporter to see if any telegrams had been sent to them at the station itself.

As Huddie and the reporter got to the telegraph desk, a redcap asked the reporter if he was Mr. Lomax. No, he answered, but he knew where Mr. Lomax was. The redcap explained there was a lady in the waiting room who had just sent a telegram to a Mr. Lomax at Wilton, Connecticut. "That's my wife! That's my wife!" shouted Huddie, and rushed back out to the waiting room. Almost at once he ran into Lomax, who had with him a woman whom the reporter later described as "a tall, sweet-faced Negro woman with a brilliant smile and lustrous eyes." It was indeed Martha, and Huddie ran to embrace her. The reporters, suddenly energized, gathered around to watch the reunion; the photographers loaded their flashbulbs, and began to shoot.

What had happened? Leadbelly wanted to know. Why wasn't Martha on the train? Martha Promise laughed. "I just got an early train by accident," she said. "I got here 20 minutes to twelve, so I just walked in here to sit down and wait till you came." In the excitement of meeting the train on the platform, no one had thought to check the waiting room upstairs. While Leadbelly had been dashing through empty cars, Martha had been sitting quietly upstairs, wondering when she could get something to eat. "Were you scared, honey?" Huddie asked. "No, I wasn't scared," said Martha. "I knew you'd find me all right. I was much more scareder on the train." The trio set out, planning to get Martha some lunch, and to get back out to Wilton. A marriage would follow as soon as they could get a license, Lomax told reporters, and Leadbelly had to get back to his busy schedule. He was set up to make forty records for a major company and was set to sing at Harvard next week. In a day or two, he could tell them the exact day of the wedding. With all the publicity about Martha coming, Lomax was worried about delaying the wedding too long. The week before, he had written his wife that if this didn't happen soon, he feared Leadbelly would be charged for violating the Mann Act—a 1910 piece of legislation that prohibited the "interstate transportation" of women for immoral purposes. There was probably little chance of this—the law was designed to curtail white slavery—but Lomax was, as usual, being cautious. And, to be sure, Huddie had promised to marry Martha as soon as she arrived and was anxious himself to get things under way. By Tuesday, the fifteenth, the pair went to the town clerk at Wilton and applied for a marriage license: It was only $5, but under Connecticut law they had to wait a full five days before they could use it. Martha also had to swear that she had in fact "secured two or three divorces" (Lomax's words). This set the date for the twentieth, and at once the media started flocking around again. That afternoon, an Associated Press photographer appeared, arguing that he needed lead time to get their photos ready for the wedding story.

The wedding promised to be a public event, and throughout the week

Huddie and Martha made their preparations like any bride and groom. Since he had signed a contract with Huddie, John Lomax started keeping a notebook of all his expenses, and the entries for the week of January 20 are full of wedding references. In between all these things, jobs continued to come in. On the fifteenth a society woman offered Leadbelly $100 to play for a cocktail party she was giving, and a few days later he sang at a party given by Lomax's other son John, Jr. On the fourteenth an executive from the American Record Company drove fifty miles from downtown to hear Huddie sing and to work out details for the upcoming recording session. Martha wasted no time in fitting in; the Monday after she arrived, she began cleaning the kitchen, made a grocery list, and walked ten miles into Norwalk to shop. Throughout it all, Huddie shouted and sang, excited and ready to step into his new career.

The ceremony itself was set for noon on Sunday, January twentieth—the earliest moment after the probationary period was up. Two of the most important guests arrived on Saturday—Margaret Conklin and Mary Elizabeth Barnicle. Huddie liked both of them and affectionately called them "Conkle" and "Bonkle." They settled in and then went with Alan and Martha to buy the wedding dress. John Lomax, Jr., had come down for the weekend, and the Saturday afternoon was spent plotting the final touches. John Lomax would give the bride away; Alan would be Huddie's best man. Officiating would be the Reverend Samuel Wendell Overton, pastor of the Bethel A.M.E. Church in Norwalk, about ten miles away. The event would be held at the Wilton farmhouse. Huddie watched over all this, beaming, and finally mentioned something that surprised everyone: his wedding day would also be his birthday. Even Lomax was a little taken aback, since Huddie had been evasive and contradictory about his age. He also announced that he would be forty-six on Sunday (though census records would make him forty-seven).

Sunday dawned with bad weather: snow and sleet. Sitting at his dining room table, Lomax worried about how the guests would arrive, whether the minister could make it the ten miles out from Norwalk, how many reporters and photographers would make the trek. But things began to jell, and the wedding party began to assemble. Three deacons of the church made it— Leonard Brown, Maurice Podd, and Sol Nichols—and Gertrude King, a friend of Barnicle and Conklin from New York, was there. Photographers from *Time* arrived, as well as reporters from the New York and Norwalk papers. At noon the bride and groom appeared.

Leadbelly had on another double-breasted suit, this one cinnamon with red stripes. Martha's wedding dress was a black silk frock, with a striped yoke and sleeves. To top it off, the groom wore white formal gloves; they were tight and uncomfortable, and Martha joked later that she had had trouble finding gloves big enough to fit Huddie's hands. The ceremony was brief and to the point; the only hitch was when Alan. the best man, dropped the ring as he was handing it to Huddie. Within minutes it was over, and Huddie found himself formally married again—for only the second time. He was no longer the restless, roaming free spirit he had been the first time; now he was nearing fifty, well into middle age, hundreds of miles from the hardships of Caddo Parish, scarred but not broken, ready at last to find a better way to live his life. If Martha was willing to commit to him, he would commit to her. He must have sensed that this would be his last marriage, and that it would last until the end.

But the reflective mood, if there was one, did not last long. Huddie "saluted his bride"; Lomax slapped him on the back; off came the formal gloves and out came the guitar. Huddie began singing:

> *I'm in love with you, honey,*
> *You said you'd love me too, honey,*
> *I'm in love with you, honey,*
> *It's funny, but it's true, honey,*
> *None but you will do, honey.*

One of the deacons shouted, and the guests applauded. The Reverend Overton, a chubby, bespectacled man who had recently returned from serving eighteen years as a missionary in Liberia, smiled in spite of himself, and Huddie rose to the occasion. He readjusted the old green twelve-string and began a new song.

> *A yellow-skinned woman keeps you worried all the time,*
> *A yellow-skinned woman makes a moon-eyed man go blind,*
> *But a dark-skinned woman makes a jack-rabbit hug a hound,*
> *And makes a dark-skinned preacher lay his Bible down.*

The Reverend Overton gasped in surprise and one of the deacons laughed, saying, "Preacher, you better hold that Bible tight!" When he had recovered his composure, the good reverend said to Lomax, "I think you made him sing that song for me. Oh my, you have to have a good deal of religion to stay around this place."

Then abruptly Huddie put down his old guitar and started to dance. He started off with the kind of tap dance he had done twenty years before in the streets of Dallas with Blind Lemon. A reporter wrote: "With a broomstick on his shoulder he shuffled and slapped and clicked his heels in the rhythm of an impromptu buck and wing." Lomax was surprised; the dancing was something new to him. "He pulls new rabbits out of his hat every day," he told the *Tribune* man. In the meantime, the deacons were urging him on. "Step it, boy, step it," cried Deacon Podd. "He's going to town," shouted Deacon Nichols. Afterward, Martha sat on Huddie's lap, smiling. It didn't matter now that she had been forced to leave her home in Shreveport on two days' notice, nor that she had endured a brutal two-day train ride, nor even that her wedding dress had been purchased off a sale rack in Norwalk, marked at $3, down from $12.95. "I've never been so happy in my life," she told a reporter.

Things started winding down, but there was a moment for John Lomax to reflect a bit for the benefit of the reporters. "This is probably the first Negro wedding that ever took place in Connecticut where a white man gave the bride away and another acted as best man. It's done in the South, but we feel differently about Negroes down there. Here in the North, you sympathize with Negroes as an oppressed race, but don't know them as individuals. In the South, though, we don't think about the race as a whole, we get to know and love the individual Negro." The reporters nodded, polite and a little confused.

Then Lomax got up and reminded Huddie that he needed to save his voice. Even though it was his wedding day, it was also a working day. At five P.M. they were scheduled to play at a special party, on a date that had been booked long before the wedding date had been set. The owner of the Brooklyn *Daily Eagle*, Preston Goodfellow, was having a cocktail party at his home on Argyle Road in Brooklyn. He had paid Lomax $50 for Leadbelly's services: to sing and play for a number of "distinguished guests." Among them was the mayor of New York, Fiorello Henry La Guardia.

18 "You Don't Know My Mind"

The house in Wilton, which would be the headquarters for Leadbelly, Martha, and the Lomaxes for the next two months, was a two-hundred-year-old New England farmhouse. It had once been owned by Francis Perkins, who was now serving in the Roosevelt cabinet as Secretary of Labor. It was hardly a cottage: there were three bedrooms upstairs, several rooms and a cellar downstairs, and a picturesque stone fence outside. It was built into the side of a hill, surrounded by venerable trees, including a massive fir that was all of eighty feet tall. From the sitting room window one could see a nearby lake. The water came from a pump, and only after Lomax moved in was there even a telephone. It was ideal for someone wanting to get away, and Lomax looked forward to getting some real work done on the book manuscript—which he continued to think he could finish in a month.

The week after the wedding made both Leadbelly and Lomax wonder if even the move to Wilton would slow down their pace. Almost every day they found themselves going back into New York for one thing or another. The most important was the start of a series of commercial recordings for the American Recording Corporation. Back on the eighth Huddie had signed a contract for this, and since then had met with the chief "artist and repertory" (A & R) man for the organization, Art Satherley. Though royalty rates were set at 2 cents per record sold, the company offered a $250 advance against royalties.

Though Lomax complained that this record company was the kind that sold their product at 25 cents each in cheap dime stores, it was probably the largest in the country in 1935. ARC had been formed from the wreckage of a number of smaller record companies that had not survived the Depression, and by 1935 it had absorbed several major labels, including the once powerful Columbia label, as well as OKeh, Brunswick, Vocalion, Cameo, Banner, and Perfect. The company issued records under these and other labels, and ranged across the pop music spectrum from cowboy singer Gene Autry to bandleader Duke Ellington. ARC had an especially popular race series that included Big Bill Broonzy, a double-entendre group called the Hokum Boys, Tampa Red and Leroy Carr, and a blues shouter named Memphis Minnie. ARC did indeed have a series of labels that were sold exclusively in dime stores for 25 cents—about a third of the 75 cents then charged by a major label like Victor. Their Romeo label, for instance, was sold through the S.H. Kress dime stores, and their Oriole label was sold through the chain store McCrory's; other labels were custom pressed for sale through Sears, Roebuck's catalogs. Usually an ARC recording appeared on five or six different labels, sometimes using various pseudonyms for the artist.

The contract called for Huddie to deliver forty songs—twenty double-sided 78 rpm records—and the plan was to record these at four sessions in January. Huddie would travel into the city, to the ARC studio at 1776 Broadway, and do ten masters a day. By modern standards, Huddie would be doing the equivalent of almost an album a day for four days; by modern standards, he would be fortunate to get one or two usable sides per day. But this was 1935, and ARC was the most cost-conscious of all the labels; the music was cut onto big wax discs, there were few retakes, and there was no splicing to fix a mistake. Blues and folk artists of the time were used to having to get their records done in the first try, and within a matter of minutes. On one day in Chicago not long before, the ARC engineers had managed to get some twenty-three blues and gospel masters done, most of them releasable. Since the company expected great things from the Lead-belly sides, they did give him the opportunity to make alternate takes on many of his titles.

Still, it was a brutal pace. On three consecutive days, January 23, 24, and 25, the singer managed his ten titles a day. He was still using the old twelve-string Stella he had brought with him from prison, and Lomax in his spare time had been searching all over New York to find him a new one. (Ironically, the factory for the Stellas was just over in New Jersey.) He finally found one, for $16.80, but not until January 30, after most of the ARC sessions were finished. Thus for these important first records, Lead-belly used his old guitar; judging from the sound on some sides, he also occasionally used a six-string guitar, probably Alan's.

Coincidentally, an old Texas connection helped to solidify the recording deal between Lomax and ARC. During his undergraduate days at the University of Texas at Austin, Maurice Woodward "Tex" Ritter had been introduced to Lomax's influential book and articles on cowboys songs in a literature class. Ritter was delighted to know that someone had collected and annotated many of the songs that he had known since he was a child. *Cowboy Songs* helped to shape his musical interests, which included religious shape-note singing, light opera, and popular songs, in addition to the cowboy tunes. By the late 1920s Ritter was breaking into show business in New York City and beginning his long recording career. Ritter struggled through the Depression, but a break came his way when he earned a spot as a member of a daily radio program on WINS, *Cowboy Tom's Roundup*, in 1933. In March 1933 he recorded a breakthrough record, "Rye Whiskey," for ARC, which became his trademark in later years. Ritter was still in New York City working on the radio in early 1935 when Lomax and Leadbelly hit town: "Mr. John A. Lomax brought him to New York and I met him the first day he was in town." It was Ritter who helped to smooth the way for his old hero, introducing him to the right people at ARC, including his own A & R man, Art Satherley.

Art Satherley was an Englishman who had worked his way up through the pioneer days of recording. He was by now the company's expert on hillbilly and race records. (He would later gain fame as the man who signed up country singer Hank Williams.) Satherley obviously saw Leadbelly's commercial value as that of a blues singer, possibly as a modern-day successor to Blind Lemon Jefferson, who had died just a little over five years before. The first two days' work was full of such classic blues, including Huddie's version of one of Jefferson's best-known songs, "That Black Snake Moan." Essentially the same as Jefferson's, Huddie's version was entitled "New Black Snake Moan." Then there was "Packin' Trunk Blues," Huddie's shortened version of the song Jefferson had recorded in Chicago in 1927 and called "Match Box Blues." In fact, on Huddie's last ARC session, not held until February 5, he forgot he had already done this song and recorded it a second time, this time calling it "Match Box Blues." Another song, "C.C. Rider," was derived from Jefferson's popular "Corinna Blues" from 1927. "Red River" was close in style to Blind Lemon, and later Huddie recorded his tribute song, "My Friend, Blind Lemon."

Missing from these sessions were several songs that Lomax had originally recorded in Angola and which Leadbelly used in his New York concerts: "The Western Cowboy," "Frankie and Albert," and "Ella Speed." Apparently these songs were not bluesy enough for Satherley and crew; like so many commercial record producers, they had a simplistic perception of black folk music. They divided folk and folklike music into two camps: Whites performed hillbilly and cowboy songs, while the black singers played blues and spirituals. A black man like Huddie, whose complicated repertoire ranged across these arbitrary lines, seemed problematic for them. They finally did consent to record "Irene," but it was never issued.

Some of the ARC songs showed Leadbelly's awareness of some of the race and hillbilly records that companies like ARC had been releasing over the last seven or eight years. However, well over half the forty songs done at this time were actually Leadbelly's own unique canon. They included versions of "Alberta" and "Roberta," old Fannin Street barrelhouse songs; "Julie Ann Johnson" and "Pick a Bale of Cotton," derived from the work songs he heard as a youth; prison songs like "Shorty George" and "Texas Penitentiary"; as well as his famous pardon songs to O. K. Allen and Pat Neff. It is easy to imagine the Lomaxes fighting to include the older tradi-

tional songs they knew from Leadbelly, while the record company men
sought to get the classic country blues that they defined as race music. In
fact, Alan Lomax found Satherley difficult to deal with. He recalls the ARC
chief during the recording shouting, "Hit it up! Hit it up!" on the wrong
beat of Huddie's performance. In terms of what was actually recorded, it
was a draw; both sides were well represented. But when it came time to
decide which of the masters to release, the ARC heads prevailed; it was they
alone who made that decision. And the releases were weighted in favor of
the blues.

The company managed to get two of the records out within a month;
they told Huddie that they were testing the waters and would see how these
did before they proceeded further. The first was "Packin' Trunk Blues"
backed with "Honey, I'm All Out and Down." Both were blues—the first
Huddie's version of the Blind Lemon song, the second what the singer
described as a "barrelhouse two-step." The record was eventually issued
under Huddie's own name on no fewer than six of ARC's labels: Banner,
Melotone, Oriole, Perfect, Romeo, and Paramount. At the same time was
issued the second disc, "Four Day Worry Blues" (learned from Era Washington) and "New Black Snake Moan." They were issued on the same set
of labels as the previous record, and everybody sat back to see what would
happen.

The records did not sell well at all—"rather disappointably," Lomax
wrote, quoting the ARC chiefs. In fact, the records must have sold far fewer
copies than did the average blues record of the day and copies now are
eagerly sought-after by collectors. It didn't seem to dawn on ARC that
Huddie's audience was not necessarily among the black families that routinely bought race records, but among northern white audiences who liked
to hear Huddie's version of "Irene" and "Governor Pat Neff." That end of
the Leadbelly repertoire ARC left languishing in its vaults. As a blues singer,
Huddie probably sounded somewhat old-fashioned in 1935; his rough, raw
"country blues" sound would have been at home in rural Texas in 1925, but
not with the black factory workers in Chicago a decade later. Five years had
passed since the death of Blind Lemon Jefferson and audiences wanted to
hear the slick double entendres of the Hokum Boys, or the clever piano and
guitar work of Leroy Carr and Scrapper Blackwell. In March, well after the
original forty sides were cut, the company contacted Lomax (with whom
their actual contract was signed) and asked to "try out" Huddie with a half
dozen more sides of "a different variety." (Huddie obliged, doing a fifth
session of all blues songs on March 25.) They were still trying to figure out
why a singer with such a national reputation could not sell records. The
company made one last attempt to market some of the sides in April 1936,
when they issued "Becky Deen, She Was a Gambling Girl" and "Pig Meat

Papa'' on their various labels. This record, too, sold poorly, and Satherley sadly wrote off the advance they had given the singer and his manager. There was no sense in throwing good money after bad, he thought; the first Leadbelly records were written off as a failure—at least in commercial terms.

The American Recording Corporation studios were state-of-the-art for 1935, and Lomax had wanted to preserve as much as he could of Leadbelly's music in them. Though rough by modern standards, the ARC studio records were generally of noticeably better technical quality than the discs the Lomaxes had made on their portable machine in the field. But the Lomaxes decided they wanted far more than than the songs ARC might choose to record; at best, they knew, this would only scratch the surface of Leadbelly's vast lode. They saw that during the coming weeks at Wilton they would have a chance to do something hardly anybody else in folk music research in that day had done: record a singer's total repertoire. Along the way, they would also record the singer's autobiography, and comments about his songs. (Both techniques are accepted methodology in modern folk music study, but they were unprecedented in 1935.) To that end, the team set up their own recording machine at Wilton, and set to work. The first of these sessions were actually practice runs for songs Huddie was planning on recording for ARC and done the week of the ARC recordings. Throughout February and March, though, the machine was left in place, and in the more relaxed atmosphere of Wilton, Huddie was encouraged to record at length, to preserve his entire repertoire for later submission to the Library of Congress. Most of the discs used were twelve-inch aluminum ones, each capable of holding up to four minutes of music.

During these months at Wilton, the Lomaxes helped Huddie explore and define his repertoire, listening to him intently night after night, day after day. They remained mildly interested in the modern songs Huddie had picked up, but they focused most of their attention on the older ones that formed the true core of his music. Alan Lomax would later recall, ''I think the most important work that I did in my own life was to be a really sensitive audience for Leadbelly'' and later singers. The efforts bore remarkable fruit. Before the Wilton sessions, Huddie had made for the Lomaxes only thirty-three field recordings featuring himself—some of these were remakes of songs he had already recorded once. Now, in the early months of 1935, Leadbelly was able to record some eighty-nine selections—the biggest part of his legacy to the Library of Congress and the source from which many of the public issues of these recordings would be drawn.

Huddie was encouraged not only to perform the songs, but to include the stories he had started telling about them. At the recent MLA meeting, Huddie had been puzzled about why some of his best songs had not gone over as well as they should have. The Lomaxes explained, "Huddie, they don't understand what you are talking about." It was not just a matter of dialect; the entire southern black culture, from the West Texas rural frontier to its harsh penal system, was alien to the white urban audience of the middle 1930s. Huddie at once grasped the problem. Alan Lomax recalled that "he began to try and put his songs in their context. It was one of the most amazing things I've ever seen done. He actually remade all of his songs from the time we were at MLA to the time we were in Wilton." For many of his best songs, Huddie created spoken interludes about the background of the song, the events surrounding the song, or his personal involvement in the song. "He created those *cante-fables* [the half spoken, partially sung introductions] in a month," said Alan Lomax. "For me that was the most remarkable thing he ever did."

Thus the Wilton recordings—and the book that eventually was based on them—are full of the rich details Huddie had added to contextualize his songs. Thus, "Whoa, Back, Buck" is framed by an explanation of how to drive oxen; "I'm All Down and Out" also describes a mule skinner who was so good he could "write 'nitials on de mule's hide." "Death Letter Blues" is sung in between accounts of a man who had left home seven years before, returning home only when his wife dies. Huddie's own story about how he left his mother to go to Fannin Street is interspersed through "Mr. Tom Hughes' Town." "Irene" inspires a *cante-fable* about a man and a woman who elope and then eventually split up.

"Frankie and Albert"—Huddie's version of the most famous of all American murder ballads, "Frankie and Johnnie"—becomes an epic. According to the Lomaxes, this performance stands as "Leadbelly's Ninth Symphony." The opening stanzas suggest just how fully the singer annotated it:

SUNG: *Frankie was a woman,*
         Ev'body know,
         Made a hundred dollars,
         Buy her man a suit of clo'es.
         Was her man, Lawd, he done her wrong.

SPOKEN: *Albert had been out all night long. When he come in that morning just befo' day, he laid down 'cross de bed. Frankie was workin' in de white folks' kitchen, an' she tol' him, says, "Now, listen, baby, I'm goin' an' cook breakfus'. You stay here an' I'll be back toreckly." Albert had his head all wrapped up in the sheet, but he was watchin' Frankie. An' no sooner had Frankie gone, the rascal got up and walked away. But Frankie didn't stay long. She had blood in her eyes already, an' she doubled right back; an' when she got home, he was gone. He had left his six-shooter under his pillow. An' she walked to de bed and looked under his pillow and found his*

cold .41 an' was on his cold trail. She went out a-walin'. She begins to
slow-trail Albert; an' here what all the boys said:

SUNG: *Frankie went a-walkin',*
               Did not go for fun,
               Had under her apron
               Albert's .41
               "Gonna kill my man, 'cause he done me wrong."

SPOKEN: *Frankie went down to the saloon where they got they whiskey an'*
beer at—on a credick right on if they ain't got no money. Whensoever
Albert want to go on a bugger-rugger, he'd go down there to get his whis-
key. So Albert had told the man, "If Frankie come, don' tell her where I
am." But anyhow you take a white man, he ain' gonna tell you no lie—ef
he know you. Ef he know bofe of you, he gonna give the woman the be'en'
of it. An' he know you got a good woman an' he know you doin' her wrong,
he gonna tell her exac'ly where you is. So she walked up to de man.

SUNG: *Frankie went down to the town saloon,*
               Called for a bottle of beer,
               Ast the lovin' bartender,
               "Have my lovin' man been here?
               He's my man, Lawd, he done me
               wrong."©

From these three-month sessions come many of the first recordings of
other songs that would become Leadbelly favorites—"Midnight Special,"
"Boll Weevil," "C.C. Rider," and "You Don't Know My Mind." But almost
two thirds of the sides were never formally made available to the public and
are less known. There was a blues ballad called "Henry Ford Blues," about
a woman who once owned a Chevrolet but now wants to drive a Ford.
There was another version of Leadbelly imitating country singer Jimmie
Rodgers's "Daddy and Home," here called "Dear Old Daddy" and replete
with a good Texas yodel. "Dicklicker's Holler," learned from an older man
in Sugarland, is a wonderful mixture of field holler and blues which Leadbelly sang unaccompanied in a molasses-slow tempo. There was a ragtime
guitar solo called "Easy Mr. Tom," which probably dated from his days in
Texas with Blind Lemon. There were bawdy songs which could never have
been published either in print or on record until recent times, songs like
"I'm Gonna Hold It in Her While She's Young and Tender" and "What You
Gonna Do with Your Long Tall Daddy" and the delightfully ribald "I Ain't
Bothered a Bit." There was "Rattler," the work song and performance

piece about the legendary hunting dog ("Rattler was a possum dog, here Rattler, here / Rattler was a nigger dog, here Rattler, here"); it included Huddie's high, keening imitation of a midnight hunt. There were old dance tunes from Caddo Parish, like "Gwine Dig a Hole to Put the Devil in It" and "Old Man Sittin' in the Corner Dyin." These were described as "hot shots" or "running one-steps" by Alan Lomax at the end of the disc.

Alan Lomax, aware that Huddie often sang a song differently from one time to another, deliberately tried to preserve two or three versions of all the major songs. It was also his job to make copies of each disc to give to George Herzog, who had been employed to make the musical transcriptions for the book. As he established song texts for the book, Alan would sometimes create composite texts from several different records. "We had, in some cases, several renditions of songs and I put together the best from all of them so the reader would encounter all of Huddie's best ideas for each song." They felt the method was justified for their intended audience. "The book was the one crack we had at an audience," recalled Alan. "We weren't interested in scholars, we were interested in people. The details of all the variants were faithfully preserved on the recordings."

It was not as peaceful and as isolated at Wilton as John Lomax had wished. Other projects kept vying for his attention, taking time away from work on *Leadbelly and His Songs* (the working title). The producers of the *March of Time* radio show had been impressed with Leadbelly's story as well as his singing. Now they were starting a film version of the program, a regular newsreel that would be a competitor to *Fox Movietone News* in theaters across the country. They would use a method similar to that used in the radio show: re-create with actors and scripts the major news stories of the day. The very first installment of the newsreel had opened at seventy first-run movie houses around the country on February 1. Each installment contained five or six separate stories, narrated, dramatized, and set to a custom musical score. After completing its first run in major movie houses, it was booked into the smaller and more remote theaters; eventually it played to some 417 theaters in 168 cities—an impressive circulation for a first episode. For the second installment, due out the first week in March, the producers wanted to use the story of Leadbelly. They loved the pure drama and conflicts present in Huddie's life and insisted that he wear prison stripes at the penitentiary scene. *The March of Time* producers reached an agreement with the Lomaxes for their help in writing a script for the segment and to help scout possible locations. An initial payment of $150 was agreed on, with more to follow later.

The plan included four basic scenes, outlining what had become the basic Leadbelly legend. The first dramatized Lomax recording the singer in prison and agreeing to take his record to Governor O. K. Allen; the second opened at a hotel, where Leadbelly, now freed, hunts up Lomax and asks to be "your man." The third focused on Martha and Huddie at home in Wilton after their wedding. And the last showed the interior of the Library of Congress, where the original field recordings were housed. Another scene, in which Leadbelly stands in the rain with his guitar and asks the Lomaxes to take his record to the governor, was apparently scrapped, though parts of it survive in the Lomax papers. *The March of Time* directors, Louis De Rouchemont and Roy Larsen, approved this idea, and on February 8 their film crew appeared in Wilton to start shooting. A hotel in South Norwalk, the Taft Hotel, was chosen to represent the hotel in Marshall where Huddie and Lomax had met the previous September. On February 10, they reconstructed the wedding at the house in Wilton; many of the original guests returned, including "Bonkle and Conkle" from New York, the preacher from Norfolk, six deacons and "deaconesses," as well as John, Jr., and Alan. The filming took much longer than anyone anticipated, running from four-forty Saturday afternoon until three-thirty Sunday morning. They were back at it again by noon on Sunday, and most of the next day, filming scenes showing Leadbelly and John Lomax on the road in Lomax's Ford V-8, and again at the hotel. Some scenes were shot ten times. John Lomax would vary a line just a little, trying to sound natural, and an off-camera voice would correct him, demanding that each line be exactly as approved by the script. Leadbelly, for his part, seemed to have little trouble with his lines, or with his singing. The film crew apparently had only one camera to use, so every scene was reshot several times from different angles, to provide room for editing. On the thirteenth, a Wednesday, the company crew even flew Lomax to Washington, where they had gotten permission to film in the Library of Congress.

The final product, after editing, emphasized the first two scenes and cut out most of the last two. With its nationwide distribution and long shelf life, the newsreel became another important building block in the Leadbelly legend. It is worth looking at in detail. In an issue of the modern *Living Blues* magazine, German scholar Herman Gebhard published a transcription of the final form of the newsreel:

March of Time Newsreel No. 2, 1935

[The opening sequence has the title "Angola, La." and shows Leadbelly and other black convicts at night near a fire. All are wearing convict clothes. Leadbelly plays his guitar. This is covered by orchestral background music that ends after a few seconds.]

ANNOUNCER: *To the Louisiana State Penitentiary goes John A. Lomax, Library of Congress curator, collector of American folksongs.*

[End of background music. Leadbelly sings and plays "Goodnight Irene" as background soundtrack. John A. Lomax records Leadbelly. His recording equipment is shown in action while Leadbelly sings. After a verse, Lomax interrupts.]

LOMAX: *Just once more, Leadbelly! [Leadbelly starts again with "Goodnight Irene." He sings another verse.]*

LOMAX: *That's fine, Leadbelly. You're a fine songster. I've never heard so many good Negro songs.*

LEADBELLY: *Thank you, sir, boss. I sure hope you send Gov. O. K. Allen a record of that song I made up about him, 'cause I believe he'll turn me loose.*

LOMAX: *Leadbelly, I don't know this governor. You mustn't expect too much of me.*

LEADBELLY: *But Gov. Pat Neff of Texas, he turned me loose, when he heard this song that I made up about him.*

LOMAX: *So you were in the Texas penitentiary, too, Leadbelly?*

LEADBELLY: *Yeah, I was serving 35 years for murder, but it wasn't my fault. A man was tryin' to cut my head off.*

LOMAX: *Mighty bad, Leadbelly.*

LEADBELLY: *I believe Gov. O. K. Allen, if you'll just send him a record of that song, I believe he'll turn me loose.*

LOMAX: *Leadbelly, I'll try it.*

LEADBELLY: *Thank you, sir, boss, thank you, sir, thank you! [He begins to play again. Scene fades. Next scene begins with a hotel entrance. Leadbelly, in jeans and with his guitar in hand, talks to the hotel clerk.]*

CLERK: *Yes, Mr. John Lomax is staying here. He's in room 109.*
[A typewriter is heard in the background.]

LEADBELLY: *Is that on the first floor?*

CLERK: *Yep.*
[Leadbelly runs up the stairs.]

CLERK: *Hey, hold on a minute!*
[Inside Lomax' room. Lomax is sitting at a table, typing. A knock at the door.]

LOMAX: *Come in!*
[Leadbelly comes in.]

LEADBELLY: *Boss, here I is!*

LOMAX: *Leadbelly! What are you doing here?*

LEADBELLY: *No use to try and run me away, boss. I came here to be your man. I got to work for you the rest of my life. You got me out of that Louisiana pen.*

LOMAX: *I—you can't work for me. You're a mean boy. You killed two men.*

LEADBELLY: *Please to don't talk thataway, boss.*

LOMAX: *Have you got a pistol?*

LEADBELLY: *No sir, I got a knife.*

LOMAX: *Lemme see it.*

[Leadbelly produces a short knife. Lomax examines it and hands it back.]

LOMAX: *What do you do with that thing?*

LEADBELLY: *I'll use it on somebody if they bother you, boss. Please boss, take me with you. You'll never have to tie your stri—, shoe strings any more, if you'll let me, long as you keep me with you.*

LOMAX: *All right, Leadbelly, I'll try you.*

LEADBELLY: *Thank you, sir, boss, thank you. [Claps his hands.] I'll drive you all over the United States and I'll sing all songs for you. You be my big boss and I'll be your man. Thank you, sir, thank you, sir.*

[End of scene. In the next scene, Leadbelly wears a suit and plays his guitar, humming and singing "Goodnight Irene." Next to him sits Martha, elegantly dressed, smiling at him.]

ANNOUNCER: *John Lomax does take the Louisiana Negro convict to be his man. Takes him north to his home in Wilton, Conn., where Leadbelly's long-time sweetheart, Martha Promise, is brought up from the South for a jubilant wedding. Then hailed by the Library of Congress' Music Division as its greatest folk song find in 25 years, Leadbelly's songs go into the archives of the great national institution. [The interior of the archives is shown, with songboooks, etc., and finally, the original copy of the Declaration of Independence. Leadbelly sings "Goodnight Irene." Close-up of the Declaration. Scene and music fade out, orchestral music, titles and signature tune. End of newsreel.]*

The similarities between this script and the original *Herald Tribune* story of January 3 are striking. Entire lines of dialogue between Huddie and Lomax are reproduced almost intact: "Boss, here I is!," "I came here to be your man," "Don't talk that way, boss," "You'll never have to tie your shoe strings anymore." Whether this was done at the insistence of the *March of Time* people is unclear; they may have felt that the initial story was so well known and so widespread that they were bound to have Lomax follow it. There are also close similarities to the script and to Lomax's long introduction to the later *Negro Folk Songs As Sung by Lead Belly*, including the incident with the knife, which seemed to genuinely bother Lomax (he even described it in his letters to Ruby Terrill). Present, too, is the broad-striped prison garb that Leadbelly first agreed to wear in public but later grew to hate. The concluding scene, which somehow manages to juxtapose the field recordings with the manuscript of the Declaration of Independence, has no dialogue at all, but ends with the sound of a large orchestra playing "Irene."

As it turned out, this sequence was the concluding segment on the second edition of *The March of Time,* released to the theaters on March 8, a little over three weeks after filming in Wilton had been completed. One of the lead stories of the edition spotlighted the rise to fame of Hitler and included a celebrated shot of the dictator sitting "in the Bavarian Alps" at his mountain retreat, staring moodily into the fire. It became one of the more famous newsreel clips of Hitler, even though the scene was completely fabricated and shot in a New York studio with a local actor playing Hitler. Given such dramatization of the international news, the fact that Leadbelly's story of Angola and Texas was filmed in rural Connecticut seems minor. At least the major characters played themselves. And if the film today seems hopelessly stereotyped and full of Uncle Tomism, it at least gives us some indication of the visual dimension of the kind of live shows Leadbelly was doing during these important early months. Moreover, it brought a sample of authentic black folk music to an audience of millions.

While most of the stories about Leadbelly during these months were written by journalists governed by sensationalism, there were a few accounts by more serious writers who were intrigued by his situation. One was William Rose Benet, who in the January 19, 1935, issue of the *New Yorker* published a lengthy poem called "Ballad of a Ballad Singer." Benet (1886–1950) was the older brother of Stephen Vincent Benet and was himself a well-respected poet who was a founding editor of the *Saturday Review of Literature;* in 1942 he was awarded a Pulitzer Prize for his works. Benet's brother had a decade earlier written a poem called "The Mountain Whipoorwill" about another southern folk musician, Lowe Stokes, who had won a Georgia fiddling contest. Both brothers were interested in folklore and folk songs, and William Rose was especially interested in the West; two of his best poems were about outlaw Jesse James, and one was called "The Horse Thief." Benet had probably met Leadbelly and Lomax at a gathering on January 5 at a party given for about fifty artists and writers; Lomax mentioned at the time that people from the *New Yorker* were present. Most of his details in the poem, though, seem, like the *March of Time* script, to come from the original *Herald Tribune* story.

"The Ballad of a Ballad Singer" begins with an account of Lomax's first meeting with Leadbelly, and with his quest for folk songs "under Southern boughs." In Angola, "marked by stripe and bar," sits Leadbelly, who could sing "as long as you please." The next several stanzas recount the story of singing for a pardon, about Huddie's hunting up Lomax for a job, about the knife incident, and about his travels with Lomax to gather songs from "convict throngs." The last four stanzas are the most interesting, describing the pair's arrival in New York. Here it becomes most obvious that the main source for the poem was the *Herald Tribune* story: there is the Leadbelly

quote about being the "famousest guitar player in the world," a quote from
"Ella Speed," and a reference to the appearances at Yale and Harvard.
Only rarely, Benet says, does a minstrel like Leadbelly arise and he wishes
the singer "a charm" that will protect him "from all harm." The references
in these stanzas show that the legend was continuing to grow. The quote
about "the famousest guitar player," which Lomax says stemmed from the
Bryn Mawr visit, had been bandied about so much that Benet could quote
it without explanation. The references to Yale and Harvard had obviously
fascinated reporters; one had said that Huddie had gone up to Yale so
members of the anthropology department could "take his measurements."
The Harvard visit hadn't actually even happened yet (it would not until
March 13). Benet apparently saw irony in the image of the giant Carnegie
Corporation gathering songs like "southern grapes." His description of
Leadbelly's scar and his voice that "made brown ladies swoon" suggests
that even New York's intelligentsia were immune from the fascination of
seeing Huddie as a "bad nigger."

The bookings continued to roll in, everything from fraternity parties to
university concerts. The rate was usually $50 to $100, plus whatever passing the hat brought. For a time, Lomax considered hiring a booking agent
to take care of the dates, but apparently he never got around to it or decided
that they couldn't afford one. In those days before computers and inexpensive telephone communication, he also handled most of the massive correspondence himself and set up dates throughout February and March. With
the book on the horizon, the records scheduled for release in a few weeks,
and the *March of Time* newsreel carrying their names across the country,
Lomax began to think that some genuine, permanent money could be
made. One letter, dated January 25, from a J. A. Rickard of a state college
called Tennessee Tech in Cookeville, offered to set up a series of engagements for the pair at colleges throughout Tennessee. Nothing came of it, but
it showed how the prospects were developing across the entire country.

The retreat to Wilton from New York City had its moments of notable
achievements and small triumphs. Huddie and Martha were finally reunited
and married. Everyone was busy with work on the book, which the
Lomaxes and Huddie hoped would broaden his audience. Leadbelly's creativity had reached a peak during the formulation of his *cante-fables* as part
of his attempt to reach more people. Offers for jobs performing at colleges
and other venues arrived at a steady clip. The future appeared bright and
completely different than it had a scant six months before when Leadbelly
was still a ward of the state of Louisiana.

Whether Lomax's ambitions were the same as Leadbelly's is difficult to
determine. Throughout January, Lomax had talked to people about his
desire to build a nest egg for Huddie and Martha, one which they could use

to return to Louisiana or Texas and buy a small farm. The farm would be stocked with pigs, cattle, and chickens, and Leadbelly would resume the kind of life-style his father Wes had had a generation earlier. Lomax said that Leadbelly had liked this idea and had even suggested that their farmhouse would have a special guest room, to be unlocked only when John or Alan came to visit. Such a dream implied that Lomax sensed the money-making was not going to last forever and that the stay in the north was temporary at best.

It is hard to get an accurate picture of the tone of the day-to-day activities at Wilton. The letters of John Lomax give, of course, only his side of the story, and often that was the reading of an aging, overworked scholar who was doing his best to deal with the cutthroat show business world of New York. At times he had nothing but praise for Leadbelly and Martha; at other times he launched into angry diatribes. "This card house can blow over from only a small puff of wind," he wrote on January 15. "He's not much of a cook," he complained at another point. "We sit on a volcano," he wrote on January 26; he felt that Leadbelly would have gone long ago if it wasn't for Martha and the isolation of the farmhouse. Leadbelly was doing pretty well, he said a day later, though he feared the singer's "vanity will explode him." He sympathized with Leadbelly concerning the brutal re-cording schedule, with its hard two-hour drive through traffic, and got him some fried chicken after the singer had had a bothersome tooth pulled. Then a week later he felt that Leadbelly was "almost impossible," but agreed to let Huddie and Martha go to Harlem because the Lomaxes had held them "to the breaking point." In a February 11 letter, Lomax tried to sum up Leadbelly for his wife; the singer was "an amazing mixture of craft, guile, cunning, deceit, ingratitude, suspicion, fawning, hypocrisy, and at times charming companion and entertainer."

Leadbelly, for his part, had reasons to be upset, too. He resented his boss's attempts to "dramatize" their programs by having the singer wear his old prison clothes—though not the stripes—with a bandanna to conceal the scar on his neck. Huddie had always been a smart dresser when he could be—this was a man whose wife had ironed and starched his coveralls before he went to work in the fields. He was fond of suits—his wedding suit was one of two classic double-breasteds he owned—and enjoyed sharply creased shirts. He must have felt odd, too, when he found out that New York audiences had trouble understanding his thick dialect and that Lomax had to occasionally "interpret" his songs to them. (No one seemed to wonder if Huddie had any trouble with the tangled New York and Brooklyn accents.) There was the matter of the money: Lomax took in all the income, even asking Huddie to turn over his hat money that in a real sense con-stituted the singer's tips. From this Lomax allowed the singer only an allowance and expenses, which he quite carefully annotated as Huddie's share of the three-way split.

Another source of tension was that John Lomax, busily piecing together Huddie's history, occasionally found him reticent or vague about details in his past. To remedy this, he began sending out letters to various people and places asking for details about the singer's early life. He wrote to relatives, to the college in Marshall, to prison wardens. By coincidence, Huddie even got a letter from Margaret Coleman, then living with her daughter in Dallas. Later she would dictate some memories about Huddie's early life. All in all, the stay at Wilton was anything but an idyllic interlude. Though Huddie continued to get along with "little boss" Alan quite well, his relationship with John was becoming frayed.

The bizarre nature of some of the New York society gatherings where the pair appeared served only to complicate matters. Most of the time, Lomax would come out first and give a little talk about Leadbelly; then he would bring the singer on, dressed in coveralls, and either John or son Alan would "name" the songs as Leadbelly sang them. Afterward, assuming the singer had done his usual job of winning over the audience, Leadbelly would pass his old hat. There were some events that were well managed and thoughtfully organized. On February 6, for example, they were invited to play at a men's organization in Garden City, New Jersey; the organizer, a former Texan named James O. Wynn, offered to drive them out in his own car, set aside a suite of rooms at the Garden City Hotel, and have Leadbelly's dinner served to him in his room. Other engagements were insulting to both Lomax and Leadbelly. On January 22, after a meeting with the prestigious Carnegie Foundation, they were asked to appear at a "swank wedding party" from five-thirty to seven P.M. Lomax took his two sons as well as Leadbelly with him and was met by an arrogant society matron who told them to hang their coats in the servants' closet and to stand in the corner out of the way. They had to encourage Leadbelly to even play, and then he finally got the crowd's attention. On the way home, they laughed about the absurd woman and the pretentiousness of the situation—made even funnier after they learned that one of the stuffiest of the guests was the son of an old friend of John's from Dallas trying to break into society. It taught Lomax a lesson, though: in some ways, he was as much an outsider to New York as was Leadbelly. This was reinforced on January 31, when the president of Hamilton College, which had tentatively booked a show with the group, read a story about Leadbelly in the *Herald Tribune* and declared that "no such disreputable person" was to be invited to the college; the scheduled date was canceled.

The real test of the touring prospects came during a two-week period in early March (March 3 through March 15). Lomax and Leadbelly set out by car for a series of college and school engagements through New York and New England. They would stay the night at Albany with Lomax's old friend Dr. Harold Thompson, who had recently arrived at the New York State College for Teachers from a long appointment as head of the English Department at Cornell University; then they would move on to Rochester on March fourth and fifth. Four days in Buffalo would follow, with dates at the College and Men's Club there, before returning to Albany on the eleventh and twelfth. Next came two concerts at Harvard and, on the way back to Wilton, a concert at Wilbraham Academy on the fifteenth. Most of these had been set up over the last two months through extensive correspondence; the Harvard date had been especially difficult to resolve.

The trip began pleasantly enough, with Huddie and Lomax staying overnight with the Thompsons at Albany, greeting an informal gathering of friends in the professor's home. The next day brought a long drive over snowy roads up to the University of Rochester, and during this time Huddie began to get depressed, asking often about how far they were getting from Martha and Wilton. There was some confusion when they arrived at Rochester (some mail had gone astray), and the pair wound up giving an impromptu concert for some two hundred students on Tuesday, the fifth. The morning of the concert, though, Lomax told Huddie to take the car if he wished and explore the town. Lomax would visit with a friend in the area in the meantime. What followed was another bizarre misunderstanding.

Lomax thought Huddie was to return by lunchtime, and when he failed to, he became concerned. He asked a music department professor to drive him through the black section of town, and learned that Huddie had been seen in the Ford with a new friend, someone he had met from Louisiana. Alarmed, Lomax went to the local police station and reported the car as lost or stolen. An all-points bulletin was issued (1934 Ford V-8, with a Texas license) and police dispatchers felt confident that they would have results in a few minutes; how many Fords were there in Rochester with Texas plates? Lomax waited for four hours, but nothing happened; news reporters began to get wind that the "lost Negro" was the famous Leadbelly, but they never figured out what was really going on. Finally Lomax returned to the dormitory where he and Leadbelly had lodged, preparing to do the night's show by himself. To his amazement, the missing car was parked in front. In his room, he found Huddie, finishing off a piece of ham and talking to "black hobo," who was his new friend from Louisiana. "I found some of my color and been stayin' with them," he explained. He was puzzled about why Lomax had gotten so concerned.

The show went on as planned, and the students cheered wildly at Huddie's songs. They had heard nothing like them at all, reflected Lomax, even though Huddie was in poor voice. (Lomax had "auditioned" him in his dorm room before the show to make sure he was up to it; he managed a passable "Death Letter Blues" and Lomax decided his voice was good enough for him to go on.) After the student concert, Leadbelly announced that he had to take his friend back home and that he had to return to a party he had left in the black section of town. He put on his hat, packed up his guitar, and headed for the car. Lomax tried to stop him, telling him flatly that he could not go; he had a drive ahead tomorrow and another important concert. Suddenly the servile Leadbelly was gone; in his place was a strong, determined, competent entertainer who had his own agenda. He had never broken singing dates, he said, and he was not planning on breaking one to fans of his own color. Lomax wasn't treating him right, he said. (His friend from Louisiana added that a "brown-skinned" lady was also involved.) But for the first time, Huddie defied his boss outright, and took off into the night. "I had lost Leadbelly," wrote Lomax.

But the next morning Huddie was back on time, dressed, reading his newspaper, ready to go. There was little, however, of the friendly chatter and small talk; Huddie seemed morose and gloomy. Lomax sensed that their relationship was changing. He had bragged to northern papers how well he understood the nature of "the Negro"; now he saw Leadbelly's face as "an ebony mask," a facade that was expressionless, dour, and difficult to penetrate. "You Don't Know My Mind," Huddie was fond of singing, and now the song began to take on new meaning. On March 6, the ballad hunter wrote to his wife that after this trip, "my last journey with Leadbelly is done."

Things don't improve when the pair got to Buffalo. Leadbelly rejected his room at the "colored" YMCA and went off into the ghetto, where he found a rough back-alley room off Williams Street. After a concert at the university that night, he refused to turn over his hat money to Lomax, and the next day he kept a stipend that one of the deans of Buffalo State Teacher's College gave him. This alarmed Lomax even more (even though he had collected $100 for the evening concert), and again he lectured the singer: He needed to get rest, eat good food, turn over his money, and not go out singing late at night for other blacks in local clubs and parties. Huddie again stood up to him; he knew how to take care of himself, he said, adding, "I ain't goin' to sing no more for you neither unless I wants to; and I ain't goin' nowhere unless you bring Marthy along too." Lomax's worst fears were starting to come true: Leadbelly was starting to "run over" him, and, he wrote home, he only hoped that they could finish the engagements and not embarrass him in front of his friends. But he had decided that this was his last attempt to lecture or improve Leadbelly.

The Buffalo stay became a nightmare for Lomax and a liberation of sorts for Leadbelly. On Friday, the eighth, the day the *March of Time* film was released to theaters nationwide, Huddie walked in on Lomax as the scholar was working at the Grosvenor Library. The singer had traded his quiet, respectable black overcoat for a new one that was green and gray with large checks. He wanted some of his money, and Lomax refused. "I want my money," he said, starting toward Lomax. Lomax thought, "The moment had come about which friends and prison wardens had warned me," and was actually expecting the singer to pull a knife. The scene was defused when a local judge came in, and as Huddie recognized him, a change came over him and (according to Lomax), the singer was his old self. He left, returning to the black part of town, where he continued singing nights to black audiences in a local barrelhouse. The night of the ninth he tried to do a concert at the University Club; his voice was totally shot from three nights singing "for his own kind," and he was barely able to croak out his songs. The audience was not impressed.

Lomax had been genuinely frightened for his life after the library scene. He asked the judge who had walked in to have a special officer shadow the singer, and a Detective Stegemann obliged; he took a knife from Huddie and even brought him to the last concert himself. Convinced that the singer had finally "got completely out of hand," Lomax had begun losing sleep. He later admitted that one of the things that most bothered him about the incident was that he was humiliated about showing his fear; "the humiliation of that will be lasting," he wrote his wife on March 17. His relationship with Leadbelly would never be the same. "I shall always regret that I have wasted my time on a person in whom gratitude or appreciation can find no place."

Leadbelly had really wanted to come on the tour to begin with, but weeks of resentment were building up. After weeks of playing to white northern audiences, many of whom were professionals or intellectuals, Huddie had finally found small, informal, like-minded black audiences in Rochester and Buffalo. These were the kind of folks on which he had built his reputation on Fannin Street and in Dallas. "I always sing too loud and too long" to such audiences, he told Lomax, to explain why his voice was shot. He never actually missed one of the scheduled shows; he simply didn't appear as early as the curfew he had been given. Lomax was no doubt hurt and genuinely frightened. He seemed mostly to worry about the fact that Leadbelly had "lost control," and that he could no longer trust him as a driver or as a friend. In a more pragmatic sense, he worried about how much all this might jeopardize Leadbelly's parole; he was still under the impression that the singer had been paroled to his care. He worried about the fate of the lecture tour, and the fact that, even in New England, they were, by this tour, breaking enough conventions without running the risk of any kind of trouble with the law.

March 8 brought a long, three-hundred-mile drive over snowy roads up through Cherry Valley to Albany. It was a tense drive, with John Lomax feeling deathly ill, and complaining to Leadbelly that he might even die in the car. Leadbelly seemed quiet, glancing over at his passenger occasionally, as if wondering what all the fuss was about. He told Lomax that he looked all right. At Albany they had three concerts set up, but the tension continued. They arrived at the Harold Thompson house and found that the family was expecting both of them to stay there as their guests. Katie Thompson, who was then twelve, recalled the evening vividly. "My family had no objections whatsoever" to Leadbelly's staying there, she said. However, the old Jim Crow rules were still in force, so Harold Thompson found, with some difficulty, a black doctor on Spring Street for Leadbelly to stay with.

The whole Thompson family sensed there was something wrong. Huddie "was in some kind of a snit, as I look back on it," said Katie. "He was just burned up about something. I imagine my father knew what it was, but I didn't." That night a concert at the college was scheduled; John Lomax had met up with Alan by now, and the two of them sat on stage that night, introducing Huddie's songs and telling his story. As soon as the concert was over, Katie remembers, everybody went back to the house, where a postconcert party was scheduled. About fifty of the Thompsons' friends, including virtually the whole English department, were planning on coming over to hear more singing. But as soon as they got in the door, "John said to Alan, 'Get hold of Martha and tell her to take the next bus. We've got to have Martha here, right now. Call Doctor So-and-so and ask if Martha can stay there.' He could tell that things had gone a little far." After the party started, Huddie refused to show his face or to play. He remained in the kitchen, where he sought refuge with young Katie and stayed apart from the rest of the adults. "He sang to me. Said, 'I'm going to stay with you, Miss Kate.' He stayed with Miss Kate and that made John livid. . . . Of course, I was thrilled. My mother kept coming in, taking peeks to see if he was drinking." He tried to teach Katie how he did the different rhythms with his feet, saying, "You can do it, Miss Kate, just like this." Later, when he was told Martha was on her way, he calmed down—but he still refused to sing, except to twelve-year-old Katie Thompson. And the next morning Katie's mother commented that "the gin had sort of disappeared that night."

Martha arrived the next morning, and Alan borrowed the Thompsons' car to pick her up. In the meantime, Leadbelly had agreed to sing at Katie's school, the Albany Female Academy:

It was a suggestion of my father's to our really incredible headmistress. Miss Trotter was an unusual woman. . . . She felt that all kinds of cultures were important, which was unusual in those days of Girls Academy. They got together before Leadbelly even came and my dad said it would be a great thing for the kids to see. She agreed and said that we could pay him. But she fixed up this plan whereby all the kids would bring pennies and Leadbelly could pass the hat. I still remember that Leadbelly stood at the front door and if you didn't have any pennies, or if you had forgotten to bring your pennies, she handed them out.

He did a marvelous concert. They never had seen anything like this. In those days, believe me, this was not the norm. I sat in the balcony, a special treat, with Alan. I don't think John even went. I remember looking down at the little kids who sat in the front rows in small chairs and they all got up and started to dance. I think it was when he started to sing "When I was a little boy" ["Ha-Ha Thisaway"], it hit them. They all started to dance and he was thrilled to pieces. I'm not sure that he'd ever done a concert at a school. But he seemed to be tickled pink, grinning from ear to ear. He had sung for three hours, then Miss Trotter had to say something about classes to attend. They passed the hat.

The concert at the college netted the team a fee of $100, and the men's club the following night brought in an additional $60. Miss Trotter's school children contributed 260 pennies, but Leadbelly seemed to enjoy that concert most of all. It was a precursor of things to come, when he would become noted for his ability to entertain children.

In letters home during these days, John Lomax said that he had told Alan about his decision to part company with the singer. The younger Lomax, who seemed to get along much better with Leadbelly, and who had few of the fears of violence that haunted his father, was "cut up" by the news. Lomax had at one time considered bringing Huddie and Martha with him to Austin, but now that had gone by the board, too. As soon as the last of the booked engagements (March 20) was done, he planned to send Leadbelly and Martha back to Shreveport.

There would be one last moment of glory, and it was to be at Lomax's alma mater, Harvard. To him this was the most important date on the tour, one he had worked hard to set up and one which he always mentioned in his interviews with newspapers. It was an utter triumph for Lomax. "At Emerson Hall in the afternoon and at Leverett House in the evening, he performed before capacity crowds," wrote a Boston reporter of the March 13 performances. The first was sponsored by the Poetry Society of Cambridge, and the other by Dean Kenneth Murdoch. Both drew students and faculty alike and both found the singer in rare form. He dressed again in new coveralls, a colored shirt, tan shoes, silk socks, and the obligatory red scarf. His new twelve-string, which Lomax had bought for him only weeks before, gleamed in the light. He sang at each gathering for about an hour, playing "with his eyes shut and his entire frame from head to toe" rocking gently to and fro with the music. Again listeners were fascinated with his manner of keeping different rhythms with his feet.

"Staid New England broke down its reserve and cheered and cheered as long as they could over the two performances," Lomax wrote the next day. Some six hundred people attended the evening show, including Lomax's mentor and famed Shakespeare scholar George Lyman Kittredge. Toasts and praises for Lomax flowed freely, and Kittredge himself, the preeminent ballad scholar and English professor of his day, introduced his former student in a most gracious and complimentary manner. The student newspaper reported that Leadbelly "played masterfully a twelve string guitar as he sang in a deep rich voice, tinged with the Louisiana dialect. He sang ballads and song grown and collected in the prisons, songs of love, funny and pathetic songs. Strumming violently on his guitar, he sang of his pardon by Governor L. K. Allen [sic] and of Huey Long. Then he danced. With the same perfection of rhythm he danced his interpretation of a duck hunt and of stylish ladies walking down the street." As the singer performed, Professor Kittredge leaned over to Lomax and whispered, "He is a demon, Lomax." When Lomax repeated the comment to Leadbelly later, the singer nodded in agreement. "The demon means the head man. That ol' man knows what he is talkin' about." Recovering somewhat from his trials of the last two weeks, Lomax wrote home, "The entire Harvard visit exceeded my wildest dreams."

The next day, though, meant a return to Wilton, and by that evening Leadbelly, the toast of Harvard, was back doing the laundry at the farmhouse. There was a last date, at the Providence Art Club on the twentieth, but John Lomax refused to accompany Leadbelly, so Alan took his place. In spite of the afterglow of Harvard, John Lomax was still determined that Huddie and Martha would leave. On Sunday, March 24, John Lomax told Huddie and Martha that they were going home. According to Lomax, this was exactly the news they wanted to hear; Huddie was packing within ten minutes. They also made a last visit to "the colored society" of south Norwalk, to bid farewell to some of the friends they had made. On Tuesday John and Allen drove Huddie and Martha into the Greyhound bus terminal in New York. Their tickets were for the twelve-forty bus. Lomax settled up his finances with Huddie by giving him a check, and the two boarded the bus. There were no dramatics, no histrionics: just Martha, standing by speechless and helpless, and Huddie unusually silent.

For John Lomax, a grand experiment was ending, and he probably had little idea of how it would echo and reverberate through the years to come. The concatenation brought about by the joining of his own skill and insight with Leadbelly's music had brought about a cultural revolution of sorts.

Folk music had made the headlines, the newsreels, the radio, and millions of average Americans were beginning to understand something about it. To be sure, Lomax had not been fully prepared for the role this thrust on him, but he was no bumbling academic who shrank from meeting the public and dealing with the media. He had made a heartfelt attempt to handle the media blitz his discovery had created; it was not he who had created the sensationalism, the "homicidal harmonizer" headlines, and he was appalled at the way in which the press had distorted the singer's life. In the end, he used the sensationalism to gain a platform by which he could try to explain and enlighten people about the nature of traditional culture, and about the importance of African American music.

The quarrels he and Leadbelly had were by no means just over money. Some were the kind of professional disagreements that any performer has with his manager; others were due to Huddie's own volatile temper and mood swings. Others stemmed from the intense pressure and public scrutiny both had been under during the three months of the New York stay, or from the Lomaxes' attempts to convince Huddie to stick with the songs of his heritage when tempted by the commercial jazz and blues of the swing era. Their parting was in some ways unfortunate, but their work—their genius—had made its mark.

19 "My Client, Huddie Ledbetter"

Huddie and Martha left New York with several heavy suitcases, a new Stella guitar, and even a concertina they had bought in Buffalo. During the stay in New York, according to Lomax's ledgers, Huddie and Lomax had managed to take in about $1,550—an impressive amount by Depression standards. This included a $250 payment for advance royalties on the ARC records, a $250 advance on the book from Macmillan, a $100 payment for the *March of Time* radio show, and a $150 partial payment on the *March of Time* newsreel. The rest was money from parties and performances as well as various hat collections. It would seem that Huddie and Martha would be returning south in good financial shape, but Huddie didn't see it that way. In the first place, his contract with Lomax meant that everything made after January 5 netted Huddie only half the income, and the modification made on February 9, adding Alan to the agreement, meant that all income after that date netted him only one third of the money. Furthermore, Lomax had kept careful accounts of any expenses—down to the 25 cents for wedding gloves he had spent for Huddie. These included money for lodging while on tour, even though John Lomax often stayed with friends—as well as suits, clothes, Martha's hairdresser, the guitar, bus fare, dentist fees, and numerous occasions in which he gave Huddie or Martha cash for general spending money. On the other hand, the list did not include any general living expenses for Martha and Huddie while in Wilton—no grocery expenses, no heating oil expenses, no laundry expenses. These, presumably, were offered in exchange for Huddie and Martha doing the cooking, cleaning, and driving.

When all the deductions were made from Leadbelly's share of the income, he wound up with, by Lomax's account, $298.94. This was an impressive sum in 1935 standards. At the bus station on March 26, Lomax gave Huddie three checks for $50 each and the balance in cash. From this cash, Huddie had to buy two bus tickets back to Shreveport, leaving little to show for three months' hard work. When they arrived at Shreveport, Martha returned to work at the Excelsior Laundry, and a couple of days later Huddie went to a local bank to cash his checks. To his surprise, he found he could not cash them. Lomax had postdated the checks; he said later that he had explained this to Martha before they left and had agreed that this was the only way Huddie would ever preserve any of the money from the New York days. Huddie had always been nervous about giving

178

money to Martha—he had refused to entrust her with railroad fare to come to New York—and even the slightest implication that she was having a say with these checks infuriated him. All the rage that had been building over the last month boiled up: the long tour to the upstate area, Lomax's anxiety around him, the meager sums he finally got from his concerts. He wrote (or wired) Lomax, demanding the checks be made good, and saying something that Lomax construed as a threat to his life.

On April 5, Lomax sent a wire to Sheriff Tom Hughes of Shreveport, the same one Huddie had sung about. He explained that Huddie Ledbetter, at the Excelsior Laundry, had threatened his life over some postdated checks. He explained that he had told Martha he was doing this, and doing it for her own protection. "Please see Ledbetter and if you think best will put cash into your hands or his as you suggest. Answer collect." Before the sheriff could really take any action, though, Huddie contacted a local attorney, W. S. Johnson, at the Ricou-Brewster Building in Shreveport. This would initiate a six-month series of legal actions he launched against his former manager. On April 6, Johnson wrote to Lomax (who was still at Wilton), explaining that his client had turned over to him three postdated checks drawn on the Republic Bank in Dallas. Each was for $50, and they were dated May 1, June 1, and July 19, 1935. His client furthermore stated that the money came from his singing and playing and should have been rightfully given to him on the spot after each performance. "He is badly in need of his money," the letter concluded, "and if what Ledbetter tells me is true, I think he is entitled to his money now instead of post-dated checks."

Between the sheriff and lawyer Johnson, Huddie managed to get his $150. Encouraged, he now asked Johnson to check into the matter of the royalties from the American Record Corporation. The ARC files show that the actual contract was signed only with Lomax, as an "agent" for Huddie. This was, in fact, not at all uncommon for ARC; many of its so-called race artists did not have contracts directly with the company, but were contracted through agents like Lester Melrose or W. R. Callaway. It was common for such agents to pay sums to their artists, usually a lump sum from the agent's pocket, and then sign an agreement whereby the record company would pay royalties to the agent himself, not the artist. It was ARC's own curious form of paternalism, built on the assumption that most blues or hillbilly artists would rather have money in hand at the time of recording than wait months or even years for royalties to trickle in. It was also easier bookkeeping for the company.

On the day Huddie left Wilton, John Lomax gave him a letter which acknowledged that Huddie *and* Martha were to receive one third of the net royalties arising from the sale of records. One third of the $250 advance had already been added into Huddie's income from New York, but now the singer asked Johnson to write directly to ARC and direct the company to provide royalty statements and any royalties, to be sent to the Ledbetters' Louisiana address. Art Satherley, ARC's head, had no real problem with doing this, but noted that the contract was with Lomax, not Leadbelly, and that before the company could release royalties of any sort, it would need a notarized letter of authority from Lomax. The problem was so far a moot point, though; the company had only released the two records, and they were not selling well. The $250 advance would have covered sales of 12,500 at 2 cents a record, and the two records issued so far almost certainly had not sold that many. Since ARC eventually issued only one other record, the royalty question soon become unimportant. The dream that both Lomax and Leadbelly had of selling thousands of each of twenty different releases remained just that: a dream.

Sometime early in May Huddie and Martha moved to Dallas. They apparently moved in with Huddie's sister Australia, who was now forty-two or forty-three years old. Whether or not the move was dictated by hard times is not clear; one source recalls that the excitement over the sheriff coming to the Excelsior Laundry cost Martha her job there. Thompson's letter had said Huddie had been badly in need of money, and even with the $150 for the checks, he and Martha might well have been broke again. There is no record of Huddie getting any kind of work in Shreveport during these months. Shortly after the move to Dallas, Huddie hired a second lawyer, E. S. Pearce, of the firm of Earl M. Deterly in Dallas. By now the *March of Time* newsreel with Huddie was being shown even in the small towns and second-run theaters, and everybody was talking about it. In a letter of May 7 to Lomax, Pearce brings up three new concerns: payments from the newsreel, a fuller accounting of the New England tour money, and possible payments from the Macmillan book.

Lomax had little to do with the newsreel; indeed, he had not himself yet been paid the complete amount due him and was upset that the newsreel people were now talking about filming a second episode in Marshall. But the Macmillan problem was another matter; although Huddie had received a third of the $150 Macmillan advance, he and his attorney felt that no official permissions had been given. Pearce wrote Macmillan's president, George Pruett, who became alarmed. On May 13 Pruett wrote to Lomax explaining that Pearce might well "restrain us from publishing your book until you have made your peace with Ledbetter." He also asked for a copy of the agreement Lomax and Leadbelly had signed—which was a generalized management contract with no specific reference to the book. "I guess you will remember that I was worried about something like this coming up," wrote Pruett. "Apparently this lawyer fellow thinks he is going to be able to shake you down for some money—or us—and maybe his chances are pretty good unless you have got some kind of document that will protect us.''

Lomax had by this time returned to Austin, where he was completing the book manuscript and dealing with an attack of arthritis. Letters from Macmillan and from the American Recording Corporation made it impossible to ignore the letters from Leadbelly's attorneys. He felt comfortable, though, that his documentation would hold up and decided to try a reconciliation of sorts with the singer. While in Wilton, he had noticed that Huddie had written to his daughter Arthur Mae, then living in Dallas with her mother, Margaret Coleman. It now occurred to him and Alan that Margaret would be an invaluable source of information about the early years of Huddie's life—years Huddie had been especially vague about and reluctant to talk about. In fact, Lomax found in his files a letter that Margaret had sent to Huddie back in February. It was a sad and remarkable plea from the singer's childhood sweetheart.

Just a few lines to you in answer to your little note wrote me in Arthur's other letter found me not feeling so well but glad to hear from you though you say that I don't care for you. Well my dear you shouldn't say that but for the way you treated me I ought not to care for you. But you no, huddie, for the sake of the child I bound to care something about you. But listen here my dear I do earnestly think you treats your chile cruel when you are making so much money you say and won't even send her one penny now. How do you think she feal? I just couldn' treat my onlest chile that way a special a girl an you know its so many things they kneeds.

You sure ought to be proud and feal great to think you have a daughter in the world grown and haven't brought no shame and disgrace upon us. You should think I am a wonderful mother to raise such a girl in this fast town and such a little salary as women make in this town. Of course she could have been more faymous if I had just had some one to help furnish the money to put her through college but as it is I thank God for her and that it is [as] well with both of us. I do hope I will meet you some day so that I can explain to you so now I am asking you this in the name of Jesus Christ the Son of God out of the depths of my heart. Please send me $5.00 five dollars I need it so bad. From Margaret.

By this time, Arthur Mae was hardly a child; she was a grown woman of around thirty-two years old, and her mother was in her late forties. Though Huddie had not seen them for some time, he had written them from Wilton, talking about his new success. He probably didn't expect to receive a letter like this back, and after he had shown it to Lomax, he was noncommittal about it. It angered Lomax that he would not send Margaret the $5, and as Lomax himself struggled to raise his three children, he felt the singer's lack of interest in his child was reprehensible. (In fact, Lomax thought Arthur Mae was the singer's only child, a fact Huddie never bothered to correct.)

John Lomax decided to write Margaret himself to ask for information about the singer's childhood, and he now wrote to Huddie to ask for the address. Huddie supplied it, and apparently sent Margaret some money, possibly hoping to defuse a bad report from her to Lomax. (Ironically, by now the $5 was probably as hard for Huddie to come by as it was for Margaret.) But Huddie also took the opportunity to get back into direct contact with Lomax and to try a little reconciliation himself. He thanks Lomax for his "letter & check," which he had sent in response to Pearce's letter—the check derived probably from the final *March of Time* payment. It was a warm, unctuous letter, asking about "Miss Bess" (Bess Brown, the Lomaxes' daughter), Alan, "Mrs. Terrill" (John's wife), and others from the Wilton days. There are no direct references to the two lawyers Huddie had hired, but there was an odd comment about "we had a lot of money to make but I could not tell the People any thing until I see you." He seemed almost desperate for Lomax to come up to Dallas and talk over a new plan Huddie had for making more money. He had some new songs he said he knew Lomax would like. In conclusion, he said: "I would like to come to Austin and play for the new Governor Hon. Mr. Allred, so if you want me come over here I will be ready to go any time." Apparently the trip to play for the governor did not pan out, and two weeks later Martha wrote another letter for Huddie, offering to sell his portion of the ARC record contract to Lomax. "We would like to know," she wrote, "if he sell this, it will not keep him from making more records if he would ever decide to make some more." They asked what Lomax would offer for their share and asked him to "please answer right back at once."

This apparently got no results, so a week later Huddie hired yet another lawyer, his third since leaving New York. This time he chose, by design or good luck, an attorney who actually knew John Lomax and had some credibility with him. Joseph Utay was a Texas football hero who had played for Texas A&M around 1905–1907 and later was a friend of Notre Dame's Knute Rockne. John Lomax had taught with Utay at Texas A&M and considered him a fair and trustworthy man. Utay wrote Lomax on June 11, bringing up all the old matters that the earlier lawyers had: the East Coast money, the records, the book, and the *March of Time*. In this letter, as in the earlier ones from Johnson and Pearce, the lawyer stressed that Huddie was not angry and that he had "not lost confidence" in Lomax. For his part, Lomax felt that if this attorney could actually get Huddie into his office to work out a definitive agreement that would settle everything, he would cooperate—even to the point of going to Dallas himself to meet with them.

He even forwarded to Utay a photostat of the January contract from New York.

Things were looking up, but when Utay explained the contract to the singer, Leadbelly was outraged. As Utay explained it in a letter of July 8, both Martha and Huddie "emphatically deny that they executed the instruments and that they at any time made any agreement with you." Had they understood the contracts, they said they would never have agreed to the 50 or 66⅔ percentages and never would have signed on for five years. Huddie felt, wrote Utay, that the two-third–one-third split for services was wholly unfair and unreasonable. Huddie now demanded two thirds of the East Coast money, a balance he figured to be $661.77. Utay was also writing to Macmillan, threatening to refuse to permit the publication of the book if an agreement was not reached. Finally, the singer no longer had any interest in selling off his ARC rights—a decision probably prompted by Utay.

The book was also being delayed on another, unexpected front. George Herzog, the distinguished ethnomusicologist from Columbia University, had been employed to make musical transcriptions for the book. The Lomaxes provided him with copies of the discs and were impressed by Herzog's precise, detailed transcriptions, which they felt made an important addition to the book. In his note about the transcriptions in the final version of the book, Herzog explains that traditional European musical notation is ill-equipped to accurately capture the idiom of "folk-blues," and that he had to insert unconventional symbols to indicate things like quartertones and unorthodox times. But Herzog had two complaints that delayed the book's progress. First, he felt that not all of Huddie's songs reflected his black American heritage and that the more white-influenced songs should perhaps be struck from the final draft. Herzog failed to fully understand that the South was the great melting pot of black African culture and white European culture, and that its music reflected this mixture. The scholar also objected to the Lomaxes' current title, *Negro Sinful Songs*, expressing the opinion that the use of the word *sinful* was not appropriate to the subject. Even when Herzog had completed his work, they had not yet agreed upon a new title. In the midst of all of the serious disputes with Leadbelly, Herzog's objections seemed minor; nonetheless, they required attention.

Throughout the summer, negotiations went back and forth. Lomax, realizing things were getting too complicated, hired his own attorney, Ed Crane, an acquaintance from Dallas. He continued to work away at the manuscript, struggling to cut and edit his account, which had turned more into a story about the Leadbelly-Lomax relationship than the full story of Leadbelly's life. Now he began to get letters from Pruett at Macmillan, who was becoming increasingly alarmed at the tone and the ability shown by Utay's letters. "We simply have to make our peace with Huddie Ledbetter before we can proceed with the publication of the book," he wrote on July 23, "for he has a common law copyright on all the material and any court in the realm would grant him an injunction the instant the book was published." Pruett was also getting concerned at the possible delays on the book; he was watching the press attention to Leadbelly slowly evaporate and was worried that there would be little interest in the book if it got out too late. He rejected several plans from Lomax, finally saying in so many words that if Macmillan was to bring out the book, it had to have a release from Huddie.

Lomax began to wonder at one point if Joe Utay had lost control of his client; he was trying to settle in good faith mainly because he trusted the lawyer and assumed he could hold Huddie to any agreement. By September the two attorneys were actively making offers, counteroffers, and concessions. One of the sticking points was the ARC contract; both attorneys urged their clients to hold on to their parts of that, regardless of what else they gave up. Ironically, that was probably the least valuable of all the items they debated, since ARC was about to decide that the Leadbelly masters were a write-off. Still, both men still thought there was real money to be made here. Lomax was angry over Utay's direct letters to Macmillan and at what he thought was Utay's blocking of the book, and at one point he even asked Crane if they could sue Utay.

Finally a settlement was worked out and an agreement was signed on September 12. Leadbelly accepted a cash payment from Lomax of $250. In exchange, he agreed to cease any kind of action against John or Alan arising from the New York management contract, to assign "all publication and other rights" to Lomax for use in the book, still called *Leadbelly and His Songs,* and to give Lomax one third of the ARC record royalties. The New York management contract was canceled and each party was released from all obligations defined by it. "Your alliance with Ledbetter is at an end," Crane wrote to Lomax that day. Hoping that the barrage of lawsuits was at an end, Lomax made plans to hole up at the Henry Zweifel ranch to push as hard as he could on finishing the book.

Joe Utay had been introduced to Huddie by Morris Fair, a mutual friend who had met the singer that summer. "He was living in Dallas with a sister on Bogel Street," recalled Fair. Apparently there was a delay in Huddie's getting his money after the settlement, and he was so broke he and Martha needed food. Morris Fair arranged credit for Huddie at a local grocery store, one located at Hawkins and Elm streets and run by Fair's relatives. Once the singer got his money, he celebrated his victory. "Leadbelly went on a gin-drinking binge," Fair recalled. "His sister called me to come over on Bogel Street. She said that Huddie's wife became upset when her husband was beating on her. And Mrs. Ledbetter walked around Huddie with a razor. Huddie was then a rather fat man. When I got out on Bogel Street he was sitting on a stump on a front yard. And he had razor cuts in a circular pattern around his midriff. But the razor hadn't cut deeply. I called an ambulance and rode with Huddie to Parkland Hospital.'' Probably because of the gin, Huddie was feeling no pain by the time they got to the emergency room, and sang for the doctors as they stitched him up. After the work was finished, he took up his guitar and sang a few more selections for the nurses and doctors. ''It was a most unusual Leadbelly concert,'' remembered Fair.

By late November, Leadbelly and Martha were needing money again. Still living in Dallas, Huddie began to hunt for some kind of work to help them get by. On Thanksgiving Day, he got a job at a local service station, where he greased and washed cars. Huddie was asking 10 cents a day wages then, and his offer was accepted. During the day, during off hours, he talked about his music, his trip to New York, and his records; while he buffed cars, he remembered how easily the money had rolled in from his singing, how his old hat would fill with $1 and $5 bills. On December 18, he took a chance and wrote Lomax again: he badly needed money and wanted to go on the road again. Neither he nor Martha was angry with Lomax, and they could make even more money this time than they did before. If Lomax couldn't go himself, would he let Alan perhaps go? The answer was an angry and thunderous no. A week or so later Huddie tried again, bringing to bear even more diplomacy. This time there was no answer.

In the meantime, though, the young manager of the service station where Huddie had been working, John W. Townsend, had been listening to the stories his new employee was telling. He had also been following Huddie's attempts to get together with Lomax and on the road again. At first skeptical, he was now convinced that Huddie was exactly who he claimed to be and that the singer was right in his insistence that there was money to be made from new tours. With Lomax uninterested in any further touring, Leadbelly began to talk with Townsend about working out something. As it turned out, Townsend's mother was also interested, and in January 1936 they signed a contract to manage and promote Huddie. To raise capital, Townsend sold his filling station and rented his house. Then he tuned up his car and made plans for them to head to New York. In February, Townsend, his mother, Huddie, and Martha started out driving to New York. The comeback was under way.

20 "Ain't It a Pity, I'm in New York City"

On March 2, 1936, Lincoln Barnett, the *Herald Tribune* reporter who had done so much to spread the
legend of Leadbelly a year before, found himself writing a new headline
about the singer: "AIN'T IT A PITY? BUT LEADBELLY JINGLES INTO CITY. EBON,
SHUFFLIN' ANTHOLOGY OF SWAMPLAND FOLKSONG INHALES GIN, EXHALES RHYME."
Leadbelly was back, full of brash confidence and very much at ease with his
new manager. As he held court for the local reporters, he showed off his
ability to improvise—an ability he had honed as far back as Dallas, but
which he had not displayed all that much on his earlier trip. When asked
how he had spent his time since his last New York trip, he chanted:

> *For a couple of months I got nothin' done,*
> *Just eatin', sleepin' and stayin' in the sun,*
> *Jes' did nothin' but take in my income.*

He had created a new song which he called "Ain't It a Pity, I'm in New York
City," and about every answer to a reporter's question seemed to form a
new stanza for it. When asked if he was glad to be back, he sung:

> *Oh, I walked up to Dallas town,*
> *The sky was blue an' the road was brown,*
> *No one give me nothin', now I got nothin' to give,*
> *Shreveport's my ol' home, but Dallas where I live.*
> *But I'm in New York City*
> *And I'll tell anybody what I like for'em to do*
> *Is catch a bus and ride up Fifth Avenue.*
> *I'm still in New York City.*
> *Ain't it a pity,*
> *I'm in New York City.©*

"Rhymes fall from his lips in the course of ordinary conversation in discon-
certing profusion," wrote Barnett, obviously impressed. He continued to
record the singer's comments about the differences between the city and his
southern home.

> *Yes, sir—too glad—it's heaven to me,*
> *The bigges' city I ever did see.*

> *Down in the South everybody tell*
> *New York City is a burnin' hell.*
> *So, ain't it a pity,*
> *I'm in New York City.*
> *Because it's heaven for me.©*

Even the harsh New York winters came in for attention:

> *I ride roun' looking at the snow and ice,*
> *An' if anybody wants to take my advice,*
> *They'll keep away from this snow and ice.©*

Like Muhammad Ali in the 1970s, or the rap artists of the 1980s, Leadbelly could cultivate rhymes at the drop of a hat. He would soon add such techniques to his performances, fascinating audiences by his odd, rhymed spoken introductions to songs. It was a technique rooted deeply in African American oral tradition, in things like drinking toasts and playing the dozens. But it was new to white audiences, and to the reporters on that March day.

One of them asked about Martha; Leadbelly smiled and went through the pantomime of lifting a phone to his ear.

> *Hello, Central, give me long distance phone.*
> *I want to talk with my baby the whole night long,*
> *Tell her 'bout the trouble and the trials that I've had —*
> *She toll me that all wasn't so bad.*
> *So, hello Central, give me that two-naught-nine,*
> *I want to talk to that gal o' mine.©*

His account of his life with Martha was in fact fairly accurate; she had, in effect, told him "that all wasn't so bad" when she had first taken him in at Shreveport after his release from jail. Barnett concluded his account by noting that all Townsend had to do was "keep the guitar-king away from the bottle and close to his strings" and give the address of Townsend's mother so those anxious to do business could find them.

Not many people did, apparently. Townsend had few of the New York connections that John Lomax had and knew virtually nothing about show business. He and Leadbelly visited the American Record Corporation offices to see if there was any interest there, but Art Satherley still had plenty of unused masters from the year before. He did agree, now that the royalty issue was straightened out, to try one more release, and in April put out the final ARC coupling, "Pig Meat Papa" and "Becky Deem, She Was a Gamblin' Gal." He took down Townsend's mother's address for his files and promised to get back to them if the record sold well. But generally things did not go well, and soon Townsend's grubstake was expended.

Sometime after this, manager Townsend, disappointed at the results of his venture, dropped out of the picture, probably returning to Dallas. Lead-belly did have one key booking—the Lafayette Theater in Harlem. This had been for two decades the most important venue for black stage shows in New York and was managed by a white man named Frank Schiffman, a former schoolteacher from the Lower East Side. During his first stay in New York, Leadbelly had seldom played for black audiences, but now Schiffman decided to try headlining him in the black community's best-known theater. Schiffman had heard all the publicity about how tough the singer was and was somewhat intimidated. He was also not sure about using down-home blues in the theater, since most of his audience was more used to the music of Duke Ellington, Andy Kirk, and Cab Calloway. For these reasons, he decided to build on the Leadbelly publicity: He devised a skit in which Leadbelly appeared on stage wearing prison garb and reenacted his pardon story. He sang in a set designed to resemble a governor's office, and the governor—apparently an actor—was so moved that he pardoned him. This happened thirty-one times a week, Schiffman recalled, suggesting that the piece was played out four or five times a day. It was a great success, he remembered; it was a sort of live version of the *March of Time* newsreel.

During the first week of April Schiffman tried booking Leadbelly into another big theater in Harlem, the Apollo. This had opened in 1934, and would later become the most important crucible for black talent in the nation. On April 4, the New York *Amsterdam News* announced that "Lead Belly, the pardoned killer" would be heading a "revue which has all the earmarks of entertainment and novelty." A cast of sixty-five "colored and white" would be supporting him, including the jazz band of pianist Willie "The Lion" Smith and two chorus lines, one "white" and one "brown." Headlining, though, was Leadbelly, "whose glorious voice and heart-touch-ing songs won him a pardon from the Governor of Texas!" Obviously Schiffman was trying to capitalize on the recent press sensationalism, but this time it didn't work at all. Black audiences stayed away in droves. Huddie shared the bill with pop singer Midge Williams and managed to get one of the few totally hostile reviews in his career. The New York *Age* critic wrote:

The week before Easter is one of the worst weeks of the whole year in the theatre. . . . The management of the Apollo, anticipating a small turnout at the box office, has placed a show on the boards that will do its share toward encouraging the folks to stay home and keep Lent.

Top billing for the show goes to George [sic] Ledbetter, alias "Lead-

belly", *a singing guitarist. The advance publicity stated that this man had been in two jails under murder charges and that the wardens, on hearing him work out on the guitar and vocally, set him free. Maybe they did, but after hearing the man myself, I'm not so sure that musical excellence prompted the two governors' actions. It may have been that both they and other inmates wanted some peace during their quiet hours. No. Leadbelly isn't the man if it's music you want.*

Leadbelly never talked much about these shows, but he must have re-sented them as much as he had the newsreel. Here it meant little to him that he was performing before black audiences; he wanted to be accepted as a singer in his own right, not as some southern primitive who had sung his way off the chain gang. At the same time, he was realizing just how hard the New York entertainment scene could be to break into, and just how much he had benefited from John Lomax's sponsorship. Lomax's reputa-tion and contacts had virtually guaranteed the singer a hearing the year before—something that, with his lack of show business experience, Lead-belly had not appreciated then. Soon he gravitated back to one of his old friends, Mary Elizabeth Barnicle, who was more than willing to accept him on his own terms. During the next few years, she became his unofficial manager, his mentor, and his entrée into the developing folk music scene in the city.

Barnicle had been born into a Scotch-Irish family in Massachusetts in the late 1890s; she had worked her way through Brown College in Vermont, then won a scholarship to Bryn Mawr. Like many early folklore enthusiasts, she studied medieval literature, and for a time even taught in England. Barnicle's social conscience caused her to give up her job there (due to the high unemployment), and to return stateside. She held positions at the University of Minnesota and Antioch College before joining the faculty of New York University about 1919. Unlike many earlier folklore collectors, who were fond of collecting old ballads from printed sources and manu-scripts, Barnicle saw folklore as a living cultural and political force. She was fascinated with fieldwork and with political and occupational folklore, genres pretty much ignored by other collectors in the 1930s. (She was also one of the first scholars to see the importance of sexual folklore, a huge and now-recognized area which was not discussed in polite academic circles of the time.) As a young woman, she had worked in the woman's suffrage movement around Providence, Rhode Island, and after she joined NYU she turned her attention to the civil rights movement, to various labor move-ments, and to the problems of poverty—especially in Appalachia. She often brought performers or speakers into her classes at NYU and tried to make her students see how folk culture related to the real world outside the classroom—especially the world of Depression-era America. Alan Lomax explained why her classes were so popular:

The way she presented her courses eventually made her the most popular teacher on the big downtown campus of New York University. She had to limit her enrollment to one hundred students per class, and there was always a waiting list for students who wanted to get in. Her classes were stimulating and highly unconventional sessions, with a demanding intellectual content, yet unrestrained in their discussion of literary, economic, political, and sexual issues. Deans and heads of departments did at times protest, but in the end they had to let Professor Barnicle go her own way.

When Barnicle had met John and Alan Lomax in January 1935, she had been fascinated with their use of field recordings and with what they were trying to accomplish. She made a special impression on Alan; she struck him as "a fine, tall horsey Irishwoman, full of fire and movement"; never before had the young collector "met anyone so learned and literate, and yet so profoundly concerned with the problems of the world." Barnicle was eager to learn about making field recordings and to see firsthand some of the South that the Lomaxes and Huddie talked about. In 1935, just after the wedding of John Lomax and Ruby Terrill, Barnicle, Alan, and the writer Zora Neale Hurston, who had just completed work on her classic book *Mules and Men*, took off on a recording trip to Florida. (Hurston at times asked Alan and Barnicle to put on blackface to protect themselves from suspicious whites; nonetheless, they were arrested once or twice.) Later Barnicle and Alan went on to the Bahamas to collect more recordings; she and Hurston had grown to dislike each other.

According to Hurston, Barnicle didn't like the way John Lomax treated either Alan or Leadbelly. She felt Alan was being "smothered" by his father's conservatism, and her frequent talks with Leadbelly back in 1935 (when John Lomax had been gone) were all that kept him "alive and believing in himself" during those troubled days. Hurston even suggested that Barnicle's request for Leadbelly to do odd jobs and work at her apartment was due to the fact that "she was attracted to him as a man by her own admission." By this time, however, Hurston was trying to warn John Lomax about Barnicle's alleged deviousness, and her comments were hardly objective. She was also convinced Barnicle was a Communist. "She like all Communists are making a play of being the friend of the Negro at present and stopping at nothing, *absolutely* nothing, to accomplish their ends. They feel that the party needs numbers and the Negro seems to them their best bet at present." In fact, Barnicle's biographer, Willie Smyth, has found little direct evidence that Barnicle was actually a member of the

Communist party. She was good friends with a number of left-wing liberal and radical activists, but friends remembered her own ideology as simply being "humanitarian."

In the midst of the Depression and the New Deal, labor leaders and social activists were searching as never before for alternate ways of making the country work. Many of these people gravitated to New York, where they held a bewildering series of meetings, rallies, debates, protest marches, and lectures. As Barnicle took Leadbelly and Martha under her wing in the spring of 1936, she helped find him work, invited him to sing for her classes (for pay), and introduced him to many people involved in the activist movement. They, in turn, found more jobs for him. Folk music and civil rights had become central issues for many of the activists of the time: An old Communist party joke had two comrades talking about an upcoming meeting, and one saying to the other, "You bring the folksinger; I'll bring the Negro." Folk music—the music of the people—was a visible and acceptable proletarian art form. It was the antithesis of the current pop music coming out of the capitalist-centered Tin Pan Alley, and with the years of hard times, it was often a source of protest.

Though earlier singer-composers like Joe Hill and "Haywire Mac" Mac-Clintock had shown how folk songs could be refashioned into protest songs, by the time the New York Communist movement published *The Red Song Book* in 1932, times had changed. Many activists felt that the protest songs in that book could best be sung in mass singing and workers' choruses, and organized such groups as the Daily Worker Chorus and the American Workers' Chorus. But in the early 1930s, activists began to meet and hear individual singers whose protest songs were modeled on older traditions. Margaret Larkin brought to New York in 1929 the songs of textile worker Ella May Wiggins, and that same year Aunt Molly Jackson, a Kentucky miner's wife who was a superb ballad singer, came to New York to sing protest songs to raise money for the miners' bloody struggle in Kentucky. As the left-wing movement, especially the Communist party, began to reject "foreign" models and embrace American tradition, their appreciation of authentic folk music grew. In New York, writes historian R. Serge Denisoff, this movement toward Americanization helped create "a nebulous audience and appreciative critics for the transplants from Harlan County [Aunt Molly Jackson's turf] and elsewhere."

Leadbelly arrived at the very start of this movement, and right in the middle of the so-called "Red Decade." Aunt Molly Jackson, another singer whom Barnicle had befriended and helped find work, was starting to emerge as an answer to the party's call for a "Communist Joe Hill." And in November 1935, a few months before Huddie returned, editors of the *Daily Worker* newspaper introduced to their readers Ray and Lita Auville,

West Virginia singers who sang folklike songs to their guitar accompaniment. Stalinists were at first enchanted, then began to complain that the Auvilles were simply too modern, too jazzlike, too sophisticated. *Daily Worker* writer Mike Gold replied that such objections tended to reflect an antipathy toward formal European music. "Would you judge workers' correspondence by the standard of James Joyce or Walter Pater? No, a folk art rarely comes from the studios; it makes its own style, and has its own inner laws of growth." This idea was formalized by the Popular Front music organization the American Music League, which in 1936 published as one of its guidelines "to collect, study, and popularize American folk music and its traditions." Though the glory years of the first left-wing folk revival would not be until 1939–1942, Huddie happened to arrive at a time when the movement was just defining itself and the role music would have in its work.

One of the people Huddie met through the Barnicle circle was Margot Mayo, who had organized the American Square Dance Group. This was a loose-knit association interested in trying to preserve some of the variety of regional, rural dancing styles. Members would meet regularly, learn new dances, and during intermission sing folk songs. Like Barnicle, she was interested in field collecting herself (she later made several field trips to collect for the Library of Congress) and lost no time in befriending Leadbelly and Martha.

During much of this time, the couple were living pretty much on relief and on what jobs Barnicle could get for them. One month Martha became quite ill and was forced to go to welfare department doctors; neither she nor Huddie were satisfied with the kind of care she was getting. Margot Mayo found out about it and referred Huddie to another doctor, one who took a look at Martha and admitted her to a hospital. Huddie was still suspicious; he feared that Martha's race—and class—would make her a second-class patient, even in a decent hospital. As the days passed, he found he was right: Martha had a hospital bed, but was not really being treated. When he mentioned this to Margot Mayo, the dance teacher hit upon a plan to bluff the hospital: she arranged for all the prominent people she knew, white or black, to telephone the hospital, inquiring about the condition of Mrs. Ledbetter. The plan worked; in a few days, Martha was operated on and was soon on her way back home.

A few months later, Mayo invited Huddie and Martha to spend a weekend at a special interracial camp where she was teaching. She recalled that Huddie was thoroughly amazed at finding such a camp, where black and white children and adults mingled socially. While he had expected New York to be an improvement over the harsh segregation of Texas and Louisiana, he had not really expected anything like this. He was, in fact, never able to really overcome his own latent suspicion of whites; Irwin Silber, who later booked him to play at various People's Songs shows, described his attitude toward whites as a mixture of suspicion and gullibility. Other friends recall that Huddie was often distrustful of whites even though he still had "the southern Negro's faith in the power of the white man."

There were other reasons for Huddie's suspicions. In October 1936, Huddie and Martha were living at 431 West 52nd Street and were seriously broke. At the suggestion of friends, they applied for assistance from the Emergency Relief Bureau of the city. This normally would have been a routine matter, but a bureaucrat in the district office recalled reading about Leadbelly in the January 1935 issue of *Time*. There was a rule that nobody could receive relief assistance unless they had been residents of the city for at least two years. On their application, Huddie and Martha had stated they had been in New York since 1933. Their case supervisor took it upon herself to write the warden at Angola to find out if this could have been so. "Mr. Ledbetter has furnished us with letters from various persons in the community who testify that they have attended his concerts in the years 1933 and 1934," wrote Mary Hamm, the supervisor. "We wonder if you would send us what information you have about Mr. Ledbetter concerning his place of residence prior to incarceration and the place to which he went after release." Warden Louis A. Jones at Angola responded back the day he got the letter. The prisoner Ledbetter served his time and was discharged on August 1, 1934. "Press reports to the contrary notwithstanding, he was released by the operation of the good time law, and not as a result of executive clemency." Jones also reported that after release, Huddie went back to Mooringsport, to his wife, who was still listed as Era Washington. It was a rather heroic attempt to check the documentation of this one case, from an agency that must have had hundreds of requests concerning other cases. As he listened to the caseworker explain why he was being denied relief, Huddie must have wondered if all the publicity he had gotten was really worth it.

Mary Elizabeth Barnicle was so intrigued with the Lomaxes and their portable disc-cutting machine that she managed to buy one herself. By the summer of 1936, after a summer's work the previous year with Alan, she had learned how to use hers. It was a bulky affair that ran off automobile batteries which leaked acid and burned holes in Barnicle's dresses. Nonetheless, she got her blank discs and began to do her own field recordings. Huddie had not made any recordings at all since he had split with John Lomax, and he soon became a frequent subject for Barnicle's machine. For the next ten years or so, he would record dozens of pieces for Barnicle, often dropping by to try out new songs he had written. But now, in August 1936, he and Martha prepared to go with Barnicle on a new trip. They had been living with her most of the summer in the farmhouse at Wilton. Now they embarked on a five-week trip back to Leadbelly's old turf. They would go to Shreveport, Dallas, New Orleans, and return up through Mississippi. Leadbelly would do most of the driving, and Shreveport would be the headquarters, where Barnicle would receive her mail.

Another of the people Barnicle introduced to Leadbelly was a folklorist, activist, and scholar named Lawrence Gellert. Born in 1896 of Hungarian immigrants in New York City, Gellert had moved to North Carolina in the early 1920s. There he gained the confidence of the black community and began doing field recordings of his own, specializing in various types of black protest songs. His singers were understandably nervous about his recording such frank songs, and he promised to preserve their anonymity as he continued his collection. Gellert's brother Hugo was involved in the publication of the socialist magazine *New Masses*, and Gellert began attracting attention by publishing some of his songs in the magazine in the early 1930s. With composer Elie Siegmeister, he collected many of these into a book, *Negro Songs of Protest*, in 1936. In late 1934, Gellert had written some strong criticism of John Lomax's collecting methods in *New Masses*, some of it directly relevant to Leadbelly. He was especially scornful of the pardon story.

He [Lomax] had the "right" connections. Could go straight to the Governor of Louisiana with a phonograph record by Leadbelly—and presto—a pardon! Between gentlemen—a "nigger's" life-time—a matter of a song! But imagine Ben Davis, Jr., editor of the Negro Liberator going to Governor Talmadge of Georgia with one sung by Angelo Herndon and getting a pardon for him! Or ditto Governor Miller of Alabama with a record sung by nine Scottsboro boys in a chorus!

He felt that John Lomax "failed to get to the heart of contemporary Negro folk lore" because "he embodies the slave-master attitude intact." If Leadbelly had felt free enough to sing some of the strong protest songs Gellert had collected, Lomax wouldn't have had the nerve to even take it to the governor, Gellert wrote. On southern chain gangs and in prisons, where Lomax got many of his songs and where he had to get permission from guards and authorities to get his subjects to sing, no black person could freely express himself. As Alan Lomax himself has noted, these songs have long existed in black oral tradition, but it was dangerous for the blacks to even sing such protest songs in private, much less sing them for a recording.

Now Gellert joined in the group that helped Huddie find work and singing jobs. He probably was also interested in the parts of the singer's repertoire that Lomax had not explored, and might have talked at length with him about this or even transcribed some of his songs. He was also interested in the legal problems Huddie had been having with Lomax, and he shared songs of his own collection with the singer.

In the meantime, John Lomax had finished the book, which was now being retitled as *Negro Folk Songs as Sung by Lead Belly*. The title was a compromise; "it was imposed on the book to satisfy Herzog's academic fears," recalls Alan, "and it helped to kill the book." There were problems reconciling variations in text between one recording and another, and in this both Alan and John Lomax helped Herzog. At one point in the spring, Herzog had transcribed some fifty-six songs; space constraints eventually meant that the team could use only forty-eight songs in the book. Among those dropped were "Way Over in the Promised Land," "Alberta" (as distinct from "Roberta"), "Old Man Settin' in the Corner Dyin'," and "You Don't Know My Mind"—the latter because Lomax found that the song had been published and copyrighted by jazz composer Clarence Williams in 1924. In fact, as he worked out the melodies, Herzog noticed that a number of them were familiar; he wrote in the book's introduction, "More than half of these melodies and texts have been published in other collections, in some other version. Others are of white parentage, some are white tunes pure and simple." John Lomax felt that this did not especially disqualify them as folk songs, since Leadbelly had learned them via oral tradition and "had practiced them for years in isolated penitentiaries." A decade later, however, Leadbelly would admit to interviewer Ross Russell that as a young man he occasionally did listen to records, and even learned songs off pieces of sheet music.

Lomax, working away on the ranch near Fort Spunky owned by his friend Henry Zweifel, had been cutting huge sections from his biographical section. At one point in November 1935 he wrote to his wife that he had "simplified the book much; cut out generalities and reflections and conclusions" and was intending to reduce the manuscript by cutting some three hundred manuscript pages. He was determined to save the sections that Alan had written, especially his "fine character study and description of Leadbelly," as well as "the stories that Leadbelly told Alan." Presumably this was all done at the behest of Macmillan, which was fearful of getting a manuscript so large the company could never print it. Lomax had gone into the project in January 1935 expecting to knock off the book in a month's hard work. In reality, he had not finished it until late March 1936.

Thus in November 1936, in time for the Christmas trade, Macmillan finally released *Negro Folk Songs as Sung by Lead Belly*. It was a big, handsome book, running to 242 pages and sporting a frontispiece photo of Huddie by Otto Hesse, made at the cost of $250. It showed the singer sitting on a stack of feed sacks in front of some old barrels, barefoot, dressed in his coveralls and bandanna outfit, strumming the Stella and singing. It had been made a year before, when Lomax had been encouraging Huddie to wear such an outfit. The introduction and biography took up some sixty-eight of the book's pages—almost a third of it—and each song was prefaced by a headnote explaining its origin or place in Leadbelly's life. Many of the songs had the spoken interludes that the singer had started using to such advantage in his New York shows.

The book was favorably received and widely reviewed. The *New York Times* printed a full-page review by the distinguished black playwright and composer James Weldon Johnson. "The story of Leadbelly is stark realism and raw life," he explained. "The Lomaxes . . . hardly do more than present their hero. They let him tell his own story [and] the result is one of the most amazing autobiographical accounts ever printed in America." Harry Hansen, writing in the *World Telegram*, called the book a "Black Epic of Horrifics." *The New Republic*'s Constance Rourke, later to gain fame as an authority on American humor, reviewed it along with Gellert's book of protest songs, and called it "in essence a novel, a drama or even an opera." The *Saturday Review of Literature*, in whose offices Leadbelly once performed, noted that "the history of popular music, some day to be written profitably, will take leaves from this contribution of the Lomaxes." Back in Dallas, the *Morning News* assigned the noted cowboy writer J. Frank Dobie to review the book, who started off his review with a personal note. "Those who know him well, know that John A. Lomax is one of the most vivid and vigorous talkers in the world, a master of concrete details that light up human beings and human motives lying way back in the dark." Dobie, too, was more interested in the Lomax biography than in the songs themselves, and concluded: "The picture of [Leadbelly] so far as my limited knowledge goes, is the most powerful picture of a negro man, excepting Emperor Jones, that has appeared in American literature."

What none of the reviewers of the time realized was that this book was also the first serious, full-length portrait of a folksinger in American literature. Other collections of folk songs, including Lomax's own, contained scraps of information and scattered details about the singers. Here, for the first time, a folk song collector had presented not only a comprehensive cross-section of the singer's repertoire, accurately transcribed from phonograph records and framed by accurate headnotes, but also a lengthy and sympathetic portrait of the singer's own life, often using his own words. It was an endeavor that fully did justice to its rich and complex subject.

To Huddie and Martha, living up on 52nd Street and arguing with the district office of the Emergency Relief Bureau to try to get some kind of welfare help, the publication of the book must have seemed bitterly ironic. It was being sold, albeit in rather small numbers, all over the city for

$3.50—enough to keep a poor family in food for a week. Yet there are no surviving letters indicating Huddie wrote either to Macmillan or to John Lomax to complain. There is some indication that he threatened legal action against the book because of things that were said in it. Huddie had delayed work on the book through his lawsuits the previous summer, but Lomax had not even finished the manuscript at that time and Huddie had no idea what it would contain. Friends, though, knew that Huddie did not like the book and never really had much good to say about it. Years later he wrote, "Don't forget because there is a book writing about my life and I don't think nothing about that book. . . . Because Lomax did not rite nothing like I told him." Alan Lomax feels that Huddie never understood the book to begin with, and that his attitude in later years probably reflected the feelings of Martha and others who knew the older Leadbelly and wanted to forget his violent past. "Yet without the violent past, the white audience never would have noticed him."

Leadbelly may not have liked the book, but the Lomaxes seem to have done a good job of transcribing his autobiography. Their headnotes for songs are generally insightful, interesting, and add a great deal to our knowledge and understanding of African American folk music. Partially because Huddie was reluctant to talk about some parts of his life, they left many facets of his life unexplored, such as the details of his relationship with Blind Lemon Jefferson. Huddie himself practiced a great deal of self-censorship; for instance, he failed to reveal the fact that he had fathered three daughters, nor was he forthcoming with the details regarding the murder of Will Stafford in 1917. Today, readers might find the Lomaxes' use of black southern dialect offensive, but this was far more commonplace and acceptable in the middle 1930s.

As 1937 rolled around, though, Huddie began to find out that the book would win him some much-needed publicity and another shot at making the big time in the commercial entertainment world. On April 19, *Life* magazine did a picture story on him, built around an outtake from the Otto Hesse session that yielded the book's frontispiece. The familiar themes were all there—not even *Life* reporters apparently bothered to check out the facts with the people down South. BAD NIGGER MAKES GOOD MINSTREL, read the headline of the story. A beautiful photo of Huddie's hands fingering the Stella was captioned, "These hands once killed a man." Martha was pictured as "her husband's manager," and photos of Pat Neff and of the Huntsville prison filled in the history. The story included the 1935 trip to New York, after which "Leadbelly broke with Lomax" and returned home. The article added, "Chastened, poor again after brief, sudden affluence, he recently returned to New York, is currently singing and playing on the radio, may well be on the brink of a new and prosperous period."

The radio prospects seemed good, but Huddie at once ran into a problem that made his anger over the book not merely a personal problem.
The radio stations would not sign a contract with him because they were
afraid that his best and most famous songs were copyrighted by Macmillan in the book. Without some kind of consent from Macmillan's legal
staff, the various radio station programmers were nervous about letting
him sing. The agreement signed the year before between Lomax, Leadbelly, and Macmillan had given to the company all publication and other
rights to the songs. It was a legitimate problem. Huddie hired an attorney
named Sol S. Perlow and opened negotiations with Macmillan. George
Pruett at once saw this was a chance to get rid of the "threatened suit"
Huddie had been talking about, the one in regard to the "defamation" in
the book, and decided to do some bartering. He contacted Lomax and by
October had worked out yet another agreement between the three. In this
document, after acknowledging the ownership by the Macmillan Company of copyright for songs in the book, the text states that "Ledbetter
now wishes to sing certain of such songs and use other material in the
said book in radio broadcasts, motion pictures, or in personal public performances." The company, as well as Alan and John Lomax, were to
permit this, but the permission specifically did not extend to "any person
other than the said Ledbetter." In exchange for this permission, and for
the sum of $10, Leadbelly "releases and forever discharges John A.
Lomax, Alan Lomax, The Macmillan Company . . . from any and all manner of action or actions, cause or causes of action, suits, claims, or demands whatever, at law or in equity, which he may have against them or
any of them, arising out of the publication of the aforesaid book, or from
any other cause whatever." In short, for agreeing to abandon any claims
against the book in the future, Huddie got back not ownership of his
songs, but merely the right to sing them in public.

Once again, though, Huddie had missed his chance. By the time he got
the Macmillan agreement, the flurry of publicity over the book had died
down. There were plenty of offers to play for labor meetings and political
gatherings, but the big-money people were less interested now. Some of
them had little understanding of or appreciation for the "simple" kind of
folk music he played. Benny Goodman had made swing and jazz the most
popular form of music in the nation, and the black singers in demand
were the ones in the mold of Cab Calloway: slick, sophisticated, and generations removed from their folk roots. This was probably the main reason why the ARC records and the Harlem stage show at the Apollo—the
singer's main attempts to appeal to the city's black community—were
failures. The pattern would continue for the next several years, and the

singer would not even associate much with the city's black community. He seldom went to Harlem and deliberately chose not to live there. Though he still did not trust whites, he was learning that they were his best audience. And they did not want, it seemed, a down-home blues singer: they wanted a folk singer.

21 "The Bourgeois Blues"

In 1937, novelist Richard Wright moved to New York from Chicago. The son of Mississippi sharecroppers, he had grown up in Memphis and knew firsthand about the great black migration from the rural South to the urban Northeast. His early publications in Chicago had included a body of Communist poetry as well as articles for the party newspaper, the *Daily Worker*. In 1937 he was still three years away from publishing his masterpiece *Native Son* and was then working on the stories that would make up *Uncle Tom's Children*, the book that would win him nationwide fame. In 1937, too, he met Huddie Ledbetter, probably at a rally or meeting. For several years he became one of Huddie's drinking buddies in New York, one of the few black friends the singer had. On August 12, 1937, Wright wrote a column for the *Daily Worker* introducing Leadbelly as a true "people's artist." The article furthered the singer's reputation in left-wing circles and was a strong contrast to the 1935 press stories about the "homicidal harmonizer." It is also one of the very few portraits of the singer by a black writer. The story begins with an account, obviously drawn from interviews with Huddie, of the singer's early life.

Huddie Ledbetter, Famous Negro Folk Artist,
Sings the Songs of Scottsboro and His People.

by Richard Wright

(Daily Worker, HARLEM BUREAU) When 50-year-old Huddie Ledbetter plants himself in a chair, spreads his feet, and starts strumming his 12-string guitar and singing that rich, barrel-chested baritone, it seems that the entire folk culture of the American Negro has found its embodiment in him.

Blues, spirituals, animal songs, ballads and work songs pour forth in such profusion that it seems he knows every song his race has ever sung.

Shaped and molded by some of the harshest social forces in American life, Ledbetter admits that he knows 500 folk songs and "maybe many more I can't count."

He makes his songs out of the day-to-day life of his people. He sings of death, of work, of balked love, of southern jails no better than hell holes, of chain gangs, of segregation, of his hope for a better life.

SANG THROUGH THE SOUTH

This hard stocky black man sang his way through the Louisiana swamp-land, the sun-baked cotton fields, and out of two state prisons, where he was sent for protecting himself against the aggression of southern whites.

Down south the white landlords called him a "bad nigger" and they were afraid of his fists, his bitter biting songs, his 12-stringed guitar, and his inability to take injustice and like it. Because they feared him and respected his hardness, they called him Leadbelly, and at the first opportunity that came their way, they threw him in jail.

This folksinger tells tales of dodging white mobs, of wandering at night to save his life, and of how he would snatch a few hours of companionship with his friends when the white folks were not looking. He tells of cutting sugar cane in the rain, of picking a bale of cotton in two days, and of seeing black men drop dead from the heat of southern suns in the cotton fields.

WINS PARDON

When Ledbetter won himself a pardon for a second time out of a southern prison by composing folk songs, the southern landlords exploited him, robbing him of his self-made culture and then turned him loose on the streets of northern cities to starve.

John A. Lomax, collector of American folk songs for the Library of Congress, heard of Ledbetter and went to see him in prison. And here begins one of the most amazing cultural swindles in American history. Lomax found in Ledbetter a man of lore, songs, tunes and adages of the South.

After recounting the familiar O. K. Allen prison story, Wright continues his passionate attack on John Lomax. "Lomax then beguiled the singer with sugary promises, telling him if he helped him to gather folksongs from other Negro prisoners in other prisons, he would make him rich." In fact, he had told the singer from the first that he could barely pay him more than his expenses. But according to Wright, when Huddie's songs were used in *American Ballads and Folk Songs*, the only credit Ledbetter got was "the 'high honor' of seeing his name in print."

After the pair came to New York, Wright continues, "Lomax gave out a vicious tirade of publicity to the nation's leading newspapers." Leadbelly was represented in these papers, and over the radio, as "a half sex-mad, knife-toting black buck from Texas." When he tried to insist on a "straight and legal contract" with Lomax, he was told the collector was saving his money for him, and that "if I gave you your money, you'd throw it away in Harlem." According to Wright, Leadbelly got only $18 for his appearance in *The March of Time* and a sum of $265 for his later concerts and travels.

Wright then explains Huddie's return to the South, his return to the Northeast with John Townsend, and his Layfayette Theater engagement. "For the second time Ledbetter was victimized by a prejudiced white southerner in a theater engagement." He still doesn't make clear exactly what happened with Townsend, but the impression is that his sudden leaving might well have something to do with the income from the Layfayette shows. As things became more desperate for Huddie and Martha, he joined the Workers' Alliance, an organization for the unemployed. Wright explains:

Finally he joined the Workers' Alliance and applied for relief. Relief authorities would not believe that Ledbetter did not have money saved from his extensive appearance on stage, and threatened to withdraw his food ticket. In return, the folksinger threatened to write a song about the rotten relief methods, and the relief authorities granted his demand.

"The folks in the Workers' Alliance are the finest I've ever known," said Ledbetter. "I feel happy when I'm with the boys here at the Workers' Alliance. They are different from those southern white men."

Wright seemed impressed that in Leadbelly's early days, "white landlords" in the South feared his "bitter biting songs." Even after he moved north, the singer continued to suffer injustices and bigotry in the big cities. It was natural that he fight back with one of the few weapons he had: his music. The fact that he could challenge and defeat the relief authorities by threatening to write a song about them was imposing. Wright and his colleagues at *The Daily Worker* were dutifully impressed; a few months later, Mike Gold, the flamboyant Communist whose ambition was to find "a thousand Shakespeares in overalls," wrote about Leadbelly again. He renewed Wright's praise of the singer and argued that the people's movement needed more authentic folk songs like "John Henry" and that people like Huddie Ledbetter were the ones to provide them.

In fact, Leadbelly himself seldom if ever actually used the word *Protest* to describe any of the new songs he was starting to write. Nor was the term heard on radio or seen much on record labels and catalogs in the mid-1930s. To be sure, there had been vernacular songs complaining about social or political problems since the days of Andrew Jackson and Davy Crockett. Civil War soldiers sang about bad food and stupid generals; homesteaders sang about about corn dodgers (biscuits) so hard you had to swallow them like a pill. But these were often humorous, throwaway songs—gripes and complaints—that had no serious hope of actually changing a social ill. The idea of using a song as a specific weapon, as a tool for social reform, was something fairly new. This harsh, acerbic art took root in the Depression-wracked 1930s. No surprisingly, popular records of the time reflected the new outrages and indignation: Workers could have their "Pie in the Sky," farmers learned to live with "Eleven Cent Cotton and Forty Cent Meat," while merchants sang "The NRA Blues." Even preachers could point out that "There's No Depression in Heaven." The city dwellers who knew little about real folk music recognized that a new tone, and a new type, of song was emerging.

Protest songs were sometimes confused with topical songs, which celebrated or chronicled current events or people in the news. These, too, had been around for a long time. When Leadbelly sang of the sinking of the *Titanic* back in Dallas in 1912, he was singing a topical song that chronicled the event without much attempt to assess blame or complain about unfairness. The earliest ballads to find their way to commercial phonograph records, in the mid-1920s, were all topical songs such as the train-wreck song "The Wreck of the Old 97," country music's first million-selling hit in 1925. The day Huddie arrived in New York City, one of the best-selling records was a lachrymose ballad about the fate of Bruno Hauptmann (the Lindbergh baby kidnapper); another, by young Gene Autry, detailed the death of country yodeler Jimmie Rodgers.

Huddie had learned earlier that he could attract attention in prison by customizing songs—either by adapting an existing song or making up a song about local specific events or people, whether it was Governor Neff he wanted to get a pardon from or a girlfriend he wanted to seduce. His quick wit and musical versatility made this almost second nature. Indeed, Leadbelly probably improvised scores of topical songs, forgetting them in a couple of weeks after they served their purpose. He soon found that the people in New York were not all that different from the audiences in Angola or Sugarland: all got a kick out of instant songs about current topics. Huddie enjoyed reading the newspapers as much as anyone else and the headlines he saw gave him ideas for a whole genre of new songs. If people tired of hearing about Pat Neff, then he could give them Jean Harlow, Howard Hughes, the *Hindenburg* airship, or the *Queen Mary* luxury liner—not quite protest songs, but pieces offering a fresh take on current topics.

Thus he soon began to add both types of new songs to his repertoire—the protest and the topical song. Though the labor movement and other left-wing organizations in New York City read of Leadbelly in the *Daily Worker* and heard him at rallies, the singer himself seemed more impressed by a small cadre of Kentucky singers he met through Mary Barnicle. Many of them had been through the bloody struggle to unionize the coal mines and had suffered the same kind of violence and injustice that Leadbelly had

endured in Texas and Louisiana. They were adept at taking the old mountain songs and recasting them as powerful protest songs. Leadbelly seemed
impressed with them and intrigued with how they did this. One of these
singer-organizers was Aunt Molly Jackson, whom Barnicle had also taken
under her wing, a woman Woody Guthrie later called a "woman Leadbelly."

Aunt Molly was a native of Clay County, Kentucky. Born there in 1880,
she married a miner and became active in the bloody struggle for coal
miners' rights in the 1920s and early 1930s. A natural ballad singer with a
huge repertoire of old songs and tunes, she began to fashion new protest
songs out of older ones, songs like "Harlan County Blues" and "I Am a
Union Woman," and in 1931 she was "discovered" by a group called the
Dreiser Committee, concerned with miners' rights and raising money to
help them. She moved to New York City and eventually toured numerous
states, speaking and singing to raise funds and promote her cause. Later her
brother Jim Garland and stepsister Sarah Ogan—two more singers and
songwriters—moved there, too. Jackson became a regular at Barnicle's
NYU classes. Leadbelly met her through Barnicle, liked her, and even
recorded a few songs with her on Barnicle's machine. As Leadbelly listened
to the Kentucky singers and sang with them, he saw that their protest music
was not very different from his personalized topical songs like "Governor
Pat Neff" and "Ain't It a Pity, I'm in New York City." He had not put much
of a political spin on his songs yet, but if this was the kind of thing his
audiences at the meetings and rallies wanted, he might give it a try.

One day Huddie met a man who was visiting Jim Garland, another
Kentuckian named Tillman Cadle. Cadle was actually born in Claiborne
County, Tennessee in 1902, to impoverished tenant farmers. At the age of
thirteen, he left school to work as a trapper boy in the coal mines for 6 cents
an hour. His brother's death in a mining accident and the constant poverty
he saw daily led him into attempts to organize miners into a union. Routinely harassed and eventually fired, he came to New York to stay with his
fellow organizer Jim Garland and to have an operation performed. There he
met Barnicle, who promptly drafted him to speak to her NYU classes; the
two hit it off, and soon he was working with Barnicle on her folk song
collecting. He also became a fixture at her Greenwich Village apartment as
he continued to do union work at the national level.

In spite of their different backgrounds, Cadle and Leadbelly seemed to hit
it off well. As Cadle recalled: "I had some of the people in New York to
kindly kid Leadbelly about me. They'd ask Leadbelly, 'How does it happen
that you get along with this hillbilly? I didn't think you liked hillbillies.' And
Leadbelly would say, 'This man here from the hills, he's got a little sense,'
and he'd mention that I wasn't prejudiced." Like Leadbelly, Cadle had seen

his share of violence; like Leadbelly, he knew dozens of old songs, blues, and even "toasts"—long, often obscene narrative poems that were normally associated with urban blacks, but which Cadle knew from hardscrabble white miners. Leadbelly soon came to trust Tillman. Tillman recalled, "Leadbelly, used to, we'd meet on the street, and he'd want to buy me a drink. If a bar was close by, he'd say, 'Let's go in this bar.' We'd go in, and he'd tell the bartender, 'Give this man a drink, and give him a good one.' And if he'd set out one of those little glasses, them little demitasses or something, Leadbelly would say, 'Man, I told you I wanted this man to have a good drink!' And then he'd set up a water glass."

Tillman also began to help Barnicle in her attempts to get Leadbelly singing jobs. He had good contacts with the labor movement and with the different organizations then active in the city. Protest meetings and rallies were going on almost every night and Cadle was well known at most of them. Once it got around that he and Leadbelly were friends, groups began coming to Cadle to ask if he could get Leadbelly to come to their meetings. Leadbelly drew a good crowd, but Cadle made sure something was in it for Leadbelly as well. Usually he suggested they take up a collection for the singer and this often netted $10 or $15. Some of the groups Leadbelly sang for during this time were the Worker's Alliance, the Workers' International Relief (raising money for Kentucky miners), The International Worker's Order, the Young Communist League, the Theater Arts Alliance, and a host of organizations raising funds for the Spanish Civil War. Always able to read an audience well, Huddie was versatile enough for almost any occasion: He could give them an old folk song or tailor a new one. An old spiritual, for instance, served as the model for "We're in the Same Boat, Brother"; an old Baptist church song from the days of tracted meetings, "Gonna Fight the Battle," took on new meaning in union rallies and meeting halls.

The links Leadbelly forged with the labor movement and the left were not pure; Leadbelly used the movement much as they used him. He seems to have been mildly sympathetic with their aims, but seldom revealed any strong political feelings on his own. Frederick Ramsey said that Leadbelly "never really felt at home with the left" and that he was not a "militant or a political. A lot of the left-wing groups had decided to make a pet out of him." Neither Pete Seeger nor Tillman Cadle recalled Leadbelly talking much about politics, and Cadle could recall the singer voting only on rare occasions. "I never heard him say anything against the Communist party," Seeger remarked. "He sang for it from time to time, but he probably would have sang for some other group if they had paid him to." Seeger also felt that Leadbelly seldom sang specifically union songs because of the long-engrained suspicion many blacks in those days had of unions. In general, though, Leadbelly did not see himself as a crusader in the same way Aunt

Molly Jackson did. To him, the protest rallies and labor meetings were simply new venues to replace his traditional black audiences that had turned their backs on him at the Apollo.

Occasionally, though, one of the causes hit close to home. Everyone agrees that the one issue Leadbelly felt strongly about was civil rights. He had found that the Northeast was as Jim Crow as Shreveport or Dallas, and he had experienced this firsthand on his early trips with the Lomaxes. Now, in June 1937, he and Martha went to Washington, D.C., in part to record more songs for the Library of Congress. Young Alan Lomax was in charge of the session—Huddie had never had the kind of falling out with him that he had had with his father—and Alan offered them lodging at his little flat near the Supreme Court building. Huddie and Martha spent the first night sleeping on the floor and were awakened by angry voices. Alan's landlord was at the downstairs entrance, shouting at Lomax, "You brought some niggers in my house? I don't want no niggers up there!" Lomax knew that his landlord could bring the Jim Crow laws down upon him and reluctantly agreed to find Huddie and Martha another place to stay.

This was easier to say than do. The Ledbetters had driven down with Mary Barnicle—in fact, Huddie had driven her car—and a mutual friend named Kip Kilmer. He was the son of Joyce Kilmer, the poet who had written the famous poem "Trees," and, as Leadbelly explained later, "was worth $90,000." The party set out to find lodging. Huddie recalled, "We rode all around in the rain. No colored people would take me in because I was with a white man." To his astonishment, he soon learned that the mixed group couldn't even go into a place to eat—even to one catering to blacks. "I had so many white people with me, he wouldn't let me in. But she told me just before I left, the colored woman did, that when I came back and didn't bring no white man, I could eat."

At some point in the search, Barnicle was feeling especially bitter about the extent of Jim Crow in the nation's capital and complained, and the whole group began joking about what a bourgeois town Washington was. Huddie perked up. He didn't know what the word *bourgeois* meant, but his poet's ear loved the sound of it. When he asked Barnicle what it meant, and after she explained it, he was even more interested in the word. There had to be some way to use it—and the whole Washington, D.C., trip—in a song. The end result was "The Bourgeois Blues," a song that would become one of his most famous and that would gain fame as one of his more sincere, heartfelt protest songs. The song came together quickly; Alan Lomax especially liked it since it describes something that happened in his own apartment. What emerged was a strong indictment of Washington, then as now living up to its nickname of "the largest city in North Carolina." One stanza was especially strong:

The white folks in Washington,
They know how,
They chunk you a nickel,
Just to see a nigger bow.©

"I got the Bourgeois Blues, and I'm gonna spread the news," ran another line, and Leadbelly did. He was singing the song a few weeks later when Richard Wright interviewed him, for Wright quoted part of it. Huddie recorded it in a New York studio in December 1938 at a session paid for by Barnicle and later donated to the Library of Congress.

His fledgling political conscience was awakened again shortly after he returned to New York. He learned about new developments in the case of the Scottsboro Boys. The Scottsboro case, as it was called, had become, in the words of one historian, "the cause celebre of American race relations in the 1930s." It had all begun in 1931, when a deputy sheriff of Jackson County, Alabama, arrested nine young black men who had been hoboing on a train. He also took off the train a number of white hobos, including two women, who claimed the nine blacks had raped them. Lynch mobs formed, but the sheriff managed to get the boys to trial, where they were convicted and eight of them sentenced to death. An appeals court soon overturned the conviction, but the state launched a second prosecution in 1933. By now public opinion, especially in the north, was rising, and offers of help began pouring in. The International Labor Defense, a group loosely associated with the Communist Party USA (CPUSA), helped the youths mount a defense, and for the next several years, the case became headline news. In 1937 a compromise was reached, whereby four defendants were freed, but the others sentenced to long prison terms.

The obvious injustice infuriated the labor unions and political activists in New York at the time. As early as 1933 the *Daily Worker* was announcing that the workers would hear a new Scottsboro song, one by L. E. Swift, called "The Scottsboro Boys Shall Not Die." It was heartfelt, but based too much on the formal European music of the day. In a few weeks Huddie had decided to try his hand at a song about it. Using the same general idea as he had with "Bourgeois Blues," he sang, "go to Alabama and you better watch out." The Scottsboro boys "they can tell you what it's all about." His advice to "all you colored people" in Harlem: "Don't you ever go to Alabama." In one of his spoken interludes in the song, he said: "If a white woman says something, it must be so, and she can say something about a colored person, if it's a thousand colored men, they kill all of 'em just for that one woman. If she ain't telling the truth, it don't make any difference. Why? 'Cause it's Jim Crow, and I know it's so 'cause the Scottsboro boys can tell you about it."

Huddie sang the new song for Richard Wright, who quoted part of it in his *Daily Worker* article. He premiered it publicly on August 13, 1937, at a special event sponsored by the Federal Workers' Project. They sponsored a moonlight sail on the steamboat *Mayflower*, which left Pier One, North River, west of Battery Park, at eight-thirty. Two of the Scottsboro mothers, Mrs. Wright and Mrs. Montgomery, were especially invited to hear the new song in honor of their sons. In later years, as the furor over the Scottsboro case died down, Huddie sang the song less. He recorded it twice for the Library of Congress, but never commercially. But in the 1930s it helped much to establish his own reputation in New York as a folksinger who could sing about relevant topics.

The success of "Bourgeois Blues" and "The Scottsboro Boys Shall Not Die" encouraged Huddie to do even more songwriting and he quickly found that topical songs got him attention and press. He wrote "The *Hindenburg* Disaster," a song about the great airship destroyed by fire as it tried to land at Lakehurst, New Jersey, on May 6, 1937. Various cowboy singers had songs out about the disaster within weeks of the crash, and the American Record Corporation even released a Victrola record of the actual radio broadcast that described the crash. By the time he went to Washington with Barnicle, barely six weeks after the disaster, Huddie had his song ready to record for Alan Lomax's microphones at the Archive of Folk Song. Like the writers of disaster ballads had done for years, Huddie added rich, full details to his story. "It was up in the world just a little too high," he sang, doubtless thinking of the *Titanic* song he had sung years before. An avid reader of newspapers, Huddie was able to select from the long accounts of such events the kind of details that caught people's imaginations. In the *Hindenburg* song he focused on a woman throwing her children out, and how people watching it roll thought it was supposed to do that, and how all that was left of the ship was the frame.

There is little element of protest in "The *Hindenburg* Disaster," nor was there any in songs like *"Queen Mary,"* about the famed ocean liner; "Jean Harlow," about the blonde film actress; or "Howard Hughes," an odd song about the reclusive billionaire, replete with references to Hughes's around-the-world flight, his girl friend Katharine Hepburn, and the World's Fair of 1939. "Get upon in the morning, / Read about Howard Hughes," went the refrain. There was a song called "Turn Your Radio On," not to be confused with the gospel song of the same name by Albert E. Brumley; this was a simple tribute to radio. "You listen in to tell what's goin' on in the world." You also listen, says the song, to WNBC if you want to listen to Huddie. There was also a song called "Quit, Joe Louis, Quit," written to the boxing champion after he defeated Max Schmeling in June 1938. Leadbelly wanted the champ to hang up his gloves and retire gracefully. This is one of several

Leadbelly songs that have been lost; people remember him singing them, but the songs were never recorded, nor ever written down, and the text has vanished. This first flush of Leadbelly's topical songs revealed his own wry humor as well as his ability to use old forms for new songs. The songs themselves form his own unique panorama of the late 1930s: a sort of Leadbelly version of *The March of Time.*

More openly political was "He Is the Man," a campaign song Leadbelly wrote for Wendell Willkie. Leadbelly was impressed with Willkie when the Republicans nominated him to run against Roosevelt in 1940. Especially interesting was Willkie's strong civil rights plank, and Leadbelly's song imagined the night of victory for the candidate.

> *Whole town was ringin',*
> *Lots of 'em was singin',*
> *Champaigne was flowin' like a river,*
> *Like water runnin' down a branch.*©

He wrote several songs about Roosevelt, including "The Roosevelt Song" (circa 1939), in which he describes the President going "all over the United States, / Tryin' to get England and Germany to hesitate." It featured his juxtaposing of the old folk patterns and imagery with the odd political realities of 1939.

> *Way across the ocean,*
> *Thought I spied a jar,*
> *Nothin' but some Germanys,*
> *Sittin' on a log.*©

His "Mister Hitler" is a cogent biographical account of the dictator's rise to fame, while "We're Gonna Tear Hitler Down" is an up-tempo war song modeled on an old sukey jump. "National Defense Blues" talks about how women began working in defense factories: "Every pay day would come, / Her check was as big as mine." (Huddie did in fact do work later on in a defense plant in California.)

The wide popularity of "The Bourgeois Blues" and Huddie's willingness to perform for a wide variety of political gatherings helped earn him a reputation as a protest singer. By the end of the 1930s, he had become part of a growing circle of folksingers and interpreters of folk songs in New York City that included Aunt Molly Jackson, Sara Ogan, Jim Garland, Tillman Cadle, Burl Ives, Pete Seeger, Josh White, and Woody Guthrie. Henrietta Yurchenco, who was in the middle of it all through her popular radio show, noted: "All of them, with the exception of Leadbelly, were politically conscious." Indeed, the whole concept of a "folksinger" was becoming associated with causes in the popular mind, an association that would linger for decades. If Leadbelly was a folksinger, then by definition he was supposed to be a protest singer. Peter Seeger, who met Huddie about 1941 and saw him at dozens of rallies and meetings, explained why this assumption was wrong. "Underneath, Leadbelly, I'm sure, had to use a great deal of discipline to keep his temper at times. . . . when he found white people willing to help him, he simply was willing to ignore our radical politics." Seeger recounts paying him to come and sing for gatherings in Greenwich Village "raising money for some radical that had been thrown in jail." Money would be raised, Leadbelly would get $10 and he was able to make at least something with his music. Another young acquaintance of Huddie's, Richard Nickson, remembers, "From all of the left-wing functions we saw him at, we just assumed that was his bias, too. . . . I think he was just glad to fit in with people who enjoyed his music, no matter his political coloration."

In later years, Leadbelly's association with the Communist party gave some friends and fans cause for concern. Though he probably never knew it, the FBI started a file on him in the early 1940s, though even they did not consider him a "subject of investigation in the central indices at FBI headquarters." The file was primarily composed of cross-references—the "mentioning of a person, place, organization or event in the investigative file on another subject," according to the FBI. Yet the CPUSA at the time did not really exploit him. Henrietta Yurchenco remembers that "it's an old myth that the Communists used him. He was fulfilling his role. He was telling what it was like to be a black man in the South." The party was one organization that "gave him every opportunity to perform," Yurchenco continued. "We adored him, we loved him, we respected him. We were the ones who were interested. No matter what you may say about the Communist party later on, at this time the things that went on were absolutely beyond reproach. The attention given to blacks, we were the only ones who did." Huddie himself was able to joke about this after the war. At a party with his friend Joe Brown, he overhears somebody say, "You be careful now, or somebody will be calling you a communist." To which Huddie replied "Oh, all us niggers is communists, you know."

Perhaps the best summary of Huddie's work with the left came from Ronnie Gilbert, later to win fame with the Weavers. "On the left," she said, Huddie "would have found friendship, understanding of his and the life that oppressed people anywhere would have to face. He would have found a sympathetic ear and he certainly would have found a deep appreciation for his music and who he was. For his dignity and an appreciation for what he was doing—that's what he would have found on the left."

22 "Good Morning, Blues"

From 1935 until early 1939, Leadbelly made no more commercial recordings. He did record some topical songs for Alan Lomax when he went to Washington in the summer of 1937, but for a time much of his recording activity was casual and took place at the flat of Mary Barnicle and Tillman Cadle. Shortly after he met Barnicle, Cadle began to look for ways to improve the old bulky machine she had, the one that ran off car batteries. "Surely to the world they must make an electric recording machine somewhere," he remembered thinking at the time. "We got acquainted with a sound engineer that worked for the American Foundation for the Blind. His name was Charles Ritter, and I asked him if there was any chance you could get an electric recording machine made today to record on. And he told me about a man out in Stamford, Connecticut, that made them. His name was Lincoln Thompson, and we went out and got him to make our first electric machine. This would have been in the late 1930s." Before then, though, Barnicle and Cadle were nervous about getting some of Huddie's new songs preserved somehow.

In the fall of 1938, Leadbelly drove Barnicle down to Middlesboro, Kentucky, but not to record; they were to pick up Sara Ogan and bring her and Jim Garland back to New York. After they got back, Barnicle took all of them—Sara, Jim, and Leadbelly—into a commercial studio called Havers Studio in New York and had them record several discs. These included Huddie's first recording of "The Bourgeois Blues" and "The Scottsboro Boys Shall Not Die," as well as his first recording with Martha, who occasionally accompanied him on old gospel songs. Later Barnicle sent the discs to the Library of Congress, where they were filed with the series of field recordings already done.

With their new machine in place, though, Barnicle and Cadle could casually record in their own apartment, and began to do so with a vengeance. They eventually preserved over six hundred such recordings, of everyone from Aunt Molly Jackson, Sonny Terry and Brownie McGhee, Jim Garland, an ex-sailor named Richard Maitland who sang sea chanties, and dozens of others. Some of these were done in New York, others in Kentucky, east Tennessee, or even the Bahamas. Barnicle donated some of these recordings to the Library of Congress, but she retained others, including about fifty by Leadbelly. Tillman Cadle recalled: "I tell people we recorded him more extensively than even the Lomaxes did, because Leadbelly kept writing songs, or making up new versions of songs, after he'd finished with the Lomaxes. We recorded all these. We recorded him much more extensively, including some songs nobody else recorded. When he wrote a new song, he would want to make a record. He'd come over and say, 'Well, I've got another new song, get that recording machine set up.' '' These included a few off-color songs, some strong political songs, and occasional duets with Jim Garland, Sara Ogan, and even Aunt Molly Jackson. (On some of the latter, Leadbelly would play guitar backup for Aunt Molly.) For years, the Barnicle-Cadle collection sat in Tillman's mountain cabin in Tennessee, unknown and even uncataloged; in the late 1980s it was finally cataloged and donated to the Archives of Appalachia of East Tennessee State University in nearby Johnson City, Tennessee. Though some of the aluminum or acetate discs have deteriorated over the years, many contain superb versions of familiar Leadbelly songs, as well as unique versions of others.

———

Nothing ever went smoothly for Huddie. On March 5, 1939, he was arrested by detectives in Manhattan for felonious assault: He had allegedly stabbed another black man with his knife. Exactly what happened is not quite clear, but his friend Brownie McGhee said Huddie had caught a man climbing in his apartment window at night and had attacked the intruder. Alan Lomax thought the incident might have stemmed from a situation in which an unwanted suitor had been bothering Martha. Whatever the case, Huddie apparently stabbed the man some sixteen times. Bond was set for $1,000, and Alan Lomax came to the rescue; he posted a $50 "premium" with a bail bondsman named Alex J. Reben in the Bronx on March 10, getting the singer out on bail. Huddie then asked Alan to visit the victim and try to persuade him to drop the charges; not surprisingly the victim declined. Trial was set for May 4. There the charge was reduced to third-degree assault, but the jury in general sessions court voted to convict. Before the judge passed sentence, he asked probation officers to check on Huddie's background, and letters went out to Angola and Shreveport to ask about the prison record and to ask if Huddie was currently wanted there. The return letter from Angola explained the singer's time, acknowledged that he was not wanted, and added, almost petulantly, that the famous pardon story was not true.

Knowing that Leadbelly was going to need money for a decent lawyer, as well as some way of supporting Martha, Alan Lomax dropped out of Columbia for the spring semester to help raise money for the singer. Various parties and benefits at places like Mary Barnicle's succeeded in bringing in a certain amount of money, but the largest share came from a commercial record deal with a new company called Musicraft—a deal that Alan set up.

On April 1, between Huddie's release on bond and his trial date, he went
into the studio on top of the Steinway Building and recorded a session of
some thirteen songs. Included were old favorites like "Fannin Street,"
"Frankie and Albert," "De Kalb Blues," and "The Gallis Pole," Huddie's
version of the centuries-old English ballad often called "Hangman, Hangman." He also did the first commercial recording of "The Bourgeois
Blues." The masters were cut on twelve-inch discs, which gave the singer
more time per song; some discs even were able to hold two songs on a side.
They were eventually issued in the form of two four-record 78 rpm albums,
some of the first such albums featuring folk music and containing biographical notes and song lyrics.

Musicraft was the first of a number of small, independent labels that
would eventually play a defining role in Leadbelly's later career. Samuel
Pruner had begun Musicraft in 1935 to record Baroque and pre-Bach organ
music. A lawyer by training, Pruner had learned about the record business
through one of his clients, Timely Records, a small New York company that
specialized in left-wing artists, but had also released African American protest songs by southern blacks in its "Negro Songs of Protest" series. Pruner
learned about the record business as he helped Timely through its financial
problems, but he also knew Jack and Dave Kapp, of the highly commercial
Decca record company. With $10,000 seed money, Pruner began his own
label, Musicraft. Gordon Mercer, a childhood friend who liked music and
electronics, became the company engineer; the company used a studio in
the Steinway Building, but was often stymied in its goals for a first-class
record by the uneven quality of the acetate onto which it had to record.
Working for $25 a week, Pruner and his friends began issuing records and
soon branched out from the Baroque pieces that had been their original goal
and embraced black folk music.

Pruner recalled: "Josh White came . . . and the Hampton Institute
Quartet, and we recorded them. We did a number of things that other
record companies simply were not doing. We weren't making any money
at it, but we were doing it for love, I suppose. We were deeply involved in
liberal causes. The plight of the black men and women in this country was
a heck of a lot worse than it is today. We even wanted to get Paul Robeson,
but Victor had him under contract."

Pruner was able to give Leadbelly an advance for the session, and this
money helped pay for Huddie's legal expenses. Alan Lomax recalled that
the advance went "from Huddie's hand to the lawyer's pocket." As it
turned out, though, Huddie didn't have to serve his full year. While he was
out on bond, he was shopping at a small store one night and stumbled into
a robbery. Intent on holding a gun on the owner, the robber did not notice
Leadbelly in the back of the store. Leadbelly moved up behind the bandit,

tackled him, and held him until a policeman arrived. When the judge heard
of this act of bravery, he was impressed and on May 20, sentenced Huddie
to less than one year at Riker's Island prison. His "good time" record
further reduced the sentence to eight months. Though the evidence suggests that Huddie had acted in self-defense in the stabbing, any further
appeals seemed too expensive and promised little hope. The court was
looking at his past and seeing him as just another middle-aged, knife-wield-
ing black man who couldn't seem to stay out of trouble. Huddie did his
time.

At the dawn of the 1940s, folk music in New York City was undergoing a
major change. Familiar faces like Aunt Molly Jackson were still around, but
they were now being joined by a new crop of younger singers, most notably
Woody Guthrie, Pete Seeger, Burl Ives, Richard Dyer-Bennet, and Lee
Hayes. Their ranks were soon augmented by newly arrived refugees from
the South—Josh White, Sonny Terry, the Golden Gate Quartet, and
Brownie McGhee—in search of a new audience. All seemed to arrive in (or
return to) New York within a few months of one another, and all would
make huge marks on the field of American folk music. Leadbelly would, in
the next few years, sing with them, broadcast with them, party with them,
and get to know them all.

Some, like Leadbelly, came from traditional southern backgrounds. Josh
White, one of the black singers, had actually followed Leadbelly as a companion to blues great Blind Lemon Jefferson. Later he used his South
Carolina background while recording for the old ARC company. He made
a good many records under names like "Pinewood Tom" and "Joshua
White, the Singing Christian," and as he became more proficient, his style
became slicker and more acceptable to urban audiences. By 1940, he was
even recording with jazzman Sidney Bechet.

Woody Guthrie was twenty-eight in 1940, fresh from the West Coast,
where he had already made a name for himself in radio; he actually came
from the Southwest, born in Okemah, Oklahoma, and later living in Pampa,
Texas, and learned the same kind of old ballads and square dance tunes that
Leadbelly had. He had never recorded commercially, but had published a
collection of his protest songs in a songbook. Burl Ives, just entering his
thirties in 1940, came from a family of singers in Illinois, and added to what
he learned there as he bummed his way around the country during the early
years of the Depression. He wanted to be an actor and found his way to New
York, where his pleasant Irish tenor and ability to dramatize his presentations landed him a CBS radio show called *The Wayfaring Stranger*.

Sonny Terry was a bluesman born in Greensboro, Georgia, a blind harmonica player and singer who made his way into New York in the late

1930s; he would later record and tour with Leadbelly. He would also later team with Brownie McGhee, a blues singer and guitarist who came from a family of African American string band musicians around Knoxville. A busker on street corners through North Carolina in the later years of the Depression, McGhee made his first records in 1940 and then he, too, headed for the big time. Terry and McGhee would later become members of the influential singing group called the Almanac Singers.

Other new players on the scene did not have so many ties with rural life and music, but came to the music with a passion, zeal, and hard-won knowledge. Richard Dyer-Bennet, for example, had studied literature and music at the University of California and traveled to Sweden, where he learned to sing both folk songs and formal art songs. He learned to play the lute as well as the guitar and was seeking to make a career out of the concert stage. Pete Seeger, who was barely twenty-one in 1940, was the son of Charles Seeger, the Harvard graduate who became one of the century's most influential ethnomusicologists. He spent a restless childhood at some of New England's better boarding schools and then discovered mountain banjo playing at a 1936 folk festival in the Smoky Mountains. Soon he decided to drop out of Harvard and accept an offer from Alan Lomax to briefly work for him at the Archive of American Folk Song at the Library of Congress. Lomax, in addition to helping Huddie, was a central figure for many of the new young singers. As historian Norm Cohen has written, "Working from his base of authority at the Library of Congress, Lomax helped many singers, traditional and urban, to find performance opportunities and expand their repertoire." Himself only twenty-five in 1940, Alan Lomax was a powerful, charismatic figure in his own right, with boundless energy and an intense dedication to folk music.

All of these newcomers were in their twenties or thirties, a full generation younger than Leadbelly, who had turned fifty-one before his trial. It was natural that many of them looked to him as a role model, a father figure, a source of advice. It was not a role he sought; few people were less pedantic or less dogmatic than Huddie Ledbetter. Yet to many of these singers, he was a powerful teacher, a superbly skilled artist who had fought battles most of them had only heard about. Henrietta Yurchenco remembers, "Woody was constantly saying that 'We are learning everything from him.' It was such fervent respect."

In March 1940 actor Will Geer, then starring in the Broadway stage production of Erskine Caldwell's controversial *Tobacco Road*, organized a benefit show. Though known to modern audiences primarily through his role as the grandfather in *The Waltons* television series, Geer was, in the late 1930s, a prominent Shakespearean actor who shared his time between Broadway and radical organizations like the New Theater League. On

March 3, he organized a "Grapes of Wrath Evening" to raise money for California migrant workers; it was held in the same theater where *Tobacco Road* was running, at midnight. Leadbelly, now out of prison, was invited to be one of the performers. The publicity described the cast as "American Ballad Singers and Folk Dancers: Will Geer, Alan and Bess Lomax, Aunt Molly Jackson, Leadbelly, The Golden Gate Quartet, Woody Guthrie, and The Pennsylvania Miners." Many of the new young singers got their first big-time exposure here; they had been playing, like Leadbelly, at small, informal gatherings of folk music fans. Here they had a chance to appear before a large, mainstream audience and get publicity from major newspapers and media. It was a watershed for the folk music movement and in some ways a turning point in American music.

Pete Seeger made his public debut that night, and Woody Guthrie was presented for the first time to an eastern audience. Pete Seeger recalls the night vividly. "There was Leadbelly on the porch, Toshi and I were in a square dance group . . . Burl Ives was there, Josh White, the Golden Gate Quartet. I sang one song, very amateurishly. It got a polite smattering of applause. I retired shame faced. . . . Leadbelly did that dance, he did the 'Duck Hunter's Dance,' where he goes on to slap the guitar." Guthrie's performance was a major success as he charmed his audience with his Will Rogers folksiness and attracted the attention of Alan Lomax, who recognized in him a major new folk music voice. "We showed 'em where singing started," quipped Woody later about the evening. "We showed 'em how come songs come to be. . . . We didn't have no fancy costumes, nor pretty legs, but we showed 'em old ragged overalls, and cheaper cotton dresses . . . shows [folk music] can be useful." Alan Lomax himself said he felt the concert was the real beginning of the folk song revival in America. It was also another beginning for Huddie: the next two years would be among his best and would propel him back into the spotlight he had once shared with John Lomax. Only now it would be on his own terms.

Shortly after the "Grapes of Wrath Evening," Huddie and Martha took pity on young Woody Guthrie and invited him to stay with them. Woody had no permanent place to live (and would not for a year); he stayed with Huddie on several occasions, sleeping on the Ledbetters' Murphy bed. He wrote a richly detailed account of life with Huddie during this time:

I came to his and Martha's apartment over on east Tenth Street and I carried my own guitar, and they begged me to stay, to eat, sing and dance there in their apartment of three little rooms painted a sooty sky blue and then smoked over with the stains from cigarettes, cigars of the rich and of the poor.

I saw Leadbelly get up in the morning, wash, shave, put on his bath robe,

and Martha would stand up in her tall way and make me get shaved,
bathed, washed, dressed, while she cooked Leadbelly his breakfast on her
charcoal flat top stove. The stove was older than me, older than Martha, but
not older than Leadbelly.

I watched him set after breakfast, look down eastwards out of his win-
dow, read The Daily News, The Daily Mirror *and* The Daily Worker. *I*
listened as he tuned up his Twelve String Stella and eased his fingers up and
down along the neck in the same way that the library and museum clerk
touched the frame of the best painting in their gallery. It was not possible
for me to count the numbers of folks that came in through Leadbelly's door
there.

The little Leadbelly apartment became a gathering point for the singers
and those who followed them. Henrietta Yurchenco recalls "He was so
concentrated on his music. He was the core figure in this folksong movement. . . . It was his house, down on the lower East Side, where everybody
who was doing any singing at all or wanted to learn, that's where they
went." Bluesman Brownie McGhee saw the apartment as a fertile musical
exchange point. "I met Woody at Leadbelly's house, I met Lee Hayes [later
member of the Weavers] at Leadbelly's house. . . . I met Burl Ives at Lead's.
Everybody else that I met . . . was at Lead's. He had Italian friends, Jewish
friends, white friends—he had all types of people at his house."

Guthrie was fascinated with Aunt Molly Jackson and her clan from "the
fascist country of Harlan County, Kentucky," who would all come to Leadbelly's house almost daily. At this time, Aunt Molly was married to an Italian
cook named Tom Stamos, and he "loved Martha and Leadbelly, danced
with everybody, laughed and cried, and came to this house because it was
the only place that he could find all of his whole tribe at once." At times
Aunt Molly would sing, then Jim Garland, then Sara Ogan, her TB causing
her thin voice to be high and dry. Guthrie: "I heard Sarah [sic] Ogan sing
her songs about getting together and shaking hands, organizing around this
whole world once, then twice. I heard her sing, 'I'm going to write you a
letter just as quick as times get better.' But 'I've got to get organized, Baby
mine.' Sarah had no guitar, and lots of times Jim did not play behind her.
Leadbelly might not play for her first verse or so. I had to keep my guitar
still so I could hear the words."

Guthrie was especially fascinated with the gentle side of Leadbelly. In
performance, the singer often played loud—as if possessed, one friend
said—and he literally thrashed the guitar. But in the quiet of the morning,
as Guthrie watched, Leadbelly played at "half speed," gently picking a tune
for friends and neighbors that dropped in and asked for one to help get them
off on their way to the store to buy coal. "He had a slow running, easy, deep

quiet way about him, that made me see that his strength was like a little ball in his hands, and that his thoughts ran as deep in color as the lights that played down from the sky and onto his face."

The folk revival also meant new chances for radio exposure. Throughout the year and through 1941, Huddie was involved in a series of radio appearances and audition programs, both at the local New York and national network levels. As early as February, Huddie appeared on a new CBS network program Alan Lomax was starting called *The American School of the Air*, which had a *Folk Music of America* series. The plan of the series was to feature different folk artists each week and to help educate the general public about folk music. Huddie was featured on the episode of February 14. In June, he and Woody Guthrie put together an audition show at WNYC in New York; Woody acted as host and announcer, and Leadbelly did seven of his favorite songs, including "Good Morning, Blues," which was becoming one of his most requested pieces. Over time Leadbelly's introduction about the blues became quite famous:

The blues is like this. You lay down some night and you turn from one side of the bed to the other, all night long. It's not too cold in that bed, and it ain't too hot. But what's the matter? The blues has got you. When you get up and sit on the side of your bed, soon in the morning, you may have a mother and a father, a sister and a brother around, but you don't want no talk out of them. They ain't done you nothing, but what's the matter? The Blues has got you. When you get up and put your feet under the table, you look down at your plate. You got everything you want to eat. Well, you get up, you walk away, you shake your head and you say, "The Lord have mercy, I can't eat and I can't sleep." What's the matter? The blues has got you and they want to talk to you.©

The song itself, replete with the introduction, Leadbelly would record no fewer than seven other times, a testament to its popularity. Next to "Irene," it was the song most associated with the singer during his later years.

Alan Lomax continued to use his connections with network radio to get Huddie some air time on other shows. In July the singer went down to audition with NBC, but, he wrote to Lomax, "It didn't work[.] i dont no what happen." In August, Lomax got CBS to try a pilot show for another new series, this one called *Back Where I Come From*. It would feature Woody Guthrie, along with other regulars such as Burl Ives, the popular gospel-singing Golden Gate Quartet, and, originally, announcer Clifton Faddiman (before his days with the Book of the Month Club). Lomax planned on using Leadbelly "as much as possible" as a regular on the show, introducing his songs and then singing them. Each show had a theme, like "the weather" or "bad men," and scripts introduced the singers and their songs. The unusual mix of folk music styles, as well as the easy interaction between white and black singers, scared off sponsors, but the network decided to give it a try anyway. Starting in September, CBS aired the show three times a week, fifteen minutes per segment, at the 10:30 P.M. time slot. Letters and offers began to come in, and soon it was obvious that the music of the show was attracting a lot of national attention. Unfortunately, director Nicholas Ray felt that, although Woody Guthrie managed to get by on the air even with a pronounced Oklahoma drawl, the listeners could not understand Leadbelly's accent. His role in the program was cut back and in some instances given to Josh White, who could speak clear, precise New York English. In some cases, in fact, Leadbelly would come on to sing one of his well-known songs, such as "Ella Speed," but when it came time for him to do his spoken interlude, White would come on and read the interlude in his cultured voice. The overall effect was ludicrous. Guthrie himself was furious and constantly berated Ray about it; he even walked off the show in October, in part because of the treatment of Leadbelly. Others, though, have other explanations for Leadbelly's problems on the show. Alan Lomax recalls, "Everyone had to read lines in this program. Huddie couldn't read his script. It was a very tightly organized show. So though we tried to use him, it was difficult."

In the meantime, Leadbelly found a more congenial home in the studios of WNYC in New York. In 1939, the station, originally part of the Public Works Administration, had become semi-independent and was one of the few places willing to program folk music. Jim Garland, Sara Ogan, and Woody Guthrie had been singing on a show called *Adventures in Music*, produced by Henrietta Yurchenco. Leadbelly had occasionally appeared on that show, and Guthrie had been busy lobbying the management to give Leadbelly his own show. By the fall of 1940 the station agreed and gave Leadbelly his own fifteen-minute show every Wednesday evening, called *Folksongs of America*. It, too, was produced by Henrietta Yurchenco, who recalled some of the details of how it worked:

He always arrived on time (I could set my clock by his appearance), neatly dressed in a double-breasted grey suit, white shirt, and dark bow tie. We would sit in my office, a little cubbyhole without windows, and plot out a skeleton script. This would be filled in with Leadbelly's own commentary once the program was on the air. Everything was improvised. Each song was preceded by stories of his life in the South. . . . We went on live, and whatever happened during that fifteen minutes happened. Leadbelly would always know. We would signal him to wind up and we would end the program. And we would announce at the end of the program what the

subject was for the next week. We would also announce that if people
wanted lyrics to the songs, we would be very happy to send them. We did.
Leadbelly had his own stationery, which was really beautiful.

The stationery, in fact, was remarkable. The letterhead took up almost the
top half of the sheet and was headlined "Sweet Singer of the Swamplands,"
the old *Herald Tribune* headline from 1935. (Apparently Huddie thought it
was an accurate enough description, despite its source.) In the center was
the legend "Huddie Ledbetter/ Leadbelly in Southern Melodies/ Only Act
Playing '12 String Guitar'/ Gun Tap Dancing." To the left and right were
small photos of the singer holding his guitar and tap-dancing.

On a typical program, Leadbelly opened by strumming and softly humming his theme song, "Irene." A formal announcer introduced Leadbelly
and most of the songs, but more often than not Leadbelly took over and
reintroduced his songs in his own way. Apparently New York listeners
understood his dialect well enough. Yurchenco recalls:

People used to call me all the time and ask, "Who writes those wonderful
scripts?" I'd say, "Gee, there are no scripts. Its really Leadbelly. I simply
hand him the lines."
He was such a powerful creature in front of that mike. He was so sure
of himself musically. So sure of who he was. . . . There was no whining on
his part. No asking for pity because he was poor, black, and discriminated
against. Nothing like that. He was always this positive creature.

Huddie became very, very proud of the program and took it all very
seriously. Once Woody Guthrie came up with him and was hanging around
at a rehearsal and script-planning session. In a playful mood, he said, "Hey,
Huddie, let me sing you a song." And he launched into a wild, ribald,
off-color song. "Leadbelly was absolutely aghast," remembered Yurchenco. "He said to him, 'You doesn't sing that song, Woody! You doesn't
sing that song on my program!' Woody was just kidding." His pride shone
along with the sheer power of his music. For the first time, Huddie was
actually in complete control of one of his media stages, and he loved it. He
also got requests for the lyrics; on one show around Christmas 1941, he
sang his children's folk song "On a Christmas Day" and had so many
requests that he had to repeat it again the next week so people who had
gotten the lyrics could now get the melody right. "Leadbelly on the air was
just galvanizing," remembered Yurchenco. "I compared him to a volcano." Thousands of listeners agreed.

The recording scene, too, was looking up. After several years of relative
inactivity, Leadbelly recorded for the nation's largest company, RCA Vic-

tor. He also began a marathon session with the Library of Congress and
Alan Lomax and began to create his first recordings for the man who would
found Folkways Records, Moe Asch.

The RCA sessions, held between June 15 and 17, 1940, were another of
Alan Lomax's efforts to get Huddie some of the attention Lomax felt he
deserved. In May he had talked RCA into doing a *Dust Bowl Ballads* album
with Woody Guthrie, and the company, interested in getting into the folk
music and educational market, was receptive to further suggestions. Lomax
had been frustrated by his inability to get the Library of Congress to release
to the public copies of the blues and work songs that he and his father had
recorded. It was Lomax's plan to have Leadbelly record some of his familiar
songs by himself, and then pair him with the Golden Gate Quartet for some
prison and work songs. As it turned out, the session yielded thirteen songs
under each format. The Golden Gate Quartet, which had been recording for
Victor and its Bluebird subsidiary since the mid-1930s, had become the
nation's best-known black quartet. They were superb singers, slick and
sophisticated, and able to do wonders with a cappella harmony. Lomax had
used them on the *Back Where I Come from Program*, and they had even
appeared on the "Grapes of Wrath Evening" relief show. Willie Johnson,
one of the quartet members, recalls that neither Leadbelly nor the quartet
were especially fond of the recording idea, but they were willing to give it
a try. "That was strictly not my slice of pie, really. Leadbelly was a rough,
railroad, logwood camp sort of style, so we just sort of backed him up." His
voice didn't really even fit in with the quartet. "We didn't even try. The idea
was I don't think Lomax wanted too much harmony, too much precision.
He just wanted some voices behind him. . . . As far as actually singing with
him, we made no attempt to. . . . We did what we were supposed to do. But
not to perfect it, because that is what Lomax did not want. He wanted it
rough, you know, and that's what he got." The quartet, in fact, learned the
songs from Leadbelly and Lomax after the first rehearsal and were versatile
enough to go into the studios almost at once. The songs that eventually were
issued in Victor album P-50, *The Midnight Special and Other Prison Songs*,
included "Pick a Bale of Cotton," "Midnight Special," "Alabama Bound,"
"Grey Goose," "Stew-Ball," and "Ham an' Eggs."

Huddie himself was not satisfied with some of the performances; neither
were the RCA people. A month after the session, Leadbelly wrote to Lomax
discussing the concerns of an RCA man named Weatherall about the words
to "Whoa Back, Buck" (probably his use of "goddamn" in the chorus) and
"Yellow Gal." "I don't know what words in there he don't like but if he
would rite them i could change the some of the words he don't like. Me and
the golden gate boys will have to make him two more free if he wants us."
Huddie by this time had the tests of the records and pronounced, "They are

swell. With the golden gate boys The Midnight Special is a killer." He did not, however, like his solo version of "Julianne Johnson." "We should [have] had the guitar in there." The album was issued a few months later, with extensive notes and song texts prepared by Lomax. It was one of the finest public presentations of Leadbelly's music: well recorded, well advertised, well documented. And the album justified its reputation as a landmark in African American folk music. By the following February 28, though, the album had sold barely five hundred copies. Back in Dallas, John Lomax got a royalty statement for half of the money paid for composer royalties.

In August, Alan Lomax invited Huddie down to Washington for a series of extensive documentary recordings for the Library of Congress. The archive had, of course, all the field recordings done in 1933, 1934, and 1935, as well as a 1937 session arranged by Alan, and a number donated by Mary Barnicle. But Lomax now had better machines and more authority to use discs and time in his own projects. In 1938 he had recorded extensive documentation on the jazz piano player Jelly Roll Morton; earlier in 1940, he had done something similar with Woody Guthrie. Now he intended to "debrief" Huddie on record, going into detail about some of the things Huddie had told him over the years but which had not made it onto the 1935 recordings.

Huddie's sessions did not turn out to be as extensive as Jelly Roll Morton's but they were impressive. Almost sixty titles were preserved, including lengthy songs and discussion of religious music, narrative accounts of Huddie's childhood, additional songs and dance calls from his early days, and some of the newer topical songs, such as "The Roosevelt Song," "Howard Hughes," and "The Scottsboro Boys." At times Alan's wife, Elizabeth, took over the interviewing chores. The discs used were sixteen inches, allowing Huddie to go on at length and to string out a song to its fullest length.

By the late spring of 1941, Leadbelly had started recording for a man who would eventually replace Alan Lomax as his recording promoter and advisor: Moses "Moe" Asch. Although these two men had different backgrounds, they shared more in common than one might at first imagine. Both came from childhoods that were totally alien to their New York City meeting ground and became united in their single-minded effort to disseminate underappreciated music to the general public. Leadbelly's association with Moe Asch marks one of the important turning points in his life.

Born in 1905 in Poland, Moe came from a large, peripatetic family. His father, Sholem, became a writer, working first for the *Jewish Daily Forward* but many years later emerging as a novelist of considerable reputation. Members of the Asch family became involved in the revolution of 1905, which raged throughout Poland at the time of Moe's birth. By his fifth birthday, Moe had visited not only Palestine but the United States. In 1912 the family had settled in Paris, a more liberal and welcoming home for Jewish intellectuals. And the Asch home became a focal point for the scholarly and artistically inclined; Marc Chagall was one of their frequent visitors.

The outbreak of World War I drove the Asches to emigrate to the United States and, like hundreds of thousands before them, they entered by way of Ellis Island. Until the early 1920s the family lived in several of New York City's boroughs, moving from one Jewish enclave to another. Moe fell down a flight of school stairs when he was thirteen and spent nearly one year under the care of his Aunt Basha, a trained nurse and dedicated socialist. Many of Moe's ideas and well-developed sense of the evils of class distinctions can be traced not only to his experiences but to his lengthy convalescence under the eye of Basha.

In 1923 Sholem announced to everyone that his writing career in the United States was stalled and that a move back to France was necessary. Just three years after the Asches had gained citizenship, Sholem moved his wife and their youngest daughter, Ruth, back to Paris. Moe's brother Nathan was just about to enter Syracuse University, while Moe and his brother John remained at a residential boarding school near Philadelphia.

Separated from his parents and unable to endure the farm work required by the school, Moe soon turned to electronics and the newly emerging field of ham radio operations for solace. This interest turned into a passion for tinkering with tubes and microphones, but it could not fully compensate for his miserable existence. Early in 1924 he fled from school and arrived at his parents' house; Sholem, learning of his son's newfound interest, encouraged Moe to enroll in the technical college in Koblenz, Germany. The technical work held great fascination for him, but he was also introduced to the folk song traditions of Europe by the multinational student body. In 1925 he stumbled upon John Lomax's *Cowboy Songs* and began to think about folk songs in the United States.

When Asch returned to the United States in 1926 he quickly immersed himself in the field of radio manufacturing. At first he worked for RCA czar David Sarnoff, who was born in the same Polish town as Sholem, but Moe's quest for a free rein and a sense of entrepreneurship soon drove him to self-employment. He free-lanced around New York City, installing sound equipment in movie theaters and providing sound systems for political rallies. About 1935 Asch was hired by radio station WEVD, owned by the leftist *Forward* magazine and named after Eugene V. Debs, to construct its studio and transmitter. WEVD's mission was to promote a forward-thinking political agenda and to broadcast recordings with which its audience would relate. Moe quickly realized that the radio station's largely Jewish audience was underserved by the record industry, which was just emerging from the devastating effects of the Depression. Ever the entrepreneur, Asch moved to fill the void. His first record by the Bagelman Sisters was issued on the Asch label in 1939 and Moses Asch's record career was quietly and inauspiciously launched.

Like his novelist father, Moe gravitated toward controversy. He harbored strong sympathies for Communists and social causes, although he did not actually join the Communist party itself; his entire personal and professional life remained entangled with the old left. But he was also entranced by the sounds of his adopted homeland. He truly embraced the notion that African American music was well worth documenting and did so with great fervor throughout his life. One of his later Folkways series was, in fact, called *Americana*, reflecting his passion for the various types of music found in the United States.

Asch's founding of his self-named label came at a propitious time. Major record companies like Victor and Columbia had paid attention to folk and ethnic music in the 1920s, when they were lean and ambitious for new markets. But by the end of the 1930s, Victor and Columbia, along with newcomer Decca, had a virtual monopoly on American pop music, and were interested only in the broadest types of mainstream music. To document folk and ethnic music, a number of small independent labels began to emerge, seeking to fill this void.

Moe Asch certainly fit the requirements of the task, for both he and his fledgling company were iconoclastic, visionary, and, above all, independent. Beginning with the first Asch releases in the late 1930s, Moses Asch remained involved with the record industry for the rest of his life. And it continued to be a struggle. Despite the favorable climate for folk and ethnic recordings, Moses Asch's timing in beginning this new enterprise was problematic for reasons beyond his control. World War II disrupted every aspect of life, including the record industry. At first the problems were merely inconvenient for the industry, such as the rationing of gasoline and tires. But then shellac, which was needed to build aircraft, fell into short supply. Record drives were organized in which citizens were asked to bring in their old Black Patti, Gennett, Superior, and Paramount records to be scrapped for the war effort. Then in late 1943 James Petrillo, head of the musicians' union, called for a ban on recording until a new contract could be worked out. While recording had slowed before then, it all but halted from late 1943 until early in 1945.

It's not entirely clear exactly when Moe Asch and Huddie Ledbetter met, but by the spring of 1941 they were talking about a recording session for the nascent Asch label. This particularly interested Huddie because, except for a lengthy, fruitful session for Alan Lomax and the Library of Congress in

August 1940, nearly a year had passed since he had recorded for RCA Victor. In May 1941 Leadbelly made his first recordings for Moe Asch. This business and professional relationship remained intact until Huddie's death eight years later.

According to the contract dated May 14, 1941, royalties were to be paid semiannually for the six recordings made at the initial sessions. At the bottom of the contract is this significant clause: "In no way does this letter [of] agreement construe that Mr. Ledbetter is held down to just these six recordings for the Asch Recording Studios. He may record for anyone else. The Asch Recording Studio is only interested in publishing these records or any others that Mr. Ledbetter chooses to make for the Asch Recording Studio." Always looking for new opportunities, Huddie no doubt wanted to keep his options open. His next commercial session, however, was for Moe Asch some seven months later.

Asch was often taken to task for his erratic, and sometimes nonexistent, payment of artist royalties. Many complained bitterly that they never received a dime in royalties from a record they made for Moses Asch. As the sole proprietor of his small empire, Asch could handle business in any way that he could get away with. Some artists were no doubt slighted. But sometimes Moe would pop up at the most opportune time with cash in hand—when the rent was due, one of the children was ill, or other debts were piling up. A few artists, like blues singer Brownie McGhee, took it all in good humor.

Moe Asch was my A-1 man. . . . I met him through Lead and we was soon recording. He gave everyone ten bucks. I don't know what was happening behind the scenes. . . . When he was down on 46th Street I would stop by to see Moe, ask him if I could have five or ten bucks. He said "I think I can." But I didn't know that he was putting this money down. I got to make records for him and he said "Don't you want to clear your sheets with me? All that money I've been giving you all along. Why don't you make me an album?" Then it flashed in my mind that I'd been getting all those five and ten dollar bills from Moe. I thought, well, that's all right.

In the beginning, at least, Asch was pretty regular about paying royalties to Leadbelly. In May and July 1941, Asch recorded an album by the singer, a set of three 78 rpm records entitled *Play Parties*. It sold for $2.50, and featured favorites like "Redbird" and "Ha Ha Thisaway." In January 1942 he followed this album up with a second one called *Work Songs of the USA Sung by Leadbelly* (see Discography). Royalty statements in the Asch files show that by April 29, 1942, about six months after its release, the children's album had sold some 492 sets—yielding Leadbelly some $29.52 in royalties at the rate of six cents an album (or two cents a record, which was in line for that day and time). The *Work Songs* set did not sell as fast, with only 173 sets sold during its first few months out. By the end of March 1943, the children's set had sold 566 copies, the work songs set only 304. It was a disappointing start, but Moe kept encouraging Huddie and even advancing him money on a regular basis. (Many of the royalty statements show the singer still owing the company against advances.) Throughout the period from May 1941 through August 1944, Leadbelly was a regular visitor to the Asch Recording Studio. And Moe Asch released a string of records that sampled Huddie's repertoire. The only break in Huddie's regular recording visits was his extended trip to the West Coast, which began in the late summer of 1944. Certainly the most interesting accounting from Asch is dated April 25, 1944, stating that Huddie was paid $250 for "10,000 #343-1 'How Long Blues' as a special run on this record." It is surprising that Huddie's cover of Leroy Carr's 1928 sold so well.

But exactly how did Asch manage to issue records while most companies were virtually shut down? First, the Petrillo ban primarily affected instrumentalists: a cappella gospel quartets such as Richmond's [Virginia] Harmonizing Four or the Willing Four escaped the studio shutdowns. Second, many of the musicians using the Asch Recording Studio were almost certainly nonunion. Woody Guthrie, for instance, did not belong to the musicians' union because he was considered to be a singer rather than a guitar player. Finally, African American musicians like Leadbelly or jazz pianist James P. Johnson were not always allowed to join the musicians' union in the early 1940s. This was especially true for black musicians below the first rank of popularity or those living in smaller cities. In Shreveport, Louisiana, the local musicians' union was not integrated until the 1950s.

During Leadbelly's trip to the West Coast Asch himself was adapting and expanding. In 1945 he added Herbert Harris as a partner and also began Disc Records as a branch of his burgeoning empire. The addition of Harris also brought the Stinson label under Asch's umbrella. Some of the single 78 rpm Leadbelly issues on Asch later appeared on Stinson and Folkways albums.

By 1946 a major reorganization had taken place. In December Leadbelly had returned from the West Coast and the Asch label was gone. It was entirely replaced by the Disc imprint in the fall of 1945, which itself gave way to Folkways in a bankruptcy action that occurred in 1947. Sometime during this period, Asch and Herbert Harris dissolved their business partnership and Moe was once more the head man of his small empire.

The first of the Leadbelly records Asch released had come out in late 1941 as 78 rpm singles on the Asch label; "Take This Hammer," to become one of Huddie's better-known songs in later years, and the famed children's

song "Ha, Ha Thisaway" were issued by Asch. Later some of these were
issued again on the Disc label. That label also brought out two early 78
albums, done on twelve-inch discs. One was simply called *Songs by Leadbelly;* the second was *Negro Folk Songs—As Sung By Leadbelly,* which
included transcriptions of the song lyrics and an early appreciation of the
singer by Frederick Ramsey, Jr. For many years, the extensive recordings
made for the Library of Congress were not easily available to the general
public, so the sides done by Asch and later appearing on Folkways became
the main way Leadbelly's music reached its audience. Nobody knows exactly how many records Asch made of Leadbelly. (After his death, Asch's
collection was taken over by the Smithsonian, and new Leadbelly recordings are still being discovered and cataloged.) Based on those sides actually
released to the public, however, the number seems over two hundred. It
constituted the singer's largest body of recorded work and was the prime
channel through which the singer would reach his audience in the 1940s.

About 1943, bluesmen Sonny Terry and Brownie McGhee came to New
York to join the Almanac Singers, a multiracial folksinging group that
would eventually give birth to the Weavers. Their paths soon crossed Leadbelly's. McGhee took a cab directly from the bus station to the flat on Sixth
Avenue where Hays, Terry, and others of the group were staying. "They
had awnings between the beds. One bathroom and one toilet." The two new
members of the group were not exactly enchanted, but both had seen
worse. Then one day Leadbelly came over to visit. After looking around, he
confided to McGhee that this wasn't the right atmosphere. He said, "I know
that you guys ain't getting enough to eat here, you can't eat no pumper-
nickel bread. You ain't used to it. Come over and live with me and Baby
[Martha]. I know you ain't making much money, but when you make
money, bring it to Baby and put it in the pot and we'll use it to set the table."
The two talked it over and agreed it sounded good. McGhee remembered:
"We went over to Lead's house, a flat, 604 East 9th Street. He had a
bedroom, a living room, and the dining room was also the kitchen. . . .
There was an antique couch in the living room and Lead said, 'You boys can
sleep on that.' " They wound up staying about a year, adding money to the
pot when they could make some, eating when Huddie and Martha did.

One of the reasons McGhee moved out had to do with what he called
Leadbelly's "code." He explains:

*There were certain stipulations Lead wanted and I didn't want to live up to
them. Rather than break that code of his: your necktie on, your shoes
shined. . . . That was his standards. You didn't carry your guitar on your
back, you carried it in a case. You had to have a case for your guitar. I never
had a case for my guitar until I met Leadbelly. "You're a professional,*

Brownie, your guitar goes in a case. And a necktie. You don't take your coat off on stage." Lead was beautiful. Neat as a pin, and clean as a brand new bottle. When he left his house going somewhere, he was always a gentleman. With his necktie, his shoes polished, his guitar in his case—it got unbearable to me. I couldn't do that. I said, "You've got to go, McGhee."

Almost everybody who knew Leadbelly during this time commented on this code: his suit, his being on time, his growing sense of professionalism. Even from his days with John Lomax, Leadbelly preferred classy, double-breasted suits to the normal down-home dress of singers like Woody Guthrie and Pete Seeger. By now he was still not getting as much concert work as he wanted—he was still writing to Alan Lomax asking for help in getting gigs—and he had made little actual money from his new commercial records. In spite of this, Huddie's radio work and his records were getting noticed. This developed even more the sense of professionalism that Brownie McGhee noticed. Leadbelly had always wanted to make it in the music world, and now he was sensing his chance. His friend Peter Seeger recalled: "He was very anxious to make it in the music world. He knew he was a good musician and full of energy, even though he was getting on in years. . . . He was trying to make it, he was thinking all of the time, 'Who can I see?' and knocking on doors." Huddie had always admired cowboy singer Gene Autry; he had even met him once, and liked to sing his songs. He also liked to watch Autry on the screen as he helped create the genre known as the singing cowboy. Now Huddie began to get ideas about Hollywood; his niece Viola Daniels said he wanted to become the nation's first black singing cowboy and to go to Hollywood. Now, in 1944, came a chance he had been waiting for: a real chance to go to Hollywood. He was ready.

23 Hollywood and Vine

By 1944 Leadbelly had lived in the Lower East Side of New York City on and off for nearly ten years. He'd been back to the South several times, but that had been for relatively brief visits to friends or for the occasional musical event. Because of his New York City base and wartime travel restrictions, nearly all of his most recent performances occurred in the Northeast. Leadbelly's musical horizons were not expanding; he'd already played in nearly all of the venues open to him and was interested in exploring new opportunities. Like the Okies who'd moved west for more fertile ground and factory jobs during the Dust Bowl days, Huddie looked toward California. The Golden West also offered some new extramusical possibilities that had eluded Huddie in the East. Most particularly was the powerful draw of Hollywood.

In New York City the stage production of *Green Pastures* drew in big crowds, and serious talk of filming *Green Pastures* in Hollywood wafted through the local acting community. Perhaps because he often traveled in artistic circles, Huddie Ledbetter's was one of the names tossed out for the part of "De Lawd." The prospect of a part in a Hollywood film so excited Leadbelly that he decided to head west on mere speculation. Stu Jamieson, a young banjoist and dancer working with Margot Mayo, recalls that Huddie's friends in New York were "excited for him, we thought that it was great. Then Margo Robinson told us that it was off because in the photos they took . . . the scar under his eye came off too shiny and they could not disguise it. He looked imposing for the part with his white hair and everything. We also had great fun thinking of a double murderer playing this character."

In most regards, Huddie simply shifted his life west. Little doubt remains that he viewed California as a golden chance to reach heretofore untapped audiences. He had a short-term regular radio program on Los Angeles station KRE, which helped to bring his name before potential employers. In addition, the left-wing tabloid *People's World* featured Leadbelly in its July 7, 1944, issue. The tabloid's writer Dolph Winebrennee observed that Huddie was a "55-year-old Negro who can sing 500 songs and is as close to being a people's artist as these United States can boast. . . . Leadbelly has progressed through singing for townspeople, governors, the Library of Congress (some 1000 records) and Cafe Society, until he is in Hollywood, where, appropriately enough, he will spend the summer working in films and singing at People's World parties around Los Angeles." Some of the legendary aspects of Huddie's life—the size of his repertoire and the number of recordings he had made for the Library of Congress, in particular— were repeated and recirculated by such articles. Even after his nearly ten years of working the media, the press never seemed to tire of Huddie's unique life.

The article further recounted his ability to create a new song through the use of oral formulas. Leadbelly had long ago mastered the ability to substitute words or phrases into previously composed songs or verses in order to create new material. And when asked to make up a song about *People's World*, Huddie responded by reconstituting a gospel hymn, "Outshine the Sun," into a new form:

> *The People's World, your name is called.*
> *The People's World, your name is called.*
> *I said it, your name is called to outshine the sun.*

With the defense industry booming and thousands of workers making their way to southern California, Leadbelly joined hundreds of other entertainers who were finding good work in the various clubs and theaters there. In 1944 the coast was also the scene of a revival of interest in traditional jazz, and Leadbelly's work songs, blues, and even ragtime appealed to these new fans who were fascinated with the roots of jazz. This also led him to another record contract, this time with Capitol, a then-new label that had just been started in Hollywood. In the summer of 1944, shortly after Leadbelly had arrived, he met an old friend on the streets of downtown Los Angeles: cowboy singer Tex Ritter. Ritter had been performing in a stage play in New York during the time Huddie had arrived with John Lomax, and was even in the audience at the Texas-Exes banquet where the singer made his public debut. (Ritter was also a graduate of the University of Texas, and had a serious interest in folk songs; in January 1935 a mutual friend had even sent several of his songs, along with an introduction, to John Lomax.) Now Ritter had emerged as a radio, film, and recording star, and had recently signed with Capitol. He urged Leadbelly to sign with the new label, and mentioned the singer to Lee Gillette, one of the Capitol executives. "One night at my house," Ritter recalled, "I had Merle Travis [composer of 'Sixteen Tons'], Lee Gillette, my A & R man that I loved so much, and I said, 'Instead of auditioning [Leadbelly] at your office, Lee, why don't you just come back to the house tonight?' My wife was overseas at that time. And Lee helped sign him and they made an album at Capitol at that time."

The "album" was actually a series of twelve sides done at three sessions in October, and recorded at the C. P. MacGregor studios; they would be some of the singer's very best commercial recordings. On one of them, "Eagle Rock Rag," would be about the only surviving example of his barrelhouse piano playing. For his accompanist, Leadbelly chose a man named Paul Mason Howard, a journeyman studio musician who played a German zither. Howard—not to be confused with the country singer Paul Howard—worked with a number of Capitol recording artists, including Tennessee Ernie Ford. The curious combination of zither, guitar, and Leadbelly's booming voice worked surprisingly well, and Capitol released most of the songs on 78 rpm records—indeed, the set remains in print today (on compact disc). Unfortunately, the Capitol sides did not sell well. In a 1956 letter to John Reynolds, Dexter wrote, "Capitol allowed Leadbelly to pick whatever tunes he preferred and also to use a zither on some of the sides, at his request. It was terribly discouraging in the months and years that followed to learn how few people would buy a record by this great interpreter, whose fame is worldwide." According to the Capitol session sheets, Leadbelly's Los Angeles address was 1727 West 37th Place, not far from present-day Hollywood and Beverly Hills. Huddie remained in Los Angeles through the fall of 1944 playing local gigs throughout Southern California. He got as far south as San Diego, but retained his Los Angeles base. Money remained a constant source of worry for Huddie. He not only worried about his own pay, but about supporting Martha, who had remained in New York City. And Huddie remained in contact with Moses Asch through the mail. In a letter to Asch on December 31, 1944, Huddie, who then lived at 1421 East 55th Street in Los Angeles in the home of George Pugh, wrote, "Please pay to Mrs. Martha Ledbetter the money from the 'Songs of Leadbelly' and pay to her the money for the 12 inch and the Play Party." Local gigs covered his California bills, but he continued to be concerned about Martha. However, there is no evidence that he returned to New York City during the winter of 1944–1945. Martha herself had taken a job working for Bestline, a cleaning establishment.

In early 1945 Leadbelly traveled north to perform in the San Francisco Bay area. He played at the usual coffeehouses, fund-raisers, and concerts that had become his staples. On February 15, 1945, Huddie performed a live program for the *Standard School Broadcast*, which was presented by the Standard Oil Company of California. Fortunately, this program, which was targeted for an appreciative audience of schoolchildren, was preserved by Standard Oil and ultimately released by Folkways. It is clear when you hear it that Huddie truly loved performing for kids and easily held their rapt attention. The incident later led a national columnist to complain about having a murderer sing for children, but the show's success overshadowed the complaints.

On Mother's Day 1945, Leadbelly was again broadcasting over the radio.

KRE in Berkeley hosted an hour-long program that was segmented in order to highlight Huddie's broad repertoire: blues, spirituals, and topical songs. This broadcast did contain a few surprises: a nice version of "House of the Rising Sun" and his cover of the pop song "Down Hawaii Way." Huddie also made this tantalizing announcement about a new break in his career:

ANNOUNCER: *Say, Huddie, I don't know if you can give out this information. We received a telephone call about two hours before you got over here saying that you had definitely been signed to play in the picture "St. Louis Woman." How about that?*

HUDDIE: *It's mighty true. I just come back here last night from that. . . .*

ANNOUNCER: *That's wonderful. Johnny Mercer is writing the music for that, isn't he?*

HUDDIE: *He's writing the lyrics, that's right.*

ANNOUNCER: *And Lena Horne?*

HUDDIE: *Lena Horne's in there, too. She's the woman that's going to be the mother. She's going to marry a man, that's what it is.*

ANNOUNCER: *You're going to be in there—that's the main thing!*

HUDDIE: *I'm going to be on the head end there.*

ANNOUNCER: *Do you know about when the picture is going to break?*

HUDDIE: *They are going to start this thing around about August.*

Like the other film projects, though, "St. Louis Woman" never developed beyond the planning stages.

Philip Elwood, music writer for the San Francisco *Chronicle*, was about to graduate from the University of California at Berkeley when he met Leadbelly. Although quite young, Elwood was experienced at setting up musical events and concerts in the Bay Area. Jazz had become his special interest, although he was getting more interested in the roots of jazz. In April 1945 he got word that Leadbelly was coming to San Francisco. At that time Rudi Blesh was writing about local jazz and ragtime, while the legendary New Orleans trumpet player Bunk Johnson was running the elevator at the local CIO hall and playing gigs on weekends. Because of his interests and connections at the university, Elwood became the point man for a Leadbelly concert. He'd heard Huddie's Bluebird and Musicraft records, but like most West Coast fans he'd never heard Leadbelly live.

Huddie was staying at the home of Ellis Horne, a jazz musician who lived on the Oakland-Berkeley border. Elwood recalls his initial meeting was laden with uncertainty: "I was rather stand-offish because I didn't know how to handle him. He also had a severe cold. He was drinking a good deal, but he talked very well. I think he had learned to talk to people who were kind of interested in him as a folk artifact, as it were. Gradually he loosened up.''

The concert itself was on a Thursday evening near the end of April. Tickets cost less than a dollar and the university had guaranteed to pay Huddie $90 for an evening's work. The hall was rather big, larger than it should have been for a solo performer. But it was the only appropriate spot on campus and Leadbelly attracted quite a crowd, so it worked out just fine. Said Elwood:

He sat right on the edge of the little lecture stage, a typical college auditorium with folding wooden seats. . . . The chairman of the music department had taken it upon himself to prepare a small lecture on the subject. Fortunately, I had gone out on stage . . . he then turned it over to me, expecting me to give a life history of Leadbelly. I had a very brief biography, so it went quickly and Leadbelly was waiting on the side. He moved along the front [of the stage] and I think that it was better without the mike. His voice was quite strong. There was quite a bit of sing-along during the whole thing.

Following a short intermission, Huddie came back out and completed his one-and-a-half-hour concert. Elwood loved the music but was most surprised by this Texas blues singer "swilling down bourbon out of a tumbler" on the university campus!

Leadbelly stayed in the Bay Area for several more weeks, playing at clubs and at venues such as the California Labor School on lower Market Street in San Francisco. In Emeryville, Leadbelly sat in at Dugan's Gay 90's Café, a very informal place with a stage, small dance area, and a traditional jazz band that Philip Elwood used to occasionally play in. Elwood recalled that it was so casual "that it was no problem to have a black guy get up on stage and play blues, which was very unusual for a basically white, workingman's bar.''

Despite this casual attitude toward Leadbelly and his music, this part of California was not immune from racism. "There was also an attempt to do some recording with Leadbelly and some of the white guys, like they'd done with Bunk Johnson,'' Elwood said. "The local musicians' union would not permit a recording to be made using a [racially] mixed band.'' (The discs were to be produced on an independent label by David Rosenbaum, and were to back the singer with clarinet player Ellis Horne and two other members of Lu Waters's popular jazz band.) Elwood contacted famed newspaper columnist Drew Pearson, who was in San Francisco writing about the United Nations. As part of his May 11, 1945, syndicated "Washington Merry-Go-Round'' column, Pearson wrote:

Discrimination at San Francisco

While San Francisco delegates attempted to build a framework to carry out the four freedoms of the Atlantic Charter, the ministers of Music Dictator James C. Petrillo were denying the right of one of America's foremost Negro singers to make music recordings if accompanied by a white pianist or any other white musicians. . . . Petrillo's Musician's Local Union 6 denied him the right to make recordings with three white musicians—Ellis Horne, Squire Girsbach and Paul Lingle.

Ed Moore, vice president of Local 6 and Secretary Jack Haywood telephoned Petrillo in Chicago to ask whether Ledbetter could play with the three white musicians and got the word "No." There has been a long standing rule in the San Francisco Bay area that Negro musicians cannot play in public with whites. But Local 6 once before stretched this rule to discriminate against Negroes even on private recordings where the public has no idea who the musicians are and whether they are white or black. The other notable case was that of 64-year-old Willie "Bunk" Johnson, one of the inventors of jazz in New Orleans at the turn of the century.

Typically, Leadbelly also performed at local, informal parties. Philip Elwood attended one of them on a Saturday night in a "large loft over a double garage in the fancy Claremont district of Berkeley on Ruble Road. I suppose there were twenty of us, mostly college age, mostly couples, some of them left-wing types. . . . None of us were quite sure what was going on, but we'd been told that Leadbelly was going to come and we were going to sing." When they arrived, Leadbelly was already there and "he was in very good shape. I can't remember if he was 'drink tired' or just tired. He was seated the whole time. The women in particular liked him. He was a powerful personality. As a personality he was rather forbidding, but then I always felt a little nervous around people like that."

Despite his previous acrimonious conflicts with John Lomax, this long-standing relationship with the elder Lomax kept Leadbelly in California into the fall of 1945. Paramount Pictures had optioned a film about the life of John Lomax, *Adventures of a Ballad Hunter*, in 1945. Rumor had it that crooner Bing Crosby was set for the lead role. No script was written, however, and the film moved no further. But Huddie traveled back to Hollywood "on spec," hoping the film would be made and that he would gain his place in celluloid history. The film's demise proved to be a major disappointment, another frustrating incident in Huddie's search to reach an audience beyond live and recorded performances.

Ironically, this trip almost certainly resulted in Huddie's second appearance on film. Two West Coast filmmakers shot silent footage of Leadbelly performing at least six selections in their backyard and living room. The footage languished for nearly two decades before Pete Seeger contacted one of the filmmakers, who sent him the material and wished him good luck with it. Seeger notes that it was "pretty amateurish. I think that he recorded Leadbelly in a studio the day before, then he played the record back while Leadbelly moved his hands and lips in synch with the record. He'd taken a few seconds from one direction and a few seconds from another direction, which is the only reason I was able to edit it. I spent three weeks with a movieola, up in my barn snipping one frame off here and one frame off there and juggling things around. I was able to synch up three songs: 'Grey Goose,' 'Take This Hammer,' and 'Pick a Bale of Cotton.' "

During this extended California trip Huddie also encountered Ross Russell, who had recently begun the Dial label, which documented some of jazz artist Charlie Parker's first important work. Russell recalls:

Leadbelly and I met at the home of a Hollywood writer and the singer took to coming into my shop. . . . When asked for old songs, unsung for years, Leadbelly would conjure them up or at least reasonable facsimiles of them after one of his Zen-like trances. At my record shop one afternoon he walked over to the piano and began playing at the keys. I was not aware that he played. After some lengthy trial-and-error experiment, as much by sight as by sound, Leadbelly found the few notes that he wanted, in the Key of G, and began pounding out an old rag called "Big Fat Mama with the Meat Shakin' on Her Bones," all the while standing, bobbing, and weaving and doing dance steps. It was a crude, unbelievably rhythmic performance.

In addition to the old songs, Russell noted the strains of violence that still dogged Leadbelly. On a joint pub-crawling adventure in 1946 along Central Avenue, Los Angeles's main black drag, Russell recalled, "Leadbelly had his 12-string guitar along, and before the third round of drinks Leadbelly had taken over the place. It was Fanning [*sic*] Street all over. Before long the attention paid him by two young women, almost 40 years his junior and escorted by manly contemporaries who resented Leadbelly's responses, were on their way to creating trouble. With some difficulty we managed to get him out of the bar and back to Hollywood."

Interestingly, Russell also suggested some common points shared by Leadbelly and Charlie Parker: "Each had an unshakable conviction in the rightness of his music, especially in the way it should be phrased. For each, there was only one right way. Both were highly skilled actors and con men, abilities which had been painfully and laboriously acquired and arose out of their experience as black men in America. They both could instant-cast roles to suit the occasion and the attitudes of those present."

August 7, 1945, a week before World War II ended, Huddie found himself down in San Diego, writing to Moe Asch.

Hello there Mr. Moe Asch

How are you today as I am all right and just sitting here the cool The sun is shining nicely today, [it] is Tuesday morning. I sang and played for the tall girl what was at the party that night. They had a packed house and they really was a nice audience [.] They sure did sing with me I did spirits song and hollers and worksongs and blues [.] They didn't want to see me go. This was my first time here so I will have a return engagement and it will be monday after this coming. Then i will leave for Chicago and I will [be] there the following Saturday night. Then you can set the Town Hall if you wants to for any night you wants to and you can share the money after the expenses is out. I will come right from the train to the place where I'm going to play [.] I will meat my wife after I'm through [.] So rite me at this address, let me no so i can Be there. address is 1610 E 49 st, Losangeles Calif

H Ledbetter

He was looking forward to coming back east, and to doing a Town Hall concert—a P.S. mentions the young dancer Sue Remos, who would be appearing with him. Apparently the Town Hall concert got postponed—it was eventually held in New York in April 1946—and Huddie was back in San Diego in October for another concert. By now he had another new manager—Irwin Parnes of Hollywood—but jobs were still not coming in regularly. As he filled out his income tax return for 1945, he showed a total income of only $1183.

He was definitely back in New York by the spring of 1946, and embarking on a series of well-publicized concerts. In March he appeared on the first show for People's Songs, Inc., held at Elizabeth Irwin High School in New York City. Described by historian Robbie Lieberman as a left-wing organization that "used their music as a battle cry for civil rights, civil liberties, and world peace," People's Songs had just been organized a few months earlier with Woody Guthrie and Alan Lomax among its board of directors. A little later he did the Town Hall concert with his friend Sonny Terry—where he was billed as "America's Foremost Folk Singer"—and later in the year another Town Hall concert entitled "We're All in the Same Boat Brother." The latter included Sonny Terry, singer Cisco Houston, Brownie McGhee, Edith Allaire, bassist Pops Foster, and dancer Sue Remos. Surviving programs show that, in spite of his increased fame and association with jazz musicians, Leadbelly was still sticking to his traditional repertoire. He was still doing the kind of blues, spirituals, ballads, and work songs that had won him his first fame. By now he had pretty much abandoned his earlier attempts to do pop or swing material; the old admonishments by John and Alan Lomax, that he remain true to his traditions and confine his repertoire to the distinctive songs he had brought with him from Texas and Louisiana, had taken hold. The only "new" song on the programs was "Hollywood and Vine," which he sang, no doubt, with a special irony.

In early December 1946, Huddie spent several days in Salt Lake City. He was slated to perform for the University of Utah Extension Division's concert series. Following close on the heels of an embarrassment Marian Anderson had recently suffered at one of the city's highly regarded hotels, the university found Huddie a room at an out-of-the-way Japanese-operated hotel, the Astoria on West Second South, which billed itself as "The West's Largest Colored Hotel." His host, Hector Lee, a young folklorist and anthropologist who directed the Utah Humanities Research Division, describes their initial meeting:

I was at first surprised that he was not tall, as I had expected, but rather shorter than average and that his speaking voice was soft. . . . The blurred heavy dialect pronunciations that I had observed in his earlier recordings had to a remarkable extent cleared up, and the man's mildness, his deferential politeness, his softness caused me to wonder for the moment how this could be the fearless singer of "Bourgeois Blues," the strong worker from the chain gang, the killer that John Lomax had found in a penitentiary, or for that matter, the great folksinger I had heard about.

Following a radio interview, Huddie once more surprised Lee. Shortly after entertaining Lee's young son and posing for a photograph, Huddie asked, "Say, Doc-a Lee, I was wonderin' could you maybe loan me a couple o' dollahs. They's a couple o' chicks down at the place where I eats that maybe I could do some business with if I jest had some money. I got money, all right, but Baby won't gimme none. If you could see your way to let me have just a couple o' dollahs, and not say nothing about it, why tonight when you come for me, when nobody lookin' I could kinda ease it back to you." Lee declined, which Leadbelly good-spiritedly accepted.

A question of money caused another misunderstanding during this same trip. Huddie was then acting as his own manager and handled all of his own financial affairs. Hector Lee's quoted fee was for two appearances, a children's concert and an evening engagement. Leadbelly became very upset when he learned that the fee covered both concerts and complained bitterly to his host throughout his stay.

The two performances Huddie gave offered a striking contrast in attitude. His concert for the children of the University of Utah's training school

proved to be a smashing success. With his usual panache, Leadbelly danced
and delighted his rapt audience. His evening concert, however, proved to
be a very different matter. It began poorly when Lee allowed him only two
drinks before going on stage. Then Huddie declined to use the microphone
and amplification system offered to him and even Leadbelly's booming
voice and twelve-string guitar could not reach all of the twelve hundred
patrons. Many in the audience attended the concert because they were
season ticket holders. Between the conditions of the hall and their lack of
familiarity with the musician, most sat on their hands. The cold, unrespon-
sive audience must have greatly discouraged the artist, for he left the stage
with a downcast look in his eye.

But the debacle was partially redeemed by a small party held the next
evening at Hector Lee's home. Lee invited a dozen friends over and in this
more intimate context, Leadbelly's genius shone through in his music.
Leadbelly's natural storytelling ability was never more in evidence and his
attentive audience leaned forward to hear him say:

*Well, I used to have just an ordinary guitar. One night I was playin' in a
place—one of them sukey-jump places—and people were drinkin' and some
was dancin' and it was warm. I was playin' there and one of my strings
broke. I jest went on playin', though. And then a pretty gal come along, and
she just leaned down over my shoulder and pushed against me—you know.
And another string broke, but I couldn't stop now. Not no how! So I jest
kept on playin' cause she was nice—fine as wine in summer time. And then
you know what? Another string broke, and I just had one string left. I played
that one string 'cause I liked that thing. But I made up my mind then that
I'd go out and get me a twelve-string guitar.*

Apocryphal or not, Leadbelly's natural bravado and his storytelling ability
must have fascinated his guests.

That night marked the end of his trip to Salt Lake City and his final stop
in the West. It was December 1946 and Huddie seemed happy only when
his guitar was in his hands and the music or stories flowed like good liquor.
Lee noted disillusionment in songs such as "The Gallis Pole" and in Leadbelly's own demeanor. He wrote:

*[Leadbelly] seemed proud that he had the means at his command of ex-
pressing the sadness of his people. It was then that he sang and spoke as an
artist. But when he spoke man-to-man without his music he showed great
personal bitterness. The Lomaxes had exploited him, he thought. I had
taken advantage of him. Everybody did. Even Hollywood had dealt badly
with him. There was talk of making a motion picture of the story of his life,*

and Leadbelly had insisted that he play the leading role himself. The fact that he was too old was irrelevant—make-up could fix that. At that time Josh White had been mentioned to play the part and this galled Leadbelly.

But before Huddie left Salt Lake City and the West, he did a very characteristic thing. He summoned his muse and created a song about Salt Lake City that contains this verse:

> *People want to know what you come here fo'*
> *I told 'em I was coming f'to sing*
> *Fo' the Salt Lake City, Utah,*
> *University. . . .*

Not great poetry, to be sure, but it expressed Huddie's need to play music and satisfy his wanderlust. But his home in New York City was calling him, and soon he was traveling back to his beloved Martha.

24 "Goodnight, Irene"

When he returned to New York, Leadbelly found the town caught up in the midst of another type of music revival. This time it was traditional New Orleans jazz. In 1938, when jazz historians William Russell and Frederick Ramsey, Jr., were researching the first real history of jazz, they rediscovered an old New Orleans cornet player named Willie "Bunk" Johnson. He had been one of the founding fathers of New Orleans jazz and a teacher of Louis Armstrong, and his dramatic comeback had caused nationwide excitement. Along with other New Orleans veterans like George Lewis, Kid Ory, and Mutt Carey, Johnson helped awaken people's interest in the older forms of jazz that had been heard in the city around World War I, when Huddie himself had visited the town. Now Johnson and other veterans were recording again, broadcasting, and getting good dates at New York clubs. Young musicians were forming bands built around the New Orleans style, and writers were busy interviewing veteran musicians and trying to find out what they could about the early New Orleans music.

Huddie found he was cited as a source for the "roots of jazz," and jazz historians like Charles Edward Smith and Frederick Ramsey, Jr., began talking to him about his musical roots. He even did several shows with Bunk Johnson's band, as well as several radio broadcasts. He went on tour with Brownie McGhee and the jazz band headed by Art Hodes, the Chicago piano player who was enjoying the crest of the New Orleans revival. They toured into the Midwest, to Cleveland, to the University of Chicago, to the University of Illinois, among others. The Duke of Iron, Billy Sanders, and the veteran blues guitarist Lonnie Johnson were also part of the tour. In spite of all the new association with jazz, Leadbelly never formally recorded with a jazz band. Like many older performers, he was used to working alone. He would occasionally agree to perform or record with a group like the Golden Gate Quartet or with friends like Sonny Terry, Brownie McGhee, and Woody Guthrie, but the idea of singing in front of a group of instrumentalists did not appeal to him. The attention paid him by the jazz historians and journalists, though, was welcome and did much to assuage the wounds he felt from his experiences with Hollywood. In April 1946 a group of journalists put together a small book about the singer, *A Tribute to Huddie Ledbetter*. Published by Jazz Music Books in London and not widely available in the States, the book was a series of essays by writers like

Charles Edward Smith, Frederick Ramsey, Jr., Albert McCarthy, and Max
Jones (who edited the compilation). It included personal profiles, a historical background, record reviews, and an early discography. "American
readers may wonder at the interest shown in Ledbetter's singing and playing by enthusiasts who, in the main, are unable to buy any of his records,"
wrote Max Jones in the book's foreward. "The fact is, his voice has quite
often been heard over the air in such BBC recorded programmes as 'America Sings,' and WNYC's 'American Music Festival.' " V-Discs, records produced for the armed forces, had also been heard during the war, so English
fans had been exposed to him for nearly a decade.

Of the various clubs he played in New York, the Vanguard seemed to be
Huddie's favorite, and his shows there are among the ones most remembered by jazz and blues fans. He had started working there before the
California trip and used to call it "The Garden." The club was actually
called the Village Vanguard and was a sort of basement room on Seventh
Avenue in Greenwich Village. At that time, the club was painted a robin's-
egg blue, with walls that tapered back to a small stage. A mural by Paul
Petroff featured things like a white horse playing the piano and a pay
telephone nailed to a tree. Owner Max Gordon, who would become a major
figure in the development of jazz in New York through this club, had an
easygoing attitude toward his performers; he let them sing or play whatever
they wanted to, with little interference—a policy which suited Leadbelly
fine.

On a typical night at the Vanguard, by nine the night's audience would
have been filing in, taking up tables along the wall and on a little elevated
section that resembled a balcony. Huddie would appear around ten o'clock.
The lights would go down, the spotlight would come on over the stage, and
the emcee for the night would announce Huddie. Talk would stop and be
replaced by applause. Frederick Ramsey has described what would happen
next:

Then a big man steps into the glare of the little spotlight. He's wearing a
tight-fitting double-breasted suit, dark shoes, a plain-colored shirt and tie,
all well matched. His hair shows grey-to-white and is close cropped. . . . His
guitar snaps around into position as he faces the audience. He places his
foot on a chair, tunes the twelve strings. While he tunes, fingering lightly,
running through "Easy, Mr. Tom," he talks to his audience. "Good evening, ladies and gentlemen—Now tonight you say that's right." His eyes
now roam around the silent room, picking out friends. "Little girl over
there in the red dress, she wants a request." The fingers pluck easily, but
he's not ready yet. He smiles, and his face shines, bronze-to-copper-to-
brown, as the light picks up the rich, beautiful pigment of his skin. "—an'

if it's a request, then you know that's best. . . . Now this is the 'Rock Island Line.' "

As the evening continued, he would do other favorites, like "Bourgeois Blues," and often an old Baptist shout song like "Walk Through the Valley" or "Meeting at the Building." "We're gonna rock church," he liked to say as he got into the slow, driving rhythm of the songs. At other times, he encouraged the audience to get into the act by joining him in a chorus. "Well, my baby say she love me,/ And my Mama love me too,/ If my baby don't love me, then I know my Mama do," Leadbelly would sing, and on the chorus his crowd would join him:

> *Well, I know she do,*
> *Yeah, I know she do,*
> *Yes, I know she do,*
> *Yes, I know she do!*

Part of the showmanship that fascinated audiences was Leadbelly's ability to change or improvise songs on the spot and to create odd, funny, rhyming introductions and explanations. Some of these resemble the rap music of the present day, a style that Leadbelly would have been right at home with; both forms have their roots in the "patter" songs of early songsters like Henry Thomas, and the toasts and dozens of black narrative folklore. "He was a very powerful stage presence," said Stu Jamieson, who as a young man was a member of Margot Mayo's American Square Dance group. "I remember how he tickled the audience at town hall concerts with his rhymes. 'It's just as fine as wine at tea time.' He could go on for hours with those things. I think it came from practice with the dozens. It was such a different humor than city audiences were used to."

At other times, Huddie would startle listeners by changing the words to some of his songs on the spot, to reflect a current situation, even an event of that evening. During the war, for example, he often changed "Rock Island Line" to include references to troop transports and wartime shipments. Instead of having the engineer sing "I got goats, I got sheep, I got cows," he had him say, "I got soldiers, I got sailors, I got guns." Junie Scales arrived in New York about 1948 from Chapel Hill, North Carolina, where he had attended school, and got Leadbelly to play for a party. Scales reflected:

I remember that he was quite taken with one girl named Mariam. And he took "Sweet Mary Blues" and adapted it to "Sweet Mariam Blues" and it was the most outrageous seduction through music that you ever heard in your life! She was quite charmed by him. At that time in his life he was in

*his late fifties and an extraordinary good-looking man. He moved with a
great deal of grace and his white hair set off this ebony face. She was quite
taken with him, and I am not sure to this day if she didn't leave the party
with him. He was certainly most attractive to her and he used his music to
plead his case most effectively.*

He was by now learning, too, how to deal with his dialect. Young fans
still had trouble with it. Ronnie Gilbert met him in 1947. "The first time I
heard Leadbelly I could not understand a word. Not word one . . . of his
singing. It was one of his things where he kind of rambles on and on and
on. But the next time I heard him, I understood every single word he said."
Henrietta Yurchenco recalled that he had been worried about this in 1940–
1941, when she first met him, and later when she knew him again in 1947.
"He was very much concerned about his southern accent. He would say to
me, 'Gee, Miss Chenco, do you think they understood what I was saying?
Because he did try really hard to change his accent. Some of his recordings
show how carefully he tried to talk. Especially his children's records." Pete
Seeger agrees: "Leadbelly, when I knew him, was trying very hard not to
get angry and to live like people are supposed to live up in New York. He
changed his way of talking so that people could understand him better."
Ironically, these changes disappointed some of his original supporters like
Alan Lomax, who felt that he was much more interesting and vital when he
first arrived in New York City.

Huddie also began to do what many performers do when they reach
middle age: think about ways to get some regular income beyond performing. More savvy now about the songwriting business, he began to wonder
if his song-writing talent might be put to use. Before he went to California,
he had visited Samuel Pruner again, for whom he had made his Musicraft
sides back in 1939. Pruner's company had flourished, and he was into all
kinds of sidelines, from pressing to making record sleeves. His new offices
were in the Brill Building, then as later a headquarters for New York music
publishers. He remembers: "Leadbelly dropped in one day to say hello to
me. Sniffing around as he always did. He never looked you in the eye, he
always looked away from you, or looked down at something. After he
dropped in a couple of times, I knew he must be looking for something."
Finally he admitted to Pruner that he "had started to write popular songs,
and then he used to come in and play them for me and my partner. I
introduced him to the pop department. You know, we were auditioning and
here was a guy with something of a reputation. Finally, it got to a point
where we were really interested in what he might produce in the pop
department."

Pruner placed Huddie under a contract that stipulated that Musicraft pay him $50 a week in order to get first refusal on his material. Pruner was confident that he could tell a good popular song from a bad one and was looking for material for the new publishing firm. The company had in fact published a song called "I Don't Want to Love You" that had become a Top Ten hit for two weeks when recorded by crooner Phil Brito in 1944. "For weeks, Leadbelly came by to try out material," Pruner recalled. One day he sang them "Irene," which appealed to Pruner very much, but he delayed buying it. Leadbelly left and did not return.

One of the causes Huddie sang for that he did care deeply about was civil rights. The war was over, and the thousands of black veterans returning home after proving themselves in combat were not in the mood for compromise and further discrimination. Nor was Leadbelly. One of his strongest songs was born out of this: "Jim Crow Blues." He started off with a reference to his friend, jazzman Bunk Johnson:

> Bunk Johnson told me, too,
> These old Jim Crowisms,
> Dead bad luck for me an' you.©

After castigating the southern states for their various Jim Crow laws and attitudes, he added:

> I want to tell you people something that you don't know,
> It's a lotta Jim Crow in the movin' picture show.©

It is one of the few times that his bitterness about the Hollywood experience crept into his music. About the same time, Huddie wrote and sang a song about Jackie Robinson, the first African American ball player to sign with a major league team. Unfortunately, Huddie never recorded or published the song, and it remains as one of his lost ballads that people remember him singing, but which we have no copy of today.

Equally intriguing is "Equality for Negroes," which shows up in none of Huddie's songbooks, nor in the Broadcast Music, Inc. list of songs he is credited with. Leadbelly thought enough of it to record it twice for Mary Barnicle and Tillman Cadle, and it appears to date from 1948. In fact, there are internal references in the song to suggest that he worked it up after listening to the 1948 Democratic convention, where a body of southern conservatives, angered over Harry Truman's stand on civil rights, walked out and formed the Dixiecrat party. They held another convention a week later and nominated South Carolina Governor Strom Thurmond for president. None of this sat well for civil rights advocates, and Huddie reflected this in his song.

Equality for Negroes

Now listen up, I'm not lying to you,
Negroes fought in World War One and Two,
The blues is like now, the blues at hand,
Fighting for a United Nations.

If the Negroes were good enough to fight, why can't we get
some equal rights?
For God made us all, and in Him we trust, nobody in this
world is better than us.

Why don't you folks realize with one another,
Like the preacher says, love thy neighbor,
You are Jewish and I am young,
Negroes have suffered some great, great wrongs.

One thing, folks, you all should realize,
Six foot of dirt makes us all one size,
For God made us all, and in Him we trust,
Nobody in this world is better than us.

I been hearing you speak 'bout that old democracy,
The diplomats, that old hypocrite speech,
Think it's about time you should cut it out,
The way Negroes is treated down South.

All in all, it's a rotten shame,
Like they're wanting to bring back slavery again,
For God made us all, in Him we trust,
Nobody in this world is better than us.

For God made us all, in Him we trust, nobody in the world
is better than us.

Huddie's performance of the song is not blueslike; it's a strong, driving piece, anticipating by fifteen years the kind of rallying songs that would be used in the civil rights struggle. How often he sang it is not clear; probably he was still honing it and working it into his repertoire when he became ill. He might not have had time to use it much, but he certainly had plans for it. It was also a song distinctly aimed at white audiences. Pete Seeger thinks it quite possible that Huddie borrowed the idea of the song from a calypso singer named Sir Lancelot, probably a guest who recorded at the Barnicle-Cadle flat. He also remembered Leadbelly doing his own version of Earl Robinson's protest song "Free and Equal Blues."

Though Leadbelly sang about civil rights, he seldom spoke out publicly about it, and this was one reason some younger blacks were now calling him an Uncle Tom. His early fondness for passing the hat, his courtly behavior and formal dress, his willingness to adapt to communicate, and even his choice of where to perform fueled these accusations. Yet, Seeger points out, "He was a man who stands up and looks you in the eye and says, 'Here is my song.' That thing about not being ashamed is important, too. He could have been put down. I'm sure that some black people said, 'Why do you sing those Uncle Tom songs? Why don't you sing some modern songs?' . . . He must have been proud of them. 'These are good songs, they are my songs, don't tell me I'm an Uncle Tom.' " As a matter of fact, Huddie was doing a good job of keeping in touch with the more modern music. In a letter from 1947 he praises the King Cole Trio (Nat King Cole's trio, which was then being widely heard on Capitol records and numerous transcriptions), jazz pianist Mary Lou Williams ("the greatest woman piano player in the world"), and Eddy Howard ("greatest man piano player of his kind"). Only the latter choice is surprising. Howard was the leader of a sweet band that had been on the radio for years, and which had recorded the versions of "Anniversary Waltz" and "Happy Birthday" heard on juke-boxes for years. Perhaps Leadbelly saw in Howard's arrangements the same thing that Louis Armstrong saw when he once commented that he loved Guy Lombardo's saxophone section. Leadbelly also continued to admire songs like Gene Autry's maudlin "The Bible on the Table and the Flag upon the Wall," and admitted that Bing Crosby sang "right nice." On the other hand, he was especially critical about one particular folksinger who was popular in the mid-1940s. "He sings right nice but he sounds like he had the wrongest kind of operation." About another folksinger, he liked to say, "He usta sing right nice but a man can't sing with a pecker in his mouth."

One document has come to light in which Leadbelly makes a statement of sorts about his own life and its relation to the civil rights struggle—a statement not couched in terms of a song. In the spring of 1947 Moe Asch asked the singer to write some sort of autobiography, probably for use as liner notes for an album or for one of the publications Asch occasionally issued. Leadbelly set to work and completed a lengthy manuscript of four densely packed handwritten pages, dated New York City, May 22, 1947. It was not quite the account of life that Asch had envisioned, and for several reasons he never published any of it. It was found in the Folkways Archives at the Smithsonian after Asch's death. But though the statement is not all that autobiographical, it is a fascinating reflection—one of the few lengthy ones that the singer produced. Since it was addressed "To whom it may concern," it seems likely that he considered it a public statement. The first part of the text is as follows:

The american peoples, this world from 1901, look where it [sic] *and what
has been done 1912—12 day of May when the Titanic sunk in the sea. When
they was getting on board, was not no colored folks on there. Was not no
negroes died on that ship. But Jack Jackson went to get on board But boss
shoved him back. And to Jack Jackson when went to get on board. We are
not hauling no coal, so Jack Jackson didn't like what the big Boss did*[.]
He went out and tried to do something about it[.] *But it was so much Jim
Crow he could not had no go and a few hours later Jack Jackson read the
Papers where the titanic went down*[.] *Then the peoples began to hallow
about that mighty shock*[,] *you might have seen Jack Jackson doing the
Eagle Rock, so glad that he was not on that ship. Ship hit the ice berg. Well,
that shows the peoples don't understand. They forget that this is a world
and one shall*[?] *build for man and i*[.] *well my friends in 1917 teen when
the war was on i couldn't go because i was in prison with 35 years*[.] *So
from there the peoples didn't understand that the negros went in there and
clan up and a little native* [nation?] *well I* [undecipherable] *peoples i dont
care what happens on Earth i no and i think we should be as one just like
the world was bilded*[.] *when my father was a living man He was a good
man and my sweet mother was a good mother they was not no old fashion
they just was on the 1925 model and the 1922 model so on every is different
things happens so now then up to 1947*[.]

*Every since 1933 i ben recording for the Library of Congress in Washing-
ton d C up untill 1941 when alan Lomax and his father stop working for
them. So then sence i haven had no manager, my experiences larned me
enuff about the peoples in the world to no how things are going*[.] *well what
cause me to go all over and sing for President FDR. Because he was the Best
man. He was a rich man But he diden not care about it just who are was
all right with him.*

Well the world is round and the usa is wrighting to be found [.] *there's
a lots of Jimcrow in the movie pitchers shows, why it the rich man got the
best go*[.] *But some day it can be done and it will be done—well guess what
it will be this is the way i feel to words*[.] *each and every one look down and
look some time think to your self and about your self because you are one
can do something about good things*[.] *you take little children's when they
father and mother a bringing them up just what they teach there child that
is just what the child will do*[.] *get a fad of this every time a white person
call a negro a nigger they are a nigger to*[.] *There are white nigers, well
there is nothing for a negro to fight about There is the whole think right
Those in our race we have a forth person in our race, get a God of this they
call the fighting kind* [undecipherable] *But this it all four of the kind a niger
fautch* [flaunts?] *a mity figer*[.] *a coon type he don't like no body*[,] *negro
he is very good a collord person they are perfict all the way* [.] *so a negro*

wants to visit a dive and want to tour Uptown he is no dam good[.] *there is white nigers so they are the same way now*[.] *i mus say this a white niger, he dont like his mother He will robe* [rob] *and steal so that shows you that is the kind of peoples that cause trouble all over this world. But i wish all the peoples would stop and weigh* [wait] *for the green lights to come on before they step on the gas*[.] *. . . the world is at a Cross road*[.] *no body noes which end to take if you never travel there before so my dear friends they still talks peace, what makes peace last, one little thing that is stop fighting races and then we will have peace*[.] *now this is another thing to those some white peoples wont take a negros word*[.] *why*[?] *because he wants to fix it like he wants to with the most white man puts the negro and the Jewish peoples in the same boat but they is a lie they are in the same boat. We think it a dam shame how the same so call peoples try to ignore there name*[.] *But they cant go over it and they cant go around it to show you about all Bands. They are jealous of each other why when you read music they play the same peace they got to play it the same way they feel*[.] *That next band might play that peace better than they do so i will move i could right up top* [undecipherable] *so i will be there. not on the air but there* [on] *Disch* [Disc] *co. There was a man sent from the Holliday magazine to take my picture*[;] *well he said he was Huties friend, well so much for nothing. They will sell the magazine and get money and i get nothing. Well that is the world makes it go round and round*[.] *That is the usa fighting to be found*[ed] *for*[.]

The material about Jack Jackson and the *Titanic* was clearly drawn from Huddie's song, but the rest of the material comes from the singer's own experiences. In an odd way, it is an affirmation of his heritage, and a statement that things for blacks were changing ("the world is at a Cross Roads"). He uses the photographer from *Holiday* as an example of the way of the world. It is a sad, weary, experienced voice, and it is unfortunate that the statement has not appeared in print before now.

Leadbelly explained his commitment to the Jim Crow fight once to his friend Joe Brown. "I'll fight Jim Crow anyplace, anytime. But when they ask me to sing at one o' their concerts, I say sho. But one of the songs I'm gonna sing is 'We all in the same boat brothar. You rock it too far to the right you fall in the waddah, rock it too far to the left you fall in the same waddah, and it's just as wet on both sides." This was part of what he was trying to say in his autobiographical statement.

Brownie McGhee remembered something almost all of Leadbelly's friends from this time commented on: the singer's complex attitude toward whites. "The first thing that Lead ever said to me was, 'If a white man call you a nigger, what do you say or do to him?' I said, 'If I don't say anything to him, I'd leave it to his dignity, because a black man isn't a nigger.

Anybody can be a nigger if he wants to be. Or if his actions tell him that he is.' That was me and Leadbelly's first conversation.'' That Leadbelly would instruct a young black friend in this way reveals something of the singer's own attitude toward even the word *nigger*. He later told a friend a story from his childhood—one of the very few he told anybody—about the term. He used to have a white boss who liked to hear him play the guitar when he was just a boy. The white man also played the guitar, but not well; even as a child Huddie was much better. On bad nights the white boss would get drunk and demand that Huddie play; he would make him play for hours, while he kept drinking. When he finally got drunk enough, he'd look up at Huddie and he'd say, ''Nigger, some day I'm gonna kill you.'' The fact that Huddie kept this story all the years of his wanderings and adventures tells us something of the hurt he felt.

Now in the late 1940s, with Leadbelly one of the lions of the folk movement, young fans were becoming extremely self-conscious about just what to call their idol. Pete Seeger recalled: ''At a party down in Greenwich Village a white college student said, 'Black people have so much better music than white people; black people can dance so much better than white people.' And he went on like this for a minute or two. Then Leadbelly just stood up and said, 'I'm proud of my race and think everybody should be proud of their race.' That was the end and this young fella just shut up.'' Stu Jamieson, still in high school at the time he knew Leadbelly, recalled heated debates among young fans at the time over ''the classification name for black people.''

Of course, Black was out in those days. And it was either colored or Negro. And Negro had bad associations because of its implications for nigger. Some of them were rather shocked to hear him [Leadbelly] kidding around with Sonny Terry and saying, ''Hey, nigger.'' There was a lot of discussion about it and after one of our broadcasts we were standing around talking. Somebody said, ''Why don't we ask Leadbelly?''

So we went over . . . and said that we were concerned that we wanted to use the correct nomenclature in talking about his race. . . . He kind of laughed a little bit and looked at me and said, ''He can call me nigger because I know him.'' He pointed to me. It was because I always called him Mr. Ledbetter. He said, ''You can call me Huddie or Leadbelly, but you better not call me nigger until you know me better.'' In short, the lesson was more what you meant rather than what you said. That didn't solve our problems in the slightest.

Another thing that people noticed during this time was the way in which the old press legend about the ''homicidal harmonizer'' haunted the singer. It became an albatross around his neck, and people who got to know him well could understand why. Brownie McGhee disliked the Lomax book so much that he literally cut it up with a hacksaw. Pete Seeger said that whenever Leadbelly was interviewed in these years, the prison subject would come up and the singer always tried to steer the conversation away from it. "He didn't attack John [Lomax], he didn't feel strong enough to attack John. . . . Alan got along well with him. Alan must have made it clear in some way that he didn't agree with his father."

In spite of these attempts, the old stories would not die. Seeger observed that "every time a newspaper article was written about him, they said two-time murderer, spent twenty years in prison, and so on. Boy, did he never want to hear about that again. . . . He could not get away from that, try as he might. When he gave concerts, I mean the radical white people, we didn't mention it; we said, 'Leadbelly, the great folk singer.' But if *Life* magazine or *Time* magazine wrote him up, they liked to quote Kittredge speaking to Lomax, 'Oh, he's a demon, that's what he is, a demon!' "

Leadbelly's income tax return for 1945 showed that his total income was $1,183, hardly a princely sum for a person who was as well known as he was. His Capitol records had not sold well, and he seldom got substantial sums of money from Moe Asch. From time to time during the last years Martha continued to work at jobs in the city, some of them almost menial. In one royalty statement for Stinson Records, an independent rival to Asch and Disc and Folkways, Leadbelly actually wound up owing the company money. His sales had not managed to cover the $15 advance he was given. On May 23, 1947, he did sign a formal contract to do an album for Disc, six numbers including "Ham n' Eggs" and "The Midnight Special," for a lump-sum payment of $750. It was one of the best record deals he had made.

His slow record sales helped fuel the frustrations Leadbelly was feeling about his career in general, and for a time it threatened his relationship with his long-suffering Martha. She had endured much with Huddie and knew exactly how to read him. The drinking, the parties, the stubborn Texas macho, even the months he spent away from her in California she could stand; he had written her regularly while in California and obviously missed her a lot. But one thing Martha did not like flaunted was unfaithfulness. A story told about them by a friend was cast as a joke, but was underneath more serious:

Now he [Huddie] says, "Take for instance, I come home and I find Baby (Martha) with another man. Whoo, I feel terrible. I wanna die. But you think I'm gonna hurt my baby, or hurt that man? What good that do anybody? I take a walk, come back later."

So Martha, his wife, says to him, "Who you trying to fool? You jus tryin'

to fix it as'in I come back and find you with another woman. And you're
hopin' I'm gonna take a walk and come back later. Well, I AIN'T!

The situation must have become more than Martha could handle in the
spring of 1947, for she did leave Huddie for a time. Exactly what happened
is unclear, but both Brownie McGhee and Pete Seeger recall the separation.
Seeger thought she went to live with friends in Brooklyn; McGhee thought
she had returned to Shreveport. Leadbelly himself wrote about staying with
a twenty-one-year-old girl from Winston-Salem, who began going with him
to concerts and parties, but nobody remembers her name. Sometime in
1948, Martha returned, the Winston-Salem girlfriend left, and the marriage
got back on course.

As always, the real money for Leadbelly was not to be made from the
glamorous world of radio and records, but from the tough, grinding world
of the concert circuit. For these, Huddie was by now able to claim respectable fees; a 1947 concert at Cornell, for instance, yielded $200, and a tour
in the Midwest in 1949 promised $400 a week. In 1946, Woody Guthrie,
Pete Seeger, and about a dozen other singers banded together to form
People's Songs. This was not actually a musical group per se, but a sort of
cooperative organization designed to promote folksingers and folk compos-
ers. It popularized the concept of the hootenanny, an informal gathering
and concert that would feature people like Leadbelly, along with Pete Seeger, Lee Hays, Woody Guthrie, and others. Leadbelly first sang for the
group in 1946, and their management/booking company, People's Artists,
helped him find concert dates both in the city and out. Leadbelly had gone
through several managers: Fred W. Ellis, from the late 1930s; Irwin Parnes
in Hollywood; and most recently Austin Wilder of Fifth Avenue in New
York.

Huddie's biggest help in managing his career in his last five years,
though, came from his own family: Tiny Robinson. Tiny was Martha's niece
and had come up to New York as a teenager around 1939 to stay with her
aunt when Leadbelly was away on the road. Tiny grew up in Caddo Parish
but moved to New York City as a young woman. She impressed singers and
visitors to the apartment with her dancing. Eventually she married and
settled in the city. She had known Leadbelly when she was a child in
Louisiana and now took an interest in his work in New York. Though she
had no real experience in managing or in show business, she knew what
was right and what was fair. She looked over the contracts Huddie was to
sign and helped him set up dates. It was Tiny who would go to Moe Asch
and remind him about overdue royalty payments—and more often than not
come away with some. And it was Tiny who read the royalty statements
closely enough to suspect that things might not be exactly right. She also

became aware of the image problems that the Lomax book had caused; and she found the Leadbelly she knew was different, a gentle man who would visit her apartment in the mornings and dance and sing 'Whoa Back, Buck" for her small son Alvin. "No matter what bad things anyone said or any bad deed done to him," Tiny recalled, "Leadbelly would never say anything about that person."

By 1948 Asch had launched Folkways Records and had started a series of LPs featuring Leadbelly's music. First was a series of ten-inch LPs, packaged in thick cardboard sleeves, often with mimeographed booklets inside giving song lyrics and sometimes notes about the songs. The earliest LPs were simply collections of older songs that had been recorded earlier, but by 1947 Asch was having Huddie cut songs especially for LPs.

Also in 1948, jazz historians Fred Ramsey and Charles Edward Smith managed to get hold of one of the new magnetic tape recorders; this was a new way of recording sound that had been discovered at about the time American troops swept across Nazi Germany in the closing days of the war. In addition to superior sound, tape gave the performer the luxury of time. Discs could only hold three to five minutes of music; tape could go on for thirty minutes or so. For artists like Leadbelly, whose songs with stories often ran up to ten minutes or more in concert, tape seemed an ideal solution. In late September, Ramsey invited Leadbelly up to his flat and, in an informal and relaxed atmosphere, showed him how the tape recorder worked. Leadbelly was fascinated with the sound and abilities of the machine and agreed to record some of his songs, as well as his personal history. The sessions continued into October and eventually included over 90 songs. Some of them Leadbelly had never recorded before; as he reminisced with Martha and Ramsey and Smith, he reached far back into his past and brought out things nobody had heard. He also talked about his childhood for the first time on record, and about his parents. Martha even helped him sing some of the old gospel songs.

In 1953, four years after Huddie Ledbetter's death, Ramsey brought these sessions to Moe Asch and released them on a series of three double albums as *Leadbelly's Last Sessions*. They would, in fact, be his last formal sessions, though some informal recordings of radio shows and concerts would be made after them. But *Leadbelly's Last Sessions* captured the singer at a late peak of his powers, sitting in a room with people he trusted, being the superb raconteur, ranging over his huge repertoire with grace and confidence, and explaining his songs to the future generations who would hear the recording. It was a fitting memorial.

The years of 1948 and early 1949 were full of tours, concerts, and possibilities. In March 1948 Leadbelly played to one of his biggest audiences ever, at a concert at the University of Illinois at Urbana. Along with Pete

Seeger, Brownie McGhee, Betty Sanders, and calypso singer Lord Invader, Leadbelly did a whole evening concert, one emceed by writer and radio star Studs Terkel. "We got paid a thousand dollars, which came down to about two hundred a person—a lot of money for those days," recalled Seeger. "At that particular college, Leadbelly stayed up almost the whole night long singing for some fraternity students in their fraternity house and he sang all of the old bawdy-house songs that he knew, and they loved him. I marveled at his stamina."

In August Leadbelly played at Lakeside-on-Erie, Ohio, for the annual convention of the International Platform Association. In October he played at Phillips Exeter Academy in New Hampshire, a few days later St. John's University in Maryland, and then Allegheny College in Meadville, Pennsylvania. In November he began a concert and lecture series sponsored in part by the University of Minnesota. Accompanied by an assistant, a young man named Austin Fairbanks, he traveled throughout the state, at one point meeting the dean of Canterbury Cathedral from England, who was visiting Minneapolis. One evening he attended a party at the home of the University of Minnesota lecture and concert coordinator, Clifford Manz. Kenneth Britzius had a tape recorder and captured another two hours of Leadbelly singing and talking about his music.

Early in January came talk of a proposed new musical to be staged in New York—not an informal hootenanny, but a serious Broadway entry. There might be a part in it for Leadbelly if he were interested, and attempts were being made to interest Ethel Waters as well. The jazz jobs continued: appearances on the WNYC Jazz Festival on radio, a $75 gig at the Jazz Band Ball in February, and an appearance on NBC's venerable "Chamber Music Society of Lower Basin Street" show. In February, too, he finally joined the Associated Musicians Union of New York. After another round of college dates, he decided to follow the lead of so many American jazzmen and try his luck overseas. On May 8, 1949, he flew to Paris to do a series of concerts there, returning on May 31.

Austin Fairbanks, working from his office out of Somerville, Massachusetts, set up the details of the tour. He felt it was important to have some kind of backup band (to help emphasize the jazz connection) and recommended trumpet player Bill Dillard along with piano players Cliff Jackson or Mary Lou Williams. Dillard eventually was used, and while in Paris he and Huddie recorded a number of masters—though little is known of them and they appear to have never been issued. In fact, some of the concerts on the trip were hardly overwhelming successes. Suffering from bad publicity, the one at the Lyceum in Paris only attracted about thirty people—though they applauded wildly when the singer encored with "I Don't Want No More of Army Life." Other concerts were better presented, with detailed program booklets containing background information on each song.

It was in Paris, though, that something far more serious came up. For some time, Huddie had been having occasional difficulty walking; he had been hospitalized once for it earlier, had managed to get back on his feet, and celebrated by writing his song "Walk Around My Bedside." Now he began to have problems again and saw a French doctor to find out what was the matter. The diagnosis was not good: amyotrophic lateral sclerosis, or Lou Gehrig's disease. It was a progressive degeneration of the nerve cells that controlled voluntary motor functions, and its victims eventually have difficulty walking, speaking, and using their hands. It was progressive and inexorable, the cause was unknown, and there was no known cure. When he got back on May 31, the word spread quickly among his friends. A planned tour of Iowa with promoter Lucius Pryor could not happen, but there was time for a concert at Orchestra Hall in Chicago with Woody Guthrie, and a special one at the University of Texas on June 15. This was a homecoming of sorts. John Lomax had died in January 1948, and he was on Huddie's mind as Huddie remembered his early days with him. He sang some of the children's songs he had sung for the collector, "Ho Day" and "Skip to My Lou," as well as the cowboy songs like "Ella Speed," "Whoa Buck Back," "Old Hannah" and other songs that had been in "the book." He sang "Rock Island Line" and remembered the first trip he had made with Lomax, to the Arkansas prison camp. He closed with two spirituals that he did with Martha, "Old Ship of Zion" and "I Will Be So Glad When I Get Home." The concert sponsors had sensed the drama of the event: they had met Huddie and Martha at the plane with a wheelchair.

Early July brought some more honors: an Award of Merit from the Oklahoma Folklore Society and a couple of attendant concerts in Oklahoma City. There were some more dates with Pete Seeger, who watched with sorrow and admiration as the disease progressed and as Leadbelly fought to continue playing. Seeger recalled, "He was deeply ashamed that his strength had left. He didn't want to be seen walking onto stage with a cane. He said, 'Let me walk on stage, I'll sit down, then you open the curtain for me. Okay?' After the performance, they closed the curtain on me, then with pain, he'd get his cane and leave the stage."

By July 19 Leadbelly was in Bellevue Hospital in New York. The disease was now advancing rapidly. There were more days back home, but they were good mostly when friends or Tiny's young son came to see him. Not enough friends came, some thought, and others were not quite sure how to deal with the tragedy. For a time he could still sing and play the guitar, but that, too, was soon gone. The day he found he could no longer play his Stella he cried.

For the last six months, his doctor was a man named Dick Blocher, and he visited Huddie regularly. He was impressed with Huddie's strength and determination, and in those days became a good friend. He later told a story about Huddie, the evening before the singer went to the hospital for the last time. He was sitting in a wheelchair, where he sat to help his breathing, and the doctor was preparing to leave. He started to move Huddie over to the bed. "Doctor, don't put me in that bed," Huddie said. Blocher responded that he needed his sleep. "You put me in that bed and I'll never get out," Huddie responded. The doctor moved him to the bed anyway, thinking he was just depressed.

Huddie died in Bellevue, Ward R6, on December 6, 1949. The official cause of death, as reported in his *New York Times* obituary, was a bone infection. The next of kin were listed as Martha, a sister, and two nieces. His daughter, Arthur Mae, of Kansas City, was also listed. The services were held at the Rodney Dale Funeral Home in Harlem. Since Huddie had joined the Elks years before, the Elks attended, and turned it into more of an event than Martha wanted. Finally the formalities stopped, and some of Leadbelly's friends got up to sing. Brownie McGhee got up to sing, and Pete Seeger sang "Ain't Gonna Study War No More." Ronnie Gilbert sang. Fred Hellerman sang. Josh White sang.

Martha took him back to Shiloh Baptist Church then. It was a long, somber train ride down home, back where Huddie once played the organ. Sometime earlier in the decade he had joined the Masons in New York City. Though he'd never been a very active member, Huddie was given Masonic rites: he had been a thirty-third-degree Mason. He was placed in his coffin shoeless, wearing his Masonic apron. There was no money at the time for a marker.

Nobody knew quite what Leadbelly's death meant then. No one could see the storm clouds ahead, the trouble ahead for the folk song movement, the protest movement, the civil rights movement. No one could foresee that the small group of friends who laughed and sang with Leadbelly would soon be scattered to the winds, leaving only their music and their ideals.

Fred Hellerman, who would soon win fame as a member of the Weavers, years later recalled his favorite memories of Huddie. "Once image sticks in my mind so clearly. Where Huddie and Martha lived . . . it was on the sixth floor of a walk-up tenement. There was a time, it lasted maybe six or eight months, and it was a sort of ritual. Every Sunday night Sonny Terry, Brownie McGhee, Tom Paley, and myself would go there. Their place, you could have eaten off the floor. Martha was really a heck of a housekeeper. We would be up there singing all night and we had to bring a bottle of whiskey. That was the entrance fee. Late at night, Huddie would get his twelve-string guitar, and then he would begin to play. By now it was really quite late. Don't forget, this was a tenement building, the walls were kind of thin. Like with a Pied Piper, sleepy little kids from all across the building would sort of wander into the apartment, come on in. Then he began entertaining. It was the most wonderful, tender picture. He really liked kids, he really related to them and they really related to him. He was something they viscerally understood. It was a wonderful thing to watch him with the kids." It was a fellowship, a music, a time that was gone forever.

Epilogue

"If Huddie had lived just a few more years, he would have literally seen all his dreams as a musician come true," Pete Seeger said. In a final, bittersweet irony, Huddie's best-known song, "Irene," became the biggest popular song of 1950. Seeger, in fact, had much to do with it; he was a member of the singing group called the Weavers, along with Lee Hays, Fred Hellerman, and Ronnie Gilbert—all old friends of Huddie's. The group had gotten a contract with the giant Decca company and finally persuaded their producer, Gordon Jenkins, a slick arranger and composer himself, to let them record "Irene." Decca bosses were still nervous about it, and Jenkins finally got the record out with a clever ruse: He issued it under the name "Gordon Jenkins and his Orchestra," with small type on the label reading, "Vocal by the Weavers." Released in July 1950, the disc was soon selling briskly all over the country; it was on jukeboxes, on radio stations, and on the Hit Parade. Country singer Ernest Tubb recorded it, electric organ virtuoso Lenny Dee did it, and even Frank Sinatra crooned it. By October, the *New York Times* was estimating that it could be heard "1,400 times a minute" over "the 2,583 radio stations, ninety-nine television stations and roughly 400,000 juke boxes in the United States." The Weavers had their biggest hit record, and a platform from which to launch other folk songs. They were also scrupulous about giving Huddie credit as composer. (Official composer credits on the ornate black and gold record labels read: Huddie Ledbetter–John Lomax.) Royalties started to pour in, and suddenly every feature writer in the country seemed to want to do a story on the singer and his song. Had he been alive, Huddie would indeed have had his choice of major record label deals, radio offers, and concert bookings.

Even before "Irene" (or "Goodnight, Irene," as it was now called), Huddie's death had not gone unnoticed. Wire services across the country carried the news and trade publications like *Billboard* listed it in the "Final Curtain" column. The *New York Times* printed his obituary as a major item, replete with a recent picture of the singer and its characteristic reference to him as "Mr. Ledbetter." But down in Shreveport his passing was hardly acknowledged: only the Shreveport *Times* ran a story, and that derived from the wire service reports. None of the four weekly newspapers serving the northern Caddo Parish and eastern Harrison County even bothered covering the funeral.

Back in New York friends and fellow musicians were determined not to let Huddie's passing go by unnoticed: They organized a tribute concert at Town Hall on January 28, 1950. Sponsored by the "Leadbelly Memorial Concert Committee" and spearheaded by Alan Lomax, the show featured a series of slides and photos depicting Huddie's life, and lots of music. Old friends like Brownie McGhee, Woody Guthrie, and Pete Seeger performed, as did jazzman Sidney Bechet and "St. Louis Blues" composer W. C. Handy. Other tributes took the form of record albums: Moe Asch began putting Leadbelly music out on the new LP format, and a generation of music fans got their introduction to traditional culture by listening to these and by reading the little mimeographed brochures that Asch enclosed in each album. These booklets offered information about Huddie's life as well as the texts of his songs.

Some of Huddie's continued success must be attributed to Folkways Records, now Smithsonian/Folkways, under the guidance of Moses Asch, who for decades kept most of his catalog of Huddie's music in print on ten- and twelve-inch albums. As 78 rpm records slowly phased out in the mid-1950s, Asch made certain that they found their way onto Folkways' long-playing records. From early ten-inch discs like *Leadbelly's Legacy, Vol. 3—The Early Recordings* to the closing installment of *Leadbelly's Final Sessions*, Asch kept nearly a dozen of Huddie's albums before the general public. He made certain that the notes were written by people who knew Leadbelly well: Charles Edward Smith, Frederick Ramsey, Jr., and Woody Guthrie. Asch also had his hand, along with Alan Lomax, in the series of "Leadbelly Songbooks" that came out in the 1950s and 1960s. These Oak Publications books contained the melody lines and lyrics to a variety of Leadbelly songs with short introductions written by many of the same people who wrote Folkways liner notes. Of the Folkways-related writings about Leadbelly, Woody Guthrie's *Leadbelly Is a Hard Name* is the most poetic, warm, and personal.

Following on the heels of "Goodnight, Irene" came a host of other singers eager to interpret Huddie's songs for the vast pop music market. The Weavers themselves followed up with an old Irish song Huddie had rewritten and arranged called "Kisses Sweeter than Wine." The Folk revival movement in the late 1950s generated even more attention to Huddie's songs, though it produced some unusual bedfellows. "Rock Island Line," the old prison song, was a hit when recorded by an English "skiffle band" headed by a singer named Lonnie Donnegan in 1956; "The Midnight Special" was a hit by country music duo the Delmore Brothers as well as rockabilly singer Johnny Rivers, who liked to sing it at the Whiskey A-Go-Go Club. "Ella Speed" became a favorite of dewy-eyed Canadian folksingers Ian and Sylvia, as well as an anthem of a popular Boston jug band led by Jim

Kweskin. One of the most performed songs in the Leadbelly canon was "Cottonfields," which Huddie sang and recorded as "the Cotton Song"; it was not until the Highwaymen recorded it and made it into a hit in 1962 that the TRO Company, which oversaw the rights to Huddie's songs, realized that no one had ever filed a copyright on it. That was rectified, and since 1962 over a hundred recordings of the song have been made.

Martha, in the meantime, remained in New York City and her house continued to be a meeting ground for musicians. Tiny Robinson, her niece from Caddo Parish, continued to look after her and Huddie's musical legacy. The Reverend Gary Davis and his wife Mary could often be found at Martha's place; in fact, from those visits Tiny became such good friends that she is also executrix of Mary Davis's estate as well as Leadbelly's. But the times were not always easy and Martha often supplemented her royalty income by doing domestic work. When Martha passed away in 1968 at the age of sixty-three she was living at 74 Midwood Street, Brooklyn, but she was buried back home in Caddo Parish. Over one hundred vehicles, escorted by police cars with their sirens on, accompanied the hearse and black limousines to the burying grounds. Because the Promises were longtime members of Republic Baptist Church, Martha was interred there following a funeral service at Shiloh Baptist Church. The service itself featured five guest preachers and was overseen by Tiny Robinson, who had accompanied the body down from New York City.

———

Leadbelly's colorful life and the legends it generated were natural subjects for a book, but no one tried it until the late 1960s. Two San Francisco science fiction writers, Dick Garvin and Ed Addeo, produced *The Midnight Special,* which was published in 1971. Garvin and Addeo drove first to East Texas, where they nosed around Dallas, focusing on its Deep Ellum section, and then headed due south to Houston. They traveled due east to Angola Prison, where they spent a day at the notorious penitentiary during the height of the hellish summer. Finally they arrived in Caddo Parish, where they spent an uneasy week. They started off by using one "whole day walking up and down Fannin Street, which was interesting because we were convinced that we were the only white people within ten miles! [We got] very suspicious looks because our car had California plates." Addeo recalls, "I had shaved my beard off because I had really been frightened by 'Easy Rider.' I'd kept my sideburns because that was still groovy. But the closer we got to Shreveport, the shorter my sideburns got. By the time we got to Mooringsport, I looked like Clark Kent." In the end they decided there wasn't enough detail to make a biography. They settled on a fictionalized account, "a dramatization of his life," as Addeo put it. Though the book was clearly identified as a roman à clef, many mistook it as completely factual—including screenwriters for a later film on Leadbelly. The book was selling well when the publisher, Bernard Geiss and Associates, suddenly went bankrupt; the book died, too. The authors had been touring to promote the book, and participated in a controversial TV appearance on Tony Brown's *Black Journal* in St. Louis—an appearance that ended in a screaming debate over their emphasis on Leadbelly's sex life.

In the mid-1970s the distinguished photographer, writer, and director Gordon Parks brought Huddie's life to the screen in the feature movie *Leadbelly*. In this film, a major black artist sought to deal with the Leadbelly legend in detail. Like the book *The Midnight Special*, Parks's film was not a true biographical work but was based on Huddie's life. As a film, Parks said, "*Leadbelly* succeeds in many ways, but it was mired in controversy and bad timing."

Parks and writer Ernie Kinoy painstakingly labored for nearly three months shaping a screenplay out of Huddie's tangled life that Parks felt they could manage. The film covers roughly 1908 until 1934 because "it was a matter of time. We just had to decide what was dramatic, what people would like better. You're lucky to get two hours and fifteen minutes . . . and we had to fight for that! They want people in and out of the theater." The rest of the preproduction work required nearly one and a half years. Parks assembled a veteran crew, but his cast was relatively unknown. Roger Mosely, perhaps best known as Tom Selleck's helicopter sidekick on *Magnum P.I.*, became the youthful Leadbelly. He remained the only name star and the film still lacked a bankable star in order to increase the budget and an exceptionally tight forty-five-day shooting schedule. Finally, the actual production of *Leadbelly* began in September 1974.

Ironically, about the time the work on *Leadbelly* began in earnest, the last close relative of Huddie Leadbetter passed away. Australia Carr, his adopted sister, had moved to Dallas by the 1930s and made her living as a real estate agent. She remained there throughout her life, living on San Jancinto Street, not far from the center of Deep Ellum. Her death came in 1974, after several years of increasing feebleness, when she was eighty-one years old. According to A. C. Carr, a relative living in Kilgore, Texas, Australia died of "old age" and was buried by the Jones Funeral Home at the Post Oak Baptist Church on the outskirts of Kilgore near other members of the Carr family. No one ever interviewed Australia Carr about her famous brother.

The film crew for *Leadbelly* was headquartered in Austin, Texas, and most of the shooting was done in the surrounding gently rolling hills and the flatter pine woods to the east. Rehearsal time and production amenities, such as a crane for overhead shots, were kept to a minimum. Brownie McGhee, Sonny Terry, Pete Seeger, Dick Rosmini, John Henry Faulk, and several others who knew Huddie personally had their hands in the film. Seeger recalled, "The prison scenes were nothing like they could have been; they didn't have the subtleties. . . . Poor Gordon Parks [almost] ran out of money. I said, 'Gordon, don't you know how phony that scene is when they sing "Goodnight, Irene?" ' He said, 'I know it, Pete, but I don't have any choice. And we've got to put it in the movie.' " Although ten to twelve weeks of shooting might have produced a more complex film, Parks delivered what he promised on time and within his allotted budget.

Just as Parks finished the basic production work, adversity arose from an unexpected source. Jessie Mae Ledbetter Baisely, Huddie's illegitimate daughter born in 1927, sought legal action against Paramount Pictures in December 1974. Baisely became concerned about the aesthetic and commercial rights of her father's life story and hired a law firm that included Melvin Belli. She first wanted an injunction against the showing of the film and charged Paramount with "unauthorized intrusion into details of the life of my father and family." Hampered by Texas statutes against the rights of an illegitimate child, she lost the suit in February 1976.

Following close to a year of editing and other postproduction work, including dubbing San Francisco blues singer Hi-Tide Harris's singing, the film was completed. It is visually appealing, reasonably accurate in its portrayal of Leadbelly's life, and features some strong performances. The musical selections are equally well crafted and fine. This was no slick blaxploitation film meant to fill ghetto theaters, but an understated and sensitive coming-of-age film. Approved and bankrolled by Frank Yablans of Paramount Pictures, hopes for the film were quashed when Barry Diller became head of the studio just as the film was to be released in 1976. Unwilling to really push *Leadbelly*, and about half a dozen other of Yablans's films, Diller quietly ordered its release. Without the proper studio promotion and media hype, *Leadbelly* languished in theaters for several weeks before sliding into oblivion. Once again Huddie Ledbetter's dream of stardom was crushed by the Hollywood egos and money shakers.

Parks had deliberately made a film with no Richard Roundtree or Diane Ross, eliminating the obvious star appeal. *Leadbelly* has plenty of violence, but no car chases or spectacular gore. The story line is compelling, but Leadbelly's own name was not enough to carry the film to create general public interest. Without Yablans to push the film, *Leadbelly* languished in advertising limbo for nearly a year. Paramount screened the film privately in New York City and a few other selected cities. The critical response from *Variety* and other printed sources was favorable and Parks was hopeful that *Leadbelly* would soon grace screens throughout the country.

Instead, *Leadbelly* dropped into oblivion. In the spring it quietly opened in Detroit, Boston, and Atlanta, outgrossing all of the other films playing in

Detroit and Atlanta. Academy award winner *One Flew over the Cuckoo's Nest*, which was running on seven screens to one for *Leadbelly*, barely edged out *Leadbelly* in Boston. Following a private screening Charles Champlagne, entertainment editor of the Los Angeles *Times*, wrote that *Leadbelly* should be acknowledged as one of the finest films of 1976. Audiences at the annual U.S.A. Film Festival at Dallas and the Philadelphia Film Festival honored it with a standing ovation. Despite this success, Paramount Pictures continued to hedge on its support and promotion of the film. Its movie ads depicted a muscular young stud with a scantily clad brown beauty glancing in his direction. The commercial success of *Mandingo* must have weighed heavily upon the minds of these Paramount promoters.

Around June 1976 Parks decided to directly confront the Paramount behemoth himself.

I had a terrible fight with Barry Diller. He called me up and said, "Look, we are doing the best that we can with the film. But we are being crucified by the press and I want you to stop it." I cussed him out on the phone . . . and called him some names about which I am a little bit ashamed. [Shortly thereafter] I sat with Barry Diller in the screening room. He sat next to me and said, "It's a marvelous film. We are going to do everything we can to promote it." I don't know if it's true, but word is, from one of his young assistants, that when they got upstairs, Diller said, "Kill it."

It appears that what Diller said upstairs is what counted, because by the end of the summer *Leadbelly* had ended its run. It played for less than two weeks at most venues.

Just as the filming for *Leadbelly* began in Austin, an unexpected controversy erupted regarding Huddie's burial place at the Shiloh Baptist Church in extreme western Caddo Parish. Perhaps sparked by the renewed commercial interest in Leadbelly, Max S. Lale of Marshall, Texas, chair of the Harrison County Historical Survey Committee, suggested that Leadbelly's body be moved and reinterred on a Texas site. He voiced his concern that "one of Texas' truly great musicians should be left to Louisiana in attention." Lale further observed that Harrison County might then host a "grass roots blues festival somewhat like the ragtime festival which Sedalia, Missouri, has to honor another great black Texas musician, Scott Joplin."

Lale's bizarre proposal predictably stirred up a local ruckus that eventually involved an entertaining mix of players. Articles with titles like TEXANS WANT BODY OF LOUISIANA SINGER and HARRISON COUNTY WANTS LEADBELLY graced the pages of Shreveport's independently owned newspaper. Irene Campbell of Marshall, a second cousin, supported the move, but was opposed by Blanch Love, who said, "Don't stir 'im, he's dead and tired of bein' worried." The local black newspaper, the Shreveport *Sun*, remained strangely mute regarding this controversy. Finally, Caddo Parish coroner Dr. Willis P. Butler put the entire matter to rest when he refused to issue a permit because no one had shown him just cause. Leadbelly's unassuming grave remains in the yard of Shiloh Baptist Church, about one mile from the Texas border on the Blanchard-Latex Road.

One side effect of all this controversy was some formal recognition for the singer by the state of Louisiana. On June 10, 1982, an official state historical marker was unveiled at the Earl Williamson Park along the shores of Caddo Lake in Oil City. The informal gathering included the usual politicians, in addition to Leadbelly's second cousins Florida Ledbetter Combs and Irene Campbell. After many years of a tangled and troubled history, the contributions of Huddie Ledbetter were finally recognized by the state of his birth. Perhaps encouraged by these small victories, Caddo Parish was not through honoring the memory of Leadbelly. The city of Shreveport was determined to do something about the crime-ridden, economically destitute bottoms. This is an overwhelmingly black section predominated by narrow shotgun houses, small businesses, and brutal poverty, which was also home to the officially recognized red-light district early in the twentieth century. In the early 1980s ninety-one percent of the residents lived in substandard homes. Shreveport's solution was to name a blue-ribbon commission and renew hope by renaming the bottoms "Ledbetter Heights." Shreveport City Council member Hilary Huckaby observed, perhaps tongue-in-cheek, that "there's a lot in a name. It will give people new hope for improving their own lives." Unfortunately, Ledbetter Heights remains one of the city's less desirable sections in which to live.

The fall of 1984 brought the ninth annual Red River Revel, an arts festival named for the river that divides Shreveport from adjacent Bossier City and which paid tribute to Leadbelly. The Revel Committee staged this tribute with an October fourth concert. Pete Seeger, Sonny Terry, and Brownie McGhee were joined by Josh White, Jr., Oscar Brand, Jean Ritchie, and local musicians in celebrating the life and music of Leadbelly. By all accounts it remains one of the best advertised and attended programs in this series.

The recent recognition of Leadbelly's legacy has not been limited to the Ark-La-Tex. On January 13, 1988, Leadbelly, the Beatles, the Drifters, the Beach Boys, and Woody Guthrie were inducted into the Rock 'n Roll Hall of Fame in a ceremony held at the Waldorf-Astoria in Manhattan. Across the country, millions of rock fans saw Tiny Robinson receive the award and reveled in rare footage of Leadbelly powering his way through "Pick a Bale of Cotton." The small Caribbean nation of Granada issued a series of stamps saluting black Americans in June 1988. Included as subjects of honor were politician William Henry Hastie, educator Mary McLeod Bethune, and Huddie Ledbetter.

By September 1988 Huddie's music was brought to an audience across the United States by way of a Showtime channel television special that paid tribute to Woody Guthrie and Huddie Ledbetter. This "All Star Tribute to Woody Guthrie and Leadbelly" consisted of an hour of songs and brief interviews filmed in recording studios, concert stages, and small clubs. The performances of Leadbelly's songs consisted of Little Richard doing "Rock Island Line," Taj Mahal doing "Bourgeois Blues," Willie Nelson doing "Goodnight, Irene," and Sweet Honey in the Rock doing "Sylvie." Simultaneously, Columbia Records issued *Folkways: A Vision Shared—A Tribute to Woody Guthrie and Leadbelly.* This release shared many of the same performers as the Showtime special, but added Bob Dylan and Brian Wilson to its lineup.

In the more than forty years since Huddie Ledbetter's death, his music has become more popular than he could ever have imagined. His impact upon American culture is undeniable; his songs appear in school song books, in Hollywood films, in the music of rappers and hard rockers, and on compact discs. (By 1992, there were over eleven compact discs by Leadbelly on the market, more than for many current MTV stars.) More important, he is for many the archetypal folksinger, the perfect image of the solitary artist sitting alone on a stage with a guitar, reaching back into his past to share his roots. It is an image somehow quintessentially American, one that reflects the basic method of all of our great writers, poets, painters, and musicians.

Americans tend to think of folksingers as people who are shy about their gifts and nervous about admitting their ambitions. Huddie Ledbetter entertained grand ambitions; from the very first he was a natural performer who reveled in being the center of attention, whether in a prison gangway or a Greenwich Village nightclub. He wanted to be a star; in the words of Grand Ole Opry fiddler Uncle Jimmy Thompson, he wanted to "throw my music across the Americay." He wanted to have a hit record; he wanted to have his own radio show; he wanted to make it in Hollywood; he wanted to be lionized in Paris. And by all rights, he should have. An incredible series of misadventures, bad timing, poor judgment, and just plain bad luck robbed him of the glory he sought. He never found a manager who was able to help him capitalize on his immense talent. Later in his life, Leadbelly was personally frustrated time and again at his failure to communicate to black audiences. He should have been bitter, not only because of the brutal southern caste system that had robbed him of his youth, but because of the callous northern music industry that robbed him of true recognition of his talent.

But he wasn't. He continued to sing and write, to share his songs, to keep his creative juices flowing. He never gave up, even at the end. During the last months, there were still plans and hopes: a Broadway show, new songs, new recordings, new tours.

Leadbelly was an intensely personal man. Though he could be a consummate public man when he chose, there were parts of his past that he guarded zealously. Alan Lomax attributed this to the Ledbetter Indian blood; others thought that parts of the past were simply too painful to cope with. Whatever the cause, this silence about so much of his life only served to fuel the legends, the sensational newspaper stories, the misinformation. In this book we have tried to separate the myths from the man, where that is possible.

We have found that many of the best-known stories about Leadbelly are simply wrong, aggrandized, or oversimplified. He did not really sing his way out of Angola prison by writing a song to the governor; he was due for "double good time" release, got it, and recognized the value of maintaining the story about it. On the other hand, he did sing his way off a prison farm in Texas, though it involved no recordings and no John Lomax. Though indeed he was a convicted murderer, he was only charged with this crime once—in 1917 in Bowie County, Texas, where he was living as Walter Boyd. We have seen that the evidence for this was very circumstantial and that a modern appeals court might well have overturned the ruling. It is quite likely that Leadbelly acted in self-defense, as he did in later altercations. He did come from a violent frontier world where stabbings and shootings were common, and while he could and did defend himself in this world, he was far from the wild-eyed "murderous minstrel" *Time* described him as in 1935.

Too many photos of Leadbelly show him as a big, rough man with an ugly scar on his neck, and too many casual fans thought of him as a loud, boisterous singer. Yet he had a rather high, gentle voice when he talked and was capable of singing with great expression and restraint. He could sound at times like an Irish tenor, at times like a radio crooner, at times like a child on the playground. Leadbelly had great love for children and they seemed to sense something special about him. Yet he seemed reluctant to acknowledge his own children. He had at least three daughters—Arthur Mae Coleman, Panthea Boyd, and Jessie Mae Baisley—but none of them by Martha.

There are other myths. Huddie did not really write "Irene," nor did he make any money from it during his lifetime. In fact, though he was widely known and recognized by people like Woody Guthrie as America's greatest living folksinger, he never did make much from his singing. Though he was often called a blues singer, he had a repertoire that extended far beyond the blues. It was an old complex Caddo Lake body of songs that came from a

266

time before the blues, a time when American music was not defined through genres, copyrights, and hit records.

What is undeniable is this: Leadbelly was the first authentic traditional singer to go before the American people and make them aware of the rich vein of folk music that lay just beneath the surface of the hard bedrock of twentieth century industrial society. He also opened the door to the wondrous and potent world of African American folk culture and shared it with millions through the shaping power of his imagination.

Toward the end of his life, Leadbelly returned to Dallas, where he had learned to busk with Blind Lemon and where he had lived with his sister Australia. Something happened there that impressed him. As he later told his friend Joe Brown:

I was sitten out in the back during intermission. Sitten there resting, playin the geetar a boy, maybe ten years old came up to me. He look at me playing the geetar. Listen to me. lookin at me. After a while he says boy you got some pritty good stuff. Ah look at him and I say, thank you son, I been tryin for almost sixty years. That boy look at me. He didn't say nothin, just listen for a while. When he 'bout ready to go, he say, "Goodbye Mr. Ledbetter. I hope you come back next year." Yuh know, when a white boy in Dallas call a nigga Mistuh, he's just learned something.

CHARLES K. WOLFE *and* KIP LORNELL

Murfreesboro, Tennessee
April 20, 1992

Notes

Preface

The Baisley-Sorrell material comes from a Houston, Texas, interview done in February 1991.

The Lake

The *WPA Guide to Texas* and the *WPA Guide to Louisiana* provide lots of interesting background on the culture of both states. The sections related to the development of Shreveport, the emergence of Caddo Lake, the importance of the timber industry, and other related matters discussed throughout this chapter are derived from these guides.

"There's no white man . . ." This Leadbelly quote comes from Frederick Ramsey, "Leadbelly's Legacy," *Saturday Review of Literature* 33 (1950), p. 60.

All the Caddo Parish population figures come from the 1910 U.S. census.

A copy of the Ledbetters' marriage license can be found in the Caddo Parish Courthouse, Shreveport, Louisiana.

Blanch Love's quote appeared in Wyolene Windham, "Huddie 'Leadbelly' Ledbetter: Some Reminiscences of His Cousin Blanch Love," *Northern Louisiana Historical Association Journal* 7.3 (1976), pp. 96–100.

Vital statistics, particularly for blacks, the poor or rural citizens, were not high priority in either rural Texas or Louisiana in the 1880s. The Caddo Parish records from the early 1900s do not include the John Wesley Ledbetter family in the Shiloh area. In fact, they fail to note many blacks in a parish that by 1910 was sixty percent African American. So the census records and memories of old friends and family members, though faded, may have to suffice.

The information about Wes Ledbetter acquiring land can be found in the deed records located in the Harrison County Courthouse, Marshall, Texas.

"No sir, my papa an' mama . . ." Quotes from Huddie via John Lomax appear in *Negro Folk Songs of Lead Belly* (New York: Macmillan, 1936), p. 4, to be subsequently referred to as *N.F.S.* We also use John and Alan Lomax's book as the principal source for the chronology and background for Huddie's early life.

"Pappa had to . . ." from *N.F.S.*, p. 5.

Quote about clearing the land comes from Charles E. Smith, "Remembering Leadbelly" in Moses Asch and Alan Lomax, eds., *The Leadbelly Songbook* (New York: Oak, c. 1962).

"Sometimes I'd wake . . ." from *N.F.S.*, p. 5.

Quote about domestic violence comes from Ross Russell, "Illuminating the Leadbelly Legend," *Down Beat* 37 (1970), p. 12.

"Son wouldn't take . . ." from J. L. Wilson, "Kinfolk Remember Their 'Leadbelly,' " Shreveport *Times Sunday Magazine*, Oct. 20, 1974, pp. 3–4.

"pretty good student . . ." from Wyatt Moore's 1972 interview with Mary Patterson.

"He was an apt . . ." from a letter in the Library of Congress—Archive of Folk Culture—"Leadbelly" files.

According to Mary Patterson, he was certainly still in school in 1900 or 1901, when he was twelve or thirteen years old; the 1900 census indicated that Huddie had the ability to read and write.

"That's what his . . ." from Moore's 1972 interview.

"But if she got . . ." from Tom Kelley, "Huddie 'Leadbelly' Ledbetter," Marshall *News Messenger*, February 28, 1988, p. 1c.

"Wasn't nothing my . . ." from *N.F.S.*, p. 6.

"When I was a small boy . . ." taken from a Library of Congress interview with Alan Lomax, AFS 2503B.

"could pick more cotton . . ." Ross Russell, *Down Beat*, p. 12.

"He worked fast . . ." and Campbell's next quote are transcribed from a brief, unpublished Library of Congress manuscript—Archive of Folk Culture—"Leadbelly" file.

"There was a right smart of 'em . . ." and his next quotes come from a Library of Congress interview with Alan Lomax, AFS 4472B4.

"He never . . ." from Library of Congress "Leadbelly" files letter.

"But once when I was . . ." and his next quotes are from a Library of Congress interview with Alan Lomax, AFS 4472B4, 2503B, and 2504A, transcribed by authors.

Marshall Lullaby

The background about Huddie's early musical activity and Campbell's quote are from Sandra Cuson, "A Marshall Lullaby," Shreveport *Times*, August 3, 1975.

"When I was a little boy . . ." from an interview released on Playboy LP 119.

"One dollar bill, baby . . ." is described more fully in *N.F.S.*, p. 115.

The version of "Ha, Ha, Thisaway" we use is from the Library of Congress performance found on AFS 145A.

"He had me playing . . ." from Moore's 1972 interview.

"through all this . . ." from Library of Congress "Leadbelly" files letter. Margaret Coleman's letter reveals some information about Huddie's first accordion and his early repertoire. John Reynolds also comments upon this in personal conversations with the authors.

"He loved . . ." from Moore's 1972 interview.

Larry Cohn talks more about "Po' Howard" in his notes to the Elektra box set, ELK 301/302.

The information about the WPA slave narratives and musical instruments is summarized by Bob Winans in a chart that accompanies an unpublished manuscript in the possession of the authors.

By 1908, Sears, Roebuck was offering a standard-sized "starter" guitar for only $1.98. This low price, combined with guitars American soldiers brought back from the Spanish-American war, made the guitar a favorite with rural musicians.

"We were kids together . . ." from Wyatt Moore's interview with Edmond Ledbetter, Longwood, LA, 1971.

Eric Partridge, *Dictionary of Slang and Unconventional English*, 7th ed. (New York: Macmillan, 1970) discusses the etymology of sukey.

"They called them sukey jumps . . ." and his next quote from the notes to the Elektra box set.

This quote from Zora Neale Hurston from *Mules and Men* (New York: Harper-Collins, 1990; orig. pub. 1935), p. 61. Her next quote comes from Paul Oliver, *The Story of the Blues* (Radnor, PA: Chilton, 1969), p. 42.

These quotes from Mance Lipscomb are from an unpublished manuscript prepared by A. Glen Myers, pp. 35–37. This manuscript is housed at the Barker History Center, University of Texas at Austin.

"De White folks . . ." from George Rawick, ed., *The American Slave: A Composite Autobiography*, vol. 1 (Westport, CT: Greenwood Press, 1972), p. 55.

"long ago that was . . ." from a performance issued on the Elektra box set.

The descriptions of the "Shoo Fly" square dance and the "buck and wing" come from the notes to the Elektra box set and from the Mance Lipscomb manuscript, pp. 38–39.

Marshall and Jean Stearns, *Jazz Dance* (New York: Macmillan, 1968), pp. 26–50, is our source for these and the later descriptions of black vernacular dance.

"He did tap dancing . . ." from Moore's 1972 interview.

"My mama used to make . . ." from the notes to Stinson LP #48.

"He used to be a secretary . . ." from Huddie's recorded comments in "Back-slider, Fare You Well," AAFS 4470 B-2, originally recorded for the Library of Congress, August 1940, and transcribed to the notes to the Elektra box set, p. 14.

"Now, they sing . . ." was originally recorded in 1940 for the LC, AAFS 4470, B-4 ("Must I Be Carried to the Sky on Flowered Beds of Ease").

"There's a lot of pretty girls . . ." from Stinson LP #19.

Huddie's explanation of meters and description of services from the notes to the Elektra box set, pp. 14–16.

Hooks's description appears in J. L. Wilson's article, "Kinfolk Remember their 'Leadbelly,'" Shreveport *Times Sunday Magazine*, undated clipping in the Special Collections, Louisiana State University, Shreveport.

"The whole family . . ." Phil Martin "Ties to Huddie," Shreveport *Journal*, September 25, 1985, p. 1.

"I never led no prayer . . ." from a Library of Congress interview with Alan Lomax, AFS 4472A-3.

"He had a deep down . . ." from Moore's 1972 interview.

Quotes about backsliding appear in the Elektra set, pp. 14–15.

Fannin Street

"As the time . . ." from Library of Congress "Leadbelly" files letter.

"Every Saturday . . ." from "Last Session," Folkways FP 2942D, Band 1.

"At 14 he started . . ." from Campbell manuscript, Leadbelly file, Archive of Folk Culture, Library of Congress.

"but jealousy . . ." from Library of Congress "Leadbelly" files letter.

"That's what his parents . . ." from Moore's 1972 interview.

"He wouldn't take nothing . . ." J. L. Wilson, "Kinfolk Remember Their 'Lead-belly,' " Shreveport *Times Sunday Magazine*, October 20, 1974, p. 3.

"Now son, don't you . . ." *N.F.S.*, p. 6.

Lomax discusses the gun incident in greater detail in *N.F.S.*, p. 7.

"Huddie was a good-looking . . ." from Moore's 1972 interview.

Huddie's mother, Sallie, had been formerly married to Joe Betts before she wedded Wes Ledbetter, and Alonzo resulted from that union.

In her unpublished typescript, Irene Campbell talks about the mysterious "Sweet Mary" (Leadbelly file, Archive of Folk Culture, Library of Congress).

The *WPA Guide to Louisiana* provides our background information about the development of early twentieth century Shreveport.

Goodloe Stuck, *Annie McCune, Shreveport Madam* (Baton Rouge: Moran, 1981), discusses the development of Shreveport's red-light district (p. 10). The later quotes about the city's bawdy section are also taken from this source.

"the most notorious . . ." from Stuck, p. 70.

". . . as fine a looking whore house . . ." is from an old gambler quoted by Stuck, p. 13.

". . . some mulatto girls . . ." from Stuck, p. 54.

"After a general . . ." from Stuck, pp. 70–72.

Huddie's description of Fannin Street and the quotes about his disputes with his family regarding his activities there are found in *N.F.S.*, p. 169.

This lengthy description of Fannin Street and Huddie's adventures with his father are found on "Leadbelly's Last Session," Folkways 29400, Side 4.

The description of Pine Top Williams and other barrelhouse piano players comes from Russell, p. 12.

"It was about 1904 . . ." from Folkways 29400, Side 4.

Banished Away

"At eighteen . . ." from Charles E. Smith, "Leadbelly—King of the 12-String Guitar," *Leadbelly's Songbook*, p. 13.

"That's the first jazz band . . ." from Smith, p. 13.

His wanderings are also discussed in Russell's article, pp. 12–13.

"We always called ragtime . . ." from Smith, p. 13.

Ramsey's quotes come from Dick Weissman's B.A. thesis, "The Relation of Leadbelly's Life and Music to the Social Environments in which He Lived," Goddard College, 1956.

"I used to be terrible . . ." from *N.F.S.*, p. 12.

The information about Lafayette's mixture comes from Dr. Michael Harris, historical pharmacologist at the Smithsonian Institution, National Museum of American History.

"perhaps Mr. Ledbetter . . ." from a letter Hurd sent to Dick Weissman on February 23, 1956.

"When I joined . . ." and subsequent quotes from the notes to the Elektra box set, p. 13.

"I was Jumpin'. . ." from a Library of Congress interview with Alan Lomax, AFS 4471A2.

"The people, all of . . ." from notes to Elektra box set, p. 13.

"the one spot in the city" from J. H. Owens, "Deep Ellum," Dallas *Gazette*, July 3, 1937.

"She was a little . . ." *N.F.S.*, p. 123.

Most of this information and quotes about Blind Lemon Jefferson come from Alan Governor's essay "Blind Lemon Jefferson," in Toby Byron and Pete Welding, eds., *Bluesland* (New York: Dutton, 1991).

Huddie talks about Blind Lemon and the *Titanic* on *Leadbelly's Last Session*, on Folkways (see discography).

Stella and Irene

"Well, I used to just . . ." Hector Lee, "Lead Belly," *Journal of American Folklore* (No. 76, 1963), pp. 135–137.

"I saw one of the old . . ." Ross Russell article, *Down Beat*, p. 13.

Background on the history of the twelve-string guitar comes from George Gruhn, "12-String Past," *Frets* (September 1988), pp. 29–30. The history of the Stella Company can be found in Tom Wheeler, *American Guitars: An Illustrated History* (New York: Harper & Row, 1982). Specific information about Huddie's style of guitar playing comes from Joe McDonald, "Jon Lundberg Re-Creating Leadbelly's 12-String," *Frets* (June, 1983), p. 32. For more about how Huddie tuned his guitar, see Julius Lester and Pete Seeger, *The 12-String Guitar as Played by Leadbelly—An Instructional Manual* (New York: Oak Publications, 1965). Finally, Tom and Mary Evans, *Guitars: From Renaissance to Rock* (New York: Facts on File, 1977, pp. 299–304) provided us with background on which picks Huddie was likely to have used.

"I was there . . ." from Campbell interview with Wyatt Moore, 1972 (from tape provided by Moore, November 1989).

Background information about Uncle Bob Ledbetter comes from his interview with John Lomax in 1940, AFS 3992–3994.

The Lomaxes reveal their concern about the origins of "Irene, Goodnight" in *N.F.S.*, p. 235.

Our thanks to Joe Hickerson, Archive of Folk Culture at the Library of Congress, for calling this version to our attention.

John Reynolds—Leadbelly fan, photograph collector and close family friend since the 1950s—was the first person to come upon these printed sources for "Goodnight, Irene."

"In an era of . . ." Maxwell F. Marcuse, *Tin Pan Alley in Gaslight* (Watkins Glen, NY: Century House, 1959). The background information about Gussie Davis can be found in [Samuel A. Floyd], "In Retrospect: Gussie Lord Davis (1863–1899)," *The Black Perspective in Music* 6, no. 2 (Fall, 1978), pp. 188–212.

Harrison County Chain Gang

All of the information regarding Wes's landholdings and dealings come from the deed books of the Harrison County, Texas, Courthouse.

"I never served . . ." from Huddie's letter to Himes, December 8, 1933, in Angola Prison file.

No newspaper or other published accounts of the 1915 trial exist. Our facts come from the files of the criminal records of Harrison County.

The Lomaxes briefly describe Huddie's chain gang experiences in *N.F.S.*, p. 10.

Tom Kelly, "East Texas Minstrel Rests in Peace in Louisiana," *Marshall News* (LSUS archives, undated), tells of Sallie's presentiment regarding Huddie.

"You go down to . . ." from *N.F.S.*, p. 11.

A tip of the hat to Joni Haldeman for pointing out and discussing with us the frontier ambience of Bowie County at this time.

Gordon Parks, "A Last Visit to Leadbelly," *New York* (May 10, 1976), p. 67, quotes Leadbelly as saying, "I was calling myself Walter Boyd then, 'cause of some other trouble." We assume that he was talking about his escape from the Harrison County chain gang.

They Called Him Walter Boyd

Our history of De Kalb comes from *Texas: A Guide to the Lone Star State, Compiled by Workers of the Writers' Program of the Works Progress Administration* (New York: Hastings House, 1940), p. 387.

Our information about Will Stafford comes from several of Joni Haldeman's interviews, which are listed in following notes.

Howard Farris's comment about Boyd was made to Joni Haldeman during a conversation in the summer of 1991.

Zeola Vaughn, in an interview with Joni Haldeman on June 18, 1991, recalled that "he could pick more cotton than [anyone]."

"snatch eight or . . ." from *N.F.S.*, p. 123.

"was a bronc rider . . ." from Barton Hamilton interview with Joni Haldeman, June 10, 1991.

"he helped my daddy . . ." and subsequent quotes from Vaughn's interview with Haldeman.

For more about Juneteenth, Charles Wilson and William Ferris, eds., see *Enclopedia of Southern Culture* (Chapel Hill: Univ. of North Carolina Press, 1989), p. 216.

"was always picking up" from Kip Lornell interview with Viola Betts Daniels, November 25, 1989, Marshall, Texas.

"I whipped the dress . . ." *N.F.S.*, p. 14; this incident is further described on pp. 12–14.

This bawdy song comes from the Leadbelly files of the Archive of Folk Culture at the Library of Congress.

"during Christmas . . ." Viola Daniels interview with Kip Lornell, November 25, 1989, in Marshall, Texas.

The Rollin' Sonofabitch

Most of the details about the relationship among Stafford, Ledbetter, and Ms. Jones comes from Joni Haldeman's interview with Margaret Cornelius on June 6 and 7, 1991.

All of the Cornelius quotes are from Haldeman's interview.

Mahaffey said this during a phone conversation with the authors on May 10, 1991.

"shooting him with a gun . . ." and other background about this incident comes from a letter to John Lomax from A. L. Buford, February 22, 1935, on file at the Archive of Folk Culture at the Library of Congress.

Accounts from the trial come from both newspaper stories and the surviving Bowie County Court records, New Boston, Texas.

The varying accounts and descrepancies related to the murder are discussed in Lee Oursler, "Lead Belly," *Shreveport Journal* (February 12, 1971), p. 4D.

In Parks's *New York* article (May 10, 1976), p. 67, Leadbelly explains, "Well I figured Alex had it coming. He drawed on me first but I got my shot off first."

"Here I was . . ." from Parks, p. 67.

"I didn't like the way . . ." from Parks, p. 67.

N.F.S., pp. 18–19, is our source for the rest of Huddie's years at Shaw.

"cracked up and lost his mind . . ." and the rest of the quotes come from Haldeman's interview with Vaughn.

Zeola Vaughn recollects a conversation with her brother Zollie, who died in 1970, and who played with Huddie. "I know my brother always said 'Look at Panthy, you see Walter Boy. She's just like her daddy.' According to government records she was born Panthea Boyd, but older members of the black community knew her as Walter Boyd's "yard child."

"The Midnight Special"

Cultural historian Mack McCormick, a folk song expert with a special interest in Texas prisons, wrote "A Who's Who of 'The Midnight Special,' " *Caravan* (1959), which informed our thinking throughout this chapter. Except where otherwise noted, all of the quotes regarding this song and its history come from McCormick's article.

"Go down ole Hannah . . ." from *N.F.S.*, p. 118.

What happened to Lethe is unclear; she did drop completely out of Huddie's life. Queen Davidson remembers that she became a Pentecostal preacher, perhaps in nearby eastern Oklahoma. She did live in Kansas City in the 1940s because Irene Campbell told us that Huddie visited her there.

"They must think . . ." *N.F.S.*, p. 20.

"He's nobody with nothing . . ." and "He says to me . . ." from Keasler, "Remembering Leadbelly," *Baton Rouge Morning Advocator* (July 7, 1988).

The famous stanza beginning "Get up in the mornin' when the ding dong rings" was printed in a collection of "Folk-Song and Folk-Poetry of the Southern Negro" in the *Journal of American Folklore* as far back as 1911.

The melody used by most singers was adapted from a 1900 ragtime tune by George Sidney and J. Bodewaldt Lampe "Creole Belle." McGintey's Oklahoma Cowboy Band from Ripely, Oklahoma, recorded the first version in 1926; the first black man to record "Midnight Special" was a blues singer from the Mississippi Delta named Sam Collins. His 1927 version came seven years before Leadbelly recorded it for the Lomaxes.

"creased up and everything . . ." from an interview done by Kenneth Britzius in Minneapolis in 1948.

The piece about the "Sugarland Shuffle" appeared in Keasler's article.

" 'Fo-Day Worry Blues"

"I remember a great . . ." from McCormick, p. 18.

Ross Russell, in *Down Beat*, 37 (1970), p. 13, describes Huddie's thoughts about joining the vaudeville circuit.

Buddy Woods, a street singer since 1925, and Eddie Schaffer recorded for Victor in May 1930 as the Shreveport Homewreckers. They returned to the studio two years later to accompany onetime governer Jimmie Davis on four bawdy songs: "Saturday Night Stroll," "Sewing Machine Blues," "Red Night Gown," and "Davis's Salty Dog." Woods later recorded for Decca with a small swing band, the Wampus Cats. Born in Natchitoches, Louisiana, Woods remained around Shreveport, working as a street hustler and troubadour. The date of his death is unknown.

Jesse Thomas was born on February 3, 1911, in Logansport, Louisiana, and himself recorded for Victor in 1928. He recorded for a variety of small labels after World War II, moved throughout Texas and California before moving back to Shreveport in 1958. In 1992 he was semi-retired but still active as a blues player.

More detailed information about the Shreveport blues scene and the Lomaxes' Library of Congress recordings can be found in *Jerry's Saloon Blues*, issued by Flyright-Matchbox Records in England.

"to keep the dust . . ." and subsequent Booker T. Washington quotes from his interview with Kip Lornell, Mooringsport, March 5, 1990.

"she was all time . . ." from an unpublished manuscript in the Smithsonian/ Folkways Collection of the Smithsonian Institution.

"regular wild cat . . ." from a story related by Frederick Ramsey.

"most all of my days . . ." from Lizzie Carey's interview with Kip Lornell, February 12, 1991, in Houston, Texas. In addition to this interview, Carey's granddaughter, Betty Baisely-Sorrell, provided many stories her grandmother had told to her over the years. She also explained that "my mother always bore the name Jessie Baisley or it was Jessie Ledbetter. They [other people] just assumed that she was related to the other Ledbetters, not the daughter of Huddie."

"in 1928, I was . . ." from Keasler article.

Monte Brown's M.A. Thesis, "Leadbelly," Northwest Louisiana State University, 1989, describes other instances of violence during this period. The most notable stories involved a knife fight with six black men who tried to wrestle away Huddie's liquor, and a killing that was successfully pleaded down to self-defense in the courts.

Betty Baisely-Sorrell talks about the bootlegging incident with Eddie Packard in her interview.

Sheriff Tom Hughes's words come from a letter to Hines in 1934 that are part of Huddie's Louisiana prison files.

Leadbelly's early version of this story is recounted in *Time* (May 15, 1939), p. 77.

Betty Baisely-Sorrell recalls that Flannagan hated Huddie with "a passion" and was out to get him through any means necessary.

"was walking down the street . . ." from Booker T. Washington interview with Kip Lornell.

Blanch Love's version comes from Lee Oursler February 12, 1971, Shreveport *Journal* article on page 4D. She was hesitant to tell the story until forty years later because "I was scared they might come get me!"

"All of them folks . . ." from Windham's article on Blanch Love in the *North Louisiana History Journal* 7, no. 3 (Spring 1976), p. 98.

Angola Penitentiary

Angola State Penitentiary underwent extensive changes during a unparalleled period of reform in 1968 when it came under the stewardship of C. Murray Henderson, who found that the conditions had not substantially changed during the thirty-four years since Huddie had walked out a free man. Angola State Penitentiary had symbolized the Old South's idea of justice, which wobbled on the brink of legalized slavery and still encouraged the unmitigated exploitation of its inmate population. The history of Angola and of reform at Angola can be found in "Profile/Louisiana," *Corrections Magazine*, Sept.–Oct., 1975, pp. 9–24, and in *Angola* (Lafayette: Southwest Louisiana State University, 1988).

"white uniforms . . ." from "The Legend of Leadbelly," *Angolite*, p. 67, Jan.–Feb., 1982.

The information about Huddie's conduct and all of his dealings with the pardon board is in his Louisiana prison file.

"Alan and I . . ." from *N.F.S.*, p. ix.

The Dollar-a-Year Man

The chronology and details of John Lomax's life are based on our close reading of John Lomax, *Adventures of a Ballad Hunter* (New York: Macmillan, 1947).

Most of the details and chronology of John A. Lomax's early life are taken from a close reading of his *Adventures of a Ballad Hunter* (New York: Macmillan, 1947), as well as James Charles McNutt's dissertation, "Beyond Regionalism: Texas Folklorists and the Emergence of a Post-regional Consciousness" (The University of Texas, 1982). We have also looked at the correspondence in the Lomax papers at the Barker Center.

"they knew that Johnny Lomax . . ." is quoted by McNutt, p. 24, from an essay by Lomax called "Peepy-Jenny."

The story about selling the pony comes from *Adventures*, p. 23.

"No, he can't *preach* much . . ." from "Sister Hattie's Manuscript," Lomax papers.

"I loved him . . ." from *Adventures*, p. 12.

A fuller description of the relationship with Nat is found in a letter from Lomax to Bess Brown, ca. January 1904, Lomax papers.

"The singing is perfect . . ." from a letter by John Lomax to Bess Brown, May 30, 1904, Lomax papers.

"sole white man . . ." from a letter by John Lomax to Bess Brown, possibly June 8, 1906, Lomax papers.

"problems connected . . ." from a letter by John Lomax to Shirley Green, July 31, 1901, Lomax papers.

"Go and get this material . . ." is quoted by D. K. Wilgus in *Anglo-American Folksong Scholarship Since 1898* (New Brunswick, NJ: Rutgers University Press, 1959), p. 160.

"sparked a great surge . . ." from Bill C. Malone, *Southern Music, American Music* (Lexington, KY: University Press of Kentucky, 1979), p. 29.

Information about the lecture circuit from McNutt, p. 134 ff.

"fierce strength and . . ." from *Adventures*, p. 11.

"I found Mr. Gordon . . ." from Deborah Kodish, *Good Friends and Bad Enemies: Robert Winslow Gordon and the Study of American Folksong* (Urbana: University of Illinois Press, 1986), p. 191.

"[Black] folk singers . . ." from *Adventures*, p. 112.

"fast-disappearing gang . . ." from *Adventures*, p. 115.

"seem suspicious of us . . ." from *Adventures*, p. 116.

"steady, monotonous beat . . ." from *Adventures*, p. 117.

"I heard for the first time . . ." from *Adventures*, p. 119.

The previous year a notorious prisoner named Charlie Frazier, along with several other of his Camp E cronies, had shot their way out of the prison in one of the most brazen escapes ever. Frazier killed six people, including the warden, with guns that were presumably smuggled in by some visitor. As a precaution against a repeat of this bloody tragedy all routine visits were prohibited at Angola, a rule that was finally phased out in 1937.

"we found a Negro . . ." from *N.F.S.*, p. ix.

"one man almost made up . . ." from John Lomax letter to Ruby Terrill, July 21, 1933.

Angola Blues Again

"So touched was . . ." from *N.F.S.*, p. 231.

Most of these letters no longer exist in Leadbelly's Louisiana prison file, but they were summarized by Becky Schroeder, an early Leadbelly enthusiast who gained access to his files in the 1950s. We are grateful to Ms. Schroeder for providing them to us. The letters that we reproduce or quote from are the few that survive in his Louisiana prison file.

"Through a twist of . . ." from *N.F.S.*, p. ix.

The "Hog Law" provision is discussed in Vivian Miur, " 'Lead Belly'—Hard Facts Not So Hard," *Second Line* (March–April 1954), p. 19.

"In nineteen and hundred . . ." from the version recorded on LC recording 46-A (March 1935).

"Your Servan, Huddie Ledbetter"

The date for Martha's birth and very early life comes from Phillip G. M. Brown, "Huddie Ledbetter," M.A. Thesis, Northwestern State University of Louisiana, 1989, p. 44.

The story about Mary and Martha being defended by Huddie can be found in the *Northwest Louisiana Historical Journal*, p. 99.

"I'se had all kinds . . ." *N.F.S.*, p. 28.

These letters from Huddie to John Lomax regarding the possibility of employment are in Leadbelly's Louisiana prison file.

At the close of one of his letters, Huddie explains that he is living at 1800 Garden Street in Shreveport but receives his mail at 1881 Garden Street.

"Come prepared . . ." from *N.F.S.*, p. 29. Lomax dates their first meeting as Sunday, September 16, but the wire preserved at the Barker History Center clearly states the twenty-second; other letters confirm the later date as well.

"Only this knife . . ." and subsequent quote from a letter from John Lomax to Ruby Terrill on September 26, 1934. This letter (composed by Lomax in Little Rock) actually describes events from the previous two days; the delay was probably an attempt to assuage his wife's fears.

"Ledbetter is here . . ." from a letter from John Lomax to Ruby Terrill on September 24, 1934.

"We sat at a point . . ." from *N.F.S.*, p. 37.

"Don't one o' you boys . . ." *N.F.S.*, p. 37.

Our description of collection at Gould and "The Rock Island Line" is based on *A.B.H.*, pp. 147–148.

A more complete history of "The Rock Island Line" can be found in Norm Cohen, *Long Steel Rail* (Urbana, IL: University of Illinois Press, 1981), pp. 472–478.

"The cuttin' by axes . . ." from Huddie Ledbetter interview with Alan Lomax, AFS 995B2.

"I don't like . . ." from letter from John Lomax to Ruby Terrill on October 5, 1934.

Huddie's reaction to the Gulf of Mexico is in a manuscript in the John Lomax file, Barker History Center.

Specific discographical references to non-Ledbelly recordings can be found in Bob Dixon and John Godrich, *Blues and Gospel Records 1902–1943* (Essex, England: Storyville Publications, 1982).

"nothin' but a nigger . . ." and the story about the red light from *N.F.S.*, pp. 41–42.

The impromptu concert and "A few nickles . . ." from *N.F.S.*, p. 42.

"welcomed your generous suggestion . . ." from a letter from Scudder in the John Lomax file, Barker History Center.

"you all will make . . ." from letter from Martha Promise in the John Lomax file, Barker History Center.

The Sweet Singer of the Swamplands

"group of negro 'boys' . . ." from John Lomax, *American Ballads and Folk Songs* (New York: Macmillan, 1933), p. xiv.

"Leadbetter is a treasure . . ." from a letter from John Lomax to Ruby Terrill on December 10, 1934.

"Leadbelly had been trying . . ." *A.B.H.*, p. 154.

Much of the chronology from this trip comes from letters sent to Ruby Terrill by John Lomax.

Details of the MLA program come from *Publications of the Modern Language Association*, 49, Supplement (1934).

"a distinguished audience . . ." from a letter to Ruby Terrill from John Lomax, December 29, 1934.

"one of the famous women's . . ." from *N.F.S.*, p. 46.

The information about the performance at Bryn Mawr and Lomax's dissatisfaction with the poor payment comes from two letters to Ruby Terrill from John Lomax, December 29, 1934, and January 1, 1935.

"When my father and I . . ." and subsequent quote from a letter to Willie Smyth for use in record album brochure to accompany "The Barnicle Recordings," Tennessee Folklore Society L.P. TFS 108.

"Tomorrow is the most . . ." *N.F.S.*, p. 48.

"If I wasn't so drunk . . ." New York *Herald Tribune*, January 5, 1935.

Martha

The Philadelphia interview done in December did not reach print until January 6, 1935.

The background material for *The March of Time* comes from Raymond Fielding, *The March of Time, 1935–1951* (New York: Oxford University Press, 1978).

John Lomax's comments on Loew come from a letter to Ruby Terrill, January 12, 1935.

"Leadbelly of this moment . . ." from a letter from John Lomax to Ruby Terrill, January 1935.

"money-getters from . . ." from *N.F.S.*, p. 53.

"disturbed and distressed . . ." from a letter from John Lomax to Ruby Terrill, January 12, 1935.

"introduced Leadbelly . . ." from notes by Alan Lomax to authors, June 20, 1992.

"We have to keep Leadbelly . . ." from a letter from John Lomax to Ruby Terrill, January 6, 1935.

"Up to now . . ." from a letter from John Lomax to Ruby Terrill, January 6, 1935.

"I have sought . . ." from a letter from John Lomax to Ruby Terrill, January 15, 1935.

John Lomax's uncertainty in New York City was commented upon by Alan Lomax in a telephone interview with the authors, April 16, 1992.

A copy of this management contract is in the Barker History Center, The University of Texas, Austin.

"In time this . . ." from a letter from John Lomax to Ruby Terrill, January 8, 1935. This and other letters provide us with the chronology for these events in New York City.

"shouting happy over . . ." from a letter from John Lomax to Ruby Terrill, January 8, 1935.

These telegrams are quoted in the New York *Herald Tribune* as part of stories about Leadbelly, the Lomaxes, and Martha on January 9 and 10, 1935.

"Martha Promise is . . ." from New York *Herald Tribune* (January 10, 1935).

"they go upstairs . . ." and subsequent newspaper quotes from the *Herald Tribune*, January 14, 1935.

"secured two or three . . ." Lomax to Terrill, January 15, 1935.

Lomax notes the following expenses: Lomax paid for Huddie's clothes, to the tune of $18 for the suit, $2.95 for the hat, $1.75 for the shirt and tie, and $3 for the shoes. On the nineteenth, Martha got her dress and Huddie got her ring; Lomax paid $3 for the dress and $5 for the ring. He even noted that the white gloves for Huddie cost 25 cents.

Details of the wedding itself come from "Lead Belly Married; He Dances and Sings," *Norwalk Hour* (January 22, 1935), and "Gay LeadBelly in Cinnamon Suit Weds Martha on 46th Birthday," New York *Herald Tribune* (January 21, 1935).

"You Don't Know My Mind"

The description of the Wilton, Connecticut, farmhouse comes from a personal interview with Tillman Cadle, Townsend, Tennessee, July 7, 1990.

Under the terms of their management contract, Lomax kept two thirds, and gave Huddie $83.34 of the ARC contract.

The Ritter quote is from Capitol Record #SKC 11241.

Huddie's "Daddy I'm Coming Back to You," which ARC thought enough of to record three takes of, was in fact his version of "Daddy and Home," the 1928 Victor hit by country singer Jimmie Rodgers. "Bull Cow" (done later, in March 1935) was a version of "Bull Cow Blues," itself a 1932 ARC hit by Big Bill Broonzy. "Yellow Jacket," from the same day's session, was the same as a Columbia recording by Memphis Minnie released seven years before. "Shreveport Jail" used the structure and some of the verses of the popular country hit "Birmingham Jail" by white singers Tom Darby and Jimmie Tarlton. Later, when ARC decided against releasing most of the Leadbelly sides done during this time, they may have been concerned about duplicating some of these vintage songs—or violating copyrights on them.

The Alan Lomax story about Satherley comes from our telephone interview with him on April 16, 1992. Quote about records selling "rather disappointably" from a letter by Lomax to Terrill, probably March 23, 1935.

Some of Leadbelly's ARC sides have never been issued at all, and others were not issued until the modern LP era in the 1960s and later.

The ARC sides were not failures in an artistic sense. Though he sounds a little nervous on some, Leadbelly did some of his best work here. He was in fine voice and at the prime of his singing career. Fortunately, many of the unissued masters were preserved, and test pressings of some of them were even given to Huddie. Over the years, many unissued ARC recordings have been issued in a variety of formats, some authorized, some not. As of 1992, all but seventeen of the unissued forty-one ARC masters had been issued in some form, and test copies of four of those are known to exist (see discography).

"I think the most . . ." and subsequent quotes from Alan Lomax from a telephone interview with the authors, April 16, 1992.

"This card house . . ." from letter by Lomax to Terrill, probably January 15, 1935.

The Benet, Lomax, and Leadbelly connections are discussed in a letter from Lomax to Ruby Terrill,

The letters from January are from Lomax to Terrill.

John Lomax's notebooks for the months of January through March show entries for $5 "cash" for Huddie, $2.50 for railroad fare, $5 for Martha to get her hair done. Even such relatively minor expenses add up quickly considering that the singer often took in $15 to $20 dollars a night.

The stories about Leadbelly during the tour of upstate New York are derived from *N.F.S.*, pp. 55–63.

Katie Thompson's accounts come from our interview with her (now Katie De Port) in Delmar, New York, on December 20, 1989.

Alan "cut up" by his father's decision to break up with Leadbelly is from John Lomax to Ruby Terrill, March 12, 1935.

"At Emerson Hall . . ." from undated clipping from unidentified Boston newspaper, ca. March 24, 1935, in Lomax papers, Eugene C. Barker Texas History Center, University of Texas, Austin.

"Staid New England . . ." from a letter from John Lomax to Ruby Terrill, March 14, 1935.

"He played masterfully . . ." from *Harvard Crimson* (March 13, 1935).

"The entire Harvard visit," John Lomax to Ruby Terrill, March 14, 1935.

An ARC representative called, wanting Leadbelly to try just a few more sides to see if something more commercial could be found. The records done so far had not sold well, and the unreleased masters did not seem promising. These last sides were done on March 25, 1935, five more blue sides, some of them derived from older commercial blues records.

"My Client, Huddie Ledbetter"

Copies of the correspondence regarding the postdated checks to Huddie and other financial matters are found in the Barker History Center.

Coleman's long letter is in the John Lomax file at the Library of Congress— Archive of Folk Culture.

The Ledbetters' warm and unctuous letter to Lomax was written from Dallas (822 Bogel Street, where he and Martha were living with Australia) on May 22.

"Ain't It a Pity, I'm in New York City"

Information about Satherley comes from his notebook, a copy of which is in Charles Wolfe's possession.

Background on the Lafayette Theater can be found in Ted Fox, *Showtime at the Apollo* (New York City: Holt, Rinehart, 1983), pp. 218–220. Quote from New York *Age* review from same source, p. 218.

The information and specific quotes about Barnicle are derived from Willie Smyth's essay in the booklet accompanying Tennessee Folklore Society, TFS 108. For more information about Ms. Hurston, see Robert E. Hemenway, *Zora Neale Hurston: A Literary Biography* (Urbana, IL: University of Illinois Press, 1977).

Hurston's contentions about the relationship between John and Alan Lomax and about Leadbelly are found in a letter to John Lomax, September 16, 1935.

"You bring the folksinger . . ." from Serge Denisoff, *Great Day A Coming* (Urbana, IL: University of Illinois Press, 1971), p. 60.

"a nebulous audience . . ." Denisoff, p. 48.

Information about Margot Mayo can be found in Dick Weissman, *The Relation of Leadbelly's Life and Music to the Social Environments in Which He Lived*, B.A. Thesis, Goddard College, Plainfield, VT, 1956.

Correspondence between case supervisor Mary Hamm and Warden Jones is found in Leadbelly's prison file at Angola.

Information about the recording machine and its uses are found in our interview with Tillman Cadle (cf. above) and from letters from Mary E. Barnicle to Lawrence Gellert, 15 Aug. 1936 and ca. 1936, supplied by Willie Smyth through Bruce Harrah-Conforth.

The aspects of Gellert's life discussed here come from Bruce Batin, *Red River Blues* (Urbana, IL: University of Illinois Press, 1986) and Denisoff. In the 1980s two albums, *Cap'n You're So Mean to Me: Negro Songs of Protest* (Rounder 4004) and *Nobody Knows My Name* (Heritage 304), brought the recordings Gellert made during the 1920s and 1930s to a wider audience for the first time.

"He [Lomax] had the 'right' connections . . ." from a letter by Gellert in *New Masses*, December 11, 1934, pp. 21–22.

Alan Lomax's comment about black protest songs comes from our telephone interview with him on April 16, 1992.

"it was imposed . . ." from a note from Alan Lomax to authors, June 20, 1992.

Leadbelly's comment to Russell comes from Russell's *Down Beat* article, "Illuminating the Leadbelly Legend," August 6, 1970, p. 14.

"simplified the book much . . ." and subsequent quotes are from a letter from John Lomax to Ruby Terrill Lomax, November 15, 1935.

"Don't forget because . . ." from a manuscript dated May 22, 1947, Asch papers, Smithsonian (see Chapter 24).

A copy of this new agreement between Macmillan, the Lomaxes, and Huddie Ledbetter is in the files at the Library of Congress. The quotes are taken from this document.

"Yet without the violent past . . ." from note by Lomax to the authors, June 20, 1992.

"The Bourgeois Blues"

Gold's comments appeared in the *Daily Worker* (January 26, 1938).

For some of these songs, see Alan Lomax, Pete Seeger, and Woody Guthrie, eds., *Hard Hitting Songs for Hard Hit People* (New York: Oak Publications, 1962). Serge Denisoff, *Great Day Coming* (Urbana, IL: University of Illinois Press, 1971) and Jim Garland, *Welcome the Traveler Home* (Lexington: University Press of Kentucky, 1983), discuss this movement at length. Our interview with Tillman Cadle also provides some of the background for this section.

"I had some of the people . . ." from Tillman Cadle interview.

"never felt at home . . ." from Frederick Ramsey interview, Federal Twist, NJ, June 26, 1989.

"I never heard him say . . ." from Pete Seeger interview on May 5, 1989.

"You got some niggers . . ." and the rest of the background for this story from our telephone interview with Alan Lomax, April 16, 1992.

"We rode around . . ." from Elektra box set, originally on the December 1938 recording for the Library of Congress.

"All of them . . ." from our interview with Henrietta Yurchenco, New York, May 23, 1989.

"Underneath, Leadbelly was . . ." from Pete Seeger interview, Beacon, New York, May 24, 1989.

"From all of . . ." from Richard Nickson interview, New York, January 21, 1991.

"a subject of . . ." from a letter to the authors that accompanied Huddie Ledbetter's FBI files, dated April 16, 1990.

"it's an old myth . . ." from Henrietta Yurchenco interview.

"You be careful . . ." from Joe Brown, "Reflections on Leadbelly," *Folk Music* 1 (June 1964), p. 37.

"On the left . . ." from Ronnie Gilbert interview, Berkeley, California, July 2, 1990.

"Good Morning, Blues"

"Surely to the world . . ." and subsequent quotes from interview with Cadle.

Alan Lomax (in a phone conversation with the authors on April 16, 1992) commented that the Library of Congress's first electrical machine was made by a man named Galwick and that Lincoln Thompson's machine was marred by the fact that it cut its grooves too shallow, rendering it impractical.

Information about the recordings and the trip to Kentucky from Willie Smyth's notes to "The Barnicle Recordings," Tennessee Folklore Society Records, TFS 108.

McGhee account of this comes from our interview with him, Lomax's from our telephone interview.

Our information about Huddie's assault charge and the events that followed are from files at the Barker History Center, notes to the Playboy album, and papers in the Leadbelly file at the Library of Congress.

Most of the material for Timely Records' "Negro Songs of Protest" series came from Lawrence Gellert's recordings.

"Josh White came . . ." from Samuel Pruner interview, Ossining, New York, May 24, 1989.

The backgrounds for Josh White, Sonny Terry, and Brownie McGhee can be found in Bastin, *Red River Blues* (see above). Woody Guthrie's history comes from Joe Klein, *Woody Guthrie: A Life* (New York: Knopf, 1980). This entire section is informed by Norm Cohen's notes to the Smithsonian Record box set *The Folk Revival*.

Pete Seeger worked for Lomax at the Archive of Folk Song for about two months; his job was to explore their holdings of banjo recordings.

"Woody was . . ." from Henrietta Yurchenco interview (see below).

Will Geer's involvement is described in Klein's biography of Guthrie. The "Grapes of Wrath Evening" was held at the Forrest Theater after the regular evening show was over.

"There was Leadbelly . . ." and subsequent quotes from Pete Seeger are taken from personal interview, Beacon, New York, May 24, 1989. For Alan Lomax's reaction to the concert, see Peter Lyon, "The Ballad of Pete Seeger," in David DeTurk and A. Poulin, Jr., eds., *The American Folk Scene* (New York: Dell, 1967).

Quotations by Woody Guthrie about Leadbelly in this chapter are drawn from a pamphlet, *Woody Guthrie/American Folksong*, in an essay entitled "Leadbelly Is a Hard Name," published by Folkways owner Moe Asch and DISC company, New York, 1947, p. 9 ff.

"He was so concentrated . . ." and subsequent quotes by Henrietta Yurchenco are drawn from personal interviews, New York City, May 23, 1989.

"I met Woody . . ." and subsequent quotations from Walter "Brownie" McGhee come from personal interviews, Oakland, California, October 14, 1989.

This version of "Good Morning Blues" is transcribed from a surviving transcription of the radio show of June 19, 1940, and later issued on Biograph LP BLP 12013.

The short letter from Leadbelly to Alan Lomax is found in the Leadbelly file at the Archive of Folk Culture, Library of Congress.

"He always arrived . . ." and the three following quotes are taken from the Yurchenco interview cited above.

"That was strictly . . ." comes from an interview with Golden Gate singer Willie (Bill) Johnson, conducted by Doug Seroff, Los Angeles, January 23 and 25, 1980, provided by Mr. Seroff.

Quotations from Leadbelly about the RCA sessions are taken from his letter to Alan Lomax, ca. June 1940, in the Leadbelly file at the Archive of Folk Culture, Library of Congress.

The biographical material on Moe Asch, as well as royalty statements and contracts, is drawn from the Asch papers recently acquired by the Music History program of the Smithsonian Institution.

"Moe Asch was my A-1 man . . ." from personal interview with Walter "Brownie" McGhee, Oakland, California, October 14, 1989. Later comments on Leadbelly's apartment and "code" come from the same interview.

"He was very anxious . . ." from Pete Seeger, personal interview, Beacon, New York, May 24, 1989.

The comment from Viola Daniels about Leadbelly wanting to be a cowboy comes from personal interview with her, Marshall, Texas, November 25, 1989.

Hollywood and Vine

"excited for him . . ." from a personal interview with Stu Jamieson, May 7, 1990, Washington, D.C., and November 2, 1990, Murfreesboro, Tennessee.

Dolph Winebrennee's column appeared in *People's World*, July 7, 1944.

The information about Tex Ritter and Leadbelly comes from Lew Curtis, San Diego, California; from Cliffie Stone, Hollywood, California; and from a letter to John Lomax from Albert Baker, January 30, 1935, in the Lomax Family Collection at Barker. The quote from Ritter (who died in 1974) comes from an undated interview on Capitol album SKC 11241 ("An American Legend," 1973).

Attempts to gather more information about Paul Mason Howard or how he met Leadbelly have been fruitless. He was apparently part of the Los Angeles folk music scene for a number of years, and some sources say he died in Santa Monica around 1978.

The letter from Dave Dexter to John Reynolds was dated June 8, 1956, and was provided to us by Reynolds.

"Please pay . . ." letter from Leadbelly to Moe Asch is dated December 31, 1944, and is in the Asch papers at the Smithsonian.

"I was rather stand-offish . . ." and subsequent quotes from Philip Elwood come from a personal interview with Elwood, Berkeley, California, March 11, 1991.

Between October 19, 1945, and January 1946, letters flew between John Lomax's Texas home and Hollywood. An agreement was finally reached, and on February 1, 1946, Paramount mailed him a check for $2,500 as an option on the film. Had the film been made, the entire payment would have totaled $25,000.

"pretty amateurish . . ." from personal interview with Pete Seeger, Beacon, New York, May 24, 1989.

This footage has rarely been seen in public, but it is currently available on videotape as *A Salute to Leadbelly—The American Folk Music Series* (Central Sun Video, P.O. Box 3135, Reston, Virginia 22901). The program was originally aired as an episode in Pete Seeger's *Rainbow Quest* series from the mid-1960s. The tape also includes Seeger's recollections of Huddie, as well as "Pick a Bale of Cotton," arguably Leadbelly's most dynamic performance on film.

"Leadbelly and I . . ." and subsequent quotes from Ross Russell are drawn from his "Illuminating the Leadbelly Legend," *Down Beat*, August 6, 1970, pp. 12–14 ff.

The August 7, 1945, letter to Moe Asch comes from the Asch papers at the Smithsonian Institution, as do the later programs of 1946 New York concerts.

"used their music as a battle cry" comes from Robbie Liberman, *"My Song Is My Weapon": People's Songs, American Communism, and the Politics of Culture, 1930–50* (Urbana: The University of Illinois Press, 1989), p. xiv.

Hector Lee recounts his experience with Leadbelly in "Some Notes on Leadbelly," *Journal of American Folklore* 76 (April–June 1963), pp. 135–140.

"Goodnight, Irene"

Frederick Ramsey, Jr., and William Russell, *Jazzmen* (New York: Harcourt, Brace and Company, 1939).

Jazz record store owner Ross Russell spent many hours interviewing Huddie in California and had plans to do a sort of antidote to the Lomax book. Ironically, the project got shelved when Russell himself got into the record business and made some of Charlie Parker's first recordings for Dial.

Ramsey's description of Huddie performing comes from "At the Vanguard—and After," in Max Jones and Albert McCarthy, eds., *A Tribute to Huddie Ledbetter* (London: Jazz Music Books, 1946), pp. 7–9.

"He was a very powerful . . ." from Stu Jamieson's interview with Kip Lornell, New York, May 7, 1990.

"I remember that he . . ." from Junie Scales interview with Kip Lornell, New York, January 21, 1991.

"The first time I heard . . ." from Ronnie Gilbert interview, Berkeley, California, July 2, 1990.

"He was very much . . ." from Henrietta Yurchenco interview, New York City, May 25, 1989.

"Leadbelly, when I knew him . . ." from Pete Seeger interview, Beacon, New York, May 24, 1989.

"Leadbelly dropped in one day . . ." from Sumuel Pruner interview, New York, May 24, 1989.

"He was a man who . . ." from Pete Seeger interview.

The quotes about popular singers are found in the Joe Brown article (see above).

"I'll fight Jim Crow anyplace . . ." from Joe Brown article.

"The first thing that Lead . . ." from Brownie McGhee interview, Oakland, California, October 14, 1990.

Huddie's childhood story about the term *nigger* comes from the Joe Brown article (see above).

"At a party down in . . ." from Pete Seeger interview.

"of course, black was . . ." from Stu Jamieson interview.

"He didn't attack . . ." from Pete Seeger interview.

In fact, there were several confrontations between the father and son over Leadbelly. On August 7, 1940, John Lomax wrote to his son complaining that "you continue to deal with a man, who apart from a turn of fate, would have murdered me."

"Every time a newspaper . . ." from Pete Seeger interview.

"Now he [Huddie] says . . ." from Joe Brown article.

"No matter what . . ." Tiny Robinson in a letter printed in *Lead Belly Letter*, 1:2 (1991), p. 8.

Leadbelly was one of the first artists to record for a long playing record. Most pop singers of the time did not have albums on the market until the early 1950s; most of them were compilations of earlier material.

"We got paid a thousand . . ." from Pete Seeger interview.

"He was deeply ashamed . . ." from Pete Seeger interview.

The story about Huddie and Dr. Dick Blocher comes from Joe Brown article (see above).

"One image sticks . . ." from Fred Hellerman interview, New York City, June 27, 1989.

Epilogue

"If Huddie had lived . . ." from Pete Seeger interview.

"1,400 times . . ." from New York *Times* (October 16, 1950).

Up until the middle of 1953, the Weavers were dividing the royalties from "Goodnight, Irene," into three equal shares: for Alan Lomax, the Huddie Ledbetter Memorial Society, and themselves. This information appears in a letter in the TRO files on the song.

Moe Asch's Folkways label, though the most prominent, was not the only company disseminating Leadbelly's music. In 1964 the first comprehensive sampling of his extensive Library of Congress recordings was issued by Elektra. This lavish three-record box set was compiled and annotated by blues scholar Lawrence Cohn, a long-standing Leadbelly devotee who'd grown to know Martha quite well. His extensive booklet included a summary of Huddie's life, lyrical transcriptions, and numerous photographs. Cohn gave the Leadbelly legend a boost again about eight years later, this time as the head of the newly formed Playboy Records. He released the tapes of Leadbelly's final recorded concert at the University of Texas at Austin from June 1949. This time he did not include a booklet, but instead a serviceable insert that included a striking montage of photographs.

In subsequent years Tiny Robinson and her second husband, Jimmy, decided to get into the record business for themselves. They formed Blue Labor Records, which issued nearly a dozen record albums, including discs by Alec Seward, Louisiana Red, and other less known New York–based blues musicians. In 1976 Blue Labor lent a hand in producing and promoting a "Leadbelly Memorial Concert" featuring Brownie McGhee, Pete Seeger, Sonny Terry, and others, which they recorded and issued on their own label. Blue Labor Records is now moribund, but in the late 1980s some of its material has been leased to Tomato Records, which has been reissuing these and other albums on CD.

"a dramatization of . . ." and other information about *The Midnight Special* comes from our interview with Ed Addeo, Mill Valley, California, April 4, 1990.

Regarding the Tony Brown incident: the pair schmoozed with Brown for two to three hours early in the day, planning to return that evening for the live broadcast. After relaxing with a bottle of wine and an early dinner, Addeo and the short-tempered Irishman Garvin arrived at the studio and submitted to makeup, light checks, and all of the other preliminaries. According to Addeo, the show opened and Brown threw Garvin the leading question: " 'Why do you boys insist on perpetuating the myth of black sexual superiority?' We just looked at each other and Dick just goes berserk; he grabs the book off of the table and he says, 'Black sexual superiority!' He opens the book randomly and rips out a bunch of pages, throws them into the air, and says 'There, we took out that section!' Pages are raining all over the set and he looks at Tony and says, 'Now, do you want to talk about something other than Leadbelly's cock?' Tony Brown went apoplectic, people started screaming, the lights went out, people started hollering. A lady came out from the front desk and said that the switchboard is lit up like Coney Island. It was total bedlam—Dick is screaming, Tony is screaming, sirens are outside, cops around. Pretty soon we look outside of the window and there's seven or eight cop cars, cops with dogs, people screaming outside on the sidewalk. I thought there was a race riot in St. Louis and everybody black was storming the station. I couldn't tell if they were after Tony or us!"

The information about Jessie Mae Baisley's lawsuit against Paramount Pictures comes from an affidavit provided to us by her daughter, Betty Baisley-Sorrell. The district court dismissed the suit without prejudice, which meant that Baisley could have refiled in California, but she declined.

The Gordon Parks information and quotes come from our interview with Gordon Parks, New York City, July 7, 1990.

The fact that so few people even know of the film is hardly surprising. To this day few people have seen *Leadbelly*. It has not gone into general release since the summer of 1976, nor is it available on videocassette. An occasional special screening is arranged, usually when Gordon Parks is speaking somewhere or as part of a retrospective of his films. More controversy lay ahead for *Leadbelly* in the form of another lawsuit filed by yet another relative. Back in Houston, Huddie's second cousin, John Ledbetter, filed a $16.5 million suit claiming that the movie was false and was portrayed in a "vile and rude manner which shock the conscious" (AP, May 22, 1976). John Ledbetter's suit was handled by three lawyers—two in Houston and another in Beverly Hills, California—over a two-year period. Family members state that at least one law firm, Smith & Velasquez from Houston, were "bought off" by Paramount because they suggested that the Ledbetters accept the $2,100 offered by the conglomerate to settle their multimillion-dollar defamation of character lawsuit. John Ledbetter claimed that Ledbetter's estate was willed to his father, Edmond, in a letter written to his aunt, Blanch Love, shortly before Huddie died. John Ledbetter further contended that Martha was Huddie's common-law wife, thereby nullifying her passage of the estate to Tiny Robinson. This suit has never reached litigation because no will of Edmond Ledbetter has ever been found and Martha very clearly wed Huddie in 1935.

"one of Texas' . . ." and "grass roots blues festival . . ." from Dallas *Morning News* (October 6, 1974).

"Texans Want Body . . ." from Shreveport *Journal* (October 10, 1974).

"Harrison County Wants . . ." from Shreveport *Journal* (October 10, 1974).

"Don't stir 'im . . ." from Shreveport *Times* (October 11, 1974).

"There's a lot in a name . . ." Dallas *News* (September 5, 1983).

In June 1988 an important exhibit of Leadbelly material opened at the University of Texas-Austin's Barker History Center. Entitled "The Midnight Special: The Life and Music of Leadbelly," it featured many original letters and other printed documents from the Lomax family papers.

The most recent entrant into the race to recognize the importance of Leadbelly is the quarterly *Lead Belly Letter*. This newsletter (edited by Sean Killeen, P.O. Box 6679, Ithaca, New York 14851) is a publication of the Leadbelly Society to "appreciate & celebrate Leadbelly Music." Each issue has a miscellany of photographs, chronologies of important periods in his life, news of tributes, and short pieces about his various live performances. This is but the latest of such attempts to keep Leadbelly's name alive among fans. Amsterdam, the Netherlands, for example, boosted the Leadbelly Memorial Club in the late 1960s.

Likewise, reissues of Huddie's material keep coming on the market. Rounder released three CDs of his Library of Congress material in the fall of 1991. RCA released his recordings with the Golden Gate Quartet in 1990 as part of its Heritage Series. At Smithsonian/Folkways, a slow but steady stream of repacked Folkways issues is planned.

Over the years there have been a number of other proposed projects revolving around the life and legend of Leadbelly that have ever come to fruition, though some of them have obvious merit. About 1970, NBC television planned an hour-long special, for which some of the preproduction work was actually completed. Following the success of the Fats Waller revue *Ain't Misbehavin'*, a group of artists and financial backers met to discuss a similar musical/dramatic venture based on the life and music of Huddie Ledbetter. Veteran film, television, and stage actor James Earl Jones wanted to do a theatrical version of Leadbelly's life in the late 1970s. More recently CBS/Columbia proposed an album of unreleased Janis Joplin material spotlighting Leadbelly tunes. The company assembled the tapes, remastered them, and circulated test pressings, which were vetoed due in large measure to very poor audio quality. It sounds as though the microphone were placed in the bathroom next to the hall in which the group played. The album would have demonstrated Joplin's abilities as a folk/blues performer, and she was backed up by a small band similar to Jim Kweskin's Jug Band.

Joe Brown's concluding anecdote is from his "Reflections on Leadbelly," *Folk Music* 1 (June 1964), p. 35.

Huddie Ledbetter
Discography
1933–1949

Key to Record Labels

AE	Allegro Elite	**LC**	Library of Congress
Alb	Aldabra [Great Britain]	**Man**	Manhatten [Italy]
Ara	Aravel [Great Britain]	**Mau**	Mauros
Arh	Arhoolie	**Mdc**	Melodisc [Great Britain]
Atl	Atlantic	**Me**	Melotone
ARC	American Record Corporation	**Mu**	Musicraft
Ba	Banner	**Or**	Oriole
Bb	Bluebird	**Pe**	Perfect
Bio	Biograph	**Plby**	Playboy
Blue	Bluestime [Great Britain]	**RCA**	Radio Corporation of America
BM	Blue Moon [Great Britain]	**Rnd**	Rounder
Cap	Capitol	**Ro**	Romeo
CBS	Columbia Broadcasting System	**Ron**	Rondo
Co	Columbia	**Roy**	Royale
Coll	Collectibles	**S/F**	Smithsonian/Folkways
De	Design	**St**	Storyville [Denmark]
Doc	Document [Austria]	**Stin**	Stinson
Elt	Elektra	**Su**	Sutton
Ev	Everest	**Te**	Tempo [Great Britain]
Fkw	Folkways	**Tel**	Telefunken [Germany]
HJCA	Hot Jazz Club of America	**TM**	Travelin' Man [Great Britain]
HMV	His Master's Voice [Great Britain]	**Vi**	Victor
JC	Jazz Collector [Great Britain]	**York**	Yorkshire

*Issues in **bold** letters are compact disc, microgroove, or tape releases or reissues. All others are 78 rpm recordings. Unless indicated, all of these companies are located in the United States. In late 1991, Document Records in Austria released virtually all of Huddie Ledbetter's Library of Congress recordings on twelve albums. The series begins with DLP 606 "1935" and ends with DLP 612 "1942."*

Huddie Ledbetter: vocal/guitar

Louisiana State Penitentiary, Angola, Louisiana, circa July 16, 1933

119-B-1	The Western Cowboy	LC
119-B-2	Honey Take a Whiff on Me	LC
119-B-4	Angola Blues	LC
119-B-5	Angola Blues	LC

119-B-6	Frankie and Albert	LC
120-A-1	Irene	LC
120-A-2	Take a Whiff on Me	LC: **Doc 544**
120-A-3	You Can't Lose Me Cholly	LC
120-A-6	Irene	LC
120-A-7	Irene	LC
120-B-5	Ella Speed	LC

Louisiana State Penitentiary, Angola, Louisiana, circa July 1, 1934

121-A	Mister Tom Hughes' Town	LC
122-A-2	I Got Up This Morning, Had to Get Up So Soon	LC
122-B	Western Cowboy	LC
123-A	Blind Lemon Blues	LC
123-B	Matchbox Blues	LC: **Elt EKL 301/2, Rnd 1044**
124-A-1	Midnight Special	LC: **Elt EKL 301/2, Rnd 1044**
124-A-2	Irene	LC
124-B-1	Irene	LC
124-B-2	Governor O.K. Allen	LC: **Elt EKL 301/2, Rnd 1044**
125-A	Frankie and Albert	LC: **Elt EKL 301/2, Rnd 1044**
125-B	Ella Speed	LC: **Rnd 1044**
126-A-1	Julie Ann Johnson	LC
126-A-2	You Can't Lose-a-Me Cholly	LC
126-A-3	Take a Whiff on Me	LC
126-B	I'm Sorry Mama	LC: **Elt EKL 301/2, Rnd 1044**

Little Rock, Arkansas, September 27, 1934

| 236-B-3 | Mister Tom Hughes' Town | LC |
| 239-A-3 | Julie Ann Johnson | LC |

State Farm, Pine Bluff, Arkansas, circa September 29, 1934

| 240-A-4 | Julie Ann Johnson | LC |

Unknown white man: vocal; **Huddie Ledbetter:** guitar

| 240-A-5 | Lover in the Green Valley | LC |

Leroy Allen: vocal; **Huddie Ledbetter:** guitar

State Farm, Tucker, Arkansas, circa October 1, 1934

| 246-B-1 | Sweet Babe | LC |

Huddie Ledbetter: vocal/guitar

246-B-3   Mister Tom Hughes' Town   LC

Gould, Arkansas, circa October 5, 1934

242-B-3   Julie Ann Johnson   LC

Shreveport, Louisiana, circa October 15, 1934

273-A-1   Boll Weevil   LC

Huddie Ledbetter: vocal-1/guitar; **Sloan Wright:** dance calls-2
Bellwood Prison Camp, Atlanta, Georgia, December 12, 1934

250-B-1   The Shreveport Jail-1   LC
250-B-2   Julie Ann Johnson-1   LC
252-A-1   Dance Calls-2   LC
252-A-2   This Morning-1   LC

Huddie Ledbetter: vocal/guitar
Wilton, Connecticut, January 20, 1935

143-A   Don't You Love Me No More   LC
143-B   Henry Ford Blues   LC

Wilton, Connecticut, January 21, 1935

44-A   Irene   LC: **Elt ELK 301/2, Rnd 1044**
44-B   Irene   LC: **Elt ELK 301/2, Rnd 1044**
44-B-2   Julie Ann Johnson   LC

New York City, January 23, 1935

16683-1   Roberta—Part 1   ARC unissued: **Fwy FP 24,
                                2404, Extra 1017, Co
                                S30035, CBS (E) 64193, TM
                                8810, Coll CK 46776, Alb
                                1004CD**

16684-1   Roberta—Part 2   ARC unissued: **Fwy FP 24,
                                2404, Xtra 1017, Co S30035
                                CBS (E) 64103, TM 8810,
                                Coll CK 46776, Alb 1004CD**

16685-1   Packin' Trunk Blues Ba 33359, Me M13326, Or
                                8438, Pe 0314, Ro 5438, Pm
                                14006, JC L2, **TM 8810,
                                Coll CK 46776**

16686-	C.C. Rider	ARC unissued: **FWP FP 24, 2404, Xtra 1017, Co S30035, CBS (E), 64103, TM 8810**
16678-1	Becky Deem, She Was a Gamblin' Girl	ARC 6-04-55, JC L124, Te R11, **Coll CK 46776**
16688-2	Honey, I'm All Out and Down	Ba 33359, Me M13326, Or 8438, Pe 0314, Ro 5438, Pm 9003, 14006, JC L2, **Coll CK 46776, Doc 544**
16689-2	Four Day Worry Blues	Ba 33360, Me M13327, Or 8439, Pe 0315, Ro 5439, Pm 14017, JC L108, Te R13, **Coll CK 46776**
16690-	You Can't Lose Me, Charlie	ARC unissued: **Co S30035, CBS (E) 64103, TM 8810, Alb 1004CD**
16691-2	New Black Snake Moan	Ba 33360, Me M13327, Or 8439, Pe 0315, Ro 5439, Pm 9003, 14017, JC L108, Te R13, **TM 8810, Alb 1004CD**
16692-	Alberta	ARC unissued: **Co S30035, CBS (E) 64103, TM 8810**

[16686 is titled "See See Rider" on Folkways FP24; 16688 is titled "All Out and Down" on JC L2; there are other minor title variations on other reissues.]

New York City, January 24, 1935

16693-	Baby, Don't You Love Me No More?	ARC unissued: **Co S30035, CBS (E) 64103, TM 8810**
16694-	Ox Drivin' Blues	ARC unissued: **Fwy FP24, 2024, Xtra 1017, Alb 1004CD, Coll CK 46776, DOC 544**
16695-1	Death Letter Blues—Part 1	ARC unissued: **Bio BLP 12013, Co S30035, CBS (E) 64103, TM 8810, Alb 1004CD, BM 1038**
16695-2	Death Letter Blues—Part 1	ARC unissued: **Coll CK 46776**
16696-1	Death Letter Blues—Part 2	ARC unissued: **Bio BLP 12013, Co S30035, CBS (E) 64103, TM 8810, Alb 1004 CD, BM 1038**
16696-2	Death Letter Blues—Part 2	ARC unissued: **Coll CK 46776**
16697-1	Kansas City Papa	ARC unissued: **Bio BLP 12013, Co S30035, CBS (E) 64103, TM 8810, BM 1038**
16697-2	Kansas City Papa	ARC unissued: **Coll CK 46776**
16698-	Mary Don't You Weep	ARC unissued
16999-	Fat Mouth Mama	ARC unissued

16704-	Red River Blues	ARC unissued: **Co S30035, CBS (E) 64103, TM 8810, Alb 1004CD**
16705-	Fort Worth and Dallas Blues	ARC unissued: **Fwy FR24, 2024, Xtra 1017, Alb 1004 CD, Doc 544**
16705-2	Fort Worth and Dallas Blues	ARC unissued: **Coll CK 46776**
16706-2	You Don't Know My Mind	ARC unissued: **Coll CK 46776**
16707-	Shreveport Jail	ARC unissued
16708-	Angola Jail	ARC unissued

[16694 is titled "Ox Drivin' " on Folkways FP24; there are many minor title variations on reissues. It is not clear which take of "Fort Worth and Dallas Blues" is used on **Doc 544.** Matrices 16700 through 16703 are not by Leadbelly.]

New York City, January 25, 1935

16755-	Julie Ann Johnson	ARC unissued
16756-	Baby Take a Whiff on Me	ARC unissued
16757-	Gonna Dig a Hole—Put the Devil in It	ARC unissued
16758-	Old Chisholm Trail	ARC unissued
16759-	Dem Blues I Got Baby (Make a New-Born Baby Cry)	ARC unissued
16760-	Pick a Bale a'Cotton	ARC unissued
16761-	Lead Belly's Pardon Song to Governor Pat	ARC unissued
16762-	Lead Belly's Pardon Song to O.K. Allen	ARC unissued

Wilton, Connecticut, February 1, 1935

| 45-A | Take a Whiff on Me | LC: **Elt, ELK 301/2, Rnd 1044** |

New York City, February 5, 1935

16806-1	Daddy I'm Coming Back to You	ARC unissued: **Fwy 2024, Xtra 1017, Coll CK 46776, Doc 544**
16806-3	Daddy I'm Coming Back to You	ARC unissued: **Bio BLP 12013, Alb 1004CD, BM 1038**
16807-	My Friend Blind Lemon	ARC unissued: **Co S30035, CBS (E) 64103, TM 8810, Alb 1004CD**
16808-	Mr. Tom Hughes' Town	ARC unissued: **Co S30035, CBS (E) 64103, TM 8810, Alb 1004CD**
16809-	I Got a Mother in the Promised Land	ARC unissued
16810-	Irene—Part 1	ARC unissued
16811-	Irene—Part 2	ARC unissued
16812-	Man, I'm in Trouble	ARC unissued

16813-	Texas Penitentiary	ARC unissued
16814-1	Shorty George	ARC unissued: **Coll CK 46776**
16814-2	Shorty George	ARC unissued: **Bio BLP 12013, BM 1038**
16815-	De Kalb Woman	ARC unissued
16816-	Matchbox Blues	ARC unissued: **Co S30035, CBS (E) 64103, TM 8810, Alb 1004CD**

[It remains unclear which take of "Daddy, I'm Coming Back to You" is used on **Doc 544.**]

Huddie Ledbetter: vocal/guitar with speech-1
Wilton, Connecticut, circa February 13, 1935

45-B	Salty Dog	LC
51-A	Angola Blues	LC
51-B	Roberta	LC: **Rnd 1044**
52-A	Careless Love	LC: **Rnd 1044**
52-B	C.C. Rider	LC: **Rnd 1045**
53-A	Governor Pat Neff	LC: **Elt ELK 301/2, Rnd 1045**
53-B	Thirty Days in the Workhouse	LC: **Elt ELK 301/2, Rnd 1045**
54-A	Ella Speed	LC: **Elt ELK 301/2**
54-B	Ella Speed	LC: **Elt ELK 301/2**
127-A	Frankie and Albert	LC
127-B	Frankie and Albert	LC
128-A	Which Way Do the Red River Run?	LC: **Rnd 1044**
128-B	Got Up in the Mornin' So Doggone Soon	LC: **Rnd 1044**
129-A	You Don't Know My Mind	LC: **Elt ELK 301/2, Rnd 1044**
129-B-1	The Western Cowboy	LC
129-B-2	Becky Dean [*sic*]	LC: **Elt ELK 301/2, Rnd 1045**
130-A	Fort Worth and Dallas Blues	LC
130-B	Got a Gal in Town with Her Mouth Chock Full of Gold	LC: **Elt ELK 301/2**
131-A	Mary Don't You Weep	LC
131-B-1	Mary Don't You Weep	LC
131-B-2	Way Over in the Promised Land	LC
132-A	Death Letter Blues-1	LC
133-A	Midnight Special	LC
133-B	The Shreveport Jail	LC
134-A	Easy Mr. Tom	LC
134-B	I Ain't Bothered a Bit	LC
135-A	Boll Weevil	LC: **Elt ELK 301/2**
135-B	Western Cowboy	LC
136-A	The Titanic	LC
136-B	Blind Lemon Blues	LC
137-A	Mr. Tom Hughes' Town	LC
137-B-1	Mr. Tom Hughes' Town	LC
137-B-2	You Cain' Loose-a-Me Cholly	LC
138-A	The Medicine Man	LC: **Elt ELK 301/2, Rnd 1045**

138-B	Red Cross Sto'	LC
139-A-1	Green Corn	LC
139-A-2	The Maid Freed from the Gallows	LC
139-B	Po' Howard	LC
140-A	Alberta Blues	LC: **Elt ELK 301/2, Rnd 1045**
140-B	Fo' Day Worry Blues	LC: **Elt ELK 301/2**
141-A-1	Hesitation Blues	LC
141-A-2	Take Me Back	LC: **Elt ELK 301/2**
141-B	Matchbox Blues	LC
142-A	Tight Like That	LC
142-B-1	Gwine Dig a Hole to Put the Devil in It	LC
142-B-2	Old Man Settin' in the Corner Dyin'	LC

Huddie Ledbetter: vocal/guitar or unaccompanied-1
Wilton, Connecticut, March 1, 1935

47-B	Blues I Got Make a New-Born Baby Cry	LC
48-A-1	Ho Day-1	LC
48-A-2	One Dollar Bill Baby-1	LC

Huddie Ledbetter: vocal/guitar
New York City, March 25, 1935

17179-1	Yellow Jacket	ARC unissued: **Bio BLP 12013, Coll CK 46776, BM 1038**
17180-1	T.B. Woman Blues	ARC unissued: **Bio BLP 12013, Alb 10014CD, BM 1038**
17181-1	Pig Meat Papa	ARC 6-04-55, JC L124, Te R11, **Coll P 13211, Doc 544**
17181-2	Pig Meat Papa	ARC unissued: **Coll CK 46776, Alb 1004CD**
17182-	Bull Cow	ARC unissued: **Co S30035, CBS (E) 64103, TM 8810, Alb 1004CD**
17183-1	My Baby Quit Me	ARC unissued: **Coll CK 46776**

[**Col P 13211** is an anthology *The Blues Are Back*, a Columbia Special Products album produced for Sedgefield Jeans!]

Huddie Ledbetter: vocal/guitar or unaccompanied-1
Wilton, Connecticut, March 1935

46-A	Governor O.K. Allen	LC
47-A	De Kalb Blues	LC: **Elt ELK 301/2, Rnd 1044**
48-B	Ain' Goin' Down to de Well No More-1	LC

49-A	Ha-Ha This-a-Way	LC
49-B	Alabama Bound	LC
50-A	In Dem Long Hot Summer Days-1	LC
50-B	Go Down, Old Hannah-1	LC
144-A	I'm All Out & Down	LC
144-B	De Kalb Blues	LC
145-A	Ha, Ha Thisaway	LC
145-B-1	Dear Old Daddy-1	LC
145-B-2	Dear Old Daddy-1	LC
145-B-3	Dear Old Daddy-1	LC
145-B-4	Dear Old Daddy-1	LC
146-A	I'm Gonna Hold It in Her While She's Young and Tender	LC
146-B	What You Goin' to Do with Your Long Tall Daddy?	LC
147-A	Dicklicker's Holler-1	LC
147-B	Bill in the Lowlands/Here, Rattler, Here	LC
148-A	Frankie and Albert	LC
148-B	Frankie and Albert	LC
149-A	Send Down Your Hand	LC
149-B	Shorty George	LC
150-A	Shorty George	LC
150-B-1	Pick a Bale o' Cotton	LC
150-B-2	Elnora	LC
151-A	Ha, Ha Thisaway	LC
151-B	Send Down Your Hand	LC
152-A	Death Letter Blues	LC
152-B	Death Letter Blues [fragments]	LC
153-A	Where De Sun Done Gone	LC
153-B	Bring Me a Li'l Water Silvy	LC
154-A	Dicklicker's Holler	LC
154-B	Whoa Back, Buck	LC
155-A	Billy in the Low Ground	LC
155-B	The Grey Goose	LC
156-A	Old Rattler	LC: **Rnd 1045**
156-B	I'm All Out and Down	LC
157-A	Frankie and Albert	LC
157-B-1	I Walked Her and Talked Her	LC
157-B-2	Billy the Weaver	LC: **Elt ELK 301/2**

Washington, D.C., June 22, 1937

993-A-1	Gwine Dig a Hole	LC
993-A-2	Polly-Polly-Wee	LC
993-A-3	Jawbone Walk	LC
993-B	If It Wasn't for Dicky	LC: **Elt ELK 301/2, Rnd 1045**
994-A	Last Night in the Evening	LC
994-B	Somethin', Somethin' Keeps a Worryin' Me	LC

995-A	Monkey Men	LC
995-B-1	I Ain't Gonna Ring Dem Yellow Women's Do' Bells-1	LC: **Elt ELK 301/2**
995-B-2	Rock Island Line-1	LC: **Elt ELK 301/2**
995-B-3	All Out and Down-1	LC
996-A-1	Hello Central	LC
996-A-2	Raccoon up the Simmon Tree	LC
996-B	Ain' Goin' Drink No Mo'	LC
997-A	New York City	LC
997-B	Queen Mary	LC: **Rnd 1045**
998-A-1	Turn Your Radio On	LC: **Elt ELK 301/2, Rnd 1045**
998-A-2	Julie Ann Johnson	LC
998-B-1	The Hindenburg Disaster	LC: **Elt ELK 301/2**
998-B-2	The Hindenburg Disaster	LC: **Elt ELK 301/2**

Huddie Ledbetter: vocal/guitar; **Sarah Garland:** vocal-1; **Jim Garland:** vocal-2
Probably New York City, circa December, 1938

2020-A-1	Old Time Religion-1	LC
2020-A-2	He's Just the Same Today	LC
2021-B	Git on Board	LC: **Elt ELK 301/2**
2023-A	Rock of Ages-1, 2	LC

Huddie Ledbetter: vocal/guitar; **Martha Ledbetter:** vocal-1
New York City, December 26, 1938

2501-A	Mama, Did You Bring Me Any Silver?	LC: **Elt ELK 301/2, Rnd 1045**
2502-B	Leaving on the Morning Train Blues	LC
2502-A-1	Scottsboro Boys	LC
2502-A-2	Outshine the Sun	LC
2502-B-1	Noted Rider Blues	LC
2502-B-2	The Bourgeois Blues	LC: **Elt ELK 301/2, Rnd 1045**
2503-A-1	Nobody Knows the Trouble I've Seen-1	LC
2503-A-2	Little John Henry	LC: **Elt ELK 301/2**
2503-B	John Henry	LC
2504-A	John Henry	LC
2504-B	Eva	LC

Huddie Ledbetter: vocal/guitar/tap-dancing-1/unaccompanied-2
New York City, April 1, 1939

GM-498-	Fannin Street	Mus 225, **St SLP 139**
GM-499-K	Frankie and Albert—First Half	Mus 223, **St SLP 139**
GM-499-A	Frankie and Albert—Completion	Mus 224, **St SLP 139**
GM-500-	Frankie and Albert—Part 2	Mus unissued

GM-501-	De Kalb Blues	Mus 226, **Coll 5183, Ev 102, St SLP 139**
GM-502-	Ain't Goin' Down to the Well No More/Go Down Old Hannah	Mus unissued
GM-503-M	Looky Looky Yonder-2/Black Betty-2/Yellow Women's Door Bells-2	Mus 223, **Coll 5183, Ev 102, St SLP 139**
GM-504-	The Bourgeois Blues	Mus 227, **Coll 5183, Ev 102, St SLP 139**
GM-505-K	Poor Howard-1,2/Green Corn-1	Mus 225, **Coll 5183, Ev 102, St SLP 139**
GM-506-	The Gallis Pole	Mus unissued
GM-507-A	The Boll Weevil	Mus 226, **St SLP 139**
GM-508-	Ain't Goin' Down to the Well No More/Go Down Old Hannah	Mus unissued
GM-509-A	The Gallis Pole	Mus 227, **Coll 5183, Ev 102, St SLP 139**
GM-509-K	Ain't Goin' Down to the Well No More/Go Down Old Hannah	Mus 224, **St SLP 139**

[These selections were issued as a 78 rpm set *Negro Sinful Tunes*, Musicraft Album 31. Dolf Rerink reports at least three different pressings for several of the Musicraft 78s from this session, which may result in other discrepancies similar to the following: GM-503-M also appears as Mus 224 (Side A) on some issues. Stinson LP was also reissued, with minor changes, on two later albums, Mt. Vernon Music 141, and Folk Arts FLP 5004.]

Huddie Ledbetter: vocal/guitar/unaccompanied-1
New York City, February 22, 1940

| BC 95 | Didn't Ol' John Cross the Water Stewball-1 |
| BC 96 | Trials Ham and Eggs |

[These selections are part of the Mary Barnicle–Tillman Cadle Collection.]

Huddie Ledbetter: vocal/guitar/unaccompanied-1; **Golden Gate Quartet:** Willis Johnson, William Langford, Henry Owens, Orlandus Wilson, vocal quartet
New York City, June 15, 1940

051295-1	Pick a Bale of Cotton	Vi 27268, **HMV MH 190, RCA 9600-2-R, Alb 1007CD, Blu 2011**
051296-	Yellow Gal	Vi unissued: **RCA 9600-2-R, Blu 2011**
051297-	Whoa Back, Buck	Vi unissued: **RCA (E) RD7576, Vi LPV505 RCA (Aus) LPV505, RCA (F) 730.615, RCA 9600-2-R, Alb 1007CD, Blu 2011**
051298-1	Midnight Special	Vi 27266, **RCA 9600-2-R, ALB 1007CD, Blu 2011**

| 051299-1 | Alabama Bound | Vi 27268, **HMV MH190 RCA 9600-2-R, Alb 1007CD, Doc 544, Blu 2011** |
| 051500- | Rock Island Line-1 | Vi unissued: **RCA (E) RCX146, Vi LPV 505, RCA (Aus) LPV 505, RCA (F) 730.615, RCA 9600-2-R, Alb 1007CD, Blu 2011** |

[Vi 27266, 27267, 27268 were issued in Victor album P50. HMV MH190 as *Leadbelly and the Golden Gate Quartet with Guitar*. RCA (E) RCX146 is an extended-play 45 rpm issue.]

Huddie Ledbetter: vocal/guitar
New York City, June 15, 1940

051501-	Good Morning Blues	BB B8791, HJCA HC98, **Alb 1007CD, Blu 2011**
051502-	Leaving Blues	BB B8791, HJCA HC98, **Alb 1007CD, Doc 544, Blu 2011**
051503-	T.B. Blues	BB B8559, **Blu 2011**
051504-	Red Cross Store Blues	BB B8709, HJCA HC99, **Blu 2011**
051505-	Sail On, Little Girl, Sail On	BB B8550, **Alb 1007CD, Blu 2011**
051506-	Roberta	BB B8709, HJCA HC99, **Alb 1007CD, Blu 2011**
051507-	Alberta	BB B8559, **Alb 1007CD, Blu 2011**
051508-1	I'm on My Last Go Round	BB B8981, **Alb 1007CD, Blu 2011**

New York City, June 17, 1940

051322-	Easy Rider	BB B8570, **Alb 1007CD, Blu 2011**
051323-1	New York City	BB B8750, **Alb 1007CD, Blu 2011**
051324-	Worried Blues	BB B8570, **Alb 1007CD, Doc 544, Blu 2011**
051325-	Don't You Love Your Daddy No More?	BB B8550, **Blu 2011**
051326-1	You Can't Lose-a Me Cholly	BB B8750, **Blu 2011**

Huddie Ledbetter: vocal/guitar/unaccompanied-1; **Golden Gate Quartet:** Willis Johnson, William Langford, Henry Owens, Orlandus Wilson, vocal quartet
New York City, June 17, 1940

051327-2	Grey Goose-1	Vi 27267, HMVSw JK2765, HMVF SG440, **RCA 9600-2-R**
051328-	Didn't Ol' John Cross the Water?	Vi unissued: **RCA 9600-2-R**
051329-1	Stew-Ball	Vi 27267, HMVSw JK2675, HMVF SG440, **RCA 9600-2-R, ALB 1007CD, Doc 544**
051330-	Take This Hammer	Vi unissued: **RCA (E) RCX146 (ep), RCA 9600-2-R, Doc 544**
051331-	Can't You Line 'Em?	Vi unissued, **RCA 9600-2-R**
051332-	Julianne Johnson	Vi unissued, **RCA 9600-2-R**
051333-1	Ham an' Eggs-1	Vi 27266, **RCA 9600-2-R, Alb 1007CD, Doc 544**

[Vi 27266, 27267, 27268 were issued in Victor album P50.]

Huddie Ledbetter: vocal/guitar/spoken-1/unaccompanied-2; **Woody Guthrie:** spoken
New York City, June 19, 1940

	Introduction-1	**Bio BLP12013, Mau LBCCL3840, BM 1038**
	I Ain't Going Down-2	**Bio BLP12013, Mau LBCCL3840, BM 1038**
	Went Out on the Mountain	**Bio BLP12013, Mau LBCCL3840, BM 1038**
	Whoa Buck-1	**Bio BLP12013, Mau LBCCL3840, BM 1038**
	Worried Blues-1	**Bio BLP12013, Mau LBCCL3840, BM 1038**
	Good Mornin' Blues-1	**Bio BLP12013, Mau LBCCL3840, BM 1038**
	You Can't Lose Me Charlie	**Bio BLP12013, Mau LBCCL3840, BM 1038**
	Boll Weevil	**Bio BLP12013, Mau LBCCL3840, BM 1038**

[These recordings, from a radio broadcast on WNYC, are also on Biograph CD-113.]

Huddie Ledbetter: vocal/guitar/speech-1/unaccompanied-2; **Alan Lomax:** speech-3
Washington, D.C., August 23, 1940

4469-A-(a)	Monologue on T.B.-1,3	LC
4469-A-1	Last Night in the Evening	LC
4469-A-2	T.B. Blues	LC
4469-A-3	How Long?	LC
4469-A-4	When the Train Comes Along	LC

4469-B-(a)	Monologue on Square Dances (or) Sooky Jumps-1,3	LC: **Elt ELK 301/2**
4469-B-1	Po' Howard	LC: **Elt ELK 301/2, Rnd 1045**
4469-B-2	Dance Calls (including "A Dollar Bill: Baby Won't You Buy Any Shoes")	LC: **Elt ELK 301/2, Rnd 1045**
4469-B-3	Gwine Dig a Hole to Put the Devil in It	LC: **Elt ELK 301/2, Rnd 1045**
4469-B-4	Tight Like That	LC: **Elt ELK 301/2**
4469-B-5	Green Corn	LC: **Elt ELK 301/2, Rnd 1045**
4470-A-(a)	Monologue On (The) Blues-1,2,3	LC: **Elt ELK 301/2**
4470-A-1	Sail On, Little Girl	LC
4470-A-2	Red Cross Sto'-2	LC
4470-B-(a)	Monologue on the Mourner's Bench-1,2,3	LC: **Elt ELK 301/2, Rnd 1046**
4470-B-1	Halleljah-2	LC: **Elt ELK 301/2, Rnd 1046**
4470-B-2	Backslider, Fare You Well-2	LC: **Elt ELK 301/2, Rnd 1046**
4470-B-3	Amazing Grace-2	LC: **Elt ELK 301/2**
4470-B-4	Must I Be Carried to the Sky on Flowered Beds of Ease?-2	LC: **Elt ELK 301/2, Rnd 1046**
4470-B-5	Amazing Grace-2	LC: **Elt ELK 301/2**
4470-B-6	Down in the Valley to Pray-2	LC: **Elt ELK 301/2, Rnd 1046**
4471-A-1	Meeting at the Building-2	LC
4471-A-2	When That Train Comes Along-2	LC
4471-A-3	The Blood Done Signed My Name-2	LC
4471-A-4	Witness for My Lord-2	LC
4471-A-5	Outshine the Sun-2	LC
4471-B-1	Let It Shine on Me	LC: **Elt ELK 301/2, Rnd 1046**
4471-B-2	Way Over in the Promised Land	LC
4471-B-3	Oh, Something on My Mind	LC
4471-B-4	How Long?	LC
4471-B-5	Swing Low, Sweet Chariot	LC
4471-B-6	Ain't Goin' Study War No More	LC
4471-B-7	Join the Band	LC
4471-B-8	Old Time Religion	LC
4471-B-9	Stand Your Test in Judgement	LC
4471-B-10	Must I Be Carried to the Sky on Flowered Beds of Ease?	LC
4472-A-1	Run, Sinners-2	LC: **Elt ELK 301/2, Rnd 1046**
4472-A-2	Ride On	LC: **Elt ELK 301/2, Rnd 1046**
4472-A-3	Prayer-1,2	LC
4472-A-4	Christmas-1,2	LC
4472-A-5	John Henry	LC
4472-B-1	John Hardy	LC
4472-B-2	Howard Hughes	LC: **Elt ELK 301/2, Rnd 1046**
4472-B-3	Bottle Up and Go	LC
4472-B-4	Cowboy Song	LC: **Rnd 1046**
4473-A-1	Leaving Blues	LC: **Rnd 1046**
4473-A-2	The Roosevelt Song	LC: **Elt ELK 301/2, Rnd 1046**
4473-A-3	The Scottsboro Boys	LC: **Elt ELK 301/2, Rnd 1046**

4473-A-4	Don't You Love Me No More?	LC
4473-B-1	Noted Rider Blues	LC: **Rnd 1046**
4473-B-2	The Gallows Song	LC
4473-B-3	So Doggone Soon	LC: **Rnd 1046**
4473-B-4	Ham and Eggs-2	LC
4473-B-5	Bottle Up and Go [fragment]	LC

Huddie Ledbetter: vocal/guitar
New York City, November 18, 1940

Ace 381   Ella Speed
[This recording is from the WABC radio show "Back Where I Come From." The matrix number was assigned in 1990 by the Smithsonian/Folkways Archive and refers to the sixteen-inch acetate upon which the music was transcribed.]

Huddie Ledbetter: vocal/guitar; **Golden Gate Quartet:** Willie Johnson, Henry Owens, Clyde Reddick, Orlandus Wilson, vocal quartet
New York City or Washington, D.C., January 1941

E 3685   Alabama Bound/On a Monday/   OWI unissued
                 Stewball/Gray Goose
[These selections were recorded by the Office of War Information for radio broadcast.]

Huddie Ledbetter: vocal/guitar; **Orleander Quartet:** George Boyd, Cecil Murray, Howard Scott, George Hall, vocal quartet-1
New York City, February 6, 1941

Ace 377	Irene, Goodnight
Ace 377	Chickens Crowing for Midnight
Ace 377	Blues in My Kitchen and Dining Room
Ace 377	Went Up on the Mountain-1
Ace 377	Good Morning Blues
Ace 377	Don't You Love Your Daddy No More-1
Ace 377	T.B. Blues
Ace 377	Irene, Goodnight

[These selections are from a radio program broadcast on WNYC. The matrix number was assigned by the Smithsonian/Folkways Archive in 1990 and refers to the sixteen-inch acetate upon which the music was transcribed.]

Huddie Ledbetter: vocal/guitar
New York City, February 12, 1941

Ace 390	Walk Through That Valley
Ace 390	Grey Goose
Ace 390	Julie Ann Johnson
Ace 390	T.B. Blues

[These selections are from a radio program broadcast on WNYC. The matrix number was assigned by the Smithsonian/Folkways Archive in 1990 and refers to the sixteen-inch acetate upon which the music was transcribed.]

Huddie Ledbetter: vocal/guitar/vocal unaccompanied-1/guitar accompaniment-2; **Oleander Quartet:** George Boyd, Cecil Murray, Howard Scott, George Hall, vocal quartet-3; **Ann Graham:** vocal-4
New York City, February 18, 1941

Ace 398	I Woke Up This Morning-1
Ace 398	I Went Up on the Mountain-3
Ace 398	Whoa, Back, Buck
Ace 398	If It Wasn't for Dicky
Ace 398	I Declare This World's in a Bad Condition-2,3
Ace 398	What Kind of Soul Has Man-2,4
Ace 398	What You Gonna Do when the World's on Fire-4
Ace 398	Hide Me in Thy Bosom-2,4
Ace 398	The Blood Done Signed Your Name
Ace 398	Gallis Pole
Ace 398	Leaving Blues

[These selections are from a radio program broadcast on WNYC. The matrix number was assigned by the Smithsonian/Folkways Archive in 1990 and refers to the sixteen-inch acetate upon which the music was transcribed.]

Huddie Ledbetter: vocal/guitar/guitar accompaniment-1; **Anne Graham:** vocal-2

New York City, February 27, 1941

Ace 384	Irene
Ace 384	Look Down That Lonesome Road-1,2
Ace 384	What Kind of Soul Has Man-1,2
Ace 384	Shorty George
Ace 384	When You Got to Sleep, Please Don't Sleep Too Long
Ace 384	Packin' Trunk
Ace 384	Irene

[These selections are from a radio program broadcast on WNYC. The matrix number was assigned by the Smithsonian/Folkways Archive in 1990 and refers to the sixteen-inch acetate upon which the music was transcribed.]

New York City, circa late February 1941

Ace 382	Irene
Ace 382	Stewball
Ace 382	Cottonfields
Ace 382	Ham and Eggs
Ace 382	Take this Hammer
Ace 382	Pick a Bale of Cotton
Ace 382	Sylvie-1,2
Ace 382	Irene

[These selections are from a radio program broadcast on WNYC. The matrix number was assigned by the Smithsonian/Folkways Archive in 1990 and refers to the sixteen-inch acetate upon which the music was transcribed.]

Huddie Ledbetter: guitar/vocal
New York City, March 13, 1941

Ace 381	Irene
Ace 381	Grey Goose
Ace 381	Boll Weevil
Ace 381	Yallow Gal
Ace 381	Ha, Ha Thisaway
Ace 381	Leaving Blues
Ace 381	Irene

[These selections are from a radio program broadcast on WNYC. The matrix number was assigned by the Smithsonian/Folkways Archive in 1990 and refers to the sixteen-inch acetate upon which the music was transcribed.]

New York City, late May 1941

SC-26-	Ha, Ha Thisaway	Asch SC26
SC-27-	Little Sally Walker	Asch SC27
SC-32-	Redbird	Asch SC32
SC-34-X	Christmas Song	Asch SC34-X
SC-34-	The Cotton Picking Song	Asch unissued
SC-35-	Parting Song	Asch unissued

New York City, July 1941

SC-79-	Skip To My Lou	Asch SC79, Disc 5071
SC-80-	You Can't Lose Me Cholly	Asch SC80

[Disc 5071 as by Leadbelly. Rev. Disc 5071 by Charity Baily. Asch SC26, SC27, SC32, SC34-X, SC79, SC80 issued by Asch as a 78 rpm album, *Play Parties in Song and Dance as Sung by Lead Belly.*]

Huddie Ledbetter: vocal/guitar; **Oleander Quartet:** George Boyd, Cecil Murray, Howard Scott, George Hall, vocal quartet-1
New York City, circa fall 1941

Ace 375	Irene
Ace 375	Yellow Gal
Ace 375	Cottonfields-1
Ace 375	Cotton Needs Picking-1
Ace 375	Grey Goose
Ace 375	Pick a Bale of Cotton-1
Ace 375	Irene

[These selections are from a radio program broadcast on WNYC. The matrix number was assigned by the Smithsonian/Folkways Archive in 1990 and refers to the sixteen-inch acetate upon which the music was transcribed.]

New York City, December 3, 1941

Ace 379	Irene
Ace 379	Pick a Bale of Cotton-1
Ace 379	We Shall Walk in the Valley in Peace
Ace 379	Look Away in Heaven-1
Ace 379	See the Sign of Judgement-1
Ace 379	Irene

[These selections are from a radio program broadcast on WNYC. The matrix number was assigned by the Smithsonian/Folkways Archive in 1990 and refers to the sixteen-inch acetate upon which the music was transcribed.]

Huddie Ledbetter: vocal/guitar
New York City, December 31, 1941

Ace 381	Irene
Ace 381	Ha, Ha Thisaway
Ace 381	Sally Walker
Ace 381	You Can't Lose Me, Cholly
Ace 381	Skip to My Lou
Acc 381	Redbird
Ace 381	Christmas Song
Ace 381	Irene

[These selections are from a radio program broadcast on WNYC. The matrix number was assigned by the Smithsonian/Folkways Archive in 1990 and refers to the sixteen-inch acetate upon which the music was transcribed.]

City College of New York, January 20, 1942

6407-A-1	Dear Mr. President	LC
6407-A-2	President Roosevelt	LC
6407-B-1	Mr. Hitler	LC: **Rnd 1046**

Huddie Ledbetter: vocal/guitar/button accordion-1
New York City, January 1942

SC-101-	Take This Hammer	Asch 101
SC-102-	Haul Away, Joe	Asch 103
SC-103-	Rock Island Line	Asch 102, Disc 6090
SC-104-	Ol' Riley	Asch 102, Disc 6090
SC-105-	Corn Bread Rough-1	Asch 101, **Stin 13, Doc 544**
SC-106-1	Old Man	Asch 103

[Disc 6090 as by Leadbelly. Asch 101, 102, 103 issued by Asch as a 78 rpm album, *Work Songs of the U.S.A. Sung by Leadbelly.* Asch SC79, SC80, 101, 102, 103 issued by Asch as a 78 rpm set *Work and Play Party Songs Sung by Leadbelly.* (Asch 341)]

Huddie Ledbetter: vocal/guitar; **Brownie McGhee:** guitar; **Sonny Terry:** harmonica
Washington, D.C., May 1942

6502-B-1   T.B. Blues   LC

Huddie Ledbetter: vocal/guitar
New York City, circa fall 1942

Ace 378   Irene
Ace 378   Don't You Love Your Daddy No More
Ace 378   Christmas Is Coming
Ace 378   Fannin Street
[These selections are from a half-hour radio program broadcast hosted by Art Hodes on WNYC. The matrix number was assigned by the Smithsonian/Folkways Archive in 1990 and refers to the sixteen-inch acetate upon which the music was transcribed.]

New York City, circa spring 1942

Ace 376   Irene
Ace 376   Way Down in Georgia
Ace 376   How Come You Do Me Like You Do?
Ace 376   Easy, Mr. Tom
Ace 376   Broke and Ain't Got a Dime
Ace 376   I'm Gonna Buy You a V-8 Ford
Ace 376   Irene
[These selections are from a radio program broadcast on WNYC. The matrix number was assigned by the Smithsonian/Folkways Archive in 1990 and refers to the sixteen-inch acetate upon which the music was transcribed.]

Huddie Ledbetter: vocal/guitar; **Sonny Terry:** harmonica-1
New York City, circa August 1943

SC-258-   On a Monday-1   Asch 343-3, Mdc 1187, **Stin 17, St SLP 139**

SC-259-   John Henry-1   Asch 343-3, Mdc 1187, **Stin 17, St SLP 139**

SC-260-   How Long Blues-1   Asch 343-1, Mdc 1140, **Stin 17**
SC-261-1   Irene   Asch 343-2, Atl 917, **Atl SD 8161, Stin 17**

SC-261-   Irene   Mdc 1151, **Stin 17, St SLP 139**

| SC-262- | Ain't You Glad-1 | Asch 343-2, Mdc 1151, **Stin 17, St SLP 139** |
| SC-263- | Good Morning Blues-1 | Asch 343-1, Atl 917, Mdc 1140, **Stin 17** |

[Atl 917 as *Leadbelly & His Guitar*. Asch 343-1, 343-2, and 343-3 as by Lead Belly and issued by Asch as a 78 rpm album *Songs by Lead Belly*, A343.]

Leadbelly: vocal/guitar/piano-1/button accordion-2/unaccompanied-3
New York City, circa October 1943

SC-270-	Cow Cow Yicky Yea/Out on the Western Plains	Disc 3002, **Stin 19**
SC-271-	Noted Rider/Big Fat Woman-1/ Borrow Love and Go	Asch 561-2B, Disc 3003, **York "The Folk Box, Vol. 1," Ev 102, Coll 5183, Stin 19**
SC-272-	John Hardy-2	Asch 561-3B, Disc 3003, **York "The Folk Box, Vol. 1", Coll 5183, Stin 19**
SC-273-	Meeting at the Building/Talking Preaching-3/We Shall Walk Through the Valley	Asch 561-2A, Disc 3001, **Stin 19, Fwy 2488, S/F 40010**
SC-274-	Fiddler's Dram/Yellow Gal/ Green Corn	Asch 561-3A, Disc 3002, **Stin 19**
SC-275-	Bring Me Lil' Water Silvy/Julie Ann Johnson/Line 'Em-3/ Whoa Back Buck	Asch 561-1B, Disc 3001, **York "The Folk Box, Vol. 1", Ev 102, Coll 5183, Stin 19**

[Disc 3001, 3002, 3003 issued as a 78 rpm album *Negro Folk Songs as Sung by Leadbelly*, Disc album 660. Asch 561-A1 through 3B were scheduled for release as a 78 rpm album, but it is unclear if it was ever issued. **Coll 5196 and EV 104** contain "On a Monday," "Defense Blues," "Keep Your Hands off Her," "Jim Crow," "Down in the Valley," "Pigmeat," "Blue Tail Fly," "Boll Weevil," and "Midnight Special." These selections are almost certainly leased from Asch or Disc material; however, their precise origins remain unclear.]

Huddie Ledbetter: vocal/guitar; **Muriel Reger:** piano
New York City, January 3, 1944

LEA-1	Careless Love Blues	"V" Disc unissued
LEA-2	We Shall Walk Through the Valley	"V" Disc unissued
LEA-3	You Know She Do	"V" Disc unissued
LEA-4	Blues Without Understanding	"V" Disc unissued
LEA-6	Good Morning Blues	"V" Disc unissued

Huddie Ledbetter: vocal/guitar
New York City, February 17, 1944

| 5126-3 | Roberta | Mus 311, **AE 4027, Vik 017, Roy 18131, Su 278** |

5127	Bill Brady	Mus 313, **AE 4027, Ron R 2021, Roy 18131, Su 278**
5128	(Black Gal) Where Did You Sleep Last Night?	Mus 312, **AE 4027, Roy 18131, Su 278**
5129	Yellow Gal	Mus 310, **AE 4027, Roy 18131, Su 278,**
5130-1	When the Boys Were on the Western Plain	Mus 310, **AE 4027, Vik 017, Roy 18131, Su 278**
5131	Pretty Flowers in My Backyard	Mus 313, **AE 4027, Roy 18131, Su 278**
5132	In New Orleans	Mus 312, **AE 4027, Vik 017, Ron 2021, Roy 18131, Su 278**
5133	John Hardy	Mus 311, **AE 4027, Vik 017, Rondo 2021, Roy 18131, Su 278**

[On **Su 278** the end of 5131 has been cut. This album is entitled, *Leadbelly Sings Ballads of Beautiful Women and Bad Men/With the Satin Strings*. These titles were scheduled for issue on **MuS LP 67,** which was never issued.]

Huddie Ledbetter: vocal/guitar; **Josh White:** vocal/guitar
New York City, April 19, 1944

| MA 60 | I've a Pretty Flower | Asch 348-3, **Stin 9** |
| MA 63 | Don't Lie Buddy | Asch 432-3, **Stin 5 & SLPX5, Des 247 & 903** |

[Stinson 5 is a 10" album, while Stinson SLPX is a 12" album.]

Huddie Ledbetter: vocal/guitar
New York City, April 23, 1944

683	How Do You Know	Asch rejected
683-1	How Do You Know/Don't Mind the Weather	Asch 331-2, **Stin 39 & 41**
684	What Are Little Boys Made Of	Asch rejected
684-1	(What Are) Little Boys (Made Of)/Let Me Hold Your Hand (All For You)/Polly Wolly (Polly) Wee	Asch 331-3, **Stin 39 & 41**
685	Skip to My Lou	Asch rejected
685-1	Skip to My Lou/Christmas Day (It's Almost Day)	Asch 331-2, **Stin 39 & 41**
686	Sally Walker	Asch rejected
686-1	Little Sally Walker/Ha, Ha Thisaway/Red Bird	Asch 331-1, **Stin 39 & 41**

[It is probably this version of "Ha, Ha Thisaway" that appears on **Life LP LA 1001.** "How Do You Know," "Little Boys," "Polly Wolly" are not on **Stinson 39;** likewise, "Christmas Day" is not included on **Stinson 41.**]

Huddie Ledbetter: vocal/guitar; **Sonny Terry:** harmonica
New York City, April 25, 1944

| MA 97 | Outskirts of Town | **Stin 5, Fkw 31006 & 2488, S/F 40010** |
| ? | Red River/Black Girl/You Don't Miss Your Water Blues | **Stin 48** |

Huddie Ledbetter: guitar-1/tap dancing-2/talking
New York City, April 25, 1944

| MA 160 | Blind Lemon (Memorial Record)-1 | **Stin 48** |
| MA 161 | Leadbelly's Dance-2 | **Stin 48** |

Huddie Ledbetter: vocal/guitar; **Josh White:** guitar-1
New York City, April 25, 1944

| MA 167 | Mother's Blues (Little Children Blues)-1 | Asch 331-3, **Stin 41** |
| MA 168 | Mo' Yet/(Little Boy) How Old Are You/There's a Limb on the Tree (Green Grass Grows All Around) | Asch 331-1, **Stin 41** |

Huddie Ledbetter: vocal/guitar; **Sonny Terry:** harmonica-1; **Woody Guthrie:** guitar-2
New York City, circa May 1944

MA 196	In The Evenin' When the Sun Goes Down-1	**Stin LP 48**
	Easy Rider (See See Rider)-1	**Fkw LP 4 & 2034**
	We Shall Be Free-1	**Fky LP 2488 & 31006, S/F 40100**
	Keep Your Hands off Her-2	**Asch AA 1/2, Stin LP 19, Fky LP 2488 & 31006, Ara AB 1002, S/F 40100**

[It is uncertain if these selections were recorded at the same session.]

Huddie Ledbetter: vocal/guitar/concertina-1; unknown vocal group-2
New York City, circa May 1944

| | There's a Man Going Round Taking Names | **Fkw LP 34, 2034 & 2488, S/F 40100** |
| | Red Bird | **Fkw LP 34 & 2034** |

Line 'Em	**Fkw LP 34, 2034 & 2488, S/F 40100**
T.B. Blues	**Fkw LP 34 & 2034**
Jim Crow Blues	**Fkw LP 34 & 2034**
Bourgeois Blues	**Fkw LP 34 & 2034**
Army Life-2	**Fkw LP 34 & 2034**
Mr. Hitler	**Fkw LP 34 & 2034**
Juliana Johnson	**Fkw LP 53**
Pig Meat	**Xtra LP 1047**
Jean Harlow	**Fkw 2488, S/F 40100**
Corn Bread Rough-1	**Arh LP 1009**
National Defense Blues	**Arh LP 1009**
Children's Blues	**Arh LP 1009**
The Blood Done Sign Your Name	**Arh LP 1009**

[It is uncertain if these recordings are from the same session. "There's a Man Going Round Taking Names," "Line 'Em," "Jean Harlow," "Corn Bread Rough," "National Defense Blues," and "The Blood Done Sign My Name" *may* also have been issued on **FWX-M 52488**—a French label that leased material from Folkways. Likewise, "T.B. Blues" and "Man Going Round Taking Names" almost certainly appear on **St SLP 139**.]

Huddie Ledbetter: vocal
New York City, circa July 1944

Cow Cow Yicky Yicky Yea	**S/F 40043**

Huddie Ledbetter: vocal/guitar; **Paul Mason Howard:** zither
Hollywood, California, October 4, 1944

397-4A	Ella Speed	**Cap H 369, Cap T 1821, EAP 2-369**
398-3A1	Rock Island Line	**Cap H 239, Cap 10021, Cap T 1821**
399-1A	Tell Me Baby	**Cap H 369, Cap EAP 2-369, Cap T 1821**
400-A1	Take This Hammer	**Cap H 369, Cap EAP 1-369, Cap T 1821, Cap (E) LC 6597, Cap TBO-1970**

[**Cap EAP 1-369** is a 45 rpm issue.]

Hollywood, California, October 11, 1944

413-3A	Irene	Cap 40130, **Cap EP 1-369, Cap LP 369, Cap 1821**
414-2A	Western Plain	**Cap EP 2-369, Cap LP 369, Cap 1821**

| 415-2A | On a Christmas Day | **Cap EP 1-369, Cap LP 369,** Cap 1821 |
| 416-3A | Backwater Blues | Cap 40130, **Cap EP 1-369, Cap LP 369, 1821** |

Huddie Ledbetter: vocal/guitar-1/piano-2/no vocal-3
Hollywood, California, October 27, 1944

457-1	Eagle Rock Rag-1 & 3	**Cap LP 1821**
457-2A	Eagle Rock Rag-2	**Cap 10021, Cap LP 238 &** 1821
458-	Meat Shakin' Women	Cap unissued
459-2A	Sweet Mary Blues	Cap 40038, Tel 80102, **Cap EP 2-369, Cap LP 369 & 1821**
460-3A	Grasshopper in My Pillow	Cap 40038, Tel 80102, **Cap LP** 1821

Huddie Ledbetter: vocal/guitar; **Paul Mason Howard:** zither-1
Hollywood, California, November 6, 1944

| | Rock Island Line-1 Jim Crow Blues | **AFRS Jubilee 107 CIC 23** |

["Rock Island Line" was released by the Armed Forces Radio Service.]

Huddie Ledbetter: vocal/guitar/children singing-1/unknown trumpet, clarinet, tenor sax, piano, bass & drums-2
San Francisco, California, February 15, 1945

Irene, Goodnight	**Fky LP 7533**
John Henry	**Fky LP 7533**
Boll Weevil-1	**Fky LP 7533**
When a Man's a Long Way from Home	**Fky LP 7533**
Good Morning Blues-2	**Fky LP 7533**
By and By When the Morning Comes-1 & 2	**Fky LP 7533**
Let It Shine on Me	**Fky LP 7533**
Everytime I Feel the Spirit	**Fky LP 7533**
Swing Low Sweet Chariot-1	**Fky LP 7533**
They Hung Him on the Cross-1	**Fky LP 7533**
Rock Island Line	**Fky LP 7533**
Julie Ann Johnson	**Fky LP 7533**
Haul Away Joe	**Fky LP 7533**
Christmas Is Coming	**Fky LP 7533**
We're in the Same Boat Brother-1	**Fky LP 7533**
Skip to My Lou	unissued

Amazing Grace   unissued
Take This Hammer   unissued
Poor Boy   unissued
[These selections were originally recorded as a "Standard (Oil Company) Broad-
cast" radio program.]

Huddie Ledbetter: vocal/guitar; **Willie:** vocal-1
Berkeley, California, circa May 12, 1945

Oh Mary, Don't You Weep
John Henry
Ella Louise
Rock Island Line
Casey Jones
Jim Crow
House of the Rising Sun
Irene, Goodnight
Tell Me How Long the Train Been Gone
Shine On Me
Nobody Knows the Trouble I Seen
Swing Low, Sweet Chariot
Oh Mary, Don't You Weep
Shout On-1
Down Hawaii Way
Skip to My Lou
All Over This World
Irene, Goodnight
[These recordings come from a program broadcast over KRE.]

Huddie Ledbetter: vocal/guitar/piano-1; **Bunk Johnson** (trumpet), **Jimmy Archey**
(trombone), **Omer Simeon** (clarinet), **Ralph Sutton** (piano), **Danny Barker**
(banjo), **Cyrus St. John** (tuba), **Fred Moore** (drums)-2
New York City, spring 1946

Yellow Gal   **Doc LP 544**
Borrow Love and Go   **Doc LP 544**
Eagle Rag Rock-1   **Doc LP 544**
Good Morning Blues-2   **Doc LP 544**
[These are "live" recordings from the New York Jazz Club.]

Huddie Ledbetter: vocal/guitar; **Sonny Terry:** harmonica-1; **Willie "The Lion"**
Smith: piano; **Brownie McGhee:** guitar; **George "Pops" Foster:** bass-2
New York City, circa June 1946

D 385   Diggin' My Potatoes-2   Disc 5085, **Stin LP 48**
D 386   Defense Blues-1,2   Disc 5085, Asch AA 1
          Easy Rider-2   Disc 5501
          Pigmeat-2   Disc 5501
          John Henry   **Fkw LP 53, Doc 544**

Huddie Ledbetter: vocal/guitar; **Woody Guthrie:** vocal/guitar; **Cisco Houston:** vocal/guitar
New York City, circa October 1946

D 669	Alabama Bound	Disc 6045, **Stin LP 5, Fwy LP 2488 & 31006, S/F 40100, Stin SLP 6**
D 670	Ham and Eggs	Disc 6043, **Stin LP 48**
D 671	Yellow Gal	Disc 6044, D 110, **Stin LP 91 & 9, Fkw LP 31006**
D 672	Stew Ball	Disc 6045, **Stin 9 & 11, Fkw LP 2488, Ara AB 1004, S/F 40100**
D 673	Gray Goose	Disc 6044, **Stin LP 48**
D 674	Midnight Special	Disc 6043, **Stin LP 6**
	Green Corn	**Fkw LP 4 & 2004**
	Fiddler's Dram	**Fkw LP 2488 & 31006, S/F 40100**

["Alabama Bound," "Stew Ball," and "Fiddler's Dram" may appear on FWX-M52488—a French label (Lechant Dumonde) that leased material from Folkways.]

Huddie Ledbetter: vocal/guitar; audience singing-1
Salt Lake City, Utah, December 1946

St. Louis Blues
Frankie and Albert-1
Irene-1
Salt Lake City
Bourgeois Blues
The Gallis Pole
We're in the Same Boat, Brother

[These selections were recorded at a party of the home of Dr. Hector Lee on a wire recorder.]

Huddie Ledbetter: vocal/guitar/piano-1/concertina-2/vocal solo-3; **Anne Graham:** vocal solo-4; **Sonny Terry:** harmonia-5; **The Oleander Singers,** vocal group-6

New York City, circa February 1947

Yellow Gal	**Fkw LP 4 & 2004**
You Can't Lose Me Cholly	**Fkw LP 4 & 2004, Stin 39**
Laura-2	**Fkw LP 4 & 2004**
Good Morning Blues	**Fkw LP 4 & 2004**
Leaving Blues	**Fkw LP 4 & 2004**
Big Fat Woman-1	**Fkw LP 4 & 2004**
Gray Goose	**Fkw LP 4 & 2004**
Pick a Bale of Cotton-6	**Fkw LP 4 & 2004, Elk Ekl 9001**
Take This Hammer	**Fkw LP 4 & 2004, Stin 12**

Bring Me a Little Water Silvy-4	**Fkw LP 4 & 2004**
Moaning-3	**Fkw LP 4 & 2004**
Meeting at the Building-6	**Fkw LP 4 & 2004, Elk Ekl 9001**
We Shall Walk Through the Valley	**Fkw LP 4 & 2004**

["Meeting at the Building" and "We Shall Walk Through the Valley" may also appear on FWX-M 52488—a French label (Lechant Dumonde) that leased material from Folkways. **Fkw FTS 31019 and Verve Folkways FV 9001**, both titled *Take This Hammer*, appear to be straight reissues of **Fkw LP 4 & 2004.**]

Huddie Ledbetter: vocal/guitar/concertina-1/rapping on guitar-2; unknown guitar-3
New York City, summer 1947

Cotton Song	**Fkw LP 14 & 2014**
Ha Ha This Way	**Fkw LP 14 & 2014**
Sukey Jump (Win' Jammer)-1	**Fkw LP 14 & 2014, Arh LP 1009**
Black Girl	**Fkw LP 14 & 2014**
Rock Island Line	**Fkw LP 14 & 2014, Elk Ekl 9001, Stin 17**
Blind Lemon Song	**Fkw LP 14 & 2014**
Borrow Love and Go	**Fkw LP 14 & 2014**
On a Monday (I'm Almost Done)	**Fkw LP 14 & 2014**
Shorty George	**Fkw LP 14 & 2014**
Duncan (and Brady)	**Fkw LP 14 & 2014**
Old Riley	**Fkw LP 14 & 2014, Stin 17**
Leavin' Blues-2	**Fkw LP 14 & 2014**
Pigmeat-3	**Fkw LP 14 & 2014**

[LPs 2004 and 2014 ("Leadbelly Legacy," Vols. 1 and 2) were also issued in combined form on a seven-inch commercial open reel tape as Phonotape Sonore Pm 143.]

Huddie Ledbetter: vocal/guitar
New York City, June 14, 1947

Green Corn	**Man LP 504**
John Henry	**Man LP 504**

[These titles come from a "This Is Jazz" radio broadcast.]

Huddie Ledbetter: vocal/guitar; **Tillman Cadle:** vocal-1; **Martha Ledbetter:** vocal-2
New York City, circa June 15, 1948

BC97	When Your Hair Turns to Silver
	Relax Your Mind

BC98	Hollywood and Vine
	Honey You Are the Only One
BC99	Gallus Pole
	We're in the Same Boat, Brother
BC100	Gallus Pole
	We're in the Same Boat, Brother
BC101	Alabamy Bound
	Equality for Negroes
BC102	Hollywood and Vine
	Honey You're the Only One
BC103	House of the Rising Sun
	He Never Said a Mumbling Word
BC104	Gonna Tear Hitler Down
	Black Girl
BC105	When Your Hair Has Turned to Silver
	Relax Your Mind
BC106	We're in the Same Boat, Brother
	Blank
BC107	Shorty George
	Blank
BC108	Gallows Pole
	Gallows Pole
BC109	Git on Board
	Not by Leadbelly
BC110	Go Down Old Hannah
	Blank
BC111	Maid Freed from the Gallows
	Not by Leadbelly/Unknown
BC112	Holes in My Pockets, Patches on My Pants
	Daddy, Let Me Lay It on You
BC113	Going to Fight the Battle Until I Die
	In the Pines-1
BC114	I Went Down in the Valley to Pray
	Blank
BC115	Little Bit O' That You Setten On Elnora
BC116	Julie Ann Johnson
	Ain't Going to Ring Them Yellow Women's Door Bells
BC117	Tight Like That
	Fiddler's Draw Don't Give a Damn

BC118   Midnight Special
        Trials
BC119   Blood Done Signed My Name
        Not by Leadbelly/Unknown
BC120   Frankie and Albert (Part One)
        Frankie and Albert (Part Two)
BC121   In Them Long Hot Summer
            Days/Ain't Going Down to the
            Well No More/One Dollar
            Bill, Baby Hooray, Hooray,
            Hooray/Dicklicker's Holler
BC122   Alberta (Part One)
        Alberta (Part Two)
BC123   Queen Mary
        Shreveport Jail
BC124   Ha, Ha Thisaway
        Bill in the Lowlands
BC125   Boll Weevil Song/Green Corn
        Ella Speed and Bill Martin
BC126   Hitler Song
        Black Girl
BC127   Equality for Negroes
        Alabama Bound
BC128   In Kentucky
        Not by Leadbelly/Blank
BC129   Baby, You Can't Do Me Like
            Corinna Done
        Alabama Bound
BC130   Don't You Weep, Don't You
            Moan/I'll Be Glad When I Get
            Home-2
        Blank
BC131   Take This Hammer
        Walk Around the Bedside
BC132   Rock Island Line/Looky, Looky
            Yonder
        Man Ploughing with Mules
BC133   Whoa Back, Buck and Gee by
            the Lands
        Honey, I'm All Out and
            Down
BC134   Old Rattler
        The Gray Goose
BC135   Prison Bound Blues
        Not by Leadbelly
BC136   Nearer My God to Thee
        Come to Jesus
BC137   New York City
        Susie Q.

[These recordings come from the Elizabeth Barnacle–Tillman Cadle Collection.
Some discs are dated June 15, 1948, and all seem to have been recorded on or near
that date.]

Huddie Ledbetter: vocal/guitar/vocal solo-1/chorus added-2
New York City, circa September 1948

11717-B-22	Tell Me Baby, What's Wrong With You	LC
11717-B-23	Take a Whiff on Me	LC
11719-A-26	Ox-Driving Man-1	LC
11719-A-27	We're in the Same Boat, Brother-2	LC

Huddie Ledbetter: vocal solo/guitar with vocal-1; **Martha Ledbetter:** vocal-2/ vocal solo-3
New York City, late September 1948

Yes, I Was Standing in the Bottom	Fkw LP 241 & 2941
Yes, I'm Goin' Down in Louisiana	Fkw LP 241 & 2941
I An't Goin' Down to the Well No More	Fkw LP 241 & 2941
Dicklicker's Holler	Fkw LP 241 & 2941
Miss Liza Jane	Fkw LP 241 & 2941
Dog Latin Song	Fkw LP 241 & 2941
Leaving Blues	Fkw LP 241 & 2941
Going Down Old Hannah-1	Fkw LP 241 & 2941
Blue Tail Fly	Fkw LP 241 & 2941
Nobody in This World Is Better Than Us	Fkw LP 241 & 2941
We're in the Same Boat, Brother	Fkw LP 241 & 2941
Looky, Looky, Yonder	Fkw LP 241 & 2941
Jolly, o' the Ransom	Fkw LP 241 & 2941
Old Ship of Zion-2	Fkw LP 241 & 2941
Bring Me a Little Water, Silvy-2	Fkw LP 241 & 2941
Mistreatin' Mama	Fkw LP 241 & 2941
Black Betty	Fkw LP 241 & 2941
I Don't Know You, What Have I Done	Fkw LP 241 & 2941
Rock Island Line	Fkw LP 241 & 2941
Old Man, Will Your Dog Catch a Rabbit	Fkw LP 241 & 2941
Shorty George	Fkw LP 241 & 2941
Stewball-2	Fkw LP 241 & 2941
Bottle Up and Go	Fkw LP 241 & 2941
You Know I Got to Do It	Fkw LP 241 & 2941
Ain't It a Shame to Go Fishin' on Sunday	Fkw LP 241 & 2941
I Ain't Gonna Drink No More	Fkw LP 241 & 2941
My Lindy Lou	Fkw LP 241 & 2941
I'm Thinking of a Friend-3	Fkw LP 241 & 2941

He Never Said a Mumbling Word	Fkw LP 241 & 2941
I Don't Want No More of Army Life-2	Fkw LP 241 & 2941
In the World	Fkw LP 241 & 2941
I Want to Go Home	Fkw LP 241 & 2941

Huddie Ledbetter: vocal/guitar; **Sonny Terry:** harmonica-1/speech-2
New York City, October 1948

Gallows Pole-2	Fkw LP 31030
John Henry-1	Fkw LP 31030
Pick a Bale of Cotton-1	Fkw LP 31030
Go Down, Old Hannah	Fkw LP 31030
Ain't Going Down to the Well No More	Fkw LP 31030
Honey I'm All Out and Down-2	Fkw LP 31030
It Was Soon One Morning	Fkw LP 31030
Whoa Back Buck-2	Fkw LP 31030
Birmingham Jail	Fkw LP 31030
Take This Hammer	Fkw LP 31030
It Was Early One Mornin'	Fkw LP 31030
Going Back to Mary	Fkw LP 31030

[These selections taken from radio broadcasts of the WNYC Jazz Festival.]

Huddie Ledbetter: vocal/guitar/vocal solo-1/guitar solo-2; **Martha Promise:** vocal-3; **Charles Edward Smith:** vocal responses-4
New York City, October 1948

New Iberia-1	Fkw LP 241 & 2941
Dancing with Tears in My Eyes	Fkw LP 241 & 2941
John Henry	Fkw LP 241 & 2941
Salty Dog	Fkw LP 241 & 2941
National Defense Blues	Fkw LP 241 & 2941
Easy, Mr. Tom-2	Fkw LP 241 & 2941
Relax Your Mind	Fkw LP 241 & 2941
Bottle Up and Go	Fkw LP 241 & 2941
Polly Polly Wee	Fkw LP 241 & 2941
Pig Latin Song	Fkw LP 241 & 2941
Hawaiian Song	Fkw LP 241 & 2941
Drinkin' Lum Y A Alla	Fkw LP 241 & 2941
The Grey Goose-4	Fkw LP 241 & 2941
Silver City Bound	Fkw LP 241 & 2941
The Titanic	Fkw LP 241 & 2941
Death Letter Blues	Fkw LP 241 & 2941
Mary Don't You Weep-3	Fkw LP 241 & 2941
He Never Said a Mumbling Word	Fkw LP 241 & 2941
Midnight Special	Fkw LP 242 & 2942
Boll Weevil Song	Fkw LP 242 & 2942

Careless Love	Fkw LP 242 & 2942
Easy Rider	Fkw LP 242 & 2942
Call It "Cry for Me"	Fkw LP 242 & 2942
Ain't Going to Drink No More	Fkw LP 242 & 2942
Birmingham Jail-4	Fkw LP 242 & 2942
Old Riley	Fkw LP 242 & 2942
Julie Ann Johnson	Fkw LP 242 & 2942
It's Tight Like That	Fkw LP 242 & 2942
4, 5, & 9	Fkw LP 242 & 2942
Good Morning Babe, How Do You Do	Fkw LP 242 & 2942
Jail House Blues	Fkw LP 242 & 2942
Well You Know How to Do It	Fkw LP 242 & 2942
Irene	Fkw LP 242 & 2942
Story of the 25 Cent Dude	Fkw LP 242 & 2942
How Come You Do Me Like You Do	Fkw LP 242 & 2942
Hello Central, Give Me Long Distance Telephone	Fkw LP 242 & 2942
The Hesitation Blues	Fkw LP 242 & 2942
I'll Be Down on the Last Bread Wagon	Fkw LP 242 & 2942
Springtime in the Rockies	Fkw LP 242 & 2942, S/F 40043
Chinatown	Fkw LP 242 & 2942
Rock Island Line	Fkw LP 242 & 2942
Backwater Blues	Fkw LP 242 & 2942
Sweet Mary-3	Fkw LP 242 & 2942
Irene-3	Fkw LP 242 & 2942
Easy, Mr. Tom-2	Fkw LP 242 & 2942
In the Evening when the Sun Goes Down	Fkw LP 242 & 2942
I'm Alone Because I Love You	Fkw LP 242 & 2942
House of the Rising Sun-3	Fkw LP 242 & 2942
Mary Don't You Weep-3	Fkw LP 242 & 2942
Talk About Fannin Street-4	Fkw LP 242 & 2942
Fannin Street	Fkw LP 242 & 2942
Sugar'd Beer-4	Fkw LP 242 & 2942
Didn't Old John Cross the Water	Fkw LP 242 & 2942
Nobody Knows You when You Are Down and Out	Fkw LP 242 & 2942
Bully of the Town	Fkw LP 242 & 2942
Sweet Jenny Lee	Fkw LP 242 & 2942
Yellow Gal	Fkw LP 242 & 2942
He Was the Man	Fkw LP 242 & 2942
We're in the Same Boat, Brother-3	Fkw LP 242 & 2942
Leaving Blues	Fkw LP 242 & 2942

[These selections are probably from more than one session in October 1948.]

Huddie Ledbetter: vocal/guitar
New York City, October 1948

Come and Sit Down Beside Me	**Fkw LP 31030**
Ha, Ha Thisaway	**Fkw LP 31030**
You Can't Lose a Me, Charlie	**Fkw LP 31030**
Rooster Crows at Midnight	**Fkw LP 31030**
Skip to My Lou	**Fkw LP 31030**
Parting Song (When You Smile-O)	**Fkw LP 31030**

[These selections taken from a radio broadcast of the WNYC Jazz Festival.]

Minneapolis, Minnesota, November 21, 1948

Black Girl (fragment)
Rock Island Line
House of the Rising Sun
House of the Rising Sun
No One Like the Girl, She Was the Only One
Talk About Governor Sam Neff
Governor Sam Neff
Ho Day (A Cowboy Song)
I Ride Old Paint
Skip to My Lou
Whoa, Old Buck
Uncle Joe
We Shall Walk Through the Valley
Let It Shine on Me
I'll Be down at the Last Bread Wagon
Polly Polly Polly Wee
The Boll Weevil
Ain't It a Shame (fragment)
The Boll Weevil (fragment)
The Grey Goose (fragment)
Ain't It a Shame
Stewball
Bourgeois Blues
Governor Sam Neff
Talk About Governor Allen
Governor O.K. Allen
A Lesson in History
Lake Superior
Mississippi River
Down in Louisiana
Goodnight Irene
Nobody in the World Is Better Than Us
Jim Crow
The Gallis Pole
Samuel Hall
Jean Harlow

I Ain't Goin' Down to the Well No More
Mississippi River
Fannin Street
Old Black Cow
Pig Latin Song (fragment)
Hawaiian Song
John Henry
Goodnight Irene (fragment)
[These selections were recorded at a private party by Kenneth E. Britzius.]

New York City, February 19, 1949

Good Morning Blues	**CIC 23, Mauros LP 11, LBCCL LP 3840**
Ain't Gonna Let You Worry My Life Anymore	**CIC 23, Mauros LP 11, LBCCL LP 3840**
Pretty Papa	**CIC 23, Mauros LP 11, LBCCL LP 3840**

[These selections taken from a radio broadcast of the WNYC Jazz Festival.]

Huddie Ledbetter: vocal/guitar/vocal solo-1; **Martha Ledbetter:** vocal-2
Austin, Texas, June 15, 1949

Irene, Goodnight	**Plby 50028 & LP 119**
Hoday, Hoday/Ain't Going Down The Well No More	**Plby LP 119**
Rock Island Line	**Plby 50028 & LP 119**
Old Hannah	**Plby LP 119**
Shine on Me	**Plby LP 119**
What Can I Do to Change Your Mind	**Plby LP 119**
Skip to My Lou	**Plby LP 119**
Mary and Martha	**Plby LP 119**
Scrambled Egg Song	**Plby LP 119**
Whoa Buck	**Plby LP 119**
John Henry	**Plby LP 119**
Backwater Blues	**Plby LP 119**
Ella Louise-1	**Plby LP 119**
I Don't Want No More of Army Life	**Plby LP 119**
Relax Your Mind	**Plby LP 119**
Irene, Goodnight	**Plby LP 119**
Old Ship of Zion-2	**Plby LP 119**
I Will Be So Glad When I Get Home-2	**Plby LP 119**

[These selections recorded live at the University of Texas.]

Huddie Ledbetter: vocal/guitar
New York City, August 4, 1949

| Don't You Love Your Daddy No More | **CIC 23, Mauros LP 11, LBCCL LP 3840** |
| You Can't Lose Me Charlie | **CIC 23, Mauros LP 11, LBCCL LP 3840** |

Special thanks to Judy Bell, Bruce Brecke, Kenneth E. Britzius, John Cowley, David Evans, Joe Hickerson, David Hoehl, Brad McCoy, Jeff Place, Dolf Rerink, Jan Schoondergang, Neil Slaven, and Pete Welding for their help in compiling this discography. It is based on Godrich and Dixon, *Blues and Gospel Records 1902–1943* and Mike Ledbetter and Neil Slaven, *Blues Records 1943–1970, Volume Two.*

Index

Copyright
Acknowledgments